Reconstructing the World Trade Organization for the 21st Century

Reconstructing the World Trade Organization for the 21st Century

An Institutional Approach

KENT JONES

OXFORD
UNIVERSITY PRESS

Oxford University Press is a department of the University of
Oxford. It furthers the University's objective of excellence in research,
scholarship, and education by publishing worldwide.

Oxford   New York

Auckland   Cape Town   Dar es Salaam   Hong Kong   Karachi
Kuala Lumpur   Madrid   Melbourne   Mexico City   Nairobi
New Delhi   Shanghai   Taipei   Toronto

With offices in

Argentina   Austria   Brazil   Chile   Czech Republic   France   Greece
Guatemala   Hungary   Italy   Japan   Poland   Portugal   Singapore
South Korea   Switzerland   Thailand   Turkey   Ukraine   Vietnam

Published in the United States of America by
Oxford University Press
198 Madison Avenue, New York, NY 10016

© Oxford University Press 2015

Library of Congress Cataloging-in-Publication Data
Jones, Kent Albert.
Reconstructing the World Trade Organization for the 21st century : an institutional approach / Kent Jones.
pages cm
Includes bibliographical references and index.
ISBN 978-0-19-936604-0 (alk. paper)
1. World Trade Organization.   2. Free trade.   3. International trade.   4. International economic
relations. I. Title.
HF1385.J669 2015
382'.92—dc23
2014024773

1 3 5 7 9 8 6 4 2
Printed in the United States of America
on acid-free paper

For Ana-Lisa and Diantha

CONTENTS

ACKNOWLEDGMENTS

Without implicating them in my own analytical approach and conclusions, I would like to acknowledge the help, guidance, and expert knowledge of many trade scholars, diplomats, and business representatives who were kind enough to submit to interviews and questions on specific aspects of this book, including: Chad Bown, Judy Dean, Linda Dempsey, Cedric DuPont, Manfred Elsig, Erin Ennis, Michael Ferrantino, Bernard Hoekman, Gary Horlick, Andrew Lang, Melissa Manwaring, John Murphy, John Odell, Don Ross, Jeff Schott, Shankar Singham, Joel Trachtman, and Frank Vargo, and WTO Ambassadors Mario Matus (Chile), Eduardo Muñoz (Colombia), Joakim Reiter (Sweden), Guillermo Valles (Uruguay), and Luzius Wasescha (Switzerland). To this list I must add a large group of WTO Secretariat officials in Geneva, as well as current and former USTR, State Department and Commerce Department trade officials in Geneva and Washington, most of whom wished to remain anonymous with regard to their frank opinions of the Doha Round and WTO processes. I also profited from comments on my work at conferences of the World Trade Institute Conference on the WTO (Berne, 2009), the Association for Global Business (New Orleans, 2010, and Washington, DC, 2012), the Atlantic Economic Society (Philadelphia, 2013), and St. Petersburg University, Russian Federation (2013). My Babson College colleague Yun-wei Gai provided econometric expertise for my presentation in chapter 5, and I am grateful to Manfred Elsig for making a critical data set available to me for that portion of the study. Sharon DeSouza, Shivangini Ghosh, Natalia Benedetti, and Patricia Yusah provided valuable research support at Babson College. I would also like to give credit for my discovery and understanding of trade policy issues to Ingo Walter and Richard Blackhurst, and to Jan Tumlir and Gerard Curzon, both now departed. I am especially grateful to the late Robert Meagher, who introduced me to the advantages of thinking about institutional matters across disciplinary lines. My final thanks go, as usual, to my wife, Tonya, who tolerated the process of my writing this book with transcendent patience and understanding.

ABBREVIATIONS

ACP	African, Caribbean, and Pacific
AD	antidumping
APEC	Asia-Pacific Economic Cooperation
ASEAN	Association of Southeast Asian Nations
BAMTA	best alternative to a multilateral trade agreement
BATNA	best alternative to a negotiated agreement
BITs	bilateral investment treaties
CAP	Common Agricultural Policy
CUs	Customs Unions
DDA	Doha Development Agenda
DSU	dispute settlement understanding
EFTA	European Free Trade Association
EIAs	Economic Integration Areas
EIF	Enhanced Integrated Framework
EPAs	Economic Partnership Agreements
FDI	foreign direct investment
FTA	free trade agreement
FTAAP	Free Trade Area of the Asia-Pacific
GATS	General Agreement on Trade in Services
GATT	General Agreement on Tariffs and Trade
GPA	Government Procurement Agreement
GSP	Generalized System of Preferences
ICSID	International Centre for Settlement of Investment Disputes
IP	intellectual property
IPR	intellectual property rights
ISA	International Services Agreement
ITO	International Trade Organization

LDCs   least developed countries
MAI   Multilateral Agreement on Investment
MC   Ministerial Conference
MFA   Multifiber Agreement
MFN   most-favored nation
MTN   multilateral trade negotiation
NAFTA   North American Free Trade Agreement
NAMA   Non-Agricultural Market Access
NTB   non-tariff barrier
NTMs   non-tariff measures
PA   plurilateral agreement
PECS   Pan-European Cumulation System
PTAs   Preferential Trade Agreements
RCEP   Regional Comprehensive Economic Partnership
ROOs   rules of origin
RTA   Regional Trade Agreement
S&D   special and differential
SPS   sanitary and phytosanitary
TNC   Trade Negotiating Committee
TRIMs   Trade Related Investment Measures
TRIPS   Trade-Related Intellectual Property Rights
TTIP   Transatlantic Trade and Investment Partnership
TTP   Trans-Pacific Partnership
UNCTAD   United Nations Conference on Trade and Development
VER   voluntary export restraint
WIPO   World Intellectual Property Organization
WTO   World Trade Organization

INTRODUCTION: WHY ISN'T THERE MORE TRADE?

Why isn't there more trade? The suspension of comprehensive Doha Round trade negotiations in December 2011, after ten long and frustrating crisis-filled years, raises this fundamental question. This study sets out to show that institutions, in particular domestic political and international economic institutions, play a major role in how much the world trades. The key to expanding trade is to build an improved institutional capacity to do so. *Institutions* in this sense are broadly defined as the rules and procedures that human beings set up to accomplish societal goals they consider to be important. They set up games we play, like baseball and soccer. They define the way we use money. They establish the functions of government and the ability of groups to influence government. And they determine the way, through laws and regulations, that we exchange goods and services, as buyers and sellers in domestic transactions, and as buyers and sellers among countries that trade. The focus in this book is on institutions because they determine how interests are translated into policies, cooperation leads to action and decisions follow a process. The lack of trade implies, in large part, shortcomings in institutions.

The case for trade in general—and for more trade through liberalizing agreements—is strong because the further gains from trade are plentiful and significant. Unexploited gains from trade, especially in services, regulatory harmonization and improved logistics, are potentially worth trillions of dollars each year in lost global GDP. Aside from making production more efficient and increasing the amount of goods and services we can consume, increased trade expands the variety of products available, spreads technology and best business practices, and promotes competition. The gains from trade are not just a benefit for large corporations doing international business but also for consumers and producers in all countries. All countries that trade tend to be better off, and trade has helped millions of people out of poverty, with millions more waiting for the chance—if only there were more trade.

Furthermore, the gains from trade are in fact embedded in the very origins of civilization, when specialization and the exchange of goods and services within the group began to improve the lives of families and communities. Anthropologists have uncovered evidence of long-distance trade that dates back as far as 140,000 years. From those early times, trade raised standards of living, and the emergence of specialization in production, combined with enticements of new, different, and better items for consumption extended the desire for exchange toward more distant locations, extending markets beyond the familiar and relatively safe confines of local villages and territories. Adam Smith's observation of the inherent human tendency to "truck and barter" has deep and ancient roots.

But there already is a lot of trade, one might say in protest to the question, so what is the problem? There is indeed more trade now than there was at the end of World War II, and its rapid growth since then coincided with the first tariff cuts under the General Agreement on Tariffs and Trade (GATT) in 1947. Seven additional GATT rounds of trade negotiations followed, driving global weighted-average applied tariff rates down to 6% by the end of the Uruguay Round in 1994, and even lower since then, to around 3% in 2010, through coun-tries' unilateral tariff cuts, preferential trade agreements and new membership in the WTO. In addition, the unprecedented establishment of a global trad-ing system of rules based on the principle of nondiscrimination, with a dispute settlement system, has stabilized trade relations and contributed to an environ-ment of economic expansion. Some may argue that, based on these facts alone, the world trading system is doing just fine. Yet we trade only as much as our institutions allow it, and the current stalemate in the Doha Round is a case in point. There is a long history of suspicion regarding international trade. One important reason that there has not been more trade across the millennia is that trade has often been dangerous, risky, expensive to pursue, and subject to territorial restrictions and arbitrary closure of markets. Trade was dangerous because traders could be ambushed, robbed, and killed for their efforts, early elements of what economists now blithely refer to as the "transaction costs of trade." Overcoming these problems gave rise to legal and economic institutions to reduce the risks and costs of distant trade. The barriers to trade inspired people to develop institutions to reduce those barriers, so that the gains from trade could be theirs.

As centralized systems of government developed, gaining control over ter-ritories, countries and empires began to erect systematic institutional barriers to trade, and this is where the problem of trade liberalization in the modern age begins. Sovereign territorial control of market access by governments made achieving the gains from trade, in many ways, dependent on a country's trade policy. While the monopoly control by governments over their territories often increased trade within the territories, it often inhibited trade from outside competitors, through tariffs and other restrictions on market access. Governments' increasing involvement in their economies added another institutional element to the issue of market access, as trade became an element of domestic economic stabilization policy. The mercantilist tradition, which has dominated many governments' attitudes toward trade over the centuries, regarded a positive trade balance to be essential to a nation's security, and this view persists to this day.

But what about those who lose from trade? It is true that not everyone involved in trade will gain from it, and those who feel threatened by it have organized political groups to oppose or limit trade. Others—mainly exporters, but also firms that import input goods—have also organized politically to support more trade. The institutions of a country's trade policy are thereby subject to the balance of power between these groups. But a distinguishing feature of trade is that the gains of the winners tend to be greater than the losses of the losers, and governments have the ability to promote economic flexibility and to redistribute some of the gains from trade through adjustment assistance and other policies, in order to minimize the impact on those who lose. The political transmission of domestic economic interests to the formulation of trade policy thereby became an important element in governments' views toward trade liberalization.

This brings us to international trade institutions. Maximizing the gains from trade on a global basis requires a framework for global trade negotiations and rules that can somehow align the interests of all participants in favor of universal trade liberalization. The GATT played this role in the years after World War II and was remarkably successful. Yet this institutional triumph, a historic landmark in international cooperation, was perhaps more fragile than it appeared to be. Finding common ground on the purpose and goals of trade liberalization in the GATT years was not always easy, but the system always seemed to find a way to conclude successful trade rounds. The major players, led by the United States and the Europeans, were developed countries with similar attitudes regarding the main issues of trade liberalization: who would lead the way on the agenda, what would be negotiated, who would participate, and where the lines would be drawn between economic policies subject to trade negotiation and those that would be off-limits. When there were problems, they managed to agree on what exceptions to make and how to avoid big and dangerous confrontations, which they accomplished by putting the difficult issues in their own boxes for special treatment. The GATT system rested on a foundation of delicate political balances and compromises, all of which were integral parts of its institutional structure. The success of the GATT made countries hungry for even more trade expansion. This ambition gave rise to negotiations for a new and expanded trade framework in the Uruguay Round, which resulted in the establishment of the GATT's successor institution, the World Trade Organization. While the WTO retained much of the structure of the GATT, any new agreement would subsequently have to follow the new or modified rules of the WTO. The test of the WTO's ability to continue the GATT tradition of multilateral trade liberalization would come in the next big negotiation, the Doha Round.

The ambitious Doha Round set out to expand market access and multilateral trade rules across a wide range of products and issues, to be packaged together as a so-called "single undertaking." Yet the path to a Doha agreement was not easy because the world and the trading environment had in the meantime changed in many fundamental ways. High economic growth had shifted from developed to developing and emerging market countries, which thereby gained negotiating power. This situation created conflict with many of the old GATT rules and procedures that the WTO had retained. Hunger for more trade brought new sectors into the negotiations, such as agriculture and services, which were politically very sensitive in many countries. Globalization had created fear and uncertainty in many countries over the impact and adjustment cost of new international competition, and institutional boundaries on what issues would be subject to trade negotiations were being challenged in an atmosphere of economic anxiety. Domestic political institutions in each of the WTO member countries had to grapple with new and difficult trade-offs in pursuing national policies on trade liberalization, and many of the new WTO members had political institutions and preferences that diverged from those of countries that had spearheaded trade liberalization in the past. Internal WTO stresses, domestic political tensions over trade in many countries, and conflicting views among WTO members on basic principles created difficult conditions for the Doha negotiations. The manifold institutional problems caused the Doha Round to lurch from one crisis to the next. While there were brief periods when the WTO members agreed to resume the negotiations and try again, they were unable to reach consensus on critical issues. The comprehensive Doha negotiations were formally suspended in December 2011. Some parts of the negotiations have continued, but a major agreement, as originally set out in the 2001 Doha agenda, no longer appears to be possible.

Why isn't there more trade? In the wake of the suspension of the Doha Round, much soul-searching has taken place. Couldn't political leaders among the major negotiating parties simply renew their commitment to complete the round? Would changes in the structure of the negotiations, or internal reforms in how the WTO operates, or the addition of new and timely topics, promote an agreement? Do new institutional structures, such as foreign aid, need to be linked to the negotiations in order to get developing countries on board? Will countries now turn to the alternative of regional and other preferential trade agreements, abandoning the WTO multilateral model of trade liberalization? This book sets out to present an institutional framework for understanding global trade liberalization as it is currently promoted—but is currently stalled—in the WTO. Its theme is that the trouble with negotiations to expand trade is essentially the result of the inadequacy of current international trade institutions to generate consensus among WTO members. The inability of the WTO as an institution to achieve new global trade liberalization is frustrating because the gains from trade liberalization are real, significant, and within reach if governments could only find a pathway to multilateral consensus.

The book begins with an assessment of what is at stake: there are enormous, but still untapped, gains from trade that can be realized through new or revived negotiations. The gains would come not only from reducing remaining tariffs and other traditional trade barriers but also from improving trade logistics, opening up services markets to trade, and harmonizing regulations. The second and third chapters form the core of the study, presenting an institutional model of the GATT/WTO system, and the institutional problems that arose in the transition from GATT to WTO and from the structure of the Doha Round. Chapter 4 recounts the difficulties of the Doha Round and examines the institutional roots of the problem, along with possible internal institutional reforms to improve the WTO's ability to achieve consensus. Chapter 5 examines "micro" institutional elements of WTO decision-making, focusing on its structure of committee and chair positions. Chapter 6 turns to the main alternative path to global trade liberalization, regional trade agreements, along with accounts of ambitious new negotiations, including the Trans-Pacific Partnership and the US-EU Transatlantic Trade and Investment Partnership. Chapter 7 examines the concept of "embedded liberalism," which referred originally to domestic economic policies that supported trade in industrialized countries under the GATT, and the possibilities of applying it to developing countries by linking aid-for-trade with trade liberalization. Chapter 8 concludes the study by exploring possible pathways back to multilateral trade negotiations, and how the institutional framework of the WTO will need to be strengthened if this is to occur. This discussion will consider, among other recent developments, the impact of the WTO's 2013 Bali Ministerial Agreement on the future of multilateral trade liberalization.

BACKGROUND

The inspiration for the proposed study came from the ongoing debate over the Doha Round debacle, and what this failure means for the future of the WTO and multilateral trade in general. Many studies examining the problems of WTO reform began appearing as the Doha negotiations began to bog down (Petersmann 2005; Steger 2010; Martin and Mattoo 2011; Meléndez-Ortiz, Bellmann, and Rodriguez Mendoza 2012; Hoekman 2012), and more general studies of negotiation deadlock and failure began to examine structural issues (Narlikar 2010; Faure 2012). I presented my early views on the reasons for the breakdown in Doha Round negotiations in my previous OUP publication, *The Doha Blues*, and in that book began to explore the institutional concept of the WTO, based on J. R. Searle's constructivist approach (Searle 1995, 2005). In the meantime, I have tried to find a unifying conceptual framework for understanding the problems of the Doha Round. Further reading on the history of world trade (Findlay and O'Rourke 2007; Bernstein 2009) led me eventually to consider the Doha Round as an example of institutional failure, based on shortcomings and/or misalignments in the WTO's capacity to carry out its mission with regard to trade liberalization. Acemoglu and Robinson (2012) contributed to my understanding of the historical importance of domestic institutions for economic growth, while a recent study by Pinker (2011) on the decline in violence and progress in international relations, based partly on the benefits of stability in promoting the gains from trade and improved economic welfare, has also persuaded me to take a broader institutional approach to global trade and the WTO. The WTO was founded as the successor to the GATT to achieve trade liberalization through a process of consensus and an agenda based on a "single undertaking" in an organization previously dominated by the United States, the European Union, and other OECD countries. The major elements of the Doha stalemate suggest strongly that, while the gains from trade still offer a compelling reason to liberalize trade, problems with the institutional underpinnings of the WTO appear to play a large role in preventing the 160 member countries, now mostly developing countries, from coming to an agreement.

Reconstructing the World Trade
Organization for the 21st Century

The Doha Round

What Went Wrong and What is at Stake?

INTRODUCTION

On July 29, 2008, the Ministerial Conference, called by World Trade Organization (WTO) Director-General Pascal Lamy in a final attempt to complete the Doha Round of trade negotiations, collapsed, thus ending the long period of postwar multilateral trade liberalization. While a partial agreement on some issues at the WTO's Bali Ministerial Conference in December 2013 was a hopeful sign that global trade agreements were still possible, the message remained clear: the WTO must adapt to the challenges of a changing world economy if broad new global, nondiscriminatory trade agreements are to take place in the future. This chapter presents the main problems of the WTO, including a summary of the problems of the Doha Round, the institutional nature of the crisis, and the importance of the development divide. It goes on to examine what is at stake in future trade negotiations in terms of the unexploited gains from trade, which go far beyond the benefits of traditional tariff cutting to include services trade and regulatory reforms. Failure to pursue further multilateral trade liberalization will not only deny significant increases in global GDP but also allow new and insidious forms of protection to creep into the global economy.

This chapter links the components of the failure of the Doha Round to the major institutional themes of the book, while also presenting the main institutional purpose of the WTO: securing the gains from trade for member countries while allowing them to maintain sovereign control over their domestic economies. If we accept that there are demonstrable gains from trade that remain on the table in the Doha Round, then why can't an agreement to achieve mutually beneficial trade liberalization take place? The structure of the WTO and its history since the end of the Uruguay Round provide some clues in this regard. While most participants will acknowledge the potential benefits of an agreement, most parties seem to view any likely Doha package as either too risky to undertake or too small to win legislative support at home.

This introductory chapter will examine the broad contours of the Doha Round problem as an institutional issue, a failure to find a framework for achieving mutual gains from trade. There are many contributing factors, but looking at the WTO negotiations as a matter of applying jointly accepted goals, rules, obligations, and procedures, a shorter list of problems can be identified. The discussion then turns to one prominent illustrative example, indicating a number of the underlying institutional problems: the conflicting positions of developed and developing countries, based in part on the bargaining "rules of engagement" in the negotiations. The narrowing scope of potential agreement that resulted from such disagreements belies, however, the vast potential for gains from trade that were left on the table, as presented in a review of the sources of gains from broad and ambitious multilateral trade liberalization. Existing estimates tend to understate the gains, due to the difficulty of quantifying regulatory barriers to trade, especially in services. While one way that multilateral negotiations can capture these gains is through reciprocal market access and agreement on new rules and integrative measures, the other is to keep the relentless forces of protectionism at bay. This point is illustrated through a review of recent developments in trade restrictions since the beginning of the financial crisis, which shows a seemingly endless capacity for bureaucratic creativity among governments in devising subtle methods of circumventing and avoiding existing disciplines against protectionism. A brief concluding section points the way to the following chapters on the institutional structure of the GATT/WTO system.

THE DOHA DEBACLE

We are already in the post-Doha period as far as global trade relations are concerned. In December 2011, for the first time in the sixty-four-year history of the GATT/WTO system, the WTO's eighth Ministerial Conference officially acknowledged that the multilateral negotiations were at an impasse (WTO 2011a), three-and-a-half years after the desperate attempt at closing a deal in July 2008. In the meantime the worst global economic downturn since the Great Depression had begun, making many governments wary of globalization and suspicious of global trade. The world appears indeed to have entered a period of global trade skepticism, with little interest in a large global package deal that had become the standard for multilateral trade liberalization. Trade ministers in Geneva finally agreed that trade talks should turn from a comprehensive Doha agreement to more focused efforts to harvest what could be salvaged, an effort that resulted in the modest agreement at the Bali Ministerial in December 2013. Yet in general WTO negotiations have moved to the back burner for many governments, as trade officials in many capitals have turned resources and attention toward the bilateral and regional trade deals they now refer to as "the only trade game in town." In the aftermath of the Doha debacle, has the WTO become irrelevant to global trade liberalization?

The good news is that the WTO is alive and well as an international organization; it is, however, just not as alive and well as a forum for the sort of big, far-reaching global trade negotiations that it was supposed to deliver. Of the WTO's three principle functions—implementing and monitoring a set of global trade rules, settling disputes among member countries, and negotiating new trade agreements—the first two continue to function well on a day-to-day basis at its headquarters in Geneva. WTO member countries enjoy the stability that comes from a rules-based global trading system, based on the work of standing committees that hash out the details and implementation of the rules, and the panel system that reviews disputes among members. These are some of the valuable "public goods" provided by the WTO to the global community: a set of trade policy rules based on nondiscrimination, the mutual gains from trade and dispute settlement that benefits all members, as long as all of them respect the rules. Membership in the WTO is a signal to the world that a country is "open for business," that it has accepted the large, accumulated body of WTO disciplines that promote reciprocal market access with WTO trading partners. As of early 2014, the WTO had 160 members, and most of the world's remaining non-member countries were negotiating to join. The WTO is doing many things right. Its predecessor institution, the General Agreement on Tariffs and Trade (GATT), was founded in 1947 with twenty-three members and shepherded the world economy through eight successful rounds of trade negotiations, over nearly five decades of trade expansion and economic growth. This success led to the founding of the GATT's successor, the more comprehensive World Trade Organization, in 1995. The WTO continued the functions of the GATT while expanding into new product areas, such as agriculture and services, created new rules to deal with an evolving trade environment, and strengthened the dispute settlement system.

And yet the WTO has failed to build on the third pillar: to provide a forum and framework for multilateral trade liberalization, and this problem cannot be ignored. A trading system that does not generate new agreements risks falling backward. The old adage, often repeated by trade diplomats during the GATT years, still applies in our day. Managing the trading system is like riding a bicycle—if you don't keep moving forward, you'll fall over. Rorden Wilkinson

(2012) criticizes such metaphors in describing the Doha Round, judging them to be overwrought and too suggestive of death, injury, and oblivion. Thus, describing the Doha Round as having died, suffering from a fatal disease, or being on life support with the plug about to be pulled, is inappropriate in his view, in that such metaphors suggest the destruction of the institution. He also finds comparison with train wrecks, "going off the rails," and the ubiquitous "falling off the bicycle" as suggesting death or catastrophic injury. While all metaphors ultimately break down in their representation when comparisons are taken into the details, the bicycle metaphor still resonates at several levels. The Doha Round is not in fact dead, although the multilateral negotiations have been suspended, but the bicycle can be said to have stopped, if not fallen over— although the riders got off the "single undertaking" Doha road and made it up a modest hill to a roadside Bali destination. Consider a bicycle built for several riders, all of whom have to agree to pedal together to keep moving forward, requiring a coordinated effort and agreement on the destination. Stopping or even falling down does not necessarily imply life-threatening injuries, but does provide the occasion for the riders to consider alternative ways to pursue the original trade agenda, or to agree upon other goals. There might be an argument about who stopped pedaling (a common blame game), but the failure to proceed may also raise the question as to whether the bicycle, designed for the easier roads (gentler slopes?) of past negotiations, is not capable of climbing the steeper hills of the Doha Round. Perhaps instead of a single multi-rider bike (as under a Single Undertaking) it makes sense to have teams on different tandem bikes that may follow different paths at different speeds. Perhaps the bicycle (or bicycles), representing the traditional negotiating forum, should be abandoned in favor of other means of transport, or even walking at a slow or steady pace in the form of deliberate, ongoing, day-to-day negotiations through standing committees in Geneva. In any case, the bicycle is an apt representation of the "technology" of a multilateral trade negotiation, requiring a concerted effort among the riders to move toward an agreed-upon destination, the package deal of a mandated Single Undertaking. Clearly, this bicycle has stopped moving. The riders are now trying to find ways toward less ambitious goals in pairs or smaller groups, along the byways of the original path. If the ambitions of the Doha Round have been scaled down in this manner, some limited trade liberalization may yet take place, but there may also be serious consequences for the global WTO system as a whole.

For example, new trade issues, methods of trading, and technologies imply the need for negotiating new WTO rules for the trading system. A changing world economy, with new trade participants, experiences new frictions and new trade disputes. The system of WTO dispute settlement is designed to sort out the meaning and enforcement of the existing rules that the members have negotiated, not create new rules and obligations on its own authority. In the absence of new rules and new market opening agreements, the existing system will be overburdened with disputes brought before it. Attempts to extrapolate existing rules to cover new situations will only cause new tensions. New global trading rules come about only after long intervals defined by the conclusion of multilateral negotiations, which will then, after several years of phase-in and implementation, need to serve the trading system until the next multilateral agreement takes place. The challenges of a changing world economy require a sustainable trading system of multilateral rules and procedures. The WTO will be able to perform this function in the future only if it can continue to negotiate new multilateral agreements. This book is about the WTO as an institution, how it failed to deliver a comprehensive Doha Round trade agreement, and how it can be reconstructed to achieve multilateral agreements in the future.

WHAT WENT WRONG AT THE DOHA ROUND?

The failure of the Doha Round to achieve an agreement after ten years of negotiation has many roots. This book sets out to use an institutional approach to provide a unified framework for understanding the many different problems that contributed to the stalemate. Chapter 4, in particular, will review the lowlights (many) and highlights (few) of the Doha Round. A brief summary of the many contributing factors to the problems of the Doha Round, which draws in part on Jones (2010), contains the following items:

(1) *The WTO membership has grown too large and diverse.* Developing countries now represent about 78% of the large and growing WTO membership, and it is difficult to achieve consensus on a package of trade liberalization measures that is meaningful and mutually acceptable to all developed and all developing countries.

(2) *The Single Undertaking was a good idea in principle, but it did not work in practice.* Having a big single package, in which "nothing is agreed until everything is agreed," was meant to provide the widest possible range of issues to trade off in the Doha Round bargaining. But there were some issues with "red lines" regarding reform on which no trade-off elsewhere was possible, such as agriculture and services, and the talks got stuck on issues for which trade-offs in other areas could not break the logjam.

(3) *There has been a change in the bargaining power of the GATT/WTO system away from dominance of the United States and European Union and toward the emerging markets.* India and Brazil joined the new

"Quad" group shortly after the Round was launched. The Quad countries, previously composed of large OECD members, had served as the foundation for agreement in the Uruguay Round, but the new, more diverse Quad contained positions that could not be reconciled among its members.

(4) *Leadership of the world economy by the United States, in particular, had diminished.* The Doha Round was therefore without an effective champion. Slowing US economic growth, controversial US foreign policies, especially in Iraq, and US presidents with either low international esteem (George W. Bush) or limited interest in trade liberalization (Barack Obama) were contributing factors.

(5) *Developing countries were "mad as hell" and refused to take it anymore.* Disappointments over Uruguay Round textiles/apparel and agricultural trade liberalization, and over the implementation costs of new obligations, caused resentment among many developing countries. The strategy for many of them subsequently focused on blocking agreements and taking particularly hard lines on concessions in the Doha Round.

(6) *Multilateral trade negotiations ran out of easy fuel and political support for reciprocal bargaining.* Lowering tariffs was relatively easy when tariffs on manufactured goods were high and countries could depend on exporter interests to push the negotiations forward. After eight rounds of trade liberalization, what remained to be liberalized was much more politically sensitive both in terms of the products (agriculture, services) and the methods of market restriction (behind the border regulations), making it difficult to muster domestic support for a trade deal.

(7) *Special and differential treatment confused the terms of reciprocal bargaining.* GATT provisions had established reduced reciprocity requirements for developing countries, but this was much more difficult to apply consistently in the Doha Round. First, several emerging markets among the developing countries now played an important role in trade liberalization, implying a need for them to increase access to their own markets. In addition, the diversity of development status among developing countries had grown, making uniform treatment of reciprocity obligations difficult. In a related matter, developing countries receiving preferential market access from programs such as the Generalized System of Preferences (GSP) were disinclined to support general trade liberalization, which would diminish their margins of preference in GSP products.

(8) *The world was distracted by other crises.* Global terrorism, global warming, and the financial crisis of 2008 drew attention away from trade negotiations and created anxieties in some quarters that linked WTO-inspired trade liberalization with these negative manifestations of globalization. In addition, although it was late in the Round, the financial crisis perversely inspired new forms of protectionism.

(9) *Business interests turned toward regional and global supply chains.* The advent of international cross investment and production linkages caused businesses to focus more on bilateral investment treaties and preferential trade agreements, which furthermore could be concluded more quickly than the seemingly endless WTO negotiations.

(10) *Countries had become wary of making binding new WTO commitments.* The global economy is changing more rapidly, putting more adjustment pressure on domestic economies. Reforms in dispute settlement now subject trade agreements to legally binding commitments, displacing the traditional diplomatic methods of the GATT. Safeguards measures were also being challenged and overturned in WTO dispute settlement, making new liberalization agreements riskier.

This list does not exhaust the possibilities of explaining the problems of the Doha Round. There were, for example, the inevitable charges that one country or another refused to negotiate in good faith, or undermined the talks at some critical point. In addition, one can criticize countries' strategies during the Round, such as the insistence of the European Union and other countries to include the "Singapore" issues on the agenda, which many developing countries had opposed from the beginning.[1] Developing countries insisted on reaching agreement on agricultural and non-agricultural market access (NAMA) before anything else could be tackled, which put the negotiations on a narrow and inflexible path (Hufbauer and Schott 2012: 3). The United States allegedly demanded additional sectoral agreements after a preliminary deal on NAMA had been reached, putting agreement out of reach (Panagariya 2013; Ismail 2012). These issues may have deepened the North-South divide for the rest of the Doha Round. Others have even taken Director-General Pascal Lamy to task for his management of the Round, especially his decision to call off the 2007 Ministerial Meeting. Yet most of these issues could have been overcome through subsequent bargaining if WTO members wanted a final agreement. WTO members made enormous investments in time and effort in the Doha Round, and one must presume that they all negotiated with the goal and expectation of achieving real and valuable benefits for their countries from an agreement. It is therefore difficult to believe that anything less than larger forces were at work that compromised their ability to conclude the negotiations.

There are many ways to slice and dice the various elements of the failure of the Doha Round. This book will approach this topic as an institutional issue. While the problems of the WTO can legitimately be analyzed from many specific economic, political, legal, and even sociological perspectives, a focus on the WTO as an institution addresses what this author sees as the central question: how can sovereign countries, all of whom stand to gain from trade, come to consensus on trade liberalization? Institutional analysis considers why the WTO exists as an organization, and the process by which its members collectively agree on pursuing its goals. It seeks to clarify both formal and informal rules regarding the rights and obligations of members, negotiations, and decision-making. It identifies what policy areas are allowable for bargaining, how the process of achieving consensus starts, and how it ends. With this framework in mind, the ten contributing reasons for the collapse of the Doha Round enumerated above can be restated, in broader fashion, in terms of the following five, partially overlapping, institutional problems:

(1) The Doha Round agenda conflicted with the limits of domestic policy sovereignty in trade bargaining, with divergences in acceptable "policy space" among WTO members.

(2) The Single Undertaking was the wrong organizing principle for the negotiations, since the Doha agenda was too large and the preferences of the large membership diverged too much on key issues to reach a single, package agreement.

(3) WTO guidelines on special and differential treatment for developing countries, rooted in earlier GATT practice, had led to contradictory treatment of developing countries regarding "special and differential" (S & D) treatment, without a clear understanding of how their reciprocity requirements would be defined in trade negotiations.

(4) A significant shift in the balance of power in WTO negotiations away from OECD countries and toward emerging markets generated dysfunctional confrontations over procedural issues, revealed gaps in understanding over the basic goals of the organization, and generated bargaining coalitions and strategies, particularly among developing countries, that led to deadlock.

(5) WTO dispute settlement reforms increased the stakes of liberalization commitments because of stricter legal disciplines, under conditions of increasing uncertainty and without increasing the practical availability of safeguards measures.

This book will focus on these aspects of the WTO's institutional crisis, first by developing a model of the GATT/WTO system (chapter 2), the problems introduced with the WTO transition and the Doha Round (chapter 3), confrontations in the negotiations (chapter 4), the role of internal governance in making the system work (chapter 5), the dangers—and possible usefulness—of regional trade agreements as alternatives to the WTO (chapter 6), the possibility of applying "aid for trade" to solve some of these problems (chapter 7), and finally, the synthesis of these issues in contemplating possible pathways back to successful multilateral trade liberalization (chapter 8).

AT STAKE: A FRAMEWORK FOR FUTURE TRADE NEGOTIATIONS

The collapse of the general Doha Round negotiations has raised serious concerns regarding the ability of the WTO to conduct multilateral trade negotiations. What is at stake in reviving the negotiating role of the WTO is its ability for all countries, developed and developing, to come together in a single forum to deliberate over market access and trade rules that will allow all countries to gain from trade on a nondiscriminatory basis. Also at stake is the WTO's ability to bring trade liberalization to new and growing sectors that have the greatest potential for increased welfare and economic growth. The most prominent example is services, which has now gone through two major trade negotiations without significant progress in promoting market access or rules liberalization. One key aspect of the Doha Round that illustrates some of the important institutional issues is the way it was presented to the WTO membership as a "development round." The well-meaning but ultimately foolish slogan of a "Doha Development Agenda" (DDA), introduced at the 2001 Ministerial Conference and still enshrined in WTO descriptions of the Doha Round, was meant to signal to developing countries that the new trade round would give special consideration to their interests. This decision represented an honest effort to address developing country disappointment in the results of the Uruguay Round, particularly over the dashed expectations of widespread gains from textile and agricultural trade liberalization, and over the implementation costs of new WTO obligations. As the discussion in chapter 7 will show, however, WTO-sponsored trade negotiations were never in a position to offer a systematic and targeted "development agenda." Institutionally, WTO negotiations are designed to bring all countries together to bargain over market access and trade rules, not development issues. Agreement is based on reciprocity in market access and consensus on a final agreement that satisfies each country's trade agendas, not the development agendas of selected participants.

In addition, trade is a transaction that is part of a process of gaining from trade, whereas development is a more fundamental process of domestic social and economic transformation. Trade can be an important part of the development process, but a multilateral trade negotiation should never be sold as a "development agenda."

WHAT NEW GAINS FROM TRADE ARE AVAILABLE?

Paul Krugman (1995) once provocatively wrote that economists kept a "dirty little secret" that "the measurable cost of protectionist policies … are not all that large." His comment was in part a jab at many trade economists he regarded as overly obsessive about reducing tariffs, even if the economic benefits of doing so were quite small. He was also evidently referring to the fact that tariff levels themselves, by the end of the Uruguay Round of trade negotiations in 1994, had fallen to historically low levels. Since the end of World War II, when average global tariff levels were still close to their Great Depression levels of around 40%, several rounds of trade negotiations conducted under the General Agreement on Tariffs and Trade (GATT) had brought the average down to 6%. By 2010 the global weighted mean tariff rate, estimated by the World Bank, was just 3%. In addition, the GATT negotiations had largely (though not completely) eliminated quota barriers to trade, which had been even more damaging than tariffs in terms of distorting markets. The traditional policy measures to restrict trade, in other words, had seemingly been brought under control through successful postwar trade negotiation, and further gains to the world economy from new trade talks would be marginal at best.

Yet it would be a mistake to belittle the value of reducing current tariff rates in today's world economy, even if the global mean is low. First of all, even low tariffs present an administratively potent barrier to trade, since any tariff, however small, still requires bureaucratic processing to document the tariffed item's value. In trade negotiations, special efforts have therefore focused on the complete elimination of tariffs in specific sectors, since the benefits of eliminating red tape and other transaction costs in moving to duty-free trade far exceed the damage done by even small tariff levels. In addition, the dispersion of tariff rates by product and by country is high. This is why the Doha Round focused so much energy on market access through tariff reductions, and on the modalities of doing so. Global agricultural tariffs, for example, are much higher than the mean for all tariffs, 19.1% according to a study by Antoine Bouët and others (2008). Within low average tariff levels, there are significant tariff "peaks," whose impact is often underestimated by averaging tariff lines without considering their impact on actual trade flows.[2] Despite low average tariffs, for example, individual tariff lines reach levels as high as 121% in the United States, 171% in Japan, 252% in the European Union, and 353% in Canada. The peaks, furthermore, do not occur randomly, but are typically designed to protect politically sensitive subcategories of goods, often by developed countries on products of export interest to developing countries, such as sugar, cereals, fish, tobacco, fruits and vegetables, and clothing and footwear (Hoekman, Ng, and Olarreaga 2001). And even if nominal tariff levels on final manufactured and processed products are low, they will have a disproportionately protectionist impact if their *effective* tariff rates are high. This occurs when the tariff structure leads to a high level of protection on domestic value added for final goods in a value chain. In this manner, low nominal tariffs may still make it economically infeasible for developing countries to export value-added "downstream" products that use their raw materials as inputs.[3]

Tariff levels among developing countries, for their part, are significantly higher than the global average and provide a barrier to exports emanating not only from the developed but also from other developing countries. The lower volume of trade in many developing countries makes their higher tariffs' impact on the world economy appear relatively small, but they are growing more rapidly than the developed world, and the larger emerging markets, including China, India, Brazil, and Indonesia, will be among the largest consumer markets in the world in the coming decades. Another important dimension of the tariff issue in developing countries is that their applied rates (as reported in most current tariff estimates) are often significantly smaller than their bound rates. WTO rules require member countries to "bind" their tariff rates at negotiated levels, which are often very high in developing countries, especially in agricultural goods. The rules forbid the country from raising tariffs above the bound levels, but they are free to reduce tariffs to lower levels—with the right to raise them again in the future up to the maximum. For example, the applied tariff for wheat in India in 2008 was 50% while the bound rate was 100%. When India negotiates in the WTO, only the bound tariffs are on the table for bargaining, which is frustrating for those seeking market access for wheat in India because India could cut its bound tariff in half—and take credit for it as a bargaining chip—without yielding any new market access for imports. What is worse, during the recent global financial crisis Brazil has chosen to raise many of its tariff lines from the relatively low applied rates to the maximum bound rates. Thus, the much larger bound rates will need to be negotiated down in order to eliminate the binding "overhang." Tariffs are no small matter!

In addition to tariffs, government subsidies represent a companion set of trade restrictions (see WTO 2006b). The WTO defines subsidies as policies that "impact the government budget and affect the production of goods" (Hoekman and Kostecki 2009).[4] Many subsidies can be justified in principle on the basis of improving the efficiency of markets, and most subsidies in general are permitted under WTO rules. WTO subsidy disciplines focus on measures that *distort trade outcomes*, especially in the case of overt export subsidies (banned under WTO rules in most cases). Depending on their magnitude and impact, domestic subsidies may also distort trade by giving artificial advantages to subsidized domestic producers, especially in agriculture, and this issue was a major bone of contention in the Doha Round. Agricultural subsidies represent a rich country's form of trade restriction, as usually only wealthier countries can lavish them on their farming sectors, especially the European Union, the United States, Japan, and other OECD countries. High-income countries collectively granted subsidy equivalents of about $191 billion annually between 2000 and 2004 (Anderson and Valenzuela 2008), with the most distorting subsidies, as measured by the WTO, totaling about $60 billion annually in 2001 (WTO 2006b: 134). Actual subsidy levels vary with market conditions and change with the legislative cycle in each country. It is clear that many developing countries would enjoy increased market access in high-income countries if these subsidies were reduced, although net food-importing countries would lose from such reductions. Much of the economic gain of reduced agricultural subsidies would go to the developed countries themselves because the market distortion from subsidies on the production side is more damaging to them than to competing developing country exporters. Although not an issue in the Doha Round, government subsidies have also distorted trade more recently in the form of large bailouts and targeted stimulus packages in response to the financial crisis of 2008 (see below). Finally, government procurement practices represent a form of subsidy, typically by favoring domestic over foreign producers of goods and services, leading to much larger costs that must be paid by taxpayers, and reducing the country's economic welfare. There is a WTO plurilateral agreement on government procurement, but its membership includes only a small subset of WTO countries and its scope is still limited. In view of the large portion of countries' GDP subject to government spending, estimated to be 15–20% on average worldwide (Lamy 2011), further liberalization of government procurement would lead to significant new gains from trade.

Krugman, in focusing on the "measurable" cost of protectionist policies as the "dirty little secret," was almost certainly referring to tariffs alone, for which estimating the cost of protection is usually a straightforward exercise. While tariffs nonetheless still represent a significant trade restriction, non-tariff measures (NTMs) represent a much larger problem for market access. They include domestic regulations, rules, and processes that have a discriminatory impact on imports. Technical standards for electronic equipment and machinery, health and safety standards for food, rules of origin, and government procurement are examples of domestic rules that potentially could have a protectionist impact on imports. Otsuki, Wilson, and Sewadeh (2001), for example, examined proposed EU standards for aflatoxin levels of cereals, dried fruits, and nuts from Africa and estimated that the EU regulations would reduce imports of these items by 64% ($670m) compared with the less onerous global Codex Alimentarius standards, with only a miniscule increase in health risk. The trade-restrictive impact can in principle be measured by identifying the gap in the price of the good subject to the NTM in the home and in foreign markets. The gap is often difficult to measure, but recent research has made progress in identifying and measuring their effects.[5] It is important to note that many NTMs have legitimate public policy purposes, especially when they are designed to protect public safety. However, they can have a protectionist effect to the extent that their implementation and enforcement put disproportionate burdens on traded, as opposed to domestically produced, products. NTMs impose additional costs on imports through extra compliance features, burdensome red tape, time-consuming procedures, and rules and regulations specifically targeting or disadvantaging the imported item. Their restrictive effects are usually more severe than tariffs, and agreements to reduce their trade-restrictive impact are more difficult to negotiate, but all the more important to put on the negotiating agenda.

Another set of trade barriers consists of infrastructure gaps in many developing countries that hinder the logistics and "facilitation" of trade. Deficient infrastructure is costly to those engaged in trade because it raises the cost of trading and often delays shipments. These problems are particularly costly for agricultural products, since delays often irreparably damage food products. Trade facilitation issues include port efficiency (port facilities, inland waterways, and air transport), customs service efficiency (including red tape and bribes to customs officials), the country's regulatory environment regarding the processing of imports and exports, and service sector infrastructure (especially Internet speed and cost). Both developed and developing countries would gain from the improvements. Financing for improved infrastructure has already begun, mainly through the World Bank and other development agencies, but coordinated efforts among the negotiating parties are needed in order to secure the improved policies and procedures necessary to achieve the gains. The potential for increased trade is large, as Wilson, Mann, and Otsuki (2005) estimate that raising trade facilitation standards in the weakest countries to half the global median would increase trade by $377 billion. Hufbauer and Schott (2013) report that full implementation of a successful trade facilitation agreement could lead to global GDP gains of $960 billion per year, an enormous benefit that exceeds the estimated benefits of reducing all countries' tariffs to zero. Trade facilitation was on the Doha Round agenda and was the major component of the Bali Agreement in December 2013. Further trade facilitation measures and infrastructure improvements beyond this agreement will lead to even greater gains.

Last but certainly not least, the impact of trade restrictions in services spans a wide variety of economic activity in the world economy. The potential for increased trade in services is enormous, in view of the fact that 70% of global GDP is linked to services, while just 20% of global trade consisted of services in 2011. Yet trade in services is growing rapidly and could grow more if trade barriers were liberalized. According to WTO figures, global trade in commercial services was valued at $4.17 trillion in 2011. For purposes of WTO services trade negotiations, there are four "modes" or categories of service delivery:

(1) cross-border supply, in which the services are transported across borders, such as banking, telecommunications, and consulting services transmitted electronically or through other means of communication across borders;

(2) consumption abroad, in which the customer crosses borders to receive the service, such tourism, medical services, and education;

(3) commercial presence, in which a service supplier in one country establishes a physical presence in the territory of another country to provide the service, such as banking, insurance and hotel services; and

(4) the presence of natural persons who cross borders to deliver the service, such as doctors, educators, consultants, and migrant workers in general.

These four categories indicate that the variety of traded services is large, from maritime shipping and air transport to retail food distribution and electricity distribution, from business, financial, and telecommunications services to the services of workers living temporarily in foreign countries. As was the case with the non-tariff measures described above, many services-related policies are based on legitimate regulations of domestic economic activities, and similarly, the protectionist component of the policies resides in discriminatory measures against foreign service providers beyond what is necessary to protect the public good. Francois and Hoekman (2010) summarize the literature on services trade and trade policy. In most cases, the restrictions on services trade take the form of domestic regulations regarding the mandatory use of domestically sourced services, barriers to the physical establishment of foreign service providers in domestic markets, barriers to foreign direct investment, and restrictions on temporary migration and work permits. It is difficult to calculate "tariff equivalents" for most services trade restrictions, since many of the barriers take the form of regulations—often discretionary—to limit the very presence of the foreign service provider in the market. However, Francois and Hoekman (2010) summarize several studies on the price/cost impact of services restrictions that estimate, for example, resulting increases in developed and developing countries, respectively, of 31% and 64% in air fares, 26% and 21% in mobile telecom prices, and 73% and 34% in international telecom prices. Borchert, Gootiiz, and Mattoo (2012) present comparative trade restrictiveness indexes for various types of services, as they are imposed in various regional country groupings. In general, the indexes show that services trade barriers in general are very high compared to goods. Trade in transportation and professional services tend to face the greatest restrictions, followed by retail, telecom, and financial services.[6] Services trade restrictiveness varies widely by region, with the highest barriers in the broader North Africa/Middle East/Asia and Pacific regions (2012: 19–24). Given the large and increasing share of services in nearly all countries in the world, trade restrictions on services appear to have a pervasive and large detrimental impact on consumer welfare, foreign investment activity, and economic efficiency. As a negotiating issue, services trade also introduces new challenges in finding modalities: practical frameworks for negotiated liberalization. Apart from purely trade-related aspects of services trade, there are often domestic regulations that reduce competition domestically, so that competition law principles will enter negotiations, a sensitive domestic policy issue.

A significant and still largely unexplored source of the gains from trade, in terms of pure economic welfare effects, lies in liberalizing restrictions on the temporary movement of persons. This is a part of services trade (mode 4) that remains politically sensitive, but of potentially great positive impact, especially for developing countries. The largest gains would occur in allowing greater access of low-skilled workers to markets of developed countries, since the gap between wage rates in this category is highest. In addition, agreements to allow greater movement of labor among developing countries themselves would also have significant benefits, since making work available in one country to large numbers of otherwise underemployed workers in other countries, even at low prevailing wages, would improve both countries' efficiency and welfare. In the case of small and landlocked, or island economies, the export of labor services through temporary migration is often the best, and in some cases essentially the only, way of gaining from trade. In most cases a large portion of the wages earned by such workers employed abroad are repatriated to their home countries.[7] Gains from trade also occur in the temporary movement of skilled labor in professional occupations such as management, teaching, consulting, and financial and business services, in which access to the market is based typically on certifications and other regulations. Fully open borders for temporary labor migration are unlikely in the foreseeable future, but the potential gains from liberalizing this activity are so large for developing countries that even partial liberalization would represent major gains, increasing the value of an agreement.

All of the trade issues described above have been the subject, to a greater or lesser extent, of the Doha Round trade negotiations. Negotiations on many of them did not get very far because, as this book will show, governments strongly resisted opening up discussions on them, especially with regard to the trade-restrictive impact of domestic services regulations. In other cases, especially in agriculture, tariff, and subsidy talks became deadlocked because of domestic political resistance in several countries. Agreement on tariff modalities in non-agricultural goods was also difficult because of bound tariff overhangs and disagreements on the burden of tariff cutting between developed and developing countries. One could conclude from this that the apparent estimated economic value of the limited trade liberalization that negotiators could realistically achieve under these circumstances was relatively small. However, one could also conclude, based on the scope of product coverage and the trade-distorting measures under discussion, that the potential for significant gains from trade is enormous. Empirical studies of the economic gains from eliminating these barriers are indeed substantial.

In contrast, therefore, to Krugman's estimation of the penny-ante stakes of trade liberalization, the real little secret—dirty or otherwise—is that the potential gains from further trade liberalization are much larger than what can be garnered from eliminating tariffs—although these gains are significant on their own. Laborde, Martin, and van der Mensbrugghe (2011) estimate that the complete elimination of all tariffs globally would result in an economic gain equal to 0.88% of world GDP annually. This may sound like a small percentage, but it would amount to over $632 billion in 2012,[8] and these gains would accrue and compound annually. Furthermore, the resulting gains would be significantly greater for developing countries (1.3% of their GDP) than for developed countries (0.76% of GDP). Gains from eliminating non-tariff barriers (NTBs) to goods trade are more difficult to calculate, but Cadot, Saez, and Maliszewska (2010) report that many studies show average global tariff-equivalent estimates of such measures of 5–10%. Their impact is therefore roughly comparable to that of the global tariff regime, implying gains from total NTB liberalization of the same order of magnitude. Most of the gains that need to be negotiated come from more obscure and nontransparent policies that discriminate against traded goods and services. Robinson, Wang, and Martin (2002), estimate the welfare effect of an ambitious services trade liberalization agreement (not including mode 4 worker migration) to be on the order of 3.7% of global GDP annually, which would be equal to over $2.6 trillion in 2012. Winters et al. (2002) estimate that partial liberalization of worker migration—developed countries allowing temporary migration of skilled and unskilled developing country workers to increase the workforces by 3%—would increase world income by approximately 0.4% of global GDP, which would be equal to about $260 billion in 2012. About half of these gains go to the developing countries of migration, including the migrating workers themselves. This figure is still probably a fraction of the possible gains from broader and more comprehensive liberalization in labor migration policy.

Adding up all the possible gains from trade for a global negotiating cycle of (for example) twenty years would be an ambitious, indeed, a monumental, undertaking, if one wanted to include everything that could be counted as, or be linked to, increased trade, and take account of spillover, competitive, productivity, and technological effects, compounded over time. It would have to include the total effects on global GDP from eliminating tariffs, trade-distorting subsidies, government procurement and other NTBs in goods and services, liberalizing domestic regulations to economically efficient levels that do not discriminate against traded items, maximizing coordinated efforts to reduce trade and logistics costs, and making possible the free movement of people across borders. Based simply on the figures mentioned in the review above, the benefits of such a world of free trade would be counted in the many trillions of dollars, perhaps 10% of global GDP annually, or more. Expressed in another way, Subramanian and Kessler (2013: 36) describe the process of trade globalization as less than half complete. Even if one were to insist on scaling down the results to reflect "political realities," the remaining gains would be enormous. Much of the total gain would accrue to developing countries, lifting hundreds of millions, if not billions, out of poverty. The "small change," as Krugman might put it, of a limited Doha Round agreement, which in any case never happened (in part perhaps because it was so small) is misleading. The real stakes of trade liberalization can be estimated in the multi-trillion-dollar boost it could bring to the world economy.

PROTECTIONISM DURING THE FINANCIAL CRISIS

A review of the gains from reducing tariff barriers and non-tariff measures still tells only part of the story when it comes to evaluating the benefits of the WTO and what is at stake in multilateral trade liberalization. There is real danger in taking a complacent attitude toward the failure of the Doha Round, relying on the existing WTO rules as a sufficient guardian of the global trading order. As noted earlier, the rules and dispute settlement dimensions of the WTO appear to be working well: none of the 160 member countries have announced any intention to withdraw, and the WTO rules and dispute settlement procedures are widely respected. However, it has also been revealing to see how the WTO system has operated under the stress of the global financial crisis, beginning in 2008, and the subsequent pressures on governments to protect their domestic industries. The prevailing view among many trade economists is that the WTO system has contained protectionism reasonably well, since there have been few violations of WTO rules. In contrast to the Great Depression of the 1930s, the disaster of the Smoot-Hawley tariffs imposed by the United States, and the global escala- tion of protectionism at the time, the 2008 financial crisis has not led to massive increases in tariffs and trade wars. During the Great Depression, global trade contracted massively, by 65% over the years 1929–33 (Irwin 1993: 103–113). The significant reduction in trade in 2009 can be attributed largely to the con- traction of GDP among major trading countries (Bown 2011: 13), along with the lack of short-term credit, which is crucial for import-export trade.

Yet a closer examination shows a disturbing trend. While most countries have respected the letter of WTO rules during the crisis, protectionist policies have nonetheless expanded in insidious ways, as noted by Evenett (2011). The pattern appears to show that protectionist adaptation has led to a progressive introduction of new trade restrictions as the crisis has lingered. According to Global Trade Alert, a database monitoring new protectionist measures, 2,134 government policy measures were implemented from November 2008 to September 2013 that were highly likely to discriminate against foreign com- mercial interests, many of which affected large categories of trade.[9] Most such measures over this period were imposed by the European Union (382), Russian Federation (247), Argentina (198), and India (124) (Evenett 2013: table 2.6). Some measures were acceptable under WTO rules, even if their impact was protectionist. For example, member countries can legally raise applied tariffs to their bound rates, and several countries have in fact done so.[10] Other measures linked with WTO rules included 517 trade restrictions based on safeguard, anti-dumping, and countervailing duty cases. Most of the measures, however, involve what Baldwin and Evenett (2009) call "murky protectionism," mea- sures not explicitly covered by WTO rules. Table 1.1 shows a breakdown of the 2,134 new protectionist measures implemented globally from November 2008 to September 2013, as reported by Global Trade Alert (Evenett 2013). The largest number (23%) are "trade-defensive" measures such as antidumping, countervailing duty, and safeguard measures, with another 12% representing tariff increases within bound levels, all disciplined by WTO rules, but show- ing a protectionist surge. More than half of the new measures, however, are "murky," including various domestic subsidies and bailouts, migration, invest- ment and export restrictions, and other measures, most of which fall outside of WTO disciplines.[11] Policies that avoid binding global trade rules, exploit loop- holes and otherwise invent new variants on protectionist policies represent

Table 1.1 STATE MEASURES TO DISCRIMINATE AGAINST COMMERCIAL
INTEREST, NOVEMBER 2008-SEPTEMBER 2013

Measure	Number of measures imposed	% of total	Number of jurisdictions imposing measures	Number of jurisdictions harmed by measures
1. Trade defense measure (antidumping)	517	23	64	90
2. Bailout/state aid measure	517	23	56	195
3. Tariff measure	263	12	76	168
4. Non-tariff barrier (not otherwise specified)	173	8	71	181
5. Export taxes or restriction	123	5	68	183
6. Investment measure	112	5	43	106
7. Migration measure	94	4	37	147
8. Export subsidy	83	4	51	199
9. Trade finance	78	3	13	195
10. Public procurement	52	2	23	137
11. Other	252	11		
Total	2,142	100		

a time-honored practice in global trade relations, so it should not come as a sur-
prise that a new and serious economic crisis will cause governments to find new
ways to favor domestic firms at the expense of foreigners. Some of this activity
can be interpreted as "safety valve" activity by governments imposing limited
protectionism while allowing the broader trading system to continue functioning. These measures raise the question, however, as to whether more efficient
domestic nondiscriminatory trade adjustment measures, combined with further trade liberalization, could secure a better outcome for the global economy.
Creative policymakers will always search for ways to get around existing rules
that limit the use of the current instruments of trade protection. During the
years of global structural change in the postwar period in many established
manufactured industries, for example, GATT rules banning the use of unilateral tariff increases and import quotas led to the introduction of "voluntary"
export restraint agreements, which were negotiated import quotas by another
name. These measures led to widespread protectionism in steel, automobiles,
and other troublesome imports, and most prominently through the "multifiber
agreement" of negotiated export quotas in textiles and clothing.

Evenett (2011) concludes that the WTO has not, in fact, stemmed the increase in protectionism in the wake of the 2008 financial crisis, based on the leeway the rules give to members, and on the measures not covered by them. This judgment may be too harsh, in that the creative circumvention of the WTO rules indicates a certain respect for the existing rules, but also indicates the work of protecting the world economy from protectionism is far from complete. The most important conclusion to draw is that keeping protectionism in check requires constant vigilance. The trend in protectionism also points, however, to the need not only of pursuing more trade liberalization, which will restrain countries from new protectionist actions, but also the urgency of negotiating new disciplines and rules. Tariffs, while still important, are no longer the main protectionist device. Governments are increasingly developing new and subtle methods of manipulating domestic regulations and subsidies that discriminate in favor of their industries and against those of foreigners.

SUMMARY

The unsuccessful Doha Round represents a watershed in global trade relations. The postwar formulas for negotiating trade liberalization, devised under the GATT, have proven to be inadequate to achieve new multilateral agreements in a more diverse global economy of changing technologies, changing trade patterns, and changing patterns of growth. The Single Undertaking did not work. Disagreements over "policy space" stymied progress on many issues, as did the gap between developed and developing countries' views on reciprocity. The pattern of bargaining power had changed and the judicialization of trade commitments had raised the stakes of new agreements, making the process of achieving consensus among the entire WTO membership much more difficult. The WTO of the future must therefore find new ways to negotiate trade liberalization. In part, this means bringing proposals for sufficient gains from trade to the table in new areas such as services and trade-related regulatory reforms in order to motivate the members to bargain for a deal, but in equal part it will be a matter of creating new institutional features and understandings that will promote the bargaining itself. The world has changed and is changing still, along with the nature of trade and trade relations. What is at stake is the existence of a global institution capable of providing the public goods of rules, dispute settlement and a negotiating forum that accommodates these changes. The alternative, as suggested by recent trends, is a fragmented collection of larger regional trade agreements and smaller bilateral and multi-party trade agreements, each with separate rules, standards, and exclusive networks of supply chains. The challenge facing a new WTO is therefore to keep globalism relevant. Its effectiveness will depend on providing a framework for trade relations and negotiations between developed and developing countries, in particular. Large gains from trade are available, capable of raising global incomes, especially in the developing world, and capable of lifting hundreds of millions out of poverty. The institutional structure of the new WTO will have to adapt to the rapid changes coursing through the global economy, including the rise of the emerging economies, changes in technology, new production and trade patterns based on international supply chains, and contentious new issues, especially those in which trade restrictions are being proposed to reach a regulatory outcome. Ultimately, the WTO will depend on its members for leadership, vision, adaptability, and creativity in forging the political coalitions necessary to get the global liberalization deals done. The following two chapters will examine the institutional structure of the GATT/WTO system, in order to provide a conceptual framework for addressing these issues.

Institutional Foundations of the GATT/WTO System

INTRODUCTION

This chapter examines the GATT/WTO system as an international institution: a set of rules and processes established by its members to regulate trade relations and trade liberalization with each other. It is the product of economic cooperation, the domestic political constraints of the participating countries, and historical circumstances. Originally founded in 1947 as the General Agreement on Tariffs and Trade (GATT), it was successful in liberalizing trade in the postwar period and eventually led its participating countries, known under the agreement as Contracting Parties, to negotiate the creation of a successor institution in 1995, the World Trade Organization (WTO), a new, broader, more inclusive system of rules, with stronger dispute settlement procedures. The GATT was established to promote trade liberalization in a narrow range of products, mainly manufactures, while setting up a system of rules and informal dispute settlement, and convened a series of eight successful multilateral trade negotiations from 1947 to1994. Its successor, the WTO, sought to expand on the GATT's ambitions, based on the success of postwar trade liberalization and the possibilities of increased trade in an expanding, robust, post-Cold War global economy. The resulting expansion of the global trading system into new product areas and rules, along with tightened enforcement measures, created tensions between its goals and its institutional means. The WTO, while maintaining its system of rules and new dispute settlement system, has not been able to generate new multilateral trade agreements in a changed global economy. This is the main problem of this study: how can the WTO get multilateral trade liberalization back on track?

The present chapter sets out to identify the origins of the GATT and the components of its institutional structure. The following, companion chapter will pursue this approach to show how the new WTO evolved to the point of stalemate in the Doha round negotiations. The institutional principles of the GATT have persisted to the present, as the WTO incorporated the GATT (in revised form) into its rules, and retained the basic institutional structure of the GATT. For this reason, both chapters and the book will refer to the "GATT/WTO system" as a single institution that has dominated global trade relations since 1947. While it is true that the WTO expanded the scope of the original GATT, the basic institutional framework has remained unchanged. The special features of the WTO in fact attempted to "stretch" this framework in new directions, with mixed results that will be the subject of institutional analysis throughout this and the next chapter.

The conceptual framework draws heavily on Searle's (2005) constructivist theory of institutions, with contributions by Ruggie (1982), North (1990), Greif and Laitin (2004), and Aoki (2007). It will recount the development of the postwar GATT system, with its limited ambitions, narrow scope, and small membership, through the challenges of a growing and structurally evolving world economy. The constructivist approach is not the only way to analyze the many-faceted institutional features of the WTO, as there are many other models of institutions in political science, economics, and law that attempt to capture various aspects of their structure and function. In addition, the underlying political economy of trade informs the institutional approach taken here: countries bargain to secure the gains from trade, while domestic political forces within countries compete for influence to pursue their own economic interests regarding trade. The present focus on Searle's constructivism is based upon his emphasis on collective intentionality and rules as the defining elements of an institution, and the rights and obligations that flow from them. These institutional components focus the analysis on the process of identifying goals and political constraints in trade negotiations, and of achieving consensus that will lead to agreement among the participating countries. The GATT/ WTO system is commonly described as a rules-based institution, and the benefits to its members depend on a jointly acknowledged goal of facilitating the gains from trade and the notion that collective adherence to the rules will make all participants better off. At the same time, the formal institutional structure of the GATT/WTO system interacts not only with the governmental institutions of its participating countries but also with other international institutions and agreements created by them, such as bilateral and regional trade agreements. In addition, the formal institutional components of the GATT/WTO system function in complementary tandem with informal attitudes, traditions, and practices of those who take part in the trade negotiations and operations of the organization in Geneva. The constructivist model captures these institutional features as part of an interactive framework. These structural elements and interactions remain essential in evaluating the challenges faced by the WTO in adjusting to a rapidly changing global economy.

The analysis begins by considering the institutional origins of trade policy, the exchange of goods and services with those outside one's community, territory, or country. The next section examines the GATT/WTO system as an institution, including its birth after the calamity of World War II, the motivations for its existence, its basic provisions, and its formal and informal institutional structures, based on Searle's model of collective intentionality, constitutive rules, deontic powers, and institutional output. There follows an account of the most important historical circumstances surrounding the original GATT, leading in particular to the system's inherent balancing act between trade liberalization and domestic economic sovereignty. This balance, in turn, embeds the GATT/WTO system in both the institutional structure of sovereign national political systems and the parallel institutions of trading frameworks that coexist with GATT/WTO rules. The last section presents a conceptual framework for institutional equilibrium and adjustment, and examines institutional challenges of the GATT years and the internal adjustments that allowed it to continue promoting trade liberalization. One major problem also arose, however, that created increasing friction in the GATT: the treatment of developing countries. The institutional response to this problem introduced a major inconsistency that increasing participation by the developing countries would exacerbate. A brief summary of this chapter's concepts introduces the next chapter's examination of the institutional crisis of the GATT to WTO transition and the Doha Round.

THE INSTITUTIONAL ROOTS OF TRADE RELATIONS: EXCHANGE AND CONFLICT

The origins of trade policy as an institution can be traced back to the long-standing human tendency to "truck and barter" beyond one's immediate community. Recent archeological evidence suggests that long-distance trade may have begun as early as 140,000 years ago and may furthermore be linked to the beginnings of human speech.[1] Exchanging goods and services, it seems, began in conjunction with exchanging words. The incentives to trade find their motivation in neoclassical trade theory, which shows the benefits to both parties of specialization in production and exchange. At the level of the basic unit of social organization, specialization and exchange began within the family, the clan, and the tribe, groups within which mutually reinforcing incentives to cooperate existed. From a welfare perspective, specialization and exchange increased the output of the family, clan, and tribal units, allowing increased efficiency and joint consumption for the group, thus increasing the incentive to cooperate. The result was not only increased social development but also, according to Hartwick (2010), the development of increased brain capacity. Productive activities within the group came to follow basic patterns of comparative advantage (hunting, cultivation, child-rearing, implement making, meal preparation, etc.), with corresponding internal exchanges of goods and services, institutionalized in assigned roles and in the social organization of the group. This organization of production and exchange increased efficiency and the joint economic welfare of all members of the group, and, to the extent that it was sustainable, minimized the transactions costs of internal trading. Social organization, in this regard, facilitated specialization and an open exchange of goods and services.

The apparently mutually beneficial gains from trade raise the question, however, of why organized societies began to place restrictions on trade. The primary concern regarding the dangers of trade can probably be traced back to the transactions cost of trade accompanying "arm's length" transactions with outsiders, especially in distant places. Traveling traders had to face unfamiliar surroundings and uncertain outcomes, and their vulnerability to attack, robbery, and capture required increased investments in resources to support the security and travel associated with the trading expedition. The added resource requirements to offset the increased transaction costs tended to reduce the amount of trade that would otherwise have occurred, leading to various efforts to create institutional structures to facilitate trade, or at least the material benefits a party could gain from trade. The advent of systematic government control over territories accelerated these efforts. One solution to the problem was to equip, train, and deploy armed escorts, or even armies, to protect the trading party. Such a security force could, if necessary or if the opportunity arose, further simplify the interaction through pillage and conquest, even though the result was not "trade" in the sense of a voluntary exchange. "If there are more of *them*, trade; if there are more of *us*, raid" would be the rule of thumb for an expeditionary force eagerly seeking access to foreign goods (Pinker 2011: 285). The history of trade thus paralleled, in part, the history of organized violence by social groups and governments, territorial aggression, and colonization. To the extent that such efforts established firm military control over territories, these one-sided institutional arrangements often had the advantage of stabilizing, and thereby facilitating, exchange within the territory, with the hegemonic power of empires, for example, controlling the conditions of trade over the areas they controlled. It was also certainly possible that a balance of

power between potential trading partners, or a benevolent view and curiosity toward the interaction with foreigners, would lead to mutually beneficial
reciprocal exchange, especially if territorial ambitions and xenophobia did not
overshadow the transaction. Early trading expeditions of this sort represented
the beginnings of bilateral trade diplomacy, another institutional response to
the problem of transactions costs. The nexus between trade and power may
also be partly responsible for the tendency of countries, through their governments, to conclude preferential trade agreements with their neighbors and
allies. To the extent that *trust* among the partners reduces the transaction cost
of exchange, a stable trade relationship with predictable and reliable gains
from trade was often more likely among countries with established cultural,
linguistic, and political relations.[2]

As societies began to consolidate control over territories, an additional element of trade policy grew out of the value of various components of the trading
process. Control over local market access could generate tariff revenue, requiring territorial control and the establishment of bureaucratic institutions for
tariff collection. The value of exclusive rights to ownership of production of
valuable tradable goods motivated the colonization of Southeast Asian Spice
Islands and other territories beginning in the fifteenth century, and the establishment of government-controlled trading companies, generating monopoly
profits for the colonizing countries and their agents. The desire to control the
most advantageous shipping routes, ports, and territorial rights-of-way also
fueled military expeditions and further colonization, and the development
of large naval forces and armies to capture and hold these assets. In general,
control over territories and large military forces represented the institutional
means of managing a country's trade, leading to competition for the monopoly
profits, and to wars fought to acquire the geographical assets to achieve them.
The monetization of commerce, furthermore, meant that governments equated
a trade surplus with the excess revenues of exports, which, in the mercantilist
age, often went directly into the government's coffers, representing an important source of funding for the state's military ambitions.

The consolidation of nation-states increased the importance of trade diplomacy. This practice derived from the arm's length private bargaining over the
terms of an exchange between two independent parties that had certainly begun
thousands of years earlier. Territorial control and centralized governments
now required, however, that trade bargainers be agents of the central power.
If trade relations are peaceful, some form of negotiated, and often reciprocal,
market access may be involved. The institutional roots of exchanges between
distant trading partners, subject to the traditional (and probably instinctive)
caution associated with the risks of exploitation or attack continued into the
modern era, as trust and familiarity often played a role in facilitating the trade

relationship. Thus, both the formal elements of state-to-state treaties and the informal elements of trust in the process of bargaining and agreement play an important role in trade relationships. The built-in desire for familiarity and reliability thus led to preferences for trading partners that were either friendly neighbors or allies in other spheres, or at least predictable in their behavior.

In the modern era of more extensive government involvement in the domestic economy, the process of market exchange became increasingly subject to domestic taxation and regulation. These internal "trade restrictions" resulted from internal political institutions that established government goals of revenue generation and protection of the public interest. Such policies could initially distinguish clearly between domestic and traded goods and services, but lower transportation costs and increased opportunities for trade led to the advent of a critical new aspect of trade policy: "Heckscher-Ohlin" trade, in which export goods of one country compete with production in the trading partner's market.[3] Until the nineteenth century, most trade took place in luxury and exotic goods that could not be produced in the importing country. However, with the industrial revolution came advancements in production technologies and lower transportation costs, creating situations in which agricultural products, for example, could be produced in large quantities in excess of domestic needs. The exported surplus would then compete with production of the same good in the importing country. With this development, trade became an issue of domestic jobs and the fortunes of local industries, whereby import competition could disrupt employment patterns and lower market wage rates and profits in a country's import-competing sectors. The growing importance of job-displacing trade also introduced the element of domestic political institutions in global trade policy, which would profoundly affect the GATT/WTO system. Trade is a matter of domestic policy, as well as foreign policy.

By the mid-twentieth century these historical elements of trade relations had created an institutional legacy that shaped the first multilateral efforts to construct a global trading system. Of particular importance was the legacy of mercantilism, which had come to dominate most countries' thinking toward trade policy. The view among governments favoring exports over imports came not only from the association of accumulated treasure won in trade surpluses with military might (especially in the means to finance it) but also from the perceived link between market access expansion abroad and economic success, and perhaps even territorial expansion in foregone eras. In addition, governments had learned the benefits of monopoly control over market access and trading routes, and would expect their trading partners to seek to do the same. The advent of Heckscher-Ohlin trade and its impact on domestic import-competing industries also reinforced this view, as expanding exports seemed an unalloyed boon to domestic output, while imports carried the risks of displacing domestic industries. The gains from trade thus continued to compete with the conflict that trade can engender among potential trading partners. The modern version of this conflict links the domestic welfare effects of trade with constituent groups in democratic societies.

The other major legacy of the thousands of years of trade relations was discrimination. Most countries had come to regard trade policy as a bilateral matter, in which playing favorites in trade relations was a natural extension of foreign policy. Centuries of competition and war over colonies, market access, and trading routes caused governments to view trade partners with a wary eye, in which control over the relationship was the best defense against exploitation. Trading on special terms with friendly countries was not only safer but could be combined with military and diplomatic strategies to seal alliances. The natural tendency of governments in any trade liberalizing initiatives was therefore to conclude bilateral or regional trade agreements with favored or "strategic" trading partners, rather than to open its markets on a nondiscriminatory basis to imports from all countries (see Mansfield and Milner 2012). According to economic trade theory such discriminatory policies reduce the gains from trade and introduce inefficiencies in global resource allocation. After all, the benefits of exchange with a favored country would be even larger (and more globally efficient) if extended to all countries. Yet the tendency of governments to "play favorites" is deeply embedded in national trade policies and presents a continuing challenge to the global trading system.

Institutions of trade continued to evolve as the twenty-first century began. The modern age of globalization, which had begun with the technological revolutions in manufacturing and transportation in the eighteenth and nineteenth centuries, reached a new stage with the technological revolution in communications and information technology in the late twentieth century (Baldwin 2006a). The ability to coordinate production activities across great distances has led to the creation of international supply chains, which has increased not only the cross-border exchange of intermediate and final goods but also cross-border investment and the demand for complementary business services and infrastructure. These arrangements tend to change international trade relations, often through regional agreements,[4] introducing new trade-offs in negotiations and diminishing, in part, the mercantilist attitude toward trade. More and more, supply chain economics means that imports create domestic jobs rather than displacing them. Another upshot of this technological development is the general increase in the volume of services trade, facilitated by improved transportation, instant communications, electronic delivery, and globalized quality standards.

It is important in this regard to acknowledge the origins of trade as the exchange between *individuals*, and that modern international trade continues to be largely a matter of private commercial entities exchanging goods and services on the basis of market-driven criteria.[5] If trade activity had remained a matter of otherwise unregulated private transactions around the globe, the institutional problems of trade would have focused on market-driven arrangements to address the private transaction costs associated with transportation, delivery, insurance, agency, security, payment, and safe passage, and North (1990) has emphasized the importance of these institutions for the development of modern commerce in general. However, the organization of human societies on the basis of nations and governments with sovereign control over their territories—and the historical legacy of conflict among them—have inevitably defined international trade as a matter for governments to regulate. The development of trade relations in the shadow of governments' broader political, social, and economic goals prevents us, contrary to neoclassical economic theory, from assuming that governments are necessarily benign agents assigned to maximize net economic welfare for their populations. North (1990, 2005), to be sure, sets the desired goal of institutions as providing a framework to reduce transaction costs and increase total economic efficiency and welfare, and this is the standard by which this study will generally judge the success of global trading institutions. Yet a system of global trade with trade policies controlled by governments must rest on institutions in which representation is by governments. Institutions, in turn, define the way in which decisions on trade policy are made on the national level, and at the international level. Successful multilateral trade liberalization is in large part the result of institutional arrangements that allow governments collectively to overcome their tendency to assert long-standing mercantilist, protectionist, and discriminatory instincts in their trade policies. Trade cooperation and liberalization must therefore follow an institutional process, subject to institutional constraints. How close can such institutions come to maximizing global economic welfare?

THE GATT/WTO SYSTEM AS AN INSTITUTION

Birth of an Institution

Institutions, according to philosopher John Searle, are "constructions of social reality" motivated by the focused "collective intentionality" of their participants.[6] A formal international institution such as the GATT/WTO system requires, furthermore, an explicit agreement among sovereign countries to construct such a reality and achieve specific goals. The establishment of a new major international institution is an important and extraordinary event, as it typically reflects a response among nations to a compelling systemic

problem that has wreaked widespread havoc among many countries, push-
ing them to action. The problem generally entails a serious or even cataclysmic circumstance, harrowing enough to motivate countries to come together
in an attempt to set the situation right. Major wars most often provide the
impetus for such rare and dramatic instances of cooperation. The Treaty of
Westphalia, for example, ended the Thirty Years War with the establishment
of a new political order in Europe based on national sovereignty. The victors, furthermore, typically have the upper hand in designing new institutions under these circumstances. In the early twentieth century, the League
of Nations was established at the end of the World War I, based largely on the
efforts of the victors in that conflict, creating a new (and short-lived) international agreement on collective security, disarmament, and peaceful dispute
settlement.

So it was that the GATT was established in 1947 after a catastrophic world
war that had been preceded by a Great Depression in most of the world
economy. The Great Depression had led to a severe fragmentation of the
global trading and financial system, including a self-destructive pattern of
beggar-thy-neighbor tariffs, which, combined with the contraction in output, led to a massive decrease in world trade (Irwin 1993). A breakdown in
international relations had followed and led to catastrophic world war. In the
aftermath, political leaders were mindful of the fact that attempts to achieve
international agreement and cooperation on trade and monetary issues during the interwar period had failed (ibid.). The victorious allied powers, led
by the United States and United Kingdom, looked back upon the interwar
failure of international economic cooperation and set out to establish a more
stable global economic order through the Bretton Woods institutions: the
International Monetary Fund, the International Bank for Reconstruction and
Development (later known as the World Bank), and, initially, the International
Trade Organization (ITO). However, the ITO was regarded by the US Senate
as too broad in its allowance of trade restrictions for domestic policy purposes
and so was never ratified. Instead, the portion of the ITO that dealt with tariff
negotiations, the GATT, was allowed to proceed, although it was not a formal
treaty and was therefore never subject to ratification.[7] Despite these domestic
political complications in the United States—which foreshadowed institutional problems for the trading system decades later—the GATT was born at a
historic moment in which many nations looked forward to a new beginning. It
was part of a new set of international institutions designed to fix the problems
of economic crisis that had plagued the world economy and contributed to the
conflagration of world war. It was also to be part of a plan to strengthen postwar economic growth among its participants, and as the Cold War between
the United States and the Soviet Union began to take shape, it became part of

the bulwark of a western strategy to protect the economies of democratic and western-leaning governments against threats of communist takeovers.

The birth of the GATT thus came about at a critical moment in history, as a response to manifestly failed international institutions of economic cooperation in the interwar period that were linked to economic disruption and war. The end of this major conflict placed the victorious allies in a rare position to design a set of new economic institutions (along with a major new political institution, the United Nations). The United States, which survived the war as the dominant economy in the world, was in a position to shape their institutional structure, even to the extent of denying final approval of the ITO in favor of a less ambitious GATT. Yet the United States also recognized that a new trading system among sovereign states, if successful, must include rules that all countries must follow.

Institutional Structure of the GATT

The original GATT was signed in 1948, with, twenty-three founding countries, led by the United States and United Kingdom.[8] Essential elements of the GATT included:

(1) specific tariff schedules submitted by each Contracting Party upon accession;
(2) common rules for trade policy accepted by all Contracting Parties;
(3) the Most-Favored Nation (MFN) principle (i.e., nondiscrimination) in trade relations;
(4) the principle of reciprocity in negotiating trade liberalization;
(5) a commitment to the peaceful settlement of trade disputes; and
(6) the independent pursuit of domestic economic stabilization policies by each Contracting Party as long as they do not impinge on the accepted trade rules.[9]

The purpose was therefore to establish a global institution to regulate trade relations and facilitate trade liberalization, while allowing member countries to maintain sovereignty over their critical domestic economic policies. Their motivation for trade liberalization—and one presumably shared by all participants—emanated from the gains from specialization and trade, and the contribution to economic growth and political stability such gains can make. The founders also recognized, in light of the disastrous experience of the interwar period, that a formal institution to promote trade liberalization would be necessary in order to overcome countries' general reluctance to reduce their trade barriers unilaterally. The motivation for maintaining sovereignty over domestic economic policy came from the growing recognition in the wake of the Great Depression of the Keynesian role of governments in combatting unemployment and stabilizing the domestic economy through macroeconomic policies. To be sure, members would not be *required* to address domestic stabilization goals with any prescribed policies, but they would have wide latitude in domestic economic policy, as long as their actions did not violate the trade rules. Thus, the focus of Searle's collective intentionality in the GATT incorporated the pursuit of the goal of trade liberalization subject to a condition: a defined scope of domestic policy autonomy.

The "policy space" for economic stabilization, in the context of trade relations, was not limited to broad-based macroeconomic fiscal and monetary measures, however, but also included specific trade-related policies to facilitate political coalitions favoring trade liberalization in the member countries. GATT rules set limits on policies to restrict trade but permitted certain time-limited "safety valves" to restrict imports, especially if they become politically troublesome, a topic to be discussed in the next section. Thus, as an institution, the GATT rested on a bargain among its member countries that balanced the pursuit of trade liberalization with well-defined room for each member to impose contingent trade restrictions. In this manner, its institutional structure simultaneously represented a balance struck within each member country's political system to manage its trade policy, therefore making GATT operations reliant on the governmental institutions of all its members. Legally, the GATT would have no impact if it were not embodied in the national laws and legislation of the Contracting Parties. In the GATT and later the WTO, governments are the only parties that have representative standing, and their negotiations and decisions emanate from the underlying national political institutions that define their role as participants in the international institution.

The necessity of a global trade institution arises because of the transaction costs of liberalizing trade, and North (1990) views the reduction of transaction costs as the principal purpose of institutions in general. Thus, the GATT/WTO system, in this view, was established specifically to reduce the transaction costs associated with reciprocal market opening agreements. There are at least four possible types of transaction cost the institution can reduce. First, it reduces the efficiency cost of conducting multiple bilateral negotiations, in favor of a comprehensive multilateral negotiation. Second, for those countries with sufficient market power to enjoy terms of trade gains from "optimum" tariffs, it eliminates the prisoner's dilemma of suboptimal Nash tariff equilibrium, in favor of a cooperative framework for reciprocal tariff reduction, improving welfare for both countries compared to the prisoner's dilemma solution.[10] Third, the GATT/WTO system of rules acts as an "anchor" of international commitments to more open trade policies, thereby allowing governments to overcome the often potent political opposition to trade liberalization at home. Finally, the institution's rules and dispute settlement process (strengthened subsequently in the WTO) provides for third-party adjudication of disputes, thereby reducing the transaction costs of bounded rationality (see Yarbrough and Yarbrough 1992). In other words, backsliding, violations of rules, and unforeseen contingencies that would compromise a member's benefits from a negotiated trade agreement would be subject to review and judgment by a dispute panel, making it more attractive for members to agree to otherwise risky market opening bargains. The GATT/WTO system therefore provides the global economy with the "public good" of rules and forums that contribute to predictability, stability, and the prospect for new and mutually beneficial trade agreements for all its members.

The GATT/WTO System: Elements of a Constructivist Approach

Ultimately, the GATT/WTO system's foundational agreement rests on shared beliefs about the benefits of trade liberalization, hence the importance of *collective intentionality*. The transaction cost reductions mentioned above, in other words, presuppose benefits that derive from the transactions that the institution facilitates, including efficiency gains, increased choice for consumers, access to new technologies, and incentives for innovation and competition, among others (see Irwin 2010: chapter 2). Without such a common belief, the institution and the collective agreement on the rules supporting this goal would not exist. It also defines the scope of the institution's activities in terms of securing the negotiated benefits of a rules-based trading system and the trade liberalization such a system makes possible. Other possible trade-related issues, involving debates over the environment, human and worker rights, development, and currency matters, tend to have limited prospects for meaningful agreement in the WTO as it stands now, based on the narrow focus of the shared belief in the gains from trade. Within the GATT/WTO system, individual countries' policies to address such trade-related issues are possible to the extent that the mutually agreed upon domestic policy space does not impinge on the negotiated benefits and obligations of the already balanced trade agreements. The GATT/WTO system focuses, under its current institutional structure, on trade alone.[11]

The GATT/WTO system pursues the goal of trade liberalization, in turn, through the establishment of what Searle describes as *constitutive rules*, which define the way that members formally interact and generate "institutional facts" or outputs, such as trade rules and market access agreements. For the

GATT, such foundational rules included the MFN provision (nondiscrimination in trade policy), reciprocity in trade negotiations, and consensus as a decision rule. Because of the importance of these rules, exceptions have been carefully defined—although not without difficulty, as will be described below. Examples include the regional (i.e., preferential) trade agreement (RTA) and antidumping exceptions to MFN, provisions for non-reciprocity for developing countries (and especially for a specifically defined roster of Least Developed Countries), and the rare instances in which voting majorities may replace the consensus rule.

The constitutive rules create institutional facts by assigning *deontic powers* to the members: rights and obligations established by negotiated regulative rules regarding tariff levels, the use of non-tariff barriers and other trade policy tools, the terms of market access among participating countries, and procedures for filing a trade dispute, for example. Deontic powers thus involve obligations that will allow foreign trade into a member's domestic market, and benefits to the same member, as its exporters have negotiated rights to enter foreign markets. Thus, the institutional framework of the GATT/WTO system creates "pooled" sovereignty among its participants, based on trade-off by each member to sacrifice absolute sovereign control over access to its domestic market in exchange for an extension of its sovereignty, through the negotiated agreement, over market access abroad.[12] GATT/WTO rules reinforce the benefits of pooled sovereignty by regulating members' use of trade policy tools that affect market access. It is noteworthy that GATT and WTO negotiations have been consistently designed as *mercantilist* pacts, in which export market access is the "benefit" and import market access is the "cost," each element being weighed and measured carefully by all members, each of which must then view the negotiated package as acceptable before consensus on a final deal can be achieved.

The third institutional pillar of the GATT generates *institutional facts*, in Searle's terminology, or output, through regulative rules, that is, specific provisions and procedures to secure mutual gains from trade for its members. There are three main types of output: negotiated trade agreements, the implementation and monitoring of the agreements, and dispute settlement. Each new GATT/WTO agreement has added new rules, and thereby new benefits and obligations for members, so that at any point in time, the existing rules represent the sum of all previously negotiated agreements. The GATT/WTO has established an elaborate system of committees to carry out these functions, the "micro" institutions of administration and implementation, including special negotiation committees, standing committees that deal with trade agreement implementation and administrative issues, and a dispute settlement body. A General Council of all members presides over the other committees, naming most chairs, coordinating meetings, and creating negotiating committees when necessary. The GATT/WTO system has therefore always had multiple functions, even when attention tends to focus on the course of major multilateral trade negotiations.

Crucial to the achievement of institutional output is the process by which representatives of member countries reach agreement. Institutions are, in the end, frameworks for human interaction, and the formal regulative rules of negotiation and decision-making, by themselves, are not sufficient to complete this process. In addition to the formal constitutive and regulative rules described above, the GATT/WTO also has to rely on informally developed rules in order to reach consensus, including discretionary methods of committee chairs in scheduling meetings, focusing the agenda, sequencing discussions, and summarizing progress at various stages. The Director-General often has a special role to play in moving member delegations toward consensus, through persuasive powers, discovering a member country's "red lines" in the concessions they can make, and establishing a reputation that inspires trust among the membership. Secrecy often plays a strategic role in the negotiations (Cot 1972). Member delegations, in turn, have their own informal rules regarding their communications with their capitals to maximize the effectiveness in representing their countries' trade interests, how responsibilities within their group are delegated, and how face-to-face negotiations are managed.

Informal "rules" of the institution are certainly not fixed, and vary according to circumstances, but especially in difficult and complicated negotiations, where multiple gains-from-trade outcomes are possible, the human elements of confidence, legitimacy, and trust may be instrumental in securing an agreement, whatever the formal positions of the negotiators might be. Economic welfare is what is on the table, but the bargaining is often a flesh-and-blood affair. In a world of uncertainty, members within a consensus-based institution must enjoy a minimum level of trust with each other—which derives, as the following discussion will show, from trust in the *system*—in order to come to a meaningful agreement to expand trade, since no one knows for sure what new technologies, production and consumption patterns, and economic and political events the future holds. Trust is in this regard an essential informal component of the GATT/WTO system. As an institutional component of the trading system trust has diverse personal, legal, and cultural dimensions. Combined, these elements of trust provide a degree of confidence among the participants that an agreement will be mutually beneficial. Personal trust is the most familiar and traditional dimension of this concept: a mutual recognition of personal integrity and truthfulness among negotiators. Among senior trade officials, such trust is built on experience and repeated interaction with individuals, and on their reputations. Legal trust, on the other hand,

relates to the predictability of the rules, and the reliability of the system of
third-party dispute settlement, or other means that can protect a participating
country from unexpected events, violations, or challenges to the rules. Finally,
cultural trust, in the context of the GATT/WTO system, is a broader understanding of shared values among participants in the institution. Confidence
in the outcome of a negotiation rests, in this regard, on shared views regarding the mutual benefits of trade liberalization, the importance of reciprocity in bargaining, and the ability of the rules to deliver these benefits to the
members' satisfaction. Trust is therefore associated with a requisite degree
of "like-mindedness" of the participants and confidence that the institution
is serving each member's trade goals. In a consensus-based institution, these
three elements of trust are crucial to the success of the institution, since all
participants must accept mutual responsibility for compliance to a set of rules
and procedures that will apply several years into the future, with unexpected
events and circumstances likely to pop up along the way. Since the institution's
value lies in part in its ability to address bounded rationality as an impediment
to agreement on rules and market access, trust is also a function of the shared
confidence in, and ultimately, legitimacy of, the institution.

   The concept of trust has received very little attention in the analysis of multilateral trade negotiations, particularly with regard to its cultural dimension.
Whereas personal and legal dimensions of trust, as described above, are familiar
concepts in the negotiations literature, global trade negotiations have evolved
significantly in recent years, and the interaction of the three elements of trust
is likely to be subject to changes in the negotiating environment. Trust seems
to be easiest to establish in times of stability, confidence, and shared expectations. The first GATT negotiations, for example, focused on narrowly defined
tariff reductions in manufactures among industrialized countries. Trust along
the three dimensions was perhaps easy to establish among like-minded negotiators on traditional trade barriers in those early years. Later, when trade talks
expanded to non-tariff barriers, negotiations were often difficult, especially
when it came to agriculture (an issue on which the United States and European
Union had different "cultural" attitudes) and regulating the global Airbus/
Boeing duopoly. Yet even in those cases, there seemed to be a common understanding of the acceptable scope of domestic policy autonomy, and a common
will to structure the negotiations so that a final agreement was possible. When
new challenges to trade liberalization arose, the like-minded industrialized
countries devised "solutions," such as a partitioning of textiles from MFN and
the use of "voluntary" export restraints. These trade policy devices violated
the fundamental principle of nondiscrimination, but the violations rested on
mutually held political values and understandings among the major industrialized countries, which allowed trade liberalization in other areas to proceed. The

marginal players in the system, the developing countries, had limited involvement in the GATT negotiations until the Uruguay Round, so their role in the question of trust did not arise at the time. It is probably for this reason that "trust" and "culture" were not considered crucial determinants of negotiating outcomes under the GATT. This situation was to change dramatically in the wake of the Uruguay Round.

A constructivist approach to institutions, with its three interlocking structures—a focused collective intentionality, a core set of constitutive rules and deontic powers, and institutional output through regulative rules—thus also has a crucial role for informal processes and trust. These formal and informal structures together provide a framework for analyzing the GATT/WTO system. Its existence requires, for example, a joint commitment to a common goal, increasing the gains from trade, with a common constraint among all participants, the maintenance of autonomy over domestic economic policy. Interaction among the members and the foundation of agreements are governed by a small set of simple constitutive rules, including MFN, reciprocity, and consensus in decision-making, from which deontic powers are derived. The institution's output consists of legislative (negotiated trade agreements), executive (implementation and monitoring of the agreements), and judicial (dispute settlement) elements. Figure 2.1 illustrates the basic institutional structure of the GATT/WTO with these structures in mind. The collective intentionality component of reduced transaction costs is linked to the necessary constitutive rules through the principal mechanisms of conducting multilateral trade. The sovereignty component is linked to constitutive rules and by the limitations on, and exceptions to, the rules. Constitutive rules create deontic powers, subject to the development status of members (to be discussed below) and the sovereignty constraint. Deontic powers become operational through the governance structure of the institution, which assigns committees powers to negotiate, to implement and monitor, and to adjudicate disputes. The domestic foundation of collective intentionality for all member countries, through the "national sovereignty" component and its subordinate elements (including the critical concept of "policy space"), is linked to the negotiation component through the bargaining process. A negotiation can lead to a new multilateral trade agreement, creating new rules and new terms of market access, which feed into the existing implementation and dispute settlement functions. An unsuccessful negotiation may lead to a "best alternative to a multilateral trade agreement" (BAMTA),[13] which for various members may be either unilateral trade policies or bilateral/regional trade agreements negotiated outside the GATT/WTO framework, or simply the status quo. In all negotiations within the GATT/WTO system, the political power structure and the participants' culture, level of trust, and experience from previous negotiations influence outcomes.

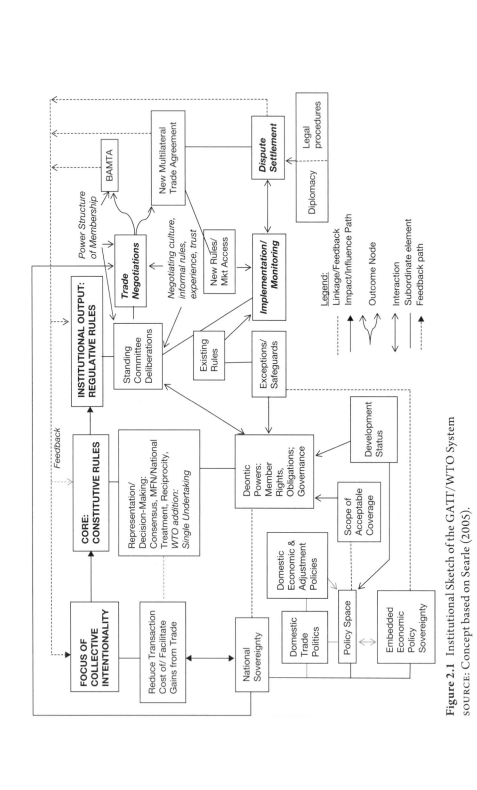

Figure 2.1 Institutional Sketch of the GATT/WTO System

SOURCE: Concept based on Searle (2005).

PATH DEPENDENCY, CONTEXT, AND EMBEDDEDNESS
OF THE GATT/WTO SYSTEM

The Great Depression had ushered in a new era of government intervention in domestic economies, especially among the richer countries, giving high priority to measures to stabilize output, prices, and employment. Increased trade could enhance growth and employment by expanding exports but also could threaten particular sectors through import competition. The problems of trade and domestic stabilization generated the compelling institutional elements of the postwar trading system, which sought to provide a framework for government trade policy and trade expansion while permitting governments to retain control over their domestic stabilization policies. Aoki (2007: 17) refers to such parallel decision-making systems as "institutional complementarities." Thus, even as the postwar trading system was being negotiated, conflict arose over how much domestic policy prerogatives could override trade commitments, and so the ambitious ITO gave way to the more narrowly defined GATT. The tension between trade policy and domestic policy defines, in many ways, the major institutional challenge that the GATT/WTO system has faced during its entire history. While governments sought through the GATT/WTO system to promote trade, the institution they built is as much a product of the advent of Keynesian intervention in domestic economies, keeping trade policy and domestic politics in constant tension.

The historical circumstances of an institution's birth have major consequences for its subsequent operation, even when the circumstances change. The GATT was founded in 1947 under the strong influence of the United States, and many of its institutional features can be traced to US trade policies at the time. The emphasis in the GATT on the MFN principle, the consensus rule, the incorporation of safeguards, antidumping and countervailing duty provisions, and the narrow scope of manufactures trade corresponded to US trade policy practices and preferences. Issues of concern to developing countries received little consideration in the rules. Kindleberger (1981) recognized the importance of hegemonic leadership in the establishment and stability of international economic institutions, and it was clear in the aftermath of the war that any effective global trade institution would involve strong US involvement in its design. Steinberg (2002) has noted the US strategy of shaping GATT governance around the consensus rule. This provision would give the US veto power over any agreement, and at the same time would give a negotiating advantage to the country or countries that could dominate the agenda setting and bargaining stages of multilateral trade negotiations. Of course, all other countries would also technically have such veto power, but it would not be easy for smaller and less politically influential countries to gain significant influence over the negotiating agenda, especially in the early GATT years, when market access requests had to come from "principal suppliers" (i.e., the major exporters) of products subject to negotiation.[14] Once the multilateral agreement was endorsed by the United States and other major players, it would be difficult for other countries to reject a take-it-or-leave-it deal. Under these circumstances, strong US influence over the process was assured. The early GATT trade rounds, largely exercises in tariff reductions, proceeded quickly. The influence of the United States over trade negotiations remained strong throughout the GATT period, even though it was declining in relative importance as the rest of the world was catching up in the postwar trade boom and economic expansion.

The design of the original GATT therefore closely followed US interests and those of other industrialized nations. Agriculture, subject to powerful protectionist lobbies in most countries, was largely exempt from GATT disciplines, and bargaining took place largely in the form of reciprocal tariff concessions among the wealthier countries on manufactured goods. This narrow scope of product coverage made adjustment to trade easier, as many sectors engaged in intra-industry trade, in which specialization within industrial sectors led to simultaneous imports and exports of similar products. Whereas lower tariffs in one sub-sector would increase imports for a country, reciprocal tariff cuts in related sub-sectors would also increase exports for that country, allowing broad industrial sectors to maintain output and employment through more intensive specialization and economies of scale. Easing the pain of adjustment, in conjunction with the general economic growth that accompanied the trade expansion, tended to neutralize some of the opposition to import competition, facilitating political coalitions favorable to more trade liberalization.

The trade-off of domestic sovereignty against extended foreign market access has its limits, however, and is part of the political balance that the GATT maintains in order to facilitate continued support for trade liberalization among the member countries. Trade policy carries implications for the country's balance of payments, income distribution, employment levels (especially at the regional level), political relationships with particular trading partners, and domestic industrial policy. In this regard the GATT/WTO system also allows each member to maintain autonomy over some aspects of trade policy. Politically, this is an important part of a country's adjustment policies to trade. In general, GATT/WTO rules do not restrain domestic monetary, fiscal, and regulatory policies, unless they have a clear impact on trade that compromises existing trade commitments, provide discriminatory treatment in favor of domestic industries, or directly promote specific export sectors. Such distinctions are not always clear, however, and what is an allowable subsidy continues to be a major issue. Members are empowered to protect their import markets against "unfair" trade, based on GATT-illegal subsidies or dumping activity, thereby providing an exception to the principle of MFN treatment. The safeguards "escape clause" allows countries to restrict imports, even if "fairly" traded, if they unexpectedly increase and cause or threaten serious injury to a domestic industry.[15] These carve-outs and exceptions are part of the trade liberalization/sovereignty trade-off in the GATT/WTO system that recognizes the necessity of contingent domestic government intervention in trade when imports become politically "dangerous" and may threaten the domestic coalitions needed to maintain commitments to multilateral trade liberalization. They are also part of a larger "embedded liberalism" that emerged in the post-World War II period (see Ruggie 1982), in which states saw the need for domestic safety nets to soften the blow from adjusting to trade competition in order to pursue a liberal global economic order.[16] The scope of trade coverage is also relevant to the adjustment problem that members face. Consensus among the original GATT members to the terms of trade negotiations and rules depended in part on its narrow scope of industrial sector coverage. Agriculture and services were generally not part of the agreement, as these sectors would involve much more difficult worker displacement and domestic regulatory complications, and domestic protection was often based on quotas (agriculture) and domestic regulation (services). All of these factors would have made negotiations very difficult and would have crossed too far over the line set up in the institution between the gains from trade and economic autonomy. Adjustment in manufactures was, if not always easy, then at least more manageable, as described above. The reduced severity of adjustment thus supported the goals of embedded liberalism. In general, trade institutions such as the GATT/WTO system represent a framework for compromise among the various domestic political forces in participating countries to find ways to capture the gains from trade.

The GATT/WTO system is based on agreements among governments and is thereby embedded in the governmental institutions of its participants. This means that the constitutive rules of the GATT/WTO are incorporated into the laws and regulations of participating governments, each of which commits to abide by the rules. In addition, domestic rules and GATT/WTO rules interact with—they affect and are affected by—each other, especially when it comes to negotiating new rules or coverage by GATT/WTO disciplines. With regard to the negotiations themselves, the global institution is embedded in the participating domestic government institutions through the transmission of each participant's agenda preferences, bargaining positions and final approval of the negotiated agreement into its domestic laws, regulations, and policies. GATT/WTO decisions require consensus, and this process requires governments to conclude internal decisions regarding the issues under negotiation and to bargain with other governments. As Putnam (1988) has noted, international negotiations involve a two-level process, in which a *domestic* agreement on a country's position is necessary to pursue an *international* bargaining position effectively. In international trade negotiations, domestic trade policy "capacity" may often be essential to forge an international agreement. The domestic adjustment problems that accompany a country's participation in trade liberalization may, for example, require the implementation of adjustment policies if market mechanisms are not otherwise functioning properly. A country's pursuit of a coherent trade bargaining position often requires the systematic involvement of private domestic trading interests, through lobbying, representation among elected officials, or indirect participation in the negotiations. Their role is also essential in the enforcement of rules and dispute settlement (see Bown 2011). Each country's ability to participate effectively in the GATT/WTO system therefore rests on the particular rules associated with its own governmental institutions, and its capacity to transmit its trade interests to its representatives in Geneva. Among participating governments, changing internal political pressures may also enter the decision-making process and affect negotiations on new issues by altering the preferred balance between trade liberalization and domestic policy space. New areas of trade liberalization inevitably collide with affected domestic economic interests, and new internal bargains must often precede new international agreements.

Embeddedness also extends to the realm of alternative international trade institutions. Countries participating in the GATT/WTO system are allowed to deviate from the MFN rule in establishing preferential, bilateral, and regional trade agreements with specific trading partners, subject to the restrictions of GATT article 24, but the associated review process has not been enforced effectively. As a result, bilateral and regional trade agreements spread without explicit article 24 approval, creating a parallel set of trade institutions to the GATT/WTO system. The long-standing tendency of countries to "play favorites" and discriminate in their trade market access policies has thus survived the earlier GATT efforts to suppress it, and in recent years has come to represent a significant alternative (or perhaps complement) to multilateral trade agreements, to be discussed in more detail in chapter 6. Goldstein, Rivers, and Tomz (2007) have described the embeddedness of the GATT/WTO system in parallel systems of preferential, bilateral, and regional trade agreements; this is another example of Aoki's "institutional complementarities," in that they, like GATT/WTO trade agreements, also develop internationally from the domestic trade policies of their participant governments. Examples include bilateral and multi-country RTAs, such as free trade agreements and customs unions, as well as largely unilateral contingent preference arrangements such as the Generalized System of Preferences (GSP), the US African Growth and Opportunity Act, the EU "Everything but Arms" initiative for Least Developed Countries (LDCs), and colonial preferences. Individual countries may also implement their own trade policies without violating GATT/WTO rules, for example, by unilaterally lowering their applied tariffs, or by taking other trade measures not specifically disciplined by these rules. These preferential trade agreements affect and are affected by the GATT/WTO system. An RTA is often the best alternative to a GATT/WTO agreement, and therefore may affect the course of multilateral trade negotiations. The GSP started as a voluntary tariff preference program offered by developed to developing countries, and was later incorporated into GATT rules, but remains under the control of "donor" countries.[17] The GSP and other forms of "special and differential treatment" are important deviations from the MFN principle, even though they are allowed under the GATT/WTO system, and may also affect the negotiations, particularly if further MFN trade liberalization threatens to erode these preferences for the recipient countries.

The embeddedness of the GATT/WTO system in domestic governmental institutions and in alternative trade institutions enters the GATT/WTO institutional structure, as shown in figure 2.1, in several ways. Domestic trade politics and processes are part of national sovereignty, which affects decision-making in the global institution in its standing committees and in the trade negotiations, as well as in trade dispute initiations. The balance of political forces for and against various trade liberalization proposals defines the allowable "policy space" the country will seek to exempt from global trade rules, which in turn affects the "embedded liberalism" safety nets and independent policy areas allowed under the global rules. Alternative trade institutions have their most prominent impact as BAMTA, especially RTAs. Preferential schemes for developing countries, which are part of GATT/WTO rules for LDCs, also indirectly affect the negotiating positions of all other participating developing countries, both through fears of preference erosion through broader trade liberalization and through expectations of what level of reciprocity they are expected to exhibit in the negotiations.

INSTITUTIONAL EQUILIBRIUM AND ADJUSTMENT IN THE GATT

The institutional model of the GATT/WTO system consists of a set of rules with the goal of reducing transaction costs of trade liberalization, subject to established boundaries of members' economic autonomy, as identified by the focus of collective intentionality, and based on common beliefs about the validity of the goals and means to achieve them. The alignment of these institutional elements creates *institutional equilibrium* if its activities move the participants toward achievement of the goals. In the case of the GATT/WTO, the equilibrium condition can be restated as the achievement of *consensus* on achieving or supporting institutional facts or outcomes: multilateral trade liberalization, the establishment and monitoring of global trade rules, and the review and resolution of disputes. A disruption of equilibrium, as through changes in critical elements of the institutional order (Greif and Laitin 2004), creates *institutional friction*, disrupting the institution's activity and calling for corrective internal action by participants in the institution so that the activity can resume. Continued, unaddressed friction can lead to *institutional disequilibrium* (failure), a breakdown in the institution's ability to function in terms of its output activities.

Institutional change is difficult to analyze because its impact depends on the complex determinants of interaction among the participants, the current ability of the institution to respond to such shocks, and a range of responses from various participants, depending on their state of knowledge, experience, relationships with other participants, and choices they face. Identifying the proper institutional reform to address the problem may therefore be elusive, and even if it is found, implementing it may require new agreements among the participants that are beyond the scope of shared beliefs that defines the institution. Greif and Laitin (2004) identify a process of endogenous institutional change in which the external forces either reinforce or disrupt the existing institutional order. Along with Aoki (2007), they adapt the concept of institutional equilibrium as a state of self-sustained behavior, driven by underlying shared beliefs, and based on the stable expectations of the players. A disruptive change, in contrast, creates institutional disequilibrium, requiring institutional change in the form of new rules in order to reattain institutional equilibrium.

Under the original GATT, eight rounds of trade negotiations were concluded, lowering the average tariffs of its members from approximately 40% at its founding in 1947 to approximately 6% at the end of the Uruguay Round in 1994. During that interval, economic growth among its members averaged 5%, compounded annually, and GATT membership expanded from the original eighteen "Contracting Parties" to 126, and under the WTO membership has grown further to 160. During the GATT period, its ability to conduct and conclude trade rounds suggested a state of institutional equilibrium, in terms of its ability to generate the necessary consensus to secure agreement. This time was punctuated, however, by internal crises for the GATT due to forms of institutional friction described above, requiring institutional adjustments, which will be the focus of this section. The GATT's successor institution, the WTO, has also faced institutional friction, but has had greater difficulty in adjusting to it, a subject to be pursued in the next chapter.

The trade environment and balance of political power evolved throughout the postwar period, and the United States saw its relative power in the institution diminishing because of the addition of many developing countries to the membership, changes in the pattern of comparative advantage in important markets, and an expansion of the trade agenda. All of these factors created institutional friction in the GATT. Institutions are by their nature conservative entities, in that they attempt to establish a stable framework of formal rules for interaction among their participants. This is the "hardware" of the institution, supported by its organizational and legal structures. Yet equilibrium also depends on the complementary functions of the institution's "software," the informal rules and processes that facilitate consensus, based on common understandings, expectations, traditions, trust, and accepted procedures. Institutional equilibrium is therefore vulnerable to external forces that alter the informal rules, such as changing structures of power and influence, the political environment, technology, and market trends, all of which tend to alter the balance of influence in decision-making and the costs and benefits accruing to their members (North 2005). In the GATT years, the cultural homogeneity that prevailed among trade officials in the leading GATT countries tended to allow the institution's informal rules and processes to operate smoothly, an important factor in dealing with instances of institutional friction.[18] The GATT faced such challenges when changes in the trade environment disrupted its ability to function according to its original purpose and design. Under such conditions, the institution must find ways to accomplish internal reforms to adapt to the change, reinvent itself, and resume its operations, or it will begin to atrophy, downgrading its goals or perhaps eventually ending its operations. The GATT faced a number of such challenges, requiring an adaptive institutional response. The examples presented here include (1) a disruptive new member; (2) disruption from changing comparative advantage; (3) new issues and plurilateral agreements; and (4) expanding membership and the difficulties of representation.[19]

A disruptive new member. The accession of a "disruptive" new exporting member tends to upset institutional equilibrium, and Japan was the most disruptive new participant in the GATT, joining in 1955. Many GATT members, fearful of surges of Japanese exports fueled by MFN market access, invoked the non-application clause (GATT article 35), which allowed a country to exclude a particular country upon accession from MFN treatment. While this was within the GATT rules, it reduced the gains from trade. Many of these countries, in attempting to normalize GATT relations with Japan, insisted on bypassing GATT disciplines by concluding discriminatory "voluntary" export restraint (VER) agreements as a condition for disinvoking article 35. As a result, Japan did receive MFN treatment among GATT members for its exports not covered

by VERs, but many such restrictions persisted into the 1990s, including a massively protectionist automobile VER on imports to the United States from
1980 to 1984, before such measures were terminated as a result of the Uruguay
Round agreement. The GATT's institutional response was therefore to allow
the Contracting Parties to suspend MFN treatment on exports of selected,
"disruptive" goods from Japan, in order to facilitate otherwise GATT-based
trade relations.

Disruptive changes in comparative advantage. GATT principles also buckled
under the pressure of shifting comparative advantage in textiles, clothing, footwear, electronics, and other manufactured products away from the established
industrialized countries toward Japan, newly industrializing countries such as
Korea and Taiwan, and several developing countries. This shift in the global
structure of trade upset the balance between MFN trade rules and domestic
policy space for many developed GATT Contracting Parties. Their response
was to carve out exceptions to the MFN rule on a sectoral basis, in the form of
several VER agreements, the most elaborate of which was the global Multifiber
Agreement (MFA), negotiated in 1974, which formalized an extensive system
of negotiated export quotas for textiles and apparel from developing countries.
This "fix" appeased protectionist lobbies in the United States, Europe, and other
industrialized countries and allowed the GATT-sponsored trade negotiations at
the Tokyo Round to be completed, but it created new and perhaps more serious
institutional problems. The MFA violated the principles of the GATT in several
ways. It was protectionist, reversing the gains from trade; it was discriminatory, violating MFN; and it introduced new import quotas, which were banned
under GATT article 11. The quota rents, furthermore, built in the incentive for
exporters to continue the trade restrictions. The MFA, along with numerous
other VER agreements, represented a form of cognitive dissonance: increasing
protectionism in order to save trade liberalization. The crisis was not resolved
until the Uruguay Round agreement terminated the MFA and banned the use
of VERs. Even then, the removal of the MFA in particular was disruptive to
many developing countries, which had enjoyed the program's quota rents and
market access security.

New issues and plurilateral agreements. Beginning with the Kennedy Round
of trade negotiations, the agenda began to expand beyond traditional tariff
cutting to include several new issues of critical interest to many Contracting
Parties, but on which agreement among the entire GATT membership was
not possible. This situation put pressure on the fundamental GATT institutional principle of consensus in decision-making. The difficulty was to find
a way to incorporate "partial" agreements into a general trade liberalization
agreement. The first of these issues was the interpretation of GATT antidumping provisions, and the Contracting Parties eventually agreed to establish a

voluntary Antidumping "Code" that would be open to all for accession, but would be decoupled from the rest of the negotiation. The Tokyo Round negotiations went on to revise the Antidumping Code and add several other Codes signed by subsets of GATT Contracting Parties, covering trade in goods such as bovine meat and dairy products, and rules on subsidies, technical barriers to trade, civil aircraft, customs valuation, government procurement, and import licensing (Jackson 1997: 75–76). Thus, it became possible to select some GATT agreements on an "a la carte" basis. This created an irregular patchwork of partial agreements that many considered to have weakened the GATT, and subsequent negotiations in the Uruguay Round eliminated most of the Codes (which became known under the WTO as Plurilateral Agreements), creating the principle of a "single undertaking" as the basis for WTO membership. However, at the time, the GATT Codes represented an institutional response to pressure for agreements on new issues by partitioning the negotiations in such a way that all parties could sign a general agreement on trade liberalization, while others could agree separately to additional agreements.

Expanding membership and the green room. A different sort of challenge arose as the GATT's membership swelled to the point where the process of reaching consensus became difficult. After the original twenty-three Contracting Parties signed the GATT in 1948, accession of new countries proceeded slowly at first, and then began to grow more rapidly in the 1960s. The vast majority of new participants consisted of developing countries, most of whom played limited roles in the early GATT trade rounds. The United States, United Kingdom, and a small number of European and other OECD countries were most active in the negotiations in those early years, and it was possible to achieve effective consensus among this small group alone, presided over by the GATT Director-General. It was during the Tokyo Round (1973–1979), however, that the number of significant participants grew to the point where consensus could no longer be reached on the basis of small group meetings. This situation required the development of a new system of consensus building based on small "green room" agreements among a core group of countries, from which a "concentric circle" method of outreach to other countries' representatives would set out to secure general consensus among all GATT countries. In this case, the informal green room measures to build consensus allowed decision-making to proceed under the acceptance by the Contracting Parties that their interests would be adequately represented, even if they were not in the green room meeting. In the GATT years, such a system was acceptable as long as developing countries were not expected to make concessions on major issues, and the smaller developed countries were confident that their interests would be well represented even if they were absent from the green room meetings. As long as the basis of trust in the system was intact, the green room worked. Green room meetings would later be challenged in the WTO, however, another subject for chapter 3.

Treatment of Developing Countries: The Great Inconsistency

As the foregoing examples show, the GATT proved capable of incremental institutional adjustment, which, even when at times violating its principles selectively, would vouchsafe the pursuit of broader trade liberalization. However, the failure of the GATT to systematically incorporate the interests of developing countries in its institutional structure was one of its most serious defects, and its attempts to redress this situation created inconsistencies in the trading system that would later come to haunt the Doha Round under the WTO. The problem of developing country participation in the GATT/WTO system raises particularly serious institutional questions. The original constitutive rules, including MFN and reciprocity in negotiations, had applied in principle equally to all GATT members, but the reduced capacity of developing countries to develop their industries and stabilize their economies, along with less developed market institutions, left them without the ability to compete in manufactures on an equal footing with developed countries. In general, trade issues of concern to developing countries received little consideration in either the rules or the negotiating agenda of the GATT. While GATT article 18 did allow infant-industry and balance-of-payments protection by developing countries, few of them found its provisions applicable and it was rarely invoked (see Curzon 1965: 211–224). Agriculture, subject to powerful protectionist lobbies in most countries, was largely exempt from GATT disciplines, despite the facts that no such exemption appeared formally in the GATT text[20] and that many GATT developing countries had a strong interest in expanding market access for their agricultural exports. The United States, however, effectively blocked GATT trade reforms in order to protect its system of agricultural price supports, backed by strong legislative lobbies.[21] Most other GATT developed countries also had strong domestic farm lobbies, resulting in extensive agricultural subsidies, price support policies, and trade restrictions. The European Common Market (later the European Union), whose Common Agricultural Policy was particularly protectionist, also maintained tight control over access to its agricultural markets. Meanwhile, developed countries also maintained higher tariffs on processed products than on raw materials, increasing the effective rate of protection on the final goods and preventing developing countries from moving downstream into value-added manufacturing, a situation that applies not only to agriculture but also to raw materials processing, textiles, and clothing.[22]

GATT Contracting Parties were well aware of the GATT's neglect of developing country interests, as the bluntly worded Haberler Report (Haberler et al. 1958), commissioned by the GATT, took the organization to task for suppressing the trade interests of developing countries (Curzon 1965: 177–185). The developed countries tried to compensate for it by adding GATT part IV, "Trade and Development," most of which played the curious institutional role of providing hortatory language with little hard rule content, exhorting developed countries to take the interests of developing countries into consideration, without any concrete obligations to do so. It did, however, establish a fateful exception to the GATT's major institutional rule of *reciprocity* in trade negotiations. The idea behind it was that developing countries had little to offer in terms of market access that would be of interest to the developed countries in the GATT; they would therefore be allowed to "free ride" on any tariff concessions concluded in GATT negotiations. Unfortunately, during that period, the GATT's focus on manufactured goods market access meant that very few tariff reductions provided meaningful new export opportunities for developing countries. Another form of compensation came later, as developing countries were afforded "special and differential" (S&D) treatment, first established in the Enabling Clause in the 1979 Tokyo Round Framework Agreement (see Hoekman and Kostecki 2009: 536–539). The S&D measures provided developing countries with preferential market access through the GSP, as well as modifications in several GATT rules (Michalopoulos 2001: 36–43). These provisions raised serious problems, however. One was that preferential market access to developed country markets through the GSP was not mandatory, but rather was dependent on voluntary (and revocable) measures offered by the individual developed countries themselves. In addition, there was a vaguely worded expectation that developing countries would one day "graduate" to developed country status, and thereby be expected to take on the full GATT responsibilities of reciprocity and full compliance with GATT rules. Yet there were no hard criteria to determine such a transition, and in fact there was not even a definition in the GATT (or later the WTO) as to what a developing country was. Only the LDCs have acquired definitive status in the GATT/WTO system, based on the United Nations list of the forty-nine "poorest of the poor" countries of the world.[23]

SUMMARY

The GATT has established a highly successful global trading order, significantly reducing tariffs and other barriers to trade, and creating a set of rules and a dispute settlement mechanism through eight multilateral trade negotiations. Its institutional structure was formed in the context of historical circumstances, economic and political power relationships, early postwar patterns of comparative advantage, and domestic lobbying forces among its Contracting Parties. In this context, the GATT's Searlean institutional structure of collective intentionality, constitutive rules, deontic powers, and institutional output, in conjunction with informal rules, processes, and mutual trust among the main decision-making countries, was able to achieve significant multilateral trade liberalization. GATT Contracting Parties did, however, have to adjust to changing circumstances, testing its ability to maintain institutional equilibrium. It stretched its own rules, but managed to keep trade liberalization moving forward. The context of the GATT's origins and early years allowed its institutional structure to function well, but its exclusion of agriculture and services from general trade liberalization, as well as its failure to include developing country interests in its agenda, set the stage for difficulties later on, beginning with the Uruguay Round. The institutional structure of the GATT would experience major pressures from the changes in the global trade environment as it transitioned into the World Trade Organization, with major negative implications for the Doha Round of trade negotiations. The institutional aspects of this crisis are the subject of the following chapter.

The GATT to WTO Transition and Institutional Crisis in the Doha Round

INTRODUCTION

The previous chapter presented an institutional model of the GATT/WTO system as a set of rules with the goal of reducing transaction costs of trade liberalization, subject to the established boundaries of members' economic policy autonomy, and based on common beliefs about the validity of the goals and means to achieve them. This chapter sets out to show how the GATT evolved, through the efforts of the participating countries, into a broader and more comprehensive trade organization, the WTO. Despite the incremental nature of this change and the retention of many institutional features of the GATT, this new organization has had serious difficulties in fulfilling a major part of its mandate: to facilitate multilateral trade liberalization. There were many problems involved in the transition from GATT to WTO, and their impact on the Doha Round, leading to its suspension, will be examined as an instance of institutional disequilibrium. The chapter begins with a discussion of the motivations for creating the WTO, including its main new features. The WTO was built on the foundation of the GATT to extend trade coverage to new sectors, introduce new sets of rules, and significantly reform dispute settlement. The discussion then turns to the conceptual issues of institutional change and the nature of institutional equilibrium. These concepts are then applied to the transition between the GATT and the WTO, and how the mismatch of institutional goals and institutional capacity created institutional friction and led to the Doha Round crisis. The main institutional gaps include (1) lack of a common understanding of the limits of national policy sovereignty, which prevents agreement on new issues; (2) the single undertaking framework, which is too unwieldy to secure an agreement; (3) the lack of a clear understanding of reciprocity for developing countries in the negotiations; (4) a significant shift in the WTO balance of power, which has hampered the decision-making process; and (5) the judicialization of dispute settlement. A corresponding set of possible institutional remedies is also discussed, which will receive further elaboration in subsequent chapters. A concluding section summarizes the problems of the WTO and the difficulties of implementing institutional change.

THE GENESIS OF THE WTO

Founded in 1995, the WTO inherited the basic governance and decision-making structure of its predecessor, the GATT, established in 1947. The success of the GATT in liberalizing trade in the postwar period eventually led its Contracting Parties to negotiate the creation of a broader, more inclusive set of rules, with broader product coverage and stronger dispute settlement procedures. The GATT had promoted trade liberalization mainly in manufactures, while setting up a system of rules and informal dispute settlement. It convened a series of eight successful multilateral trade negotiations (MTNs) from 1947 to 1994. Its successor, the WTO, sought to expand on the GATT's ambitions, based on the success of postwar trade liberalization and the possibilities of increased trade in a robust, post-Cold War global economy. This was an exercise in *incremental institutional change*, an effort by GATT participants (led by the United States, the European Union, and other large countries) to modify the existing institutional rules in order to expand the benefits of its underlying goal: the gains from trade. Yet the resulting expansion of the global trading system into new product areas and rules, along with tightened enforcement measures, created tensions between its goals and its institutional means, eventually leading to institutional friction and crisis in the Doha Round.

The desire by the GATT Contracting Parties to expand the institution's scope and coverage encountered the problem that the existing constitutive rules were unable to accommodate the new desired outcomes. Part of the gap lay in product coverage. Due to the success of the GATT before the Uruguay Round, global average tariffs in manufactured goods had been whittled down well below 10%. There were new opportunities for trade expansion in services, a rapidly growing sector in trade, where the larger rich countries, in particular, had comparative advantage. Developing countries, largely relegated to the sidelines in the GATT rounds, were also eager to expand market access in agriculture, still heavily protected in most markets, and wanted a return to GATT disciplines for textiles, clothing, and other manufactures, in which market access in many developed countries had been restricted by the MFA and VERs. In order to achieve these goals, developing countries would have to participate more actively in multilateral trade talks, contrary to previous negotiating practice under the GATT. The developed countries were well disposed to support a greater role for developing countries, many of which in the meantime had been growing rapidly, thus creating valuable import markets. The scent of a bargain between developed and developing countries was in the air.

There was also interest in expanding the rules to cover increasingly important details in rules, such as technical barriers to trade and sanitary/phytosanitary standards. The United States, in particular, also wanted an agreement on trade-related aspects of intellectual property, since patents, copyrights, and trademarks for US-based pharmaceutical, technology-oriented, and entertainment industries were not protected in much of the world. In the absence of binding global rules on intellectual property, the United States had resorted to unilateral protection through its own "special 301" procedures—a parallel trade institution—and many countries acknowledged the need for a new agreement to discipline such measures. There was, in addition, widespread support for a tighter dispute settlement process, since the GATT rules allowed the losing side in a case to veto the dispute panel's judgment, so that enforcement relied largely on informal diplomatic arrangements that emanated from a general systemic commitment to the dispute process.[1] However, dispute cases were becoming more contentious as postwar trade expanded and new issues arose, leading to calls for a more legally binding process. There was also dissatisfaction with the fragmentation of the GATT rules that had developed as a result of the ability of countries to selectively join certain GATT Codes on an à la carte basis.[2] Many countries took the position that the Codes fragmented and weakened the global trading system. Another problem along these lines was the differential and casually enforced terms of accession to the GATT. Many developing countries had joined the GATT on the basis of generous protocols of accession that did not require strict trade liberalizing measures (Jones 2009: 288–290). Developed countries, in particular, wanted to secure GATT rights and obligations on a more concrete, legally defensible basis.

It is also important to recognize the *zeitgeist* that dominated the Uruguay Round years. There was a palpable optimism regarding trade liberalization that prevailed in the years leading up to the foundation of the WTO. Postwar economic expansion had created generally positive views toward the principle of trade liberalization, reinforced by the trends in deregulation led by President Ronald Reagan in the United States and Prime Minister Margaret Thatcher in the United Kingdom in the 1980s. Many developing countries had been encouraged in the earlier postwar period to adopt import-substitution and infant-industry protectionism as a development strategy, but in the meantime this path had come to be regarded as a failed experiment. Most of the rapidly growing developing countries were the ones opening up to trade (even if there was often continued government involvement in resource allocation), and some developing countries even began to lower trade barriers unilaterally. The fall of the Berlin Wall, and subsequent dissolution of the Soviet Union, seemed to signal a definitive triumph for open-market capitalism, as embodied in the "Washington Consensus."[3] The number of countries joining the GATT expanded rapidly, with thirty-seven new accessions during the Uruguay Round years 1986–1994 (Jones 2009).

The new World Trade Organization, created as part of the final Uruguay Round agreement, officially became an international organization with member states (no longer "Contracting Parties"), and with the legal personality to sign agreements with states, unlike its predecessor, the GATT. It retained the basic institutional principles ("constitutive rules") of the GATT—most-favored nation status, consensus in decision-making, reciprocity in negotiations—and it also retained the GATT's concept of embedded domestic economic policy sovereignty, although the boundaries of domestic sovereignty in the new WTO framework, in an evolving trade environment and with broader participation, may not have been clear. Under the terms of the Uruguay Round's new "single undertaking" rule (see below) all GATT members were required specifically to join the new WTO in order to continue the benefits they enjoyed under the GATT. Revised GATT (1994) provisions replaced the original GATT (1947) and became part of an expanded set of agreements and rules, extending the framework of trade liberalization to agriculture and services, introducing new agreements on technical and health-related trade barriers, and providing a binding system of dispute settlement.

The motivations to build a new, expanded trade institution that was to become the WTO reflected a genuine desire by nearly all participants in the GATT to sustain and build upon its earlier successful trade negotiations. However, in some critical areas the WTO severely stretched the original institutional framework of the GATT, and future events would test the strength of these new features. First, the WTO incorporated agreements based on a "single undertaking," meaning that all members in principle had to take part in all constituent agreements, with a few exceptions.[4] It also implied that any future trade negotiations would likewise proceed as a single-undertaking package. New product coverage in the WTO included agricultural goods and services, two broad sectors that each exhibit widely diverging national interests among WTO members. While the Uruguay Round had not created much new market access in these areas, but rather had established mainly frameworks for rules and trade liberalization, it was hoped that future negotiations would make progress in opening up these markets. Yet including national agricultural and services policies (the latter governed largely through domestic regulations) in multilateral trade negotiations posed a potential conflict with the informal rule of embedded domestic policy sovereignty. Trade liberalization above a minimal level of opening in agriculture and services appeared for many countries to lie on the other side of the "red line" of acceptable limits for global trading rules to penetrate national "behind the border" laws and regulations. For this reason, the Uruguay Round made little progress in achieving trade liberalization in these areas. A similar problem arose with the inclusion of legally binding rules regarding Trade-Related Intellectual Property Rights (TRIPS), an area of widely diverging experience among WTO members, and one in which many members had no national legal framework for enforcement. Finally, the Uruguay Round that created the WTO had succeeded in bringing developing countries into the bargaining process, but WTO practice had carried over, and even expanded, S&D treatment of developing countries in the negotiations. Developing countries had insisted on these "affirmative action" measures, but they were designed under GATT conditions, in which trade negotiations had focused on rich-country manufactures, and non-reciprocity by developing countries was acceptable. In the Uruguay Round, for the first time, developing countries were being asked to offer concessions. Could the new WTO reconcile these contradictions?

INCREMENTAL INSTITUTIONAL CHANGE AND EQUILIBRIUM

The establishment in 1947 of a new global institution, the GATT, was an example of discontinuous change from the existing fragmented global trading system in place immediately following World War II. Starting from a clean slate, the initiative of the Bretton Woods agreement had created new global economic institutions that bore the mark of the victorious western allies, particularly the United States. Once such an institution is created, its operation is dependent on the effectiveness not only of the "hardware" of its formal rules, stated goals, and organizational structure but also of its complementary "software" of informal rules established by the prevailing historical, political, and economic forces, traditions, and circumstances of its founding. The GATT itself set up the formal rules, and governments and diplomats worked together, within the political and economic constraints of their time, to forge multilateral trade agreements. The path dependency of the institution would create potential problems, however, when the circumstances of the trade environment and the goals and perceptions of the participants changed. Ironically, the very success of the GATT generated the desire for more ambitious trade liberalization. Yet expanded goals often require new or modified institutional features to support them. The GATT therefore faced the need for incremental institutional change to match its new ambitions, which in turn, created friction in the institution as a whole.

Institutional change, as described in chapter 2, is difficult to analyze because of the complex interaction of the institution's components when confronted with an important change in its environment. Institutional equilibrium, in this context, refers to the ability of the institution's ability to create the "output" that is the goal of its collective intentionality. In the case of the WTO, the equilibrium condition rests on stability in its three constituent functions: maintaining the rules, administering dispute settlement, and negotiating new trade agreements. The disruption of equilibrium in the WTO, through changes in critical elements of the institutional order (Greif and Laitan 2004), created institutional friction. In response to such pressure, the institution can re-establish institutional *equilibrium* if it can implement internal adjustments that allow the members to renew their ability to achieve their goals. This definition of equilibrium raises two important questions. First, since achieving consensus is a process that takes place over time, one can ask at what point a lengthy negotiation creates "disequilibrium" and whether a more limited outcome represents success. Next, since the WTO has created three broad categories of institutional facts, is equilibrium necessary in all three in order for the institution to be in equilibrium?

For the negotiating function of the WTO, equilibrium can be restated as the achievement of, or movement toward, *consensus* on achieving or supporting new institutional facts or outcomes through multilateral trade liberalization. For the dispute settlement function, equilibrium is tied to the legitimacy of the panel rulings and processes seek to resolve disputes, and the eventual compliance of countries to these rulings, to the extent that normal WTO-based trade relations can take place.[5] Equilibrium in the monitoring and implementation function requires the cooperation of member country representatives and WTO Secretariat officials in the more technocratic activities and details of trade policy. Of the three WTO functions, the negotiating part is most important, since dispute settlement and implementation exist only as the result of negotiated agreements that established their frameworks and rules. Once they were established, they developed their own legitimacy, allowing them to continue their functions without further progress in multilateral trade negotiations, but even in these functions, equilibrium may not be sustainable in the absence of further agreements on the rules, as will be discussed below.

GATT/WTO trade negotiations have become lengthier over time, often with contentious delays, and it is tempting to say that the parties are by definition in disequilibrium until they finally come to an agreement. From an institutional perspective, however, one can judge equilibrium to prevail as long as the parties involved continue to *use the institution's framework in a joint effort to move toward consensus.* The distinguishing feature of the Doha Round in this regard is that, in contrast to all previous GATT negotiations, parties to the Doha Round formally agreed to suspend negotiations on their original agenda in 2011, a decision unprecedented in the GATT/WTO era, while simultaneously pursuing BAMTA measures, especially through RTA negotiations.[6] Thus, by this standard, the WTO failed to achieve the comprehensive, multilateral trade agreement it set out to achieve in 2001, and one can therefore speak of "disequilibrium" in the WTO's legislative function. Even so, it is important to remember that the Doha Round is not "dead," as the parties have continued to negotiate on subsets of the original agenda and concluded a partial agreement on specific issues at the December 2013 Bali Ministerial.[7] Any such limited agreements would be disappointing, but better than nothing. Yet the main problem with a severely incomplete conclusion to a multilateral WTO trade round is that the participants will see the limited payoff as an invitation to resort to alternative trade agreements on a bilateral or regional basis, leading, at worst, to a sort of entropy in the WTO's negotiating function. While such agreements have been negotiated outside the GATT/WTO system before, such as the formation of the European Common Market in 1958 and the North American Free Trade Agreement (NAFTA) in 1994, they took place in addition to, and often in conjunction with, concurrent multilateral trade negotiations. As the Doha Round began to stall, the proliferation of regional trade agreements appears in part to be a response to the sluggish WTO talks, and thereby represents possible evidence of WTO disequilibrium. And while WTO negotiations have continued in Geneva in the meantime, there has been a perceptible refocusing of policy attention by large WTO countries toward regional trade negotiations, a subject to be explored in more detail in chapter 6.

At the same time, it is important to note that the WTO does not currently consist of the Doha negotiations alone, but rather carries on day-to-day, and by most accounts successful, operations among its standing committees that deal with implementation and monitoring issues, and in the Dispute Settlement Body. In this regard one can distinguish between the *static* equilibrium of existing formal rules-based activities and the *dynamic* equilibrium of generating new trade liberalizing measures. Implementation, monitoring, and dispute settlement activities are based on existing formal institutional rules and cannot formally create new rights and obligations for WTO members. As long as the existing rules enjoy legitimacy among the WTO membership, their application will enjoy static institutional equilibrium in those defined functions. Thus, it is important to parse the equilibrium question according to the various functional outputs of the institution. In this sense, the negotiating part of the WTO appears to be in dynamic disequilibrium, while the monitoring and dispute settlement parts are in static equilibrium. While this approach to the question allows a differentiated and partially favorable diagnosis of the WTO's performance, one should keep in mind that there are important linkages among the three functions that raise warning signs. Existing rules will support the current trading system only as long as new trade issues and circumstances do not create serious problems among trading partners. Similarly, dispute settlement can resolve issues cleanly only if the relevant rules are adequate to guide the panels that decide them. In the absence of new negotiated rules to address new issues, unresolved disputes can begin to undermine the entire institutional framework of the WTO.

If the WTO is in legislative disequilibrium, what has caused it? The Searlean approach described in the previous chapter provides a framework for understanding the nature of institutional friction in the GATT/WTO system. The institution's performance is usually judged by the quality and volume of its output, as perceived by the members and by its overall impact on members' economic well-being. Under the original GATT, eight rounds of trade negotiations were concluded, and the expanding roster of participating countries enjoyed robust economic growth. During the GATT period, its ability to conduct and conclude trade rounds suggested a state of institutional equilibrium, even if this time was punctuated by internal crises due to forms of institutional friction described in chapter 2, requiring institutional adjustments. The GATT's successor institution, the WTO, has also faced institutional friction, but has had greater difficulty in adjusting to it. These issues are the subject of the following sections.

CHALLENGES TO INSTITUTIONAL EQUILIBRIUM: THE WTO AND THE DOHA ROUND

The trade environment and balance of political power evolved throughout the postwar period, as the United States saw its relative power in the institution diminishing, the addition of many developing countries to the membership, changes in the pattern of comparative advantage in important markets, and an expansion of the trade agenda. All of these factors created institutional friction in the GATT, and many of them continued to generate friction in the WTO. The WTO finds itself in such a crisis because of its inability to complete comprehensive multilateral trade agreements, despite the large potential gains from further trade liberalization. Furthermore, there is a growing need for negotiations on new rules on trade-related government policies involving the environment, climate change, and food and resource security goals, along with state trading, exchange rate, and development policies. Inevitably, the absence of progress in evolving areas of concern could lead to trade disputes that are dumped onto the dispute settlement system without adequate guidelines for resolving them. To return to an analogy described in chapter 2, as the trade environment changes, it may be necessary to alter both the hardware (formal rules) and the software (informal rules, understandings, and procedures) in order for the institution to continue to function effectively, or to accommodate new functions. The need for new hardware to achieve the institution's goals—reforms in formal procedures, new product coverage, new committee structures, new monitoring rules, and so on—is usually easy enough to identify, if difficult to construct, as was shown by the arduous eight-year-long Uruguay Round. But what is particularly difficult is to recognize, design, and construct the new "software" that is needed: ways of bargaining over the new issues, managing the demarcation line that defines domestic policy sovereignty, overcoming past resentments and the rigid thinking that belongs to past circumstances, and finding ways to establish confidence and trust in new negotiating environments. When it comes to multilateral trade negotiations, the hardware and the software together must function in an effective manner to allow the WTO members jointly to set an agenda, find acceptable trade-offs in market access and rules reforms, and reach consensus on a package of agreements. In this sense, the basic hardware of the negotiations, which had worked in the Uruguay Round, seemed to be in place. But the Doha Round appeared to have a "software" problem.

The Single Undertaking and New Product Areas

Table 3.1 connects the most significant new institutional elements of the WTO with their immediate impact at the end of the Uruguay Round and beginning of the WTO era, and with the Doha Round. The single undertaking rule, for example, was understandably regarded by many as the key to reaching a broad consensus on all the new WTO issues and unifying the system of rights and obligations for all members. It did in fact lead to the conclusion of the Uruguay Round, what will probably remain its one brief, shining moment. It could have provided the framework for a large package of Doha Round agreements, if the diversity of basic views on market access among major players on agriculture and services had not been so great. By the time the Doha negotiations required negotiators to make meaningful progress on liberalization in these sectors, it became clear that the WTO membership exhibited huge divergences in bargaining positions, making a single undertaking "package" deal virtually impossible. This problem was linked with the very extension of WTO coverage into these new and politically sensitive sectors. Having succeeded in introducing

Table 3.1 SIGNIFICANT FORMAL INSTITUTIONAL CHANGES IN THE TRANSITION FROM GATT TO WTO

New feature	Motivation	Initial impact	Implications for Doha Round
Single undertaking (initiated in Uruguay Round)	Avoid GATT à la carte; Create broad range for trade-offs	Motivated all GATT countries to join WTO; created "Grand Bargain"	Made consensus process more complicated; contributed to gridlock
Addition of agriculture	Gap in GATT coverage; heavy protection; developing country interest in MTN	Little progress in Uruguay Round trade liberalization	Difficult to pry from domestic protection; North-South fault line
Services agreement	Gap in GATT coverage; growing trade sector; developed country interest in MTN	Framework only: few commitments on market opening in Uruguay Round	Reluctance of countries to open behind-the-border regulations of key service sectors
TRIPS	US unilateral 301 enforcement; importance for United States in MTN	Compliance difficulties for developing countries, which lost welfare from transfers	Still a sore point for developing countries, which are warier of making commitments in new areas
Participation of developing countries	Expand liberalization to get larger agreement	Developing countries get "Grand Bargain" but are disappointed in MFA, TRIPS results	Resentment from Uruguay Round; "policy space" arguments to resist concessions
New dispute settlement understanding	No teeth in GATT dispute settlement	Improved implementation, but "missing cases"	Legalization of commitments undermined diplomacy
Reform of safeguards	Replace use of VERs, AD as emergency protection	Increased application, but DSU challenges inhibited their use	Reduced safety net may have discouraged trade liberalization
New accession procedures	Tighten entrance requirements	Bilaterals extract WTO + concessions; delays in joining	Concessions fatigue; disengagement from MTN?

negotiating frameworks (if little else) for these sectors in the Uruguay Round, many negotiators evidently overestimated the ability of the bargaining process to overcome what should have been obviously high political hurdles in achieving meaningful liberalization in them. Agriculture, as noted earlier, had been largely exempted from GATT disciplines due to strong domestic support for protection in the United States, and later the European Union. In the Doha Round, India proved to be the most intransigent opponent to liberalized agricultural market access at home, due to the vulnerability of its hundreds of millions of farmers to import competition. Services trade liberalization was perhaps even more problematical, since much of the sector was subject to domestic regulations, another national sovereignty issue. In short, a Doha Round agreement including agriculture and services proved to be extremely difficult to negotiate among a disparate set of countries, many of which jealously guarded their sovereignty over these sectors. The single undertaking and the new product coverage thereby contributed to an institutional breakdown in the WTO's ability to secure consensus.

TRIPS and Developing Country Participation

Other institutional elements of the GATT to WTO transition contributed to the North-South divide in the Doha Round. Principal among them was the TRIPS agreement, which introduced global protection for holders of patents, copyrights, trademarks, and geographical indications. The logic of introducing this issue into the WTO was largely political, as indicated earlier: the United States, which had been unilaterally enforcing its own intellectual property rights (IPR) laws, bargained aggressively for a universal TRIPS agreement. As part of the final Uruguay Round package, it became part of a "grand bargain" that also included an end to the MFA and VERs, which developing countries had demanded. Unfortunately, this package was not balanced in terms of welfare effects. The TRIPS allowed a few developed country holders of IPRs, mainly the United States, Germany, France, and Switzerland, to reap large additional profits at the expense of all other countries, particularly developing countries, which had few IPRs. The end of VERs and the MFA would perhaps have partially offset this transfer from poorer to richer countries, but the emergence of China as a major exporter of clothing, textiles, and many other manufactured goods eroded the ability of other developing countries to gain the additional market shares they expected from the Uruguay Round reforms. In addition, developing countries gave up the quantitative market access guarantees, along with "quota rents" transferred to them by VER-type arrangements. Both TRIPS and the unexpected shift in comparative advantage in clothing to

China thus ended up reducing the welfare gains from the Uruguay Round for many countries, and especially developing countries.

Perhaps more damaging from an institutional perspective was the fact that the inclusion of intellectual property in the Uruguay Round undermined the basic expectation that trade liberalization would unambiguously benefit all parties. Unlike traditional market opening measures, which in principle result in gains from specialization and exchange for all parties, the TRIPS essentially protects the monopoly rights for IPR holders, a zero-sum game, at least in the short run.[8] The counterargument is that developing countries would gain from TRIPS through the encouragement it would give to foreign direct investment, which would enhance the transfer of technology and skills to those countries, and that they would also eventually gain from their own IPR as their stake in innovation increased. However, for many developing countries, these benefits may be smaller than the cost of IPR compliance and occur much later.[9] Furthermore, even if the Uruguay Round as a whole was beneficial to all or nearly all countries (which it probably was), the prospect that a single negotiating issue would systematically reduce the welfare benefits of an agreement for certain countries would make them wary of engaging in new trade agreements, particularly with regard to unfamiliar issues whose welfare impacts are uncertain, such as services. What is worse, the "grand bargain" debacle may have motivated many developing countries, feeling that they had been hoodwinked into the Uruguay Round deal, to pursue a "distributive" strategy in the Doha Round, in which they would demand that all (or most) new bargaining concessions come from the developed countries. Their claims are that the Doha Round should provide compensation for developing countries to offset the disappointing results of the Uruguay Round and to cover the implementation costs of TRIPS, customs valuation, and standards. The developing country backlash may also have contributed to the newfound claims by many of them for "policy space" in trade negotiations, effectively moving the demarcation line for domestic policy autonomy forward to encompass trade barriers as development tools that should be exempt from reciprocity expectations. This claim found support in GATT article 18, which, as described in chapter 2, allowed developing countries to pursue infant industry protection. The upshot of this contradiction was to create confusion regarding the reciprocity requirements for developing countries in the Doha Round. Since reciprocity and a common understanding on the limits of members' domestic economic policy sovereignty have always been fundamental to successful bargaining in the GATT, the divergence in views on these institutional elements created a huge obstacle to reaching consensus in the Doha Round. As Eichengreen and Uzan (1993) have noted, a negotiation is likely to fail if the participants' domestic institutions bring different conceptual frameworks to the table.

Judicialization of Trade Agreements

The Uruguay Round had marked a definite shift from trade diplomacy to trade law, an understandable response to the perceived need to define more clearly the rights, obligations, and dispute procedures associated with the functioning of a global trading system. The most prominent example of this trend in the transition from GATT to WTO was the new dispute settlement system, which established a "negative consensus" veto requirement in order to override a dispute panel decision, replacing the GATT system, in which any Contracting Party (including the losing party in the case) could veto acceptance of the panel decision. The GATT system had actually operated reasonably well, if informally, through peer and systemic pressure, which typically resulted in behind-the-scenes negotiations to resolve the dispute. Trade diplomacy shouldered the burden of solving these problems, which had prevented seriously divisive issues from disrupting peaceful trade relations among the Contracting Parties. Such diplomacy was still important in the revised dispute settlement understanding (DSU), especially in settling disputes early in the process. But panel decisions now carried heavier consequences: a losing respondent in a case would have to bring its trade policy measure or practice into compliance with the panel ruling, or else face potential retaliatory "withdrawals of concessions" by the complainant. After a ruling, there was now much less flexibility in settling the dispute, aside from appealing the result to the newly formed Appellate Body.

Despite criticisms of the DSU in its ability to ensure compliance with WTO rules (see Bown 2011), most observers regard it as a major positive accomplishment of the Uruguay Round, largely successful in maintaining the integrity of the WTO system. However, the DSU subtly changed an important element of trade negotiations strategy. Henceforth, the terms of any multilateral agreement would require implementation in the shadow of future DSU enforcement. Member countries would have to anticipate the fastidious legal scrutiny of its trading partners in implementing negotiated concessions and binding decisions by the DSU panel in case of a judgment. Under these circumstances, countries became much more careful in what they would offer in a negotiation, so the anticipation of increased legal exposure of a Doha agreement may have constrained countries in bargaining on new trade issues, where benefits may be more uncertain and DSU challenges may be more likely. The problem of uncertainty could in principle be managed through the availability of "safeguard" emergency protection measures (GATT article 19), which were in fact revised in the Uruguay Round in an attempt to make their use more attractive. However, many countries had in the meantime successfully challenged the use of safeguards in the DSU, so that their use has been limited. As the legal implications of an agreement become more important, it seems, the political and diplomatic elements become less reliable in protecting a country's trade interests, a departure from GATT practice. Consensus may have become more elusive as a result.

These concerns raise the subtle, but fundamental problem of "globalization anxiety" in negotiating trade agreements in the twenty-first century. In principle, all trade negotiations are about the future, since the sequence of concluding a multilateral agreement, ratifying and implementing it, and enduring possible challenges under dispute proceedings roll out over several years before the next trade agreement is reached. Surprises are sure to be in store for all the participants: for example, the ascent of China as an exporting power just as the Uruguay Round had ended, the controversy over the international AIDS medicine crisis that threw the TRIPS agreement into turmoil, the rapid rise of trade based on international supply chains in the late twentieth century, and the unexpected role of the Internet and other communications breakthroughs in affecting trade. Technology itself, aside from its trade effects, is rapidly changing economies and job opportunities around the world. Adjusting to such changes is not a new problem, but governments regard the rate of change as worrisome because of its potentially rapid and unexpected impact on the domestic economy and income distribution. Safeguards protection, as noted above, may not be enough to provide "insurance" against new and unexpected trade disruptions or circumstances. The real underlying problem is a lack of adjustment to changing trade and technology opportunities and competitiveness in the countries themselves, often the result of slow domestic policy response and poor domestic economic flexibility. Under such conditions openness can be politically risky, making global trade liberalization less attractive.

A related but distinct problem associated with the legalization of WTO rights and obligations can be found in the revised accession procedures. Under the GATT system, many countries had joined the agreement without extensive entry obligations, although entry requirements tightened during the Uruguay Round. Under the new WTO rules, applicants for membership had to undergo an extensive process of negotiation and review, unilaterally reforming their economies and governance to comply with WTO rules. In addition, accession negotiations increasingly involved numerous bilateral negotiations with existing WTO members, leading to unilateral "WTO-plus" concessions by the applicant, over and above the obligations of existing WTO members (Jones 2009; Charnovitz 2007). Aside from creating resentment among new members, the accession process may have created a sort of "concessions fatigue," especially with regard to WTO-plus measures, which consequently reduced their interest and participation in the Doha Round. The most prominent country in this category may be China, which, after joining the WTO in 2001 with steep tariff cuts and numerous additional obligations and restrictions, maintained a low profile throughout the Doha negotiations. Squeezing too many concessions out of new WTO members, especially China, may therefore have inadvertently deprived the Doha Round of some negotiating "fuel" and limited the role of a potentially influential country in the bargaining sessions.[10]

Other Institutional Shocks

The transition from GATT to WTO revealed the difficulties that accompanied the attempt to expand the scope and capacity of the global trading system when important new elements of legitimacy, responsibility, and consensus building were not in place. Further evidence of the problem of managing institutional change can be found in how the WTO has responded to shocks to the system. The GATT faced similar problems, as noted in the previous chapter, and those examples provide a good basis for comparison with the WTO's handling of the situation.

China: A disruptive new member. For the GATT, the entry of Japan into the agreement in 1955 posed the problem of a "disruptive" new exporter that could upset institutional equilibrium. China has played this role since joining the WTO in 2001. In the case of Japan, many GATT members insisted on suspending MFN treatment by imposing discriminatory VER arrangements against "troublesome" Japanese exports in order to normalize GATT relations with Japan on other products. Later, the accession of China into the WTO led to similar fears. However, after VERs were officially banned as a result of the Uruguay Round, the WTO solution was to impose a special protocol of accession on China, with many unprecedented anti-disruption provisions, including a special safeguards and antidumping clauses that would apply for the first twelve and fifteen years, respectively, of its WTO membership.[11] In this case institutional learning managed to maintain general MFN discipline through a somewhat discriminatory accession protocol, whose safeguards provisions have been used more sparingly than was the use of VERs against Japan. Antidumping cases against China since joining the WTO, while numerous, have been fewer than during its comparable pre-WTO period, when countries could pursue antidumping cases against it outside of WTO disciplines (Bown 2010). At the same time, China continues to be a "disruptive" force in the WTO, in that its massive exporting capacity in labor-intensive goods raises fears among many countries, both developed and developing, of surges in Chinese exports that could threaten their domestic industries, as well as other exporting countries' market shares abroad. Any trade liberalization in goods that China exports will be negotiated in the shadow of these fears until its ability to disrupt politically sensitive markets is offset by the prospects for other WTO members to gain new and valuable access to Chinese domestic markets.

Expanding membership and the green room. By the time the Tokyo Round (1973–1979) took place, the number of participants in GATT negotiations grew to the point where consensus could no longer be reached on the basis of small group meetings. As a result, the GATT introduced the use of small-group "green room" agreements, from which a "concentric circle" method of outreach to other countries' representatives would set out to secure general consensus among all GATT countries. This system worked reasonably well as long as its legitimacy was recognized by those countries not included in green room meetings, for which the Director-General oversaw the list of invitees, and where the outlines of a final agreement were often shaped. Growing developing country participation in WTO negotiations generated conflict over this arrangement, however, as many countries felt excluded from the decision-making process. There has been a two-pronged institutional response to this problem. The Director-General, beginning with Michael Moore, redoubled his efforts to include in green room meetings representatives from all countries with a strong interest in the topic of the meeting, or at least make sure that all representative points of view were included. In addition, following the meeting, open communication with the rest of the WTO membership would ensure that all members would be informed about the deliberations. In addition, WTO members have adapted to this institutional problem of representation by forming more coalitions to enhance their joint representation on major issues, thus extending green room representation to all members of a coalition as long as one member is included in the green room meeting. These institutional adjustments have generally been successful, although there is still concern about the adequacy of green room representation when unexpected crises arise.

The problem of a changing bargaining power in the WTO. The GATT came into existence, as described earlier, under the strong influence of the United States, which had emerged from World War II as the dominant global political and economic power. While US influence did not dominate the GATT completely, it did create a sort of hegemonic stability in the global trading system of the noncommunist world. Consensus on any significant agreement in the GATT typically began with the United States and other key developed country players, such as the United Kingdom and later the European Common Market countries. Even at the beginning of the Doha Round under the WTO, the key "inner circle" players in managing consensus were the "Quad" countries: the United States, European Union, Japan, and Canada. As noted earlier, the GATT's original focus on the trade interests of industrialized countries, along with its legacy of US trade policy features, required strong US influence and support in order to maintain its successful functioning. As the postwar recovery and global economic expansion progressed, however, the relative dominance of the United States began to decline. By the 1980s, many developing countries were growing more rapidly than the developed countries and were also becoming more prominent traders. This phenomenon did not pose an economic problem for the trading system as much as an institutional one. As the relative influence of the United States and other industrialized countries declined, the terms of reaching consensus began to change. Just a few years after the Doha Round began, India and Brazil entered the "inner circle" of the negotiations, with China maintaining a quiet but influential presence. In this new negotiating environment, the more divergent interests of the major players created much greater challenges in finding broad and balanced agreements, or in some areas, in finding any agreement at all. For the first time, multilateral trade negotiations involved direct confrontation over fundamentally differing attitudes over the role of agriculture, services, and intellectual property between developed and developing countries. As the role of trade in development entered the negotiations, a more important existential question for the WTO also emerged: did all WTO members still share a common understanding of the gains from trade and the negotiating process to achieve them?

Supply chains and bilateral investment treaties. Finally, a new and more subtle development in trade has recently emerged that is likely to challenge the WTO system for years to come. Breakthroughs in technology and communications have "unbundled" the production process to an unprecedented degree, leading to increasingly extensive, and regionally integrated international supply chains (see Baldwin 2006b). The problem for the WTO and multilateralism is that such arrangements have encouraged preferential (i.e., discriminatory) trade liberalization through highly detailed bilateral investment treaties (BITs), which also include provisions for foreign direct investment and other policy reforms tailored to the partnership between the investment-seeking ("technology") country and the host ("factory") country, as well as a separate tribunal to adjudicate disputes. This phenomenon will receive further treatment in chapter 6, as it is part of the broader trend in regional trade agreements. For the WTO, perhaps the most serious implication of BITs is that they replace the traditional reciprocal exchange of market access commitments with an exchange of foreign investment and associated technology, training and other benefits, for intermediate goods market access, favorable terms of foreign direct investment, and supporting economic policy reforms. The best outcome would be to bring both supply-chain trade and foreign investment regimes under multilateral discipline, but steps to introduce such measures into the WTO have been largely unsuccessful so far.

Table 3.2 summarizes the institutional response of the WTO to disruptions, juxtaposed with those of comparable disruptions during the GATT years, along with subsequent impacts on the GATT/WTO system. In some cases, the GATT or WTO response has served to allow multilateral trade to continue. Responses to the new members (Japan and China), for example, stretched institutional provisions to accommodate the fears of disruption, although they compromised MFN treatment. The introduction of the green room, and the WTO response to developing country objections to it, has generally been successful, as the question of representation itself does not seem to be hampering the process of decision-making.[12] Dealing with new and difficult trade issues remains a major problem for the WTO. The earlier GATT response to comparative advantage shifts, which was to abandon its principles on MFN and banning quantitative restrictions by allowing VERs, briefly kept multilateral trade liberalization going, but was unsustainable, and led to the secondary (and necessary) response of eliminating such measures. Protectionist measures now flow to antidumping and other contingent protection measures, which are still a problem, but are within traditional GATT/WTO rules. Efforts to introduce WTO disciplines to agriculture and services have generally been unsuccessful, beyond establishing frameworks for future negotiations, as there appears to be a lack of consensus on how, if at all, to extend trade rules into these sensitive sectors. This institutional issue, along with the role of developing countries in MTN negotiations—along with the related shift in bargaining power that has brought Brazil and India into the Quad—reflect the serious problems that have prevented consensus in the Doha Round. Expanding WTO coverage into other new areas, such as supply-chain-related trade and investment, will be equally daunting, as the WTO does not presently have the institutional machinery, capacity, or experience to conduct negotiations on this or many other new issues.

In this connection, a major "software" issue seems to have emerged in the WTO in conjunction with the institutional problems discussed in this section: the issue of "trust." As noted in chapter 2, trust appeared not to be a major problem during the GATT years, even if the bargaining was hard and lengthy, as shown by the capacity of the negotiators to compartmentalize disagreements or come to mutual agreements on bending the rules. Even the change in bargaining power that came with the European Common Market bloc did not seem to slow down the GATT's ability to conclude trade rounds. This was probably a result in large part of the stability of the GATT system in those years, with countries in leadership roles marked by a common outlook and common economic structures creating a common negotiating culture, and higher value placed on informal processes. It would in contrast be easy enough to say, based on accounts of acrimonious remarks and accusations and confrontational

Table 3.2 Institutional Disruption and Internal Change in the GATT/WTO System

Type	Example(s)	Institutional response	Subsequent impact
Disruptive new member	Japan (1955), subject to article 35 exclusion	Allow export restraint, violating MFN	Article 35 lifted, continued VERs until WTO, antidumping
	China (2001)	Special protocol of accession	Special safeguards, fear of China trade persists
Expanding membership/ participation	Small group quorum not possible—Tokyo Round	Introduce green room deliberations	With WTO reforms, remains in use (with modifications to maximize representation)
	Increased developing country membership	GATT Part IV (1964)	Hortatory language with little impact; delayed response (see next item)
	Developing country bargaining disadvantage 1970s–1990s	Enabling clause: special/differential treatment	Developing country engagement, but preference erosion; reciprocity problem
	Green room issue: Seattle, Cancun	More inclusiveness, communication	Improved transparency; coalition building
	Developing countries expected to reciprocate	Uruguay Round: Grand Bargain Doha Round: continued S&D treatment	Uruguay Round hangover. Doha Round: North/South divide; policy space claim, gridlock over modalities

(continued)

Table 3.2 CONTINUED

Type	Example(s)	Institutional response	Subsequent impact
New trade issues	NTBs (Tokyo Round)	Codes based on partitioned consensus	Reform: WTO single undertaking for most issues
	Agriculture (Uruguay Round; Doha Round)	Uruguay Round framework; tariffication	Doha Round impasse
	Services (Uruguay Round)	Uruguay Round framework only	Doha: Little progress on new market access
Shift in comparative advantage	Textiles	MFA	Uruguay Round: terminated
	Steel, autos, electronics, footwear, etc.	Voluntary Export Restraints (VERs)	Reform: Uruguay Round outlawed; increased use of antidumping
Major change in bargaining power	European Common Market/European Community/European Union (beginning 1958)	United States, European Union share decision-making, lead Quad	Longer rounds, unresolved conflicts, but MTN consensus still possible
	Emerging markets during Doha Round	Change in Quad to include Brazil, India	Continued pressure on MTN consensus process
Supply-chain trade	Factory Asia, EU network, NAFTA	RTAs, BITs	Change in bargaining terms reduces role of WTO

behavior, that many WTO delegates during the Doha Round "didn't trust each other."[13] Yet such an observation is likely to conflate personality with political conflict and institutional problems. Trust is usually understood in terms of confidence in the personal truthfulness and honest motivations of one's negotiating partner. There may be a lack of trust in this sense in the Doha Round in some cases, but the absence of personal trust would surely have been present in previous rounds as well. What is more likely in the Doha Round is that structural differences and fault lines between different countries' interests and perceptions have fueled cynicism and suspicion among the delegations that outcomes in such a complicated negotiation can be tilted toward the interest of some parties and away from others. Such perceptions may come simply from the unprecedented divergence in negotiating interests, for example, between the rich farming sector of the United States and the subsistence farming sector in India. Differences in countries' access to, and capacity to interpret, information and expected outcome scenarios may also play a role. If you know the other party has an information advantage, you are less likely to have confidence in the terms of a proposed agreement. Memory and experience also play a role in these perceptions. Did the United States and other countries supporting the TRIPS agreement in the Uruguay Round know at the time about the heavy transfers from poorer to richer countries, and the implementation costs the poorer countries would bear? Such memories were still fresh in the Doha Round. Inconsistency and confusion over the years regarding the GATT/WTO expectations on developing country reciprocity could raise suspicions about the terms of certain proposals, such as some developing countries' view that trade facilitation efforts by developing countries to improve the efficiency of their own trade logistics should be regarded as a "concession," demanding compensation over and above the infrastructure aid and efficiency improvements by developed country donors in the process.[14] Suspicions may be directed not so much at individuals as at informal processes and procedures, for example, the power of committee chairs to manage meetings and draft negotiating texts. Finally, it is not just developing country negotiators that are distrustful. The high stakes of a package deal made many developed (as well as developing) country negotiators wary of the mediation roles of chairs, especially the Director-General. With the stakes so high of a large package deal with many new legal obligations and possible DSU enforcement, the traditional acknowledgment of the Director-General as an "honest broker," common during the GATT years, appears to have evaporated.[15] Confidence in the genuineness of other countries' negotiating "red lines" may thereby also come into question. Little research exists on the culture of WTO negotiations. While the "trust" issue may persist independently, the institutional problems themselves may have contributed to the tensions in the Doha Round, as suggested by the discussion in chapter 2. One way to relieve the stress that they have imposed upon negotiators over a long period may therefore be to find solutions to the underlying institutional problems, which would improve the willingness to compromise, and thereby, to move toward consensus.

REMEDIES? AN INSTITUTIONAL APPROACH

The foregoing account of institutional problems suggests that the current WTO system cannot create the conditions to deliver consensus on multilateral trade liberalization. Five major sources of disruption, with overlapping impacts on important institutional elements, include:

(1) an increasingly diverse membership, with increased developing country participation, which challenged the traditional WTO understanding of reciprocity obligations and acceptable policy space for negotiation;

(2) new issues, especially agriculture and services, which also raised questions of policy space, and complicated efforts to meet consensus requirement for single undertaking;

(3) a significant shift in the balance of power in WTO negotiations toward emerging markets, leading to increased resort to BAMTA measures and deadlock;

(4) the judicialization of WTO dispute settlement, increasing the stakes of liberalization commitments under conditions of increasing uncertainty; and

(5) Supply-chain trade, which increases the attractiveness of BAMTA measures, and for which the WTO framework cannot currently offer a framework for bargaining.

Figure 3.1 illustrates the impact of these disruptive elements on the WTO, based on the institutional model introduced in chapter 2. The highlighted boxes show the disruptive forces, and the arrows indicate the primary institutional component they affect. The change in the balance of power in the WTO, shifting influence toward the large emerging markets, has changed the original power structure of membership established under the GATT, previously dominated by the United States and European Union. The more balanced bargaining power that now includes China, India, and Brazil has disrupted the traditional negotiating framework and led to deadlock for most of the Doha Round. In the absence of progress in MTN, the large countries in particular have turned to BAMTA, especially in the form of RTAs that they can more

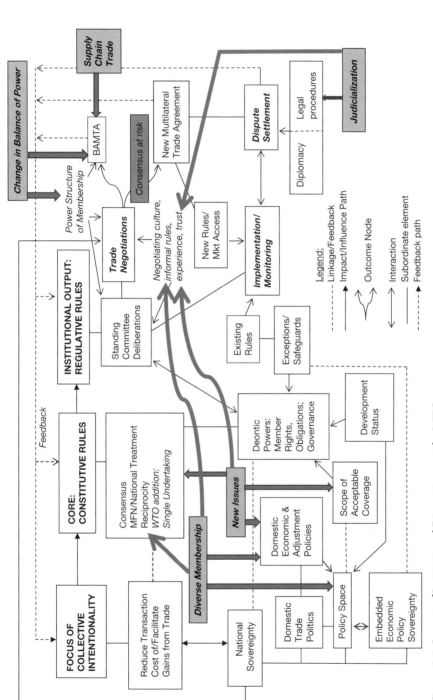

Figure 3.1 Impact of Institutional Disruptions on the WTO
SOURCE: Concept based on Searle (2005).

easily dominate as individual hub countries. Similarly, the increasing importance of trade occurring through international supply chains, linking specific
foreign investment and behind-the-border issues among partner countries,
has increased the attractiveness of BAMTA in the form of RTAs and BITs.
Disruptions have also entered the collective intentionality and core constitutive elements of the WTO. The increasing diversity of the WTO membership in
terms of economic development and domestic trade interests, for example, has
altered the balance among members regarding domestic capacity to manage
trade adjustment, which has also eroded shared understandings of policy space
and reciprocity. These factors have shrunk the zone of possible agreement and
complicated the process of reaching consensus on many issues. The emergence
of new issues in the WTO, such as services, intellectual property, and agriculture, has compounded this problem by altering the boundary lines of mutually
acceptable policy space and issue coverage. The judicialization of dispute settlement enforcement, for all its benefits in addressing conflict among members,
has also created an institutional challenge by making WTO members more
cautious of making new commitments.

Several of these factors, as shown in figure 3.1, thus also affect the conduct
of the negotiations themselves. Increasing diversity among WTO members,
the scope and complexity of an expanding negotiating agenda, and the DSU's
judicialized "sword of Damocles" hanging over any new WTO obligations have
jointly increased uncertainty over the value of outcomes to many countries. At
home, there appears to be more difficulty in getting political support for a large
trade deal. At the negotiating table, the lack of commonly recognized obligations of reciprocity and the boundaries of domestic policy space have reduced
the zone of possible agreement. The more equal bargaining power among
developed and developing countries has not been accompanied by a workable
framework of give-and-take, of leadership, and of trust among negotiators that
can replace the informal institutions of the GATT. In short, these institutional
disruptions have undermined many critical elements needed for building consensus under the terms of the single undertaking. Rebuilding the ability of the
WTO to generate new multilateral agreements will therefore require repair
work on the institutional machinery of generating agreement from the vast
reservoir of the gains from trade.

Table 3.3 summarizes these institutional problems and possible responses
to them. Three main categories of institutional response arise out of the current landscape of international trade relations: reforms in WTO rules and
practices, ranging from minor to very ambitious; the regional/preferential
agreement (RTA) pathway; and increased "coherence" between the WTO
and other international institutions. The conservative side of the first school
of thought is that the needed changes to unblock the path to consensus on a

Table 3.3 SUMMARY OF INSTITUTIONAL PROBLEMS IN THE WTO AND POSSIBLE SOLUTIONS

Institutional problem	Possible solutions	Pro-trade impact	WTO implications, challenges
Domestic policy sovereignty	RTAs	Selective agenda reduces domestic opposition; experimentation with new issues	May allow new issues to be tested among "like-minded" countries
	Domestic adjustment policies	Reduces domestic opposition	Facilitates WTO negotiations
	Aid-for-trade (developing countries)	Lower domestic constraints on bargaining	See developing country entry below; are transfers sufficient?
Single undertaking	WTO reform: unpack agenda, remove single undertaking requirement	Allows narrower agreement on issues not in need of additional cross-bargaining	Quicker results, but fragmentation of WTO obligations, reduced scope of bargaining, results
	Plurilateral agreements	Self-selected participation	Open to all WTO members to join later; risk of removing cross-bargaining incentives
	WTO reform: "Critical Mass" replaces full consensus	Lower threshold for agreement	Precedent in previous negotiations; danger of free riding; limited applicability?
	RTAs	Smaller group simplifies bargaining; limited trade liberalization better than none; possible trade diversion	Create incentives to return to WTO bargaining? Undermines MFN, danger of fragmentation of global trading system
	WTO reform: issue-by-issue platforms and coalitions	Facilitate convergence of country bargaining positions	Departure from traditional negotiating dynamics
	WTO reform: abandon summitry; use ongoing technocratic bargaining in standing WTO committees	Incremental agreement outside limelight of high-profile Ministerials	Requires countries to delegate trade liberalization to technocratic process

(continued)

Table 3.3 CONTINUED

Institutional problem	Possible solutions	Pro-trade impact	WTO implications, challenges
Power shift in WTO bargaining	RTAs	Large countries regain control of (regional) trade liberalization	Depends on openness of arrangement: defensive trade blocs would undermine WTO
Terms of developing country bargaining	WTO reform: establish rules for reciprocity, "graduation"	Set expectations for negotiating trade-offs	Requires contentious bargaining over rules
	Coherent aid-for-trade with international aid institutions	Close trade capacity gap, facilitate bargaining	WTO lacks institutional ability to include aid-for-trade in formal negotiations
Judicialization of disputes; rapid change in global economy; uncertainty	New safeguards	Provide "insurance" against major trade disruptions	Problems: overuse, abuse; detrimental if used as substitute for domestic adjustment
Supply-chain trade, FDI, related behind-the-border measures	Bring BITs, RTAs under WTO discipline	Multilateralize BIT, supply-chain regimes	Negotiating common rules, acceptable dispute settlement will be difficult

multilateral trade agreement can come from the players rather than the institutional rules of the WTO system. Until the 2011 suspension of the Doha Round, in fact, a widespread view among many WTO negotiators and observers was that the Round could be concluded if only major players would simply redouble their negotiating efforts, stiffen their political will, and work harder for negotiating flexibility in their home capitals. Perhaps a change in political leadership or representation here and there would also be required. While many of these changes may indeed still be necessary to get closer to a multilateral agreement, in the meantime this view has given way to proposals for changes in the structure of the negotiations, such as abandoning the single undertaking and "unpacking" the Doha agenda into smaller clusters of issues, on which consensus is more likely. A victory along these lines was achieved at the Bali Ministerial in December 2013.[16] Taking this approach one step further, a more permanent change would be to abandon the "single undertaking" requirement as a WTO rule altogether, through increased reliance on plurilateral agreements. This approach is already in the works with efforts to revive the services negotiation through a plurilateral agreement among WTO members willing to take part, with the understanding that, once concluded, it would be open to any other WTO members willing to join it on the common terms of accession. The WTO consensus rule on new plurilateral agreements may prevent this solution, however (see chapter 4). Another departure from normal consensus procedures would be to designate some specific negotiations as being subject to "critical mass" agreement, in which case effective "consensus" would be achieved based on agreement among countries collectively representing a high (perhaps 80%–90%) amount of the affected trade. At the same time, all WTO members would receive MFN treatment. This method was used to conclude the Telecommunications, Financial Services, and Information Technology Agreements in the early years of the WTO and precedents for this approach go back to the Tokyo Round agreement of 1979 (see Low 2011; Gallagher and Stoler 2009). Finally, a new agreement on more reliable safeguard measures, as part of future broader MTNs, might be able to address the anxieties of many WTO members over the uncertainties of future trade disruptions that may be preventing broader trade liberalization in general. Efforts in the Uruguay Round to make safeguards more effective as a "safety valve" encountered difficulties, however, as it was (and continues to be) difficult to balance the protective preferences of countries with disrupted import markets against the competitive claims of the disrupting exporters.

More radical departures from current WTO rules and practices, or extending WTO disciplines to new areas, would require major changes in thinking among WTO members. Some observers, including some negotiators, are convinced, for example, that the summit-based multilateral negotiating sessions are no longer workable, especially since major new trade issues require technical knowledge that trade ministers and heads-of-delegation cannot competently discuss or judge in high-stakes summitry. Trade specialists from country delegations in Geneva, who deal with major issues on a daily basis in standing committees, could, in this view, conduct ongoing lower-level negotiations and make more progress in reaching eventual consensus than their high-profile political counterparts can achieve in the confines of a week-long summit. Such a technocratic approach would require a reorganization of the negotiations, with periodic (and perhaps stand-alone) "breakthroughs," nurtured by what some researchers regard as "epistemic" communities of informed experts among the permanent WTO delegations (see Lang and Scott 2009). Another possibility for improving the process of achieving consensus would require a more advanced development of coalitions, with issue-by-issue "platforms" around which countries could openly carry out the negotiations (see Jones 2010: chapter 6). The necessity of forming coalitions and identifying with a platform would tend to soften extreme positions and perhaps identify bargaining trade-offs and compromises more quickly. With regard to WTO reform proposals, the complexities of interaction make it difficult to pinpoint elements for repair, since there are many moving parts in the process of reaching consensus, and any internal reforms themselves would require consensus.

The second type of remedy that many countries are already pursuing with a vengeance outside the WTO is the RTA, mainly in the form of bilateral or multi-country free trade agreements (FTAs). Such agreements have been recognized by the GATT/WTO throughout the years, but generally discouraged by its multilateral aspirations. However, if the goal is global trade liberalization, then one possible pathway to it could be a "multilateralization" of the preferential agreements, a topic to be pursued in chapter 6. Such preferential agreements would therefore play the role of steppingstones to more inclusive agreements and ultimately to a WTO agreement. The key to transforming this approach into an ally of multilateral liberalization would be a "momentum" effect growing out of the eagerness of those outside major trading pacts to join them (or return to WTO negotiations). Similarly, a WTO "supply chain" agreement could possibly multilateralize the thousands of BITs that regulate supply-chain trade and foreign investment. There is no guarantee that such agreements could be brought under general WTO discipline, but there are strong domestic political motivations for countries to conclude them, so it is important to consider them as part of a multilateral strategy. Such agreements play a role in the response to several of the WTO's institutional problems, including domestic policy sovereignty, the single undertaking, and the shift in bargaining power. In general, RTAs and BITs simplify bargaining by limiting the number of countries involved in the negotiations and limiting the agenda. Large players in the WTO, especially the United States and the European Union, can reassert bargaining power in RTAs that has eroded in the WTO, and they have been active in the post-Doha period in pursuing them.

A more globally ambitious institutional solution to issues surrounding the terms of developing country participation in WTO negotiations would combine "aid-for-trade" and other external support for developing countries with their capacity to negotiate trade liberalization on more equal terms with developed countries. This approach touches on both the "policy space" and reciprocity problems in WTO negotiations, and it would seek to close the gap in development infrastructure and remove general downside risks of market opening, for example, guarantees to replace lost tariff revenue. Such efforts are already underway, with mixed results, through the WTO-led Enhanced Integrated Framework, the Bali Agreement on trade facilitation, and various other aid-for-trade initiatives. This issue will be pursued in chapter 7. From a WTO institutional perspective, the challenge is to forge workable relationships and activities among and between various international institutions in such a way as to facilitate multilateral trade liberalization. The traditional model and constraints of WTO bargaining would require significant alterations in order to incorporate aid-for-trade into negotiated agreements.

Reconstructing the institutional framework for multilateral trade liberalization will also require at least two additional elements. One is a restoration of what was earlier described as "trust," based on a shared understanding among all members of the benefits of trade liberalization, the meaning of reciprocity, and confidence in the WTO rules and procedures themselves. This is the institutional "software" that must complement whatever "hardware," in terms of formal institutional machinery, is used to improve the prospects of generating consensus for multilateral agreements. In addition, countries must have or improve the necessary domestic political institutions that can facilitate the inevitable adjustment to trade liberalization, such as measures to promote labor market flexibility and capital market efficiency. Domestic institutions must also be capable of transmitting the country's economic interests in trade liberalization into its policy-making and negotiating agenda. These domestic institutional features are important in keeping the boundaries of countries' domestic policy sovereignty from drifting too far away from the possibilities of negotiating new market access. If trade adjustment is too painful politically, for lack of policy mechanisms to soften the blow, and if there is inadequate lobbying in the country to argue for more foreign (or import) market access, then the prospects of trade liberalization will be severely diminished.

SUMMARY AND CONCLUSION

The WTO continued the process of implementing and monitoring the accumulated rules and procedures of its predecessor, the GATT, and it has been successful in maintaining day-to-day stability in the global trading order: the implementation and dispute settlement functions of the WTO are operating effectively, for the time being at least. Yet the Uruguay Round, with its far-reaching reforms that led to the formation of an expanded institution, the WTO, set new goals without building the additional institutional capacity needed to support them. This chapter has identified several sources of institutional friction that have contributed to the current state of disequilibrium in the WTO's negotiating function, including internal factors such as the single undertaking rule, judicialization of dispute settlement, and the decision to introduce new product coverage in the negotiations, as well as external shocks such as increased participation by a diverse membership, the change in bargaining power structure, and the emergence of supply-chain trade as a new source of bilateral agreements. The circumstances that prevailed in the early GATT years—a focus on manufactured goods, early postwar patterns of comparative advantage, leadership by the United States and European Union, and a largely passive role for developing countries—were consistent with political support for trade liberalization among the developed countries that dominated the institution. In those early years, changes in the trading environment that led to institutional friction could be addressed with temporary fixes that kept the negotiating function running successfully.

In the WTO, however, new sources of institutional friction have led to institutional misalignment. First, market access negotiations expanded into agriculture and services without consideration of the importance of product coverage boundaries in maintaining political support among member countries. Without the proper institutional balance between the trade liberalization agenda and domestic economic autonomy that defined members' collective willingness to bargain, meaningful progress on agriculture and services would be stymied by a lack of shared beliefs regarding the trade-offs between liberalization and autonomy. In addition, the legacy of the GATT framework for developing countries, based on passive free riding and special and differential treatment, was inconsistent with the requirements in the WTO for a more equal partnership at the bargaining table. The GATT experience showed that meaningful trade liberalization required tough trade-offs based on reciprocity. Significant bargaining gains in terms of market access had to be paid for with the hard currency of "concessions," that is, reciprocal market access or comparable trade reforms of equal value to the negotiating partner. Only then could negotiators return home and claim victory in the face of opposition from import-competing sectors. Yet the decision to make the Doha negotiations a "development round" left a large gap in the perceptions between many developing and developed countries as to what reciprocity means. Finally, the power structure and diversity of membership of the WTO has evolved since the GATT era, and the new relationships have appeared to make consensus more difficult to achieve. And on top of these difficulties, the WTO requires that multilateral trade agreements represent a single undertaking, now more difficult than ever to negotiate in the context of the diversity of both the trade agenda and the interests of its enlarged membership. Together, these problems also contributed to an erosion of trust among both developed and developing country diplomats at the WTO, not necessarily because they suspected that their interlocutors were bargaining in bad faith, but at least in part because many members, both developed and developing, lacked confidence in proposed Doha Round agreements to achieve meaningful gains from trade and balance countries' rights and obligations in a predictable and politically acceptable manner.

These difficulties have brought the negotiating mandate of the WTO to the brink of institutional failure. Some combination of institutional reforms and alternative negotiating pathways will be needed in order to restore the ability of the WTO to generate multilateral trade liberalization. The key is to find institutional avenues that will remove impediments to achieving *consensus* in trade bargaining. Possible remedies include internal WTO adjustments and reforms, such as relaxing the single undertaking requirement, increasing the use of plurilaterals, expanding the use of "critical mass" majorities in achieving an agreement, and reforming internal governance and negotiating procedures. The use of regional trade agreements, which has already emerged as a popular alternative to the moribund Doha Round, may also provide a framework for an eventual return to Geneva-based multilateralism. More ambitious efforts to coordinate aid-for-trade with WTO trade negotiations may also play a role in the reconstruction of the WTO, although such initiatives will require either further reforms of the WTO, or unprecedented international coordination between the WTO and other institutions, or both. The study now turns to a closer look at these problems and possible remedies.

Impediments to Doha Round Consensus and The Search for WTO Solutions

INTRODUCTION

This chapter examines the institutional shortcomings of the WTO in its failure to complete a comprehensive agreement at the Doha Round of trade negotiations. Following up on the presentation of the GATT/WTO institutional model of chapters 2 and 3, it focuses on the decision-making structure of the WTO, especially as it pertains to trade negotiations, and how the gulf between developed and developing countries imposed unprecedented pressures on the WTO's consensus process. Changes in the WTO's negotiating environment, along with the historical legacy of the GATT and especially the Uruguay Round, have affected the negotiating environment, making it much more difficult for WTO members to reach consensus on a multilateral trade agreement. The analysis is organized as follows. The first section presents information on the formal structure of WTO decision-making. The next section examines the WTO's informal rules and the ways in which they may affect negotiating outcomes, while the third section focuses on the legacy of the Uruguay Round. The following sections address the issues of bargaining power and the problem of asymmetric bargaining power in an evolving trading system, the development of the GATT/WTO decision-making process over the years, especially the role of the Director-General and checkered performance of the WTO Ministerial Conference, and various internal WTO pathways to improve the chances of achieving consensus: "critical mass" negotiations, plurilateral agreements, and internal decision-making reforms. The final section summarizes the main points of the chapter, including the institutional impediments to consensus in the WTO, and considers various alternative pathways to a more effective system that later chapters will explore.

WTO DECISION-MAKING AND THE PRINCIPLE OF CONSENSUS

At the top of the WTO organizational chart stands the Ministerial Conference, consisting of the highest-level trade officials of the member countries, who meet every two years in various locations around the world, and sometimes at the Geneva headquarters, and must approve any final WTO agreements on behalf of their governments. Beneath this body, the WTO General Council runs the day-to-day operations of the organization and names most WTO committee chairs. Subordinate to the General Council are the three Councils for trade in goods, for trade in services, and for trade-related aspects of intellectual property rights (TRIPS), as well as several separate standing committees and working groups that deal with specific trade and administrative issues. In addition, the General Council oversees a special Trade Negotiations Committee, chaired by the Director-General, which convenes when multilateral trade negotiations are in progress. This committee, in turn, has several subcommittees that correspond to the various negotiating groups. This chapter will focus on decision-making within the Doha Round Trade Negotiations Committee, its subcommittees, and other WTO bodies, such as the General Council and the Ministerial Conference, which play important roles in decision-making during the negotiations.

WTO negotiations in general seek to liberalize trade through the reciprocal expansion of members' market access and through reforms in trade policy rules. The central institutional feature of GATT/WTO decision-making is that final agreement on a negotiation must be based on *consensus*, and in such a large organization, attaining consensus is difficult. Article IX of the Agreement Establishing the WTO shows that this principle was to be carried over from the GATT, its predecessor: "the WTO shall continue the practice of decision-making by consensus followed by the GATT 1947" (WTO 1995b).[1] In its reliance on consensus, the WTO is unlike other international institutions, such as the United Nations, World Bank, and International Monetary Fund, in which significant decision-making powers are relegated to smaller executive groups. The WTO does not define consensus explicitly. Kenworthy (2000) and Hoekman and Kostecki (2009) note that consensus is regarded in diplomatic practice as "the absence of dissent," which represents agreement that is weaker than unanimity. "Consensus" in the WTO means that there is no open opposition to the agreement under consideration. Members may not like the decision,

but are nonetheless willing to join the consensus if they believe it is the best
outcome available to them. Finding the basis for consensus among the WTO
membership is therefore the "holy grail" of any WTO multilateral deliberation,
since no final agreement on most issues is possible without it.

The major reason for the consensus rule is national sovereignty. The WTO,
in liberalizing trade, creates a public good of reducing the transaction cost
of countries in achieving gains from trade, which requires a joint agreement
among its members to open their markets on a reciprocal basis. The economic value of the gains from trade provides the incentive for WTO members to trade some "sovereign" control over their market access in exchange
for these gains as they extend to access to all WTO members' markets. At
the same time, as Steinberg (2002) has noted, the dominant founding country behind the GATT, the United States, also determined that the protection of its sovereignty in the consensus rule in this manner would allow it to
exercise strong influence over the outcome of negotiations. As Low (2011)
notes, consensus-based decision-making gives the advantage to large countries, which can exercise political leverage upon smaller country holdouts in
a negotiation. Meanwhile, the trading system itself is sustainable as long as
most members gain sufficient value from the agreements and the rules, even
if the distribution of the gains may not be completely "fair" in the eyes of
all participants, in terms of the distribution of benefits of market access and
trade rule reforms.[2]

WTO rules apply on a most-favored nation (MFN) basis, so that market
access improvements are spread automatically to all members. In addition,
the WTO, in following up on the structure of the GATT Uruguay Round,
has required that all subsequent trade negotiation agreements be concluded
on the basis of a "single undertaking," that is, all negotiated elements must
be accepted by all members as a single package. The purpose of this rule is
to maximize the scope of negotiations, and thereby allow bargaining across
diverse trade issues, thus broadening the possibilities of reaching consensus
among a large and diverse membership. The Uruguay Round agreement was
based on this principle, which continued with the Doha Round negotiations
under the WTO. In pursuing the goal of gaining consensus in a multilateral
trade negotiation, the WTO Trade Negotiating Committee (TNC), chaired
by the Director-General, and its subcommittees must knit together a single
package of reciprocal market access and rule "concessions" by its members
across all negotiating issues, subject to consensus. The formal structure of
the committees is defined by its scope, by its chair, and by a basic set of rules
the chair must follow in the committee's deliberations, topics that chapter 5
will pursue in more detail.

INFORMAL PROCESSES OF DECISION-MAKING

The formal structure of WTO committees, procedures, and rules for chairs provides an outer framework for trade negotiations that has proven to be insufficient, on its own, to achieve consensus on multilateral trade agreements in the GATT/WTO system. In order to begin the negotiations, for example, the General Council must identify the specific negotiating groups for the negotiations that form the basis of the TNC subcommittees. This is an important and often controversial part of the agenda-setting process, exemplified by the tenuous last-minute compromise that finally launched the Doha Round in October 2001. After the negotiating agenda is set, bargaining must narrow the differences in country positions on many technical and complicated issues, which typically require informal discussions that go beyond the confines of the formal meeting structure. The need for informal negotiations to push the talks toward consensus arises from two elements of the GATT/WTO system: the mercantilist nature of bargaining, and the increasing complexity of the negotiations over the years. In formal trade negotiating sessions, negotiators are expected by their governments and domestic constituents to fight for maximum benefits at minimum cost. In GATT/WTO bargaining, the main currency of "benefits" is foreign market access achieved for the nation's exporters, and the "costs" (known as "concessions") are in the form of domestic market access offered to foreign imports. In addition, rules that facilitate market access for a country's exports are also benefits, while rules expected to lead to more of a country's imports, or fewer exports, or which are burdensome in financial or bureaucratic terms, go into the cost (concessions) column. Clearly, it is impossible to have general multilateral trade liberalization on a reciprocal basis unless all bargainers "concede" some market access and rules reforms to foreign interests, and it is this element of a final agreement that in fact allows each country to claim victory in winning new market access for its exporters. During the negotiations, however, concessions are the subject of difficult and politically sensitive bargaining. Negotiators are reluctant to be observed in the act of making concessions, as domestic lobbies, especially in import-competing industries, are likely to scream bloody murder about them if they entail significant and uncompensated adjustment costs to firms and workers. A trade agreement, in other words, is rarely achieved without domestic political controversy for each negotiating country. In this regard, the desired element of secrecy is best protected by informal meetings, so that confidential side deals and issue linkage can help to move the negotiations closer to consensus—if in fact consensus is possible. Ultimately, any final WTO agreement requires a consensus in the General Council as the basis for formal approval at the plenary session of the Ministerial Conference that concludes the negotiation. The problem is that negotiators are typically reluctant to reveal any flexibility at the outset of negotiations, especially in formal meetings.

If a major impasse in the negotiations occurs, its resolution typically requires intense bargaining led by the Director-General in a "green room" meeting,[3] which cannot, for practical purposes, include all delegations, hence the Director-General, as chair of the TNC, must use discretion in whom to invite, when to meet, and what to discuss. During Ministerial Conferences, the green room meetings are often co-managed by the Conference chair, and on other occasions the meetings the Chairman of the WTO General Council presides.[4] The informal meetings are held at the chair's discretion, and no official minutes of the meetings are taken. [5] The associated practices of secrecy and confidential communications are not easily accommodated by formal rules (see Cot 1972). Such meetings are typically designed to make possible a frank discussion of issues within a group that is small enough to allow meaningful dialogue, but inclusive enough to assure that an emerging consensus can be taken to the larger WTO membership as the basis for an agreement. In a typical trade negotiation scenario, decision-making that moves toward a final multilateral agreement must then proceed from a breakthrough green room agreement outward in the manner of "concentric circles" to the rest of the WTO membership until final consensus is achieved (Blackhurst 2001). Before the Doha Round, various types of these informal arrangements were often instrumental in concluding the eight rounds of multilateral trade negotiations under the GATT. The typical pattern of "concentric circles" that applied from the time of the Tokyo Round (completed in 1979) through the Uruguay Round (completed in 1994) was for an agreement to emanate from a US-EU agreement, which could then be used as a basis for agreement with other influential OECD countries, then influential developing countries, followed by other developing countries, which then sets up broader approval in the General Council, for final formal approval by the Ministerial Council (see Kanitz 2011a: 63). The list of participating countries in the green room talks depends on the issue.[6] To this day, the United States and European Union are always present, and until the Doha round were typically joined by their "quad" partners, Japan and Canada. Over the course of the Doha Round, the core group evolved so that Brazil and India replaced Japan and Canada, although these countries remained influential in the negotiations. The upshot of this development is that, in the Doha Round, the path to consensus through "concentric circles" changed; it requires not only US-EU agreement (still often difficult enough) but also agreement with India, Brazil, and perhaps several other countries or coalitions such as the developing G20, reflecting the important change in WTO bargaining power to be discussed below.

THE LEGACY OF THE URUGUAY ROUND

The Uruguay Round was the great watershed in the evolution of the GATT/ WTO system, and its legacy has profoundly affected decision-making in the WTO. The Uruguay Round negotiations, which lasted from 1986 to 1994, expanded the coverage of the original GATT to include greater coverage of agriculture and services, sought to bring all manufactured sectors outside GATT disciplines back into the fold, such as textiles, automobiles, and steel, and introduced intellectual property into trade policy enforcement. Agreements on all these issues would henceforth be subject to a much more formalized dispute settlement procedure. The Uruguay Round also introduced the participation of developing countries as major players in the negotiations, as many issues of importance to them were finally on the agenda.[7] In retrospect, the major problem with the Uruguay Round for the future WTO was that it brought new and more difficult issues to the negotiating table, but with only the traditional GATT-based tools and mechanisms to manage decision-making. The negotiations themselves benefited from the optimism that prevailed at the time of global deregulation, led by the United States and the United Kingdom, the end of the Cold War, and the strong belief of many that trade liberalization would facilitate rapid and uninterrupted economic growth for both developed and developing countries. The agricultural and services negotiations were, in the end, disappointing from a global perspective, going little further than establishing frameworks for future talks. Of greater importance was the disappointment perceived by developing countries of the "Grand Bargain" that linked an end to the Multifiber Agreement (MFA) in textiles trade with the TRIPS agreement favored by the United States in particular. The MFA reforms to liberalize trade were heavily back-loaded and thereby delayed, and the emergence of China as the leading textile exporter reduced textile trade liberalization's benefits for other developing countries. At the same time, the TRIPS negotiations had masked its distributional effects: a bonanza for countries holding IP rights, while imposing a potentially large drain on IP-using countries' economic welfare, especially developing countries'.[8] The TRIPS agreement also failed to foresee the global AIDS crisis, pitting medicine-importing developing countries against developed medicine suppliers insisting on their IP rights. This controversy eventually led to a revision of the TRIPS, allowing mandatory licensing of critical drugs by developing countries for serious diseases.

The Uruguay Round was the original GATT's last hurrah in the sense that all the participants, caught up in the moment of establishing an ambitious new trade organization, the WTO, accepted the traditional GATT informal processes in moving toward consensus on the basis of the "Grand Bargain."

Developed countries were happy to continue the GATT traditions in the Uruguay Round, while the developing countries, eager finally to have a role in global trade and to get redress for the long-standing textile restrictions and agricultural market distortions cause by rich-country subsidies, joined the hopeful march toward a new WTO. Yet the unfinished issues of the Uruguay Round would lead later to the demand to renegotiate leftover Uruguay Round "implementation issues" before any new trade negotiations, an issue bitterly pursued by many developing countries as part of the Doha Round debate. As for the "Grand Bargain," it was later regarded by many developing countries as a "bum deal." The seeds of discord over WTO decision-making were thus planted before the WTO was born. Developing countries carried their resentment into the discussions regarding a new, WTO-sponsored trade round, and the traditional GATT decision-making framework, with a broader agenda requiring approval by a larger, more diverse and fractious membership, would be placed under extreme pressure.

BARGAINING IN CHANGING GLOBAL TRADE ENVIRONMENT

Bargaining power in the WTO is determined by a combination of GDP, economic growth, population, and trade volumes, combined with the country's global trade ambitions and the leadership that emanates from all of these elements. Particularly important is a high volume of imports that increases the value of foreign access to the country's markets. Odell (2000) regards a country's access to large and varied trade flows as a key determinant of its "best alternative to a negotiated agreement" (BATNA), which in the context of the WTO can be restated as the "best alternative to a *multilateral* (trade) agreement" (BAMTA).[9] The United States and the European Union, for example, account for more than half of all world trade, and their BAMTAs are based on their ability to negotiate bilateral agreements among each other and with selected trading partners that affect a significant amount of world trade.[10] Table 4.1 shows the top importing countries of the world in 2011 and their changing shares of world imports since 1977. In the period since then, China, Korea, and Hong Kong have shown the most dramatic increases, while the United States, the top EU exporters (EU-5), and Japan have all declined in world import share. Table 4.2 shows per capita GDP growth during this same period, a possible indicator of the size of current and future potential import markets. Subramanian and Kessler (2013: 2) estimate that 75% of the developing world has been closing the per capita income gap with developed countries by about 3% per year since the late 1990s. Again, China leads the list, but other large emerging markets

Table 4.1 Share of World Imports (%), 1977-2011, for Top Ten Countries, Selected Years

	1977	1987	1997	2007	2011
Other	42.10	36.96	44.20	46.37	47.00
EU-5	32.64	32.60	25.05	23.19	20.56
United States	15.57	18.24	15.95	14.00	12.33
China	0.69	1.86	2.53	6.84	9.70
Germany	9.85	9.82	7.90	7.55	7.06
Japan	6.93	6.49	6.01	4.45	4.78
France	6.86	6.81	4.82	4.52	3.93
United Kingdom	6.13	6.63	5.44	4.45	3.58
Italy	4.67	5.40	3.73	3.66	3.15
South Korea	1.05	1.76	2.57	2.52	2.93
Netherlands	5.14	3.93	3.16	3.01	2.83
Hong Kong, China	1.01	2.08	3.70	2.63	2.70

SOURCE: Euromonitor International from International Monetary Fund (IMF), International Financial Statistic.

such as India, Indonesia, Korea, and (more recently) Brazil, have also exhibited much higher per capita growth than the relatively stagnant United States and Japan, and large EU countries.[11] A country's BAMTA may also depend in part on its current economic growth rate; thus a country may find it easier to walk away from further trade liberalization if it is sustaining a high growth rate. China, for example, which already made significant trade concessions upon joining the WTO in 2001, has remained conspicuously quiet during Doha Round negotiations, perhaps deciding that further Doha Round concessions were not necessary in sustaining its 10% annual growth rate, although this may change, as its growth since 2010 has declined, with 7.25% growth projected in 2014.[12] India and Brazil, on the other hand, have increased their role in the WTO more than their proportional growth in global trade by taking leadership roles in representing the developing world.

Kindleberger (1981) emphasizes hegemonic leadership in creating stability for international economic systems, a principle that applied to decision-making and consensus in the GATT/WTO negotiations until the Doha Round, since progress in trade negotiations typically followed initiatives by large countries. Changes in WTO bargaining power that led to a more widely shared influence among several countries have evidently weakened the ability of the members to reach consensus (Narlikar 2012). McMillan (1988) notes, furthermore, that trade negotiations typically have multiple potential equilibria, based on the large set of various liberalization measures that are all welfare-improving,

Table 4.2 ANNUAL AVERAGE REAL GDP PER CAPITA GROWTH, 1976-2010, SELECTED COUNTRIES

	1976–80	1981–85	1986–90	1991–95	1996–2000	2001–05	2006–10
China	5.2	9.3	6.3	11.0	7.6	9.1	10.6
India	0.9	2.9	3.8	3.2	4.0	5.4	7.1
Indonesia	5.4	3.4	5.2	6.2	-0.4	3.4	4.6
South Korea	5.4	6.4	8.6	6.7	3.7	4.0	3.5
Brazil	4.2	-1.1	0.2	1.5	0.5	1.5	3.4
Germany	3.5	1.5	2.9	1.7	1.9	0.5	1.4
Japan	3.5	3.6	4.5	1.1	0.8	1.6	0.4
France	2.9	1.0	2.7	0.8	2.3	0.9	0.1
United States	2.7	2.3	2.2	1.2	3.1	1.5	0.1
United Kingdom	1.8	2.1	3.1	1.4	3.1	2.0	-0.3

SOURCE: World Bank, World Development Indicators.

but achieving any agreement requires a coordination of expectations through leadership of the strongest participants in order to generate a "focal point" and one particular equilibrium as a targeted outcome. The particular bargaining agenda is therefore "path-dependent," and leadership by key countries plays a crucial role, not only in setting the agenda but also in facilitating an agreement. However, since the GATT's founding in 1947, experience has shown that large countries, acting on their own, cannot completely control GATT/WTO negotiations, no matter how strong is the value of their BAMTA, since a multilateral trade agreement typically extends its benefits and obligations to its participants well beyond those that pertain to regional trade agreements that serve as the main alternatives to WTO agreements.

Bargaining power may therefore affect WTO decision-making as a potential way for larger and more powerful countries to increase control over a sequential bargaining process. Steinberg (2002), for example, regards WTO consensus-based decision-making as a two-part process. It starts with early-stage "law-based" bargaining on the scope of the agenda, using procedural rules that accommodate a broad range of negotiating issues to satisfy the widest possible membership. As negotiations proceed to the later stages of bargaining, asymmetrical "power-based" bargaining tends to prevail, when the large trading powers assert their leverage to conclude the negotiations on terms favorable to themselves. It is worth noting in this connection that countries may anticipate the dangers inherent in agenda setting at the early stages, as India apparently did in the 2001 Doha Ministerial that launched the Round, when it objected to the inclusion of the Singapore issues, a topic that some developed countries, in particular the European Union, insisted on including. Ambiguous language was added on this point, allowing the negotiations to begin, but only delayed a major confrontation at the 2003 Cancun Ministerial (see below). Hamilton and Whalley (1989) identify three stages of multilateral negotiations: agenda-setting, proposal development, and subsequent end-game bargaining. In their view, the bargaining model focuses on a "political optimum" based on income distribution that favors certain groups in the domestic market.[13] By controlling the agenda, at least as it moves toward its later stages, and leaving other participants outside the green room with a "take-it-or-leave-it" decision, those in control of the process may be able to avoid the more difficult political sacrifices that a "balanced" agenda would otherwise impose on them. They may then move toward their politically optimal outcome, perhaps at the expense of weaker participants. Weaker countries, in turn, would then be expected to try to counteract the bargaining imbalance either by (1) making sure they get into the green room as full participants; (2) forming alliances, especially with green room participants that can effectively represent their interests; or (3) forming effective alliances among "outsiders" that are sufficiently strong to block the strong country proposal. The drawback of a blocking strategy is that it raises the stakes by putting all possible negotiated gains at risk. The larger danger of blocking strategies that result from bargaining power confrontations may come from their tendency to erode the level of "trust" among negotiators that is needed to get any agreement at all.[14]

It is important to add that such informal meetings may also allow asymmetrical bargaining power to assert itself, as strong bargainers attempt to threaten or cajole weak bargainers in efforts to break their opposition or resistance to proposals supported by the strong. Such behavior will threaten the entire negotiation to the extent that (1) the assent of weaker bargainers becomes essential to reach a final agreement; (2) the bargaining positions of weak and strong players diverge more widely; and (3) weak countries can resist efforts to break their opposition (as, for example, through disciplined coalitions). Figure 4.1, adapted from Hoekman and Kostecki (2009), illustrates in schematic form the possible issues of asymmetric bargaining power in such a negotiation. The point X_0 shows an initial status quo position for two bargaining units in the negotiation, a "strong" bargainer and a "weak" bargainer. The vertical and horizontal axes measure changes in the value of bargaining outcomes for each player, so that the coordinates of any bargaining outcome X represents the net change in each bargainer's welfare as a result of the agreement implied by that point.[15] In this sense, we judge "value" as it pertains to the bargainers' political objective function and perception that will determine an acceptable agreement: the net value of increased market access paid for with a politically

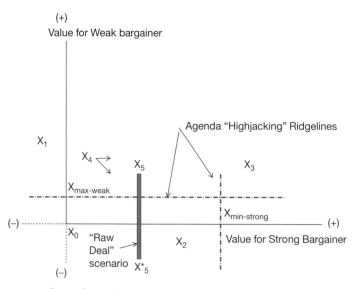

Figure 4.1 Payoff Coordinated with Bargaining Asymmetries Value for Weak Bargainer

acceptable level of concessions to foreign imports. We can therefore assume that consensus will require the outcome coordinates to lie within the upper right quadrant of the ridge lines defined by the horizontal and vertical axes that emanate from X_0, based on each country's BAMTA. Thus, by definition, no agreement could occur at points X_1 or X_2, where one or the other party would be at a position inferior to its status quo. In contrast, of the available outcomes shown, X_3 would be Pareto-optimal, as any other outcome would leave at least one party worse off.

Informal decision-making arrangements could affect the bargaining set and outcome in various ways. If, for example, the strong bargainer were to use its influence in informal discussions early in the negotiating process to gain control of the negotiating agenda, and take the opportunity to remove from the agenda tariff reductions that would benefit the weak country's exports, and include new topics or issues of strong potential benefit to the strong bargainer, then new bargaining boundaries could be established, as shown by the dashed lines $X_{max-weak}$ and $X_{min-strong}$. In this manner, the strong bargainer would be attempting to reposition the negotiating ridge lines in its favor, with outcomes for itself such as $X_{min-strong}$ and those to its right and outcomes for the weak bargainer at $X_{max-weak}$ or less. Many developing countries claim, on this point, that the United States and the European Union typically use such agenda hijacking to minimize their exposure to demands to open their agricultural markets, and that the United States took this approach to assure the inclusion of TRIPS on the Uruguay Round agenda.

Intimidating or bullying behavior by the strong bargainer against the weak behind the closed doors of informal meetings could also result in a forced movement from the weak bargainer's initial proposed point X_4 to positions further to the right, either horizontally or in a downward vector to the right, as shown by the arrows. The latter case would constitute a zero-sum win for the strong and loss for the weak. Another example of the disparity in bargaining power, which may often reflect an asymmetry in information, would be for the strong bargainer to get the weak bargainer to accept what the strong knows is a risky or uncertain outcome, valued initially at X_5, showing significantly positive value assumed by the weak bargainer. However, the ultimate result, fully understood only well after the agreement is completed, shows that the value for the weak is actually negative at X_5^*, while the strong cashes in on its gains. The terms of such a deal may not be the direct result of informal meetings, but the lack of detailed information or analysis of it may contribute to the final outcome. Many developing countries claim that the US inclusion of TRIPS in the Uruguay Round falls into this category, with unexpectedly high implementation costs and few immediate benefits for poorer countries and large increases in IP profits in rich countries. Another example often cited along these lines is the agreement to end the MFA textiles restrictions in the Uruguay Round, which ultimately saw apparel exporters failing to gain expected export benefits due to the unforeseen impact of China's entry into the global market.

These scenarios suggest that strong bargainers, such as the United States and European Union, would be able to drive hard bargains against all weaker players, and always attain favorable outcomes for themselves, such as point X_s or better in figure 4.1. After all, in theory the strong need only allow minimal negotiating gains, if this is the best outcome on offer, in order to achieve such a lopsided agreement. Many statements by developing country WTO delegates in Jawara and Kwa (2004) suggest that this view is widespread. However, the informal processes to achieve consensus, in conjunction with constraint of the single undertaking, have more likely led to a negotiating stalemate, as the Doha Round experience has shown. Shifts in bargaining power in favor of the large, high-growth developing countries such as India, Brazil, and China have created an effective counterweight to the United States and European Union in WTO negotiations, for example. The introduction of a new, strong bargainer with a divergent agenda, or a sufficiently strong coalition of countries, often joined together primarily by their opposition to the traditionally strong countries' bargaining positions, may collectively demand that the agenda boundaries move in the coalition's favor.

The formation of new coalitions among WTO members has in fact represented an important internal adaptive mechanism to the expanded membership and increasing diversity of trade interests, especially among developing countries (see Narlikar 2003). Diego-Fernandez (2008), in contrast, notes that many coalitions have arisen on specific WTO issues that include both developed and developing countries. The advantage of coalitions is that they can facilitate information sharing, and if interests are adequately aligned, can increase the bargaining power, not to mention the representation, of the group. Odell (2010) also notes that smaller countries can leverage public opinion in their favor in WTO negotiations, as, for example, in the revision of TRIPS rules on mandatory licensing and the African cotton group's appeal to popular support for ending US cotton subsidies. Coalitions of developing countries have also gained in influence, such as the WTO G20 group, which succeeded in removing the so-called Singapore issues from the Doha agenda at the Cancun Ministerial meeting. At the same time, it is important to remember that one country can speak for others only on issues of strong common interest. Neither the developed nor the developing world is unified in its bargaining positions on most WTO issues.

Because of the consensus requirement, such "agenda blockers" or "coalitions of the unwilling" are more capable of collapsing the bargaining space to a null set, rather than to move a specific agenda toward agreement among all parties.

In this context, whatever "bullying" by the strong against the weak that may have occurred during the Doha Round may have in part reflected the declining bargaining power of the traditionally dominant players, such as the United States and European Union. In addition, the memory of a perceived bad deal can affect subsequent negotiations, as many developing countries, who felt deceived in the Uruguay Round, were twice shy in the Doha Round. And all countries now know that any new WTO agreements will be enforced by a strengthened dispute settlement system, raising the stakes of any concessions offered. Adaptive negotiating behavior by both weaker and stronger countries has therefore led to a much more cautious approach to any new or unfamiliar issues, based on the uncertain outcomes of trade liberalization in these areas.

EVOLUTION OF THE DECISION-MAKING PROCESS

Figure 4.2 illustrates the trend in GATT/WTO membership since its founding in 1947, along with the terms of the nine Directors-General who have served and the duration of the nine trade rounds that have occurred during this time, with the Doha Round still incomplete. This timeline provides a useful framework for examining the changes in the GATT/WTO system that have affected the process of achieving consensus. Membership began with just eighteen founding members in 1947 and grew slowly at first, but then rapidly during the 1960s and again during the Uruguay Round from 1986 to 1994. At first, membership consisted of ten developed and eight developing countries,[16] but after Japan joined in 1955, further increases in membership consisted almost entirely of developing countries. As of 2014, three-quarters of the WTO membership of 160 could be counted as developing countries, and the changing profile of membership has increased the diversity of trade interests at play in trade negotiations and has also changed the environment in which consensus is sought.

The expanding negotiating agenda had a major impact on decision-making in the GATT/WTO system. Until the beginning of the Uruguay Round in 1986, GATT negotiations focused squarely on goods trade among its developed country members. The first seven rounds of GATT trade negotiations dealt primarily with trade liberalization in manufactured goods of interest to developed countries, while textiles and some other products of interest to developing and newly industrializing countries became subject to agreements outside of GATT disciplines, such as the Multifiber Agreement (MFA) and other Voluntary Export Restraints (VERs). In general, developing countries were not expected to offer reciprocal concessions; they could free ride on most of the tariff reductions. This was because Part IV of the GATT and "special and

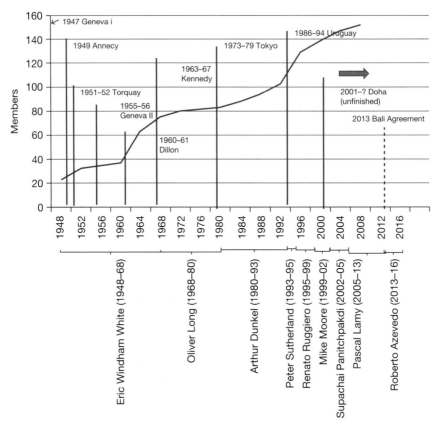

Figure 4.2 GATT/WTO Membership, Directors-General, and Trade Rounds, 1947–2014

differential treatment" introduced in the Tokyo Round allowed developing countries to take a largely passive role, with no requirement for reciprocity in market opening proposals.[17] Their interests were for the most part not on the agenda until the Uruguay Round. Especially in the early GATT trade rounds, the main issue was industrial tariffs, and while negotiations were often difficult, the negotiating framework for reciprocal concessions could be made relatively simple.[18] As non-tariff issues arose during the Kennedy and Tokyo Rounds, the GATT partitioned them into separate plurilateral negotiations, in which smaller groups could achieve consensus on narrower issues. In sum, consensus during most of the GATT years could take place along a narrower band of issues, with a smaller group of developed countries of similar outlook and economic structure.

Informal decision-making in the early years of the GATT thus operated in a more favorable negotiating environment than in the WTO period. Leadership was important during the early GATT period, as the United States dominated GATT negotiations, and decision-making relied principally on US initiatives and its bilateral consultations with the United Kingdom and other GATT members. As the European Union (founded in 1958 as the European Common Market) gained importance in world trade, the GATT membership expanded, and the complexity of issues increased. The need for a more structured system of consultation developed, focused on the United States and European Union. While these two countries still had to work with other countries to achieve consensus on multilateral trade deals, this pattern of shared dominance continued through the Uruguay Round agreement. The path to negotiated agreements in the GATT was often slow and painful, marked by periodic stalemates, walkouts, and negotiating brinkmanship, features that later characterized the Doha Round as well. The ability of the GATT to avoid the gridlock typically began with a broad and inclusive approach to formulating the agenda, subject until the Uruguay Round to the narrower scope of GATT bargaining, in order to accommodate as many countries' trade interests as possible. The sequence of substantive negotiations began with individual negotiating groups based on "principal supplier" and "multilateral balancing" rules, moving then from bilateral to multilateral bargaining in market opening discussions.[19] In order to achieve a final agreement, the Director-General began to employ "green room" meetings at critical stages during the Tokyo Round (1973–1979).

The Role of the Director-General

What has also become apparent in historical hindsight is that consensus was probably easier to achieve in those years when a shared ethos of trade diplomacy dominated trade negotiations. The first three Directors-General, Eric Wyndham White, Olivier Long, and Arthur Dunkel, served long terms. They were trained as trade diplomats and exercised considerable influence among the GATT representatives, and often played key roles in negotiations, exemplified by the "Dunkel Draft" that formed the basis of the final Uruguay Round package. Their ability to use informal meetings and green rooms to move toward consensus was considerable. Julio LaCarte Muro, the Uruguayan diplomat who has served the longest of any official in the GATT/WTO system, related the following anecdote about the first GATT Director-General (or Executive Secretary, as he was known at first), Eric Wyndham White[20]:

> On one occasion there was a very big argument. Nobody could agree on anything on this particular issue, opinions were sharply divided and a new meeting was called to try to find a solution. At the beginning of the

meeting, Wyndham White patted his pocket and he said "I've got the solution right here." Everybody clamored, "Well, go on, say it." And he replied, "I'll say it, provided you agree beforehand you'll accept it." Without dissent, everybody complied with his condition. He pulled out the piece of paper, read it, and that was the end of the problem. This gives you a notion of the authority the Executive Secretary had at that time. (LaCarte 2011)

It also provides a notion of how the conditions in which informal processes take place in multilateral trade negotiations have changed since then. Contrast the previous anecdote with Blustein's (2009) account of one of the many breakdowns in the Doha Round, this one in 2008, when Director-General Pascal Lamy attempted to present a compromise text on agriculture to a green room meeting that included representatives from the United States, European Union, and Brazil, as well as India's trade minister, Kamal Nath:

"I reject everything," Nath said. ... Putting on his jacket, he rose to leave and headed for the door, prompting Lamy to practically leap out of his chair after him. "Kamal, please stay and listen to the others," the director-general said. ... Nath returned to his seat ... showing his disregard for the proceeding by concentrating on his BlackBerry and excusing himself several times from the room to get food and to meet with outsiders. (Blustein 2009: 265)

By the Doha Round the job of the Director-General to move the major parties toward consensus had become much more difficult than in Wyndham White's day, as the negotiations pitted countries with highly divergent trade interests against each other on divisive issues such as agriculture. The WTO negotiation, in an age of skepticism regarding globalization, had become a highly visible, politically charged event. Such a defiant attitude of a developing country would be met with cheers at home, and Blustein's report of verbal abuse from other quarters against Lamy probably earned approval in many developed country capitals as well. The reduced informal authority of the Director-General also raises the question of "trust," as discussed in chapters 2 and 3. Many US trade officials acknowledge that they are unwilling to grant the Director-General, and the WTO Secretariat in general, the influence over negotiating outcomes that they often exercised in the past,[21] and other delegations appear to have adopted this view (Elsig 2009, 2011). The reason for this change in attitude appears to lie in the fact that the WTO has "legalized" trade commitments and thereby raised the stakes of the negotiations to the point that governments are wary of allowing informal mediation by the Director-General to influence the outcome. In addition, the changing balance of power in WTO bargaining left the United States, European Union, and other OECD countries less confident that green room negotiations would allow them to protect their trade interests. In the past, informal GATT negotiations had typically pitted the United States and other economies of similar structure against each other on a narrower range of issues. In the WTO, these countries must now face off against large developing countries on high-stakes and politically sensitive issues, in which OECD country concessions would result in disruptive adjustment problems at home in agriculture and in many industrial sectors. Large developing countries with newfound bargaining power may also be wary of Director-General mediation for the same reason from their point of view. To the extent that this unwillingness to allow the Director-General to broker agreements holds sway among negotiating countries, it is not surprising that committee chairs' and the Director-General's powers to bring the parties toward consensus have been weakened. A large measure of the intangible power of informal processes, including the structural elements of "trust," which appear to have contributed significantly to consensus in earlier GATT rounds, is thereby undermined in the context of WTO negotiations.

In the meantime, the Director-General's position passed, after the career trade diplomat Arthur Dunkel's term, to politicians with considerable experience in trade, beginning with Peter Sutherland, a former EU commissioner. In addition, the Director-General's nationality became an issue. These changes reflected the increasingly political nature of trade negotiations and also signaled a weakening of the Director-General's position. The issue of developing country representation in the Director-General's chair reached a peak in the 1999 selection process, which pitted Mike Moore of New Zealand against Supachai Panitchpakdi of Thailand. WTO members were split, but in general, developing countries predominantly supported Panitchpakdi, and a compromise led to each getting a three-year term. Subsequently, new rules regarding the Director-General's appointment sought to increase transparency and spell out the procedures and timetables more explicitly (WTO 2003). After Panitchpakdi's term ended, the selection process became much less contentious, as Pascal Lamy of France won two consecutive four-year terms, from 2005 to 2013, and he faced no opposition in his second appointment. By that time, it had become clear to most WTO members that the Director-General of the WTO did not have the same influence as the Director-General of the GATT in earlier years. The Doha Round, by 2005, had shown that it was no longer possible for the Director-General unilaterally to sequester the negotiators and shape a final deal. In this regard, an experienced but neutral party such as Lamy—with diminished powers—was the only sort of Director-General on which consensus would be possible at that time. In addition, to the extent that continued trade negotiations were possible at all, it was better not to switch the Director-General in mid-stream. Advocacy for developing, or developed, country agendas was apparently not the determining factor in the selection of the Director-General during the Lamy years. However, representation of the developing world was still an issue, as Lamy's successor, chosen in 2013, was Roberto Carvalho de Azevêdo, Brazil's trade ambassador to the WTO. His selection indicates in part the increased standing of Brazil's leadership role in the WTO in recent years, along with Azevêdo's independence of both the United States and European Union.[22] Azevêdo's ability to manage the consensus process would be tested early in his term, at the December 2013 Bali Ministerial meeting, a topic to be discussed in chapter 8.

The Problems with Ministerial Conferences

Because the role of the Director-General as an active broker in multilateral trade negotiations had diminished, the new structure of top-level WTO decision-making was proving to be ineffective. The WTO Agreement mandated a meeting of the Ministerial Conference (MC), a summit of top trade officials of all members, every two years. This measure appeared to be designed to keep trade issues at the forefront of national policy making, and presumably move trade liberalization initiatives forward expeditiously. However, this approach to managing the global trading system was very risky, since trade summitry presupposes extensive preparation and pre-negotiation before politicians are ready to make a public show of international agreements, and any unresolved differences will get high-profile exposure. The Singapore MC in 1996, for example, ended up showcasing growing developing country dissatisfaction with WTO decision-making, especially regarding the use of green rooms (Blackhurst 2001). Things got worse at the Seattle MC in 1999. At that time, WTO had only recently finished bickering over the compromise Director-General selection of Moore and Panitchpakdi, and they were in increasing disarray over how to launch an ambitious new round. Little progress was made on getting a draft agenda ready beforehand, and the MC was therefore probably doomed before it began, even when the street protests and disruptions are taken into account. These circumstances left the hosting chair, US Trade Representative Charlene Barshevsky, with the difficult job of moving the fractious membership toward the launch of a new Round. Her partisan approach to the job, along with her ill-advised last-ditch recourse to an exclusive green room meeting in a vain attempt to forge a final communiqué, left many developing country delegates furious, and was responsible in part for delaying by two years the launch of the Doha Round (see Pfetsch 2009). The green room negotiations themselves failed to forge an agreement, and even if it had, there was a strong likelihood that the rest of the membership would have rejected it. Perhaps more important was the perception among WTO delegates from many developing countries that they had been openly neglected and marginalized in the attempt to forge a "WTO consensus" in their absence.[23]

The backlash from developing countries at the Seattle Ministerial prompted the new Director-General, Michael Moore, to establish more inclusiveness in green room meetings, and communication between attendees and those outside the meeting. Since then, the Director-General has managed the list of invited members to WTO green room meetings very carefully. Yet the MC and green room problems continued. After the 2001 MC in Doha had launched the new trade round on the basis of a fragile and dubious compromise regarding the agenda,[24] new fissures emerged at the subsequent Cancun MC in 2003. The Quad countries had made preparations for Cancun in the traditional manner, through a series of green room, "mini-lateral" and bilateral meetings, which had also included larger developing countries such as India and Brazil. There were, however, numerous issues of contention that remained as the Cancun meeting began, including a number of divisive issues that had been papered over in the original 2001 Doha Declaration, such as the Singapore issues, as mentioned earlier. At Cancun, the European Union and the United States, in particular, attempted to use green room bargaining to emphasize certain agenda items of special interest to them, while minimizing progress on issues that were politically sensitive to them at home. Now that serious negotiations had begun, countries were applying their own interpretation of the Doha text regarding concrete negotiating commitments, and these interpretations diverged significantly. The green room process had therefore not achieved internal consensus even among its participants, but many countries had hoped that differences could be overcome in the Cancun Ministerial meeting. Many developing countries expressed growing disillusionment with the Doha agenda, some of which joined together to form the WTO "G20" alliance, including large countries such as China, India, Brazil, and Indonesia.[25] They came to Cancun demanding more concessions from the Quad countries on farm trade, while a small group of African countries also demanded reductions in US cotton subsidies, on which the United States took a hard line. The European Union, for its part, insisted until very late in the Cancun meeting on including the Singapore issues, which many developing countries adamantly refused to consider. As the meeting proceeded, many participants hardened their positions, and as the political will for compromise failed to materialize, the meeting collapsed. While there were many contributing factors that led to the failure of the Cancun Ministerial, it appeared that green room procedures, at least in its traditional one-country, one-voice format, had become ineffective as a process of achieving compromise and moving toward consensus.

In particular, this breakdown marked the end of the Quad as the "inner circle" of the concentric circles model. Arguments over the agenda and how it would be finalized revealed deep rifts among the WTO membership, but del Castillo (2011) believes that the chair of the MC, Mexican Economics Minister Ernesto Derbez, mismanaged the green room process and prematurely adjourned the entire conference.[26]

The raucous and divisive Cancun Ministerial came to epitomize the North-South divide in the Doha Round, and the inability of the WTO to bridge the development gap of its members in bargaining over the gains from trade. It was in this sense the nadir of the WTO as an institution, to that point, in terms of its role as a deliberative body. Several observers recall an atmosphere of exultation among many developing country delegations, which saw the collapse of the meeting as a triumph, after years of marginal status in the decision-making process, of their concerted efforts to block the developed country agenda. One trade official from a large developed country recalls, in the aftermath of Cancun, a developing country delegate accosting him with the comment, "See, now you've finally received your comeuppance."[27] US Trade Representative Robert Zoellick chastised the "won't do" countries and declared that the "can do" countries would take their trade negotiations elsewhere (Zoellick 2003). Pascal Lamy, EU Trade Commissioner at Cancun at the time, declared the WTO to be a "medieval organization" (Price 2003). A forum for cooling down the emotional tempers of Cancun was in order. It is noteworthy that the subsequent 2004 Framework Agreement, which put the Doha Round back on track for a few years, was the result of a special meeting of the WTO General Council in Geneva, away from the harsh light of a high-profile MC.[28] After that, MCs have been decidedly less ambitious in their agendas, and in 2007 the WTO General Council agreed to abandon the biannual MC altogether. In the meantime, major Doha negotiating sessions were moved to "mini-ministerial" meetings. This set the stage for negotiating breakdowns in 2007 (Potsdam) and 2008 (Geneva), after failed efforts to agree upon basic negotiating modalities (formulas for cutting tariffs and other trade-distorting measures) and the terms of agricultural liberalization.[29] The divisions among members on fundamental negotiating issues were too deep to allow any foreseeable hope of concluding a Doha Round single undertaking, and the impasse was formally recognized at the December MC (WTO 2011a). Some observers still regard the entire WTO decision-making process as overly dependent on the presence of fair and balanced leadership in the committee chairs and the Director-General, which according to some is still lacking.[30] Notwithstanding the lingering concerns of the ineffectiveness of informal practices themselves, there is increasing concern that decision-making within the WTO has simply become a prisoner to severe divergences in bargaining positions, leading to overpowering gridlock.

How can one therefore judge, in the end, the effectiveness of WTO formal and informal decision-making institutions? Inclusiveness and alleged unfairness will probably always be a problem in the WTO, as long as decision-making processes remain incapable of conducting negotiations at all times in plenary sessions, with full transparency. Yet green rooms and other informal meetings and discussions among smaller groups will continue to be necessary to allow for meaningful bargaining on major issues. WTO chairs of committees and the Director-General will come and go, some more effective than others in mediating contentious and difficult issues. It seems in this regard that the success of WTO decision-making seems often to rest on the razor's edge of the chairs' competency in managing the negotiations (see Odell 2005). However, the circumstances of a negotiation are still the result of many vectors of trade interests, memories of earlier negotiations, and expectations, all beyond the chairs' control. As trade interests in the WTO have diverged, the issues have become more wide-ranging, complicated, and often technical in nature. At the same time formal multilateral negotiations must follow a single undertaking framework. As a result, the prospects for finding common ground to complete a comprehensive Doha Round agreement, in the current negotiations, have evidently diminished close to zero.

POSSIBLE INTERNAL WTO REMEDIES

Achieving consensus is the holy grail of any WTO multilateral negotiation, and this chapter has highlighted the problems WTO members encountered in the Doha Round to find it. The traditional informal processes of negotiating committee chair and Director-General mediation, leadership, and persuasion, developed in the early years of the GATT, appeared to facilitate consensus under the circumstances of those times. These included a narrower negotiating agenda among similar countries, negotiations conducted by trade diplomats with a common understanding of the goals of trade liberalization, and a willingness by them to trust the Director-General and the committee chairs to informal negotiating processes. While the issues were always "political" for each delegation, which had to achieve support at home for the outcome, they were not so strongly *politicized* and subject to ideological divides over the benefits of trade. Finally, there was a clearer path to consensus when the United States and the United Kingdom (later the European Union) and a few other OECD countries could forge a preliminary agreement, which could then spread through "concentric circles" to acceptance by other members, with developing countries largely on the sidelines.

These circumstances have clearly changed, and the question is whether the WTO, through either incremental or more radical institutional reforms, will be able to deliver to its members the goods (and services) of successful trade liberalization in the future. The challenges include a shift to a multipolar bargaining structure, the increasing divergence of fundamental trade interests among members, the expanded membership and scope of negotiating issues, and the increasingly complicated nature of bargaining. Over the years, the GATT exhibited incremental internal institutional adjustment to changes in product coverage, the size of its membership, and the diversity of its membership, as shown in chapter 2. However, this chapter has argued that more recent circumstances have either altered or undermined some of the foundational elements of the WTO as an institution. The WTO members have responded with internal and incremental shifts in its decision-making structure, such as adopting a deliberately more open and transparent green room process and the official designation of the Doha Round as a "development" round, which unfortunately had the unintended consequence of allowing many developing countries to regard WTO bargaining to have different rules for developing, as opposed to developed, countries. The most dangerous assumption was that trade negotiations could be built on one-sided concessions by developed countries, a violation of the underlying WTO principle of reciprocity in trade bargaining.

These problems represent an accumulation of transaction costs in achieving global trade liberalization. Table 4.3, in summarizing the problems of reaching consensus, provides additional detail to the five major institutional problems of the WTO identified earlier in table 3.3. More detailed discussion of many of these items will take place in subsequent chapters. For example, issues whose proposed solutions largely involve RTAs, such as policy space, shifting bargaining power, and diverging trade interests (items 1, 3, and 4) will be taken up in chapter 6. Those dealing with developing countries and aid-for-trade, including reciprocity, trade capacity, and the alleged Uruguay Round "bum deal" (items 5, 6, and 7) will be discussed in chapter 7. Domestic adjustment issues (item 10) will be part of the wrap-up discussion in chapter 8. The discussion here will focus on internal WTO reforms to improve the process and prospects of achieving consensus, by addressing the problems of the single undertaking (item 2), dispute resolution and uncertainty (items 8 and 9), and representation in deliberations (item 12).

Critical Mass

The discipline of a single undertaking was meant to unify all rights and obligations of WTO members and prevent "free riding," but the Doha Round

Table 4.3 IMPEDIMENTS TO CONSENSUS IN THE WTO AND POSSIBLE RESPONSES

Impediment to consensus	Institutional impact	Possible remedies
1. Political limits on policy space	Differences among members prevents consensus	1. RTA alternative (chapter 6) 2. Domestic adjustment 3. Aid-for-trade (chapter 7)
2. Single undertaking plus breadth of negotiating agenda	Transaction cost of achieving universal balance of concessions	Unpack negotiations, plurilaterals, use "critical mass" consensus rule
3. Shift in balance of negotiating power	Narrows acceptable zone of agreement; diverging interests lower capacity for trust	1. Formal consultative body to provide reality check 2. Use RTAs to test BAMTA (chapter 6)
4. Divergence of trade interests	Smaller zone of possible agreement	1. Improved information 2. Use RTAs to test BAMTA (chapter 6)
5. Terms of reciprocity	Uncertain calculation of trade-offs	Aid-for-trade; new reciprocity understanding (chapter 7)
6. Uruguay Round "bum deal" perceived by developing countries	Weakened trust, encourages distributive strategy	1. Use RTAs to test BAMTA (chapter 6) 2. Smaller negotiations to rebuild trust
7. Lack of negotiating capacity, poor bargaining coordination with capitals	Inability to assess value of concessions	1. Information sharing, enhancement through coalitions 2. Aid for trade information support (chapter 7) 3. Subsidized Geneva participation

(continued)

Table 4.3 CONTINUED

Impediment to consensus	Institutional impact	Possible remedies
8. Dispute settlement judicialization	Cost of concessions rises	1. Restructure negotiations to better internalize costs, benefits 2. Improve domestic adjustment assistance to reduce concession burden
9. Bounded rationality	Uncertain value of concessions	1. New safeguards 2. Contingency "insurance" through Aid for Trade (chapter 7)
10. Rigid factor markets at home; protectionist lobbies,	Reduced flexibility in bargaining	Domestic adjustment assistance, reforms to improve flexibility, mobilize pro-trade political lobby
11. Weakened status of Director-General, chairs, Secretariat	Weakened effectiveness of mediation, support services	Create stronger formal role for Director-General, Secretariat; invest in developing competent chairs (chapter 5)
12. Large number of negotiating countries	Transaction cost of information sharing, bargaining	1. Formal consultative body 2. Coalitions, platforms representing issue positions

showed how difficult negotiations in particular sectors can be if all members are required to abide by a general set of obligations. Some observers have proposed using "critical mass" consensus in certain sectors, which means that consensus could be achieved with something less than all members' assent to a proposal, but all members would nonetheless receive MFN treatment of the benefits of the resulting trade liberalization (see Low 2011). The basic principle is that consensus would be defined as agreement among countries representing a large percentage of total trade in the product, for example 90%, with unconditional MFN application that applies to all other WTO members. Precedents for such an approach go back to the GATT years, but are found more recently in the Information Technology Agreement, Financial Services Agreement, and the Agreement on Basic Telecommunications Services, all concluded under WTO auspices with more than 90% consensus. In these cases, a relatively small number of countries was responsible for most of the trade in these products, who agreed in undertaking the negotiated disciplines, but also agreed to allow non-signatories the same market access without opening their own markets on a reciprocal basis. One can see in these cases that "free riding" is not particularly troublesome, as most non-signatories do not export the products involved. The problem is that there are only a few sectors that lend themselves to such agreements, generally those in high-tech products or services, with production dominated by a small number of countries, so that free riding is of minimal concern. However, the original critical mass agreements on technology-related markets listed above are now ripe for renegotiation, based on changes in markets and in the underlying technologies, so this negotiating approach is still highly relevant to those sectors.

The more difficult question is how such an approach could be used in a broader WTO negotiation such as the Doha Round. Gallagher and Stoler (2009) propose using it to achieve an agreement in agriculture, the single most contentious sector in multilateral trade negotiations. They identify a group of fifty-three countries (including the European Union as one), for example, that represent 90% of all agricultural imports and exports in five major product categories and suggest that a series of critical mass negotiations on these and other products could achieve consensus more easily than under the traditional consensus rule. They acknowledge that critical mass would not make it easier for countries with high levels of protection, like Japan and Korea, to liberalize, but the point is that the number of countries needed to reach an agreement would be smaller. To this concern, one must add, however, the problem of larger countries with very high or prohibitive agricultural tariffs, such as India, which may therefore not appear to account for much trade (and could theoretically free ride), but whose *potential* import markets would dictate inclusion in the

consensus requirement. Despite these reservations, critical mass can be a useful approach to global trade liberalization, although it will be most applicable
in high-technology sectors such as those described above, where the free-rider
problem is minimized. If in fact a smaller subset of countries can reach 90%
trade-based consensus on a contentious issue, then it should by all means be
considered either as part of the structure of a larger multilateral agreement, if
it would be instrumental in securing a package deal, or on a stand-alone basis.
For broader agreements that would require smaller groups and special rules, or
that might require waivers on MFN treatment, the only general WTO option
appears to be an annex 4 (plurilateral) agreement.

WTO Salvation through Plurilaterals?

The unsatisfactory experience with the Doha Round's single undertaking has
sparked initiatives to unpack the agenda and deal with issues along smaller
dimensions and with smaller numbers of "like-minded" participants. In this
context, negotiating a WTO plurilateral agreement (PA) would appear to be
a viable alternative. The recent interest in PAs stems from efforts to propose
new ways in which the WTO can be brought back into the business of trade
liberalization, even if it takes the form of partial agreements among subsets
of members. Hoekman and Mavroidis (2013) consider plurilaterals to be at
least partial substitutes for RTAs, and fear that failed attempts to add new
plurilaterals to annex 4 will only lead to greater negotiating activity outside
the WTO, with the consequent fragmentation of rules and legal disciplines to
settle disputes. PAs would enjoy the institutional legitimacy of being part of
the WTO, and their existence could not be challenged legally (Hoekman and
Mavroidis 2013: 2). They would enjoy WTO Secretariat support and be subject to WTO dispute settlement procedures. They would also, in principle, be
open to accession by other WTO members, extending the benefits to all of an
expanding agreement. However, adding a new agreement to annex 4 is not easy.
The main barrier is Marrakesh Agreement article X.9, which states that adding
a new PA to annex 4 requires *consensus* among all WTO members. Thus, even
though not all WTO members would be signatories, all WTO members must
nevertheless agree to the *existence* of such an agreement.[31] The approval process required to establish new PAs is an important issue that has not yet been
tested, and it is not clear how the general WTO membership would respond to
such proposals. Many nonparticipants may want to join later, and those who
consider blocking it would have to contemplate the alternatives that would be
pursued instead, perhaps an RTA (see chapter 6) or other trade agreements
outside the WTO. It is also possible that large-country proponents of the PA

would provide inducements or apply pressure to nonparticipant holdouts that are blocking consensus.

PAs have institutional predecessors in the Code Agreements of the Kennedy and Tokyo Rounds: numerous such agreements were concluded among subgroups of GATT Contracting Parties, applicable only to the signatories. As noted in chapter 3, major trading powers in the subsequent negotiations of the Marrakesh Agreement pointedly sought to remove the "GATT à la carte" fragmentation of the Codes in favor of a unified single undertaking agreement that would be the foundation of the WTO. Four of the Codes were "grandfathered" as separate plurilaterals into the WTO, while the others were subsumed in the general WTO rules. In 1997, two of the plurilaterals (on dairy products and on bovine meat) were actually terminated by consensus of the General Council, as WTO members decided that these sectors were best administered by the WTO Agriculture and Sanitary/Phytosanitary (SPS) Agreements. Their termination has left just two plurilaterals in the WTO: the Government Procurement Agreement (GPA) and the Agreement on Trade in Civil Aircraft. The GPA is the more important of the two, as terms of access to government procurement are still actively negotiated, the agreement is in force and new countries have joined the agreement.[32] From the outset, its obligations and benefits applied only to the signatories, hence it is a conditional MFN agreement. For this reason, it is held up as the prototype for new plurilateral agreements in the WTO. If the institutional machinery is already in place, why not use it to harvest unfinished Doha agreements, and include agreement among like-minded WTO members on new issues as well? Hufbauer and Schott (2012) propose five such agreements, on issues including: services, currency undervaluation (WTO-IMF coordination), greenhouse gases, zero-for-zero industrial tariffs, and state-owned enterprises. Nakatomi (2012) also proposes numerous plurilaterals, some extending existing WTO disciplines on a conditional MFN basis, others delving into new areas such as competition and international supply chains.

One might wonder why some WTO countries might object to such agreements, if they can simply choose not to sign them and leave the signatories to their own devices. Hufbauer and Schott (2012) recall, for example, the willingness of GATT Contracting Parties to accept the Tokyo Round GPA Code, and later its incorporation into WTO annex 4 at the Uruguay Round, knowing that its benefits (like its obligations) applied on a conditional MFN basis. It is important to remember, however, that the GPA was never envisaged as an integral part of Tokyo or Uruguay Round cross-issue bargaining; it was always a stand-alone negotiation not connected to other issues, allowing it to be partitioned from the rest of the negotiations. GPA was in fact specifically exempted from GATT article III national treatment disciplines.[33] In addition, most countries that chose not to sign it are likely to have regarded government procurement as an "off-limits" policy area, too close to national sovereignty, and therefore not subject to reciprocal trade bargaining. In contrast, the circumstances of at least some of the proposed PAs are quite different. Negotiations on a proposed PA, the International Services Agreement (ISA), began in early 2013. The ISA represents a change of thinking among many WTO members, who previously saw services as providing critical trade-offs in a larger Doha package deal.[34] While large countries with comparative advantage in certain services sectors were eager to bargain for more market access, the wide range of services included in the four modes (see chapter 1) meant that all countries faced uncertainties over the impact of services liberalization, which may have been difficult to balance against the value of other, more traditional market access and rules proposals in the Doha Round. For now, it seems, those involved in these negotiations view a partitioning of services into a separate negotiation to be the best way to make progress on trade liberalization in this sector. But this motivation presents a problem for the other WTO member countries: the proposed ISA represents an attempt to pursue by other means what failed in the Doha Round. The subgroup of ISA signatories would be harvesting value from unused Doha bargaining chips among themselves, while non-signatories would be coming away from the Doha Round with nothing. At the same time, how and whether an ISA plurilateral would meet approval by WTO consensus remains unclear. China, India, and Brazil, in particular, have opposed a PA in services. Furthermore, it is not clear how WTO dispute settlement would operate in an ISA, since the agreement is likely to be based in part on bilaterally negotiated market access sub-agreements, and retaliation within services alone may not be sufficient to ensure compliance.

It is important to add that the ISA could be negotiated alternatively as a "regional" WTO agreement under General Agreement on Trade in Services (GATS) article V, in which case it would not require consensus approval as an annex 4 agreement.[35] In fact, progress in the ISA negotiations may be spurred on independently by regional (RTA) negotiations such as those on the Trans-Pacific Partnership (TTP) and the Transatlantic Trade and Investment (TTIP), which will also address services trade liberalization (see chapter 6). If there is strong interest among the ISA countries in concluding such an agreement, a GATS article V agreement probably represents the path of least resistance within the WTO system of rules. It seems in any case that, in the foreseeable future, trade liberalization in services, the fastest growing sector in world trade, will be carved out of cross-sectoral talks that were previously linked to the Doha Round's single undertaking. However, if the ISA or any other offspring negotiation of the Doha Round takes the form of a PA, WTO approval would require the support of those who cannot reap the same value out of the negotiations, and it is not difficult to imagine that they would object, or perhaps demand some compensation on other issues in exchange for their support. For this reason, many of the proposed PAs, especially those that would harvest an unfinished Doha negotiating issue, would probably require quid pro quo bargaining chips in other areas in order to facilitate the necessary WTO membership support in order to achieve annex 4 approval. Thus, bargaining over introducing new annex 4 agreements could turn into renewed versions of Doha Round squabbles. In addition, some plurilateral issues would involve initial rule-making with implications for future signatories, and many WTO countries would be loath to approve the addition of such agreements to annex 4 if they felt their benefits from future participation would be compromised by rules they could not affect at their inception, or if the agreement itself were intended to constrain the actions of specific countries. For this reason a plurilateral on state-owned enterprises is unlikely. Finally, some proposed plurilaterals involve issues such as trade effects of currency valuation that non-signatory countries might oppose on principle, since they could affect all WTO countries, implying the need for general negotiation and approval on the issue by the entire membership, if not separate action by the IMF (see chapter 8).

Some types of agreements, however, might have a better chance of garnering the requisite WTO approval, especially if they involved shared commitments, especially on new issues, with no discriminatory or other negative impact on non-signatories. For example, proposals for aid-for-trade funding[36] or for tariff revenue or preference erosion contingency funds among donor countries would probably encounter little opposition and could thereby make possible MFN policy reforms in the corresponding negotiations. A PA on more ambitious international supply-chain rules might also be possible if the spillover effects of expanding global supply chains introduced bargaining chips for both technology-hub countries and "factory" countries, as described by Baldwin (2012) and the discussion in chapter 6. The growth in new regional supply chains in the future could attract the interest of the WTO membership at large in establishing such an agreement, which may in fact be the best way to introduce new WTO discipline to RTAs and BITs. Until some modification of the consensus rule is implemented (by consensus, of course) in the WTO, it is unlikely, however, that many new PAs will be approved. In the meantime, the focus on RTAs, BITs, and other agreements outside the WTO system is very likely to continue as the fastest paths to trade (and associated foreign investment) liberalization.

WTO Governance and Decision-Making

Among those examples of WTO internal transaction costs prompting calls for institutional reforms are the difficulties of establishing effective representation for all members and of inclusiveness in agenda setting. A more subtle problem comes from the perception among many developing countries that the WTO system itself is simply unjust, which increases the cost of bargaining (see North 1990: 76; more generally Brown and Stern 2012). Addressing these problems will be no easy task. Many observers, including the authors of the Sutherland Report (Sutherland et al. 2004), the Warwick Commission (2007) and Blackhurst (2005), among others, have proposed a formal WTO "consultative group" of selected members, ideally representative of the entire membership, which would be able to manage and promote multilateral negotiating agendas, and presumably help to avoid stalemate. Others have proposed a more prominent role for the Secretariat (including the Director-General) in providing information, setting negotiating agendas and assisting more directly in the negotiations, that is, closer to the role it had in the earlier years of the GATT (see Nordström 2005; Elsig 2009). Tempting as these proposals are, it does not appear that there is a currently viable way of finding an institutional process that would allow such reforms to take place. Proposals for a consultative group have fallen on deaf ears at the WTO, and the strong desire among at least some members to limit the Secretariat's, and particularly the Director-General's, role does not bode well for any expansion of its powers.

Therefore, opening up the multilateral negotiating process may also eventually require the scope of negotiating issues for large countries to broaden into new and "uncomfortable" areas for concessions that they had previously kept at bay. In this regard, progress in complicated multilateral negotiations may require a more active market in side payments (foreign aid or other non-trade-related items) in order to avoid "hold-up" problems, although such compensation would probably have to occur outside WTO agreements. For this reason, WTO negotiations will require new modes of multi-country leadership in setting trade agendas and initiatives, as well as cooperation and compromise among all members, which, as chapter 8 will show, represent an important element of the process of getting trade negotiations back on the multilateral track. At the same time, there seems to be no substitute for large country leadership and compromise in the WTO, and the green room and other informal institutions appear destined to continue. Smaller states will find it increasingly important to form effective alliances—to influence decision-making both inside and outside the green room—in order to make progress on their trade agendas (see Jones 2010: chapter 4). Yet increased flexibility in the structure of the negotiations appears to be necessary in order to avoid the straitjacket of an "all or nothing" bargain on an oversized agenda.

SUMMARY: WTO CONSENSUS AS AN INSTITUTIONAL PROBLEM

After the successful GATT-led negotiations from 1947 to 1994, the inherited institutional machinery of consensus in the WTO was no longer working in the Doha Round. Whereas US leadership in the GATT, along with the European Union and other major OECD countries, was effective in generating consensus on the agendas, and with the membership, of the GATT years, conditions had changed in the WTO. Agendas were broader, more ambitious, and apparently often outside the common policy ground of trade negotiations. Differences in trade interests among major countries, now including emerging market countries such as Brazil, India, and China, had become wider. Major resentments of developing countries regarding the outcomes of the Uruguay Round carried over to the Doha Round. Mutual trust in the Director-General-led process of consensus building had weakened in the context of the higher stakes of an agreement under a strengthened DSU. As a result, the negotiating process slowed down and stalled, frustrating everyone, and leading to a suspension of the comprehensive Doha negotiations. The question remained: could the WTO, within its current rules, somehow regain its role in leading global trade liberalization? Some WTO features and provisions, such as critical mass negotiations and plurilateral agreements, show some promise in expanding trade agreements under certain conditions. Yet the scope of promoting a global trade agenda in these cases is limited. Critical mass requires overwhelming support by major trading countries on specific sectors in order to be effective, while plurilateral agreements require WTO consensus for any new agreement. Similarly, the internal decision-making process has benefited from the increased coalition activity that has occurred, but the implementation of new proposals for a select "consultative" body or other similar steering committee would essentially require WTO consensus, which is not in evidence.

The following chapters will explore other avenues of possible change in the WTO and in parallel institutions in the global economy. The next chapter revisits the decision-making process in the WTO in more detail by exploring the nature of committee chair representation, and what this might mean for future WTO leadership. Chapter 6 examines the omnipresent issue of regional trade agreements (RTAs) and how they may establish incentives to return to multilateral trade bargaining. Chapter 7 explores the role of "embedded liberalism" for the GATT's success and the possibility that an extension of this idea to aid-for-trade and other trade capacity-building measures for developing countries may help provide the means for aligning their WTO participation more closely with reciprocal bargaining. The WTO will regain its role in promoting multilateral trade liberalization in the future to the extent that it can improve the conditions of achieving consensus.

WTO Governance and Committee Chair Representation

INTRODUCTION

The institutional analysis of the Doha Round has suggested that the WTO's informal institutions—the established patterns of leadership and methods and processes of decision-making—have become less effective. While chapters 3–4 have examined, among other factors, the problems of the green room and negotiations summitry, this chapter examines the institutional structure of decision-making in WTO committees, highlighting the pattern and determinants of committee chair appointments by the WTO's General Council (GC). The motivation for this inquiry lies in the nature of decision-making in WTO negotiating and standing committees, in which committee chairs can potentially influence agendas, as well as negotiating and implementation outcomes. Since the founding of the WTO in 1995, developing countries, now representing about 78% of the WTO membership, have raised the issue of fairness in country representation, especially with regard to multilateral trade negotiations. Jawara and Kwa (2004), for example, claim that the power structure of WTO governance is biased against the interests of developed countries, through their lack of access to positions of influence in the organization, and the power of existing committee chairs to dominate negotiating texts and agendas. In this regard the trend in committee chair appointments in the major WTO governing and negotiating committees may indicate the degree to which developing country influence in the WTO has changed in recent years. In addition, many subsidiary WTO committees deal with administrative matters and specific implementation issues associated with WTO rules and market access agreements, in which representation as chairs may help determine the degree of developing country participation in

day-to-day WTO trade relations. At the same time, the importance of committee chairs in trade negotiations, and in the efficient implementation of
the WTO agreements, suggests the benefits of a meritocratic system of chair
selection, with selection based on ability and experience, subject to distribution criteria that reflects the development and regional status of the WTO
membership. In testing this hypothesis, statistical evidence is presented to
infer the criteria used by the GC in their committee chair appointments by
nationality from 1995 to 2011.

The chapter is organized as follows. The following section presents information on the formal structure of WTO committees and the importance of
informal committee chair practices, followed by a brief discussion of the meritocratic model of chair selection. The subsequent sections briefly summarize
events that led to discontent with WTO governance by many developing countries, and the role of the Ministerial Conference chairs and Directors-General
in the overall chairmanship issue. There follows a presentation of empirical
evidence regarding WTO chair appointments in terms of developed and
developing country representation, based on a set of panel data that allows a
more detailed analysis of chair appointments by country. Further discussion
focuses on additional patterns within committee groupings and the frequency
of individuals serving as chairs. The final section summarizes the statistical
results and offers a perspective of the role of WTO chairs in the larger issue
of WTO governance and implications for developing country representation
in the future. The GC's emphasis on the ability and experience of chairs, combined with the technical expertise that many WTO delegates develop in their
day-to-day deliberations, also suggests a possible role for committees in future
trade negotiations.

INSTITUTIONAL MICROSTRUCTURE OF THE WTO

The three main functions of the WTO—negotiation, implementation, and
dispute settlement—are carried out by the delegations of the member countries in Geneva, aided by a small WTO secretariat of support staff and trade
specialists.[1] As in other large representative organizations, most of the WTO's
work is done in committees controlled by the member countries, subdividing
negotiating, dispute resolution, and implementation and administrative issues
into specialized deliberations, each led by a committee chair. The WTO does
not use formal rules of member representation in allocating chair appointments, so this task falls to the GC, to be discussed below. At the very top
of the WTO organizational chart stands the Ministerial Conference (MC),
essentially a summit gathering of trade ministers, who meet every two years

to discuss negotiating agendas.[2] The MC must formally approve any major WTO agreements on behalf of the member governments. Beneath this body, the WTO GC oversees day-to-day operations, plans MC meetings and negotiations, and appoints most WTO committee chairs. The GC meets in plenary session about twelve times a year and consists of the heads-of-delegation for all WTO members. This same body also convenes as the Dispute Settlement Body and the Trade Policy Review Body, but for each of these major committees there is a separate chairperson. Subordinate to the GC are also several standing committees and working groups, including three Councils for trade in goods, for trade in services, and for trade-related aspects of intellectual property (TRIPS). The Goods and Services Councils, in turn, oversee subordinate committees on specialized topics. In addition, the GC oversees the Trade Negotiations Committee (TNC), which convenes when multilateral trade negotiations are in progress, and creates subsidiary committees focusing on specific negotiating issues. In the Doha Round, there have been ten such subcommittees, dealing individually with market access in goods, agriculture (with a subcommittee on cotton), and services; trade facilitation, TRIPS, Dispute Settlement, Rules (antidumping, subsidies, regional trade agreements), trade and environment, and trade and development. There are also two "plurilateral" committees, which are linked with agreements of subsets of WTO members who have signed separate agreements on civil Aircraft and Government Procurement. Membership on these committees is therefore restricted to signatory members. Each chair appointed to a committee reporting to the GC or its subsidiary committees is subject to an annual appointment cycle. One additional set of committees under the GC comprises the Working Parties on WTO accession, one for each country negotiating entry into the WTO, and their activities often span several years, with various phases of greater or lesser activity. Chairs of these Working Parties often serve for several years, although in long accession negotiations (of which there are many) chairpersons will often be changed.

As noted in earlier chapters, WTO decision-making is based on *consensus*, and in such a large organization, attaining consensus is difficult. Committee chairs thus often face the challenge of moving contentious negotiations or discussions toward a consensus position. While the WTO Agreement itself generally delegates chair appointments to each individual committee.[3] WTO practice has developed a centralized procedure that places the decision squarely with the GC (see WTO 2012). This arrangement suggests that the GC anticipated from the early years of the organization that representational balance of the WTO members through chair appointments would be an issue requiring systematic control. The WTO GC chair presents a single list each year, usually in February, naming chairs to all active committees, which must be approved by consensus, after lengthy consultation and bargaining with the WTO membership, with no changes. The one exception to the one-year rotating terms is the chair of the TNC itself, to which the GC has, at its discretion during the Doha Round, named the Director-General on a continuing basis. The Director-General is thereby placed in a pivotal role in multilateral trade negotiations, as described in chapter 4. In addition, the GC has established a broad set of principles that committee chairs of the MC and the GC must follow in a document known as "WT/L/161" (WTO 1996). Aside from several procedural rules for the course of meetings, the chair is given "complete control of the proceedings" (ibid., rule 17) and is normally expected to preside over the meeting as a neutral party rather than as a representative of his or her country (ibid., rule 15). In general, committees must follow the principles outlined in WTO article IX (WTO Decision Making), in particular the practice of consensus (ibid., rule 28). Beneath the MC and GC in the WTO organizational structure, other WTO committees have adopted rules specific to their issue coverage, but they mirror the general rules in document WT/L/161 (Kanitz 2011a: 14–16).[4]

THE STRUCTURE OF WTO COMMITTEES

There are three basic types of committees to which the GC appoints chairs: (1) those that oversee major WTO activities, (2) those that engage in multilateral trade negotiations on specific issues, and (3) those that implement or administer existing agreements. The first group has standing representation from every WTO member and includes the triumvirate of the GC, Trade Policy Review Body (TPRB), and the Dispute Settlement Body (DSB), as well as the Goods and Services Councils and the TRIPS Council. The trio of GC, TPRB, and DSB are the highest level administrative committees, with head-of-delegation representation of each member country, and the Goods and Services Councils (subordinate to the GC) oversee the activities of other subordinate committees. The second group consists of active trade negotiating committees, whose chairs are often decisive in the success or failure of the deliberations in reaching agreement (see Tallberg 2010; Odell 2005, 2009; Ismail 2009). The third group, subordinate to the Goods and Services Councils, conducts much of the quotidian work of the WTO, including details of operations and rules implementation, as well as discussion of ongoing issues. Most attention and research devoted to WTO committee chairs has focused on the Doha negotiating committees and the GC, which prepares and oversees the negotiating agenda, and ultimately controls the Round. Even before the negotiations begin, for example, the GC must identify the agenda of items that will be negotiated, and, once the agenda is agreed, establish the specific negotiating groups. This is an important and often controversial part of the agenda-setting process, exemplified by the tenuous last-minute compromise that finally launched the Doha Round in October 2001 (see Das 2002). During the negotiations themselves, bargaining must narrow the differences in country positions on many technical and complicated issues, which typically require informal discussions that go beyond the confines of the formal meeting structure. Ultimately, any final WTO agreement requires a showing of consensus at the GC that concludes the negotiation, but negotiators are typically reluctant to reveal any flexibility in open, formal meetings. Chairs, in pursuing their primary goal of achieving consensus, must often use off-the-record, confidential meetings to discover negotiators' "reservation" positions. In addition, the chair's personal powers of mediation and persuasion, which may be crucial in achieving progress toward consensus, often require informal tools, such as negotiating drafts "on the chairs' personal responsibility" (see del Castillo 2011: 147), a particular sequencing of issues under discussion, the timing of meetings, and the management of one-to-one informal "confessional" meetings with chief negotiators.[5] The committee chairs' discretion therefore often plays a role in the course of the negotiations. Odell (2005) considers WTO chairs in general to have a significant impact on the negotiations, for good or for ill.

Within the day-to-day ongoing administration and implementation of WTO agreements and rules in Geneva, many other committees play a much less dramatic and less visible role in trade relations. These committees are subordinate to the GC and to the Goods and Services Councils. GC subordinate committees include "talking shops" (trade and development, trade and environment; working groups on trade and investment, transfer of technology), as well as administrative (WTO budget/finance) and monitoring (balance of payments, regional trade arrangements) bodies.[6] Committees subordinate to the Goods and Services Councils focus on technical issues of implementation of WTO agreements.[7] The importance of these committees, and of the chair appointments to them, has been the subject of debate. Unlike negotiating committees, which have a "legislative" role in the WTO, these committees cannot create new rights and obligations for members.[8] However, Stewart (2011) maintains that WTO administrative governance is creating a framework for global administrative law, while noting that its powers are currently weak. Lang and Scott (2009) claim that WTO administrative committees have created international "epistemic communities" of specialized trade policy experts and practitioners who discuss important trade issues and potential conflicts informally, outside the dispute settlement and formal negotiating frameworks. These forums can thereby stabilize trade relations and forestall trade disputes, an observation also made by Mavroidis (2011: 380). Steinberg (2010) is skeptical that such committees can attain any independent power to resolve trade disputes, since the positions taken by representatives on them are tightly controlled by their countries. Yet it is difficult to dispute the notion that the ongoing deliberations of specialized trade officials, meeting constantly with their peers on topics of mutual interest, have the potential to influence everyday trade relations, as well as future negotiations. Progress in cooperation on trade policy is certainly possible if pursued quietly, in the interstices of the WTO's day-to-day administrative process. To the extent that this is true, the chairs of such committees will also play an important role in the process, perhaps closer to the role of mediator and facilitator among committee members than what a "bureaucratic caretaker" model might suggest. It is also important to remember that chair service on these committees may lead later to chair service on higher level and trade negotiating committees.[9]

DEVELOPING COUNTRY DISCONTENT

Concerns with the balance of representation in WTO decision-making emerged shortly after the founding of the WTO. Disappointment among developing countries in the results of the Uruguay Round regarding back loaded textiles liberalization, intellectual property compliance costs, and limited progress in agriculture liberalization raised objections to the entire system of WTO governance, and by implication, the alleged use of committee chairs to promote developed country agendas.[10] The issue of representation continued to fester as a result of the use of "green room" meetings at critical negotiating junctures, as noted in chapter 4's discussion of the collapse of the Seattle (1999) and Cancun (2003) Ministerial Conferences. Subsequently, the Director-General has managed the list of invited members to WTO green room meetings very carefully, but the issue of inclusiveness continued to raise the question of representation in all WTO committee meetings. Many developing countries in the WTO, especially the smaller and poorer countries, continue to have limited representation capacity as a result of their lack of sufficient resources to staff and run a Geneva-based mission that can effectively pursue their trade interests (see Michalopoulos 2001; VanGrasstek 2008; Laker 2013). The agreement of the WTO membership to a "Doha Development Round" implied an effort to ensure that developing country interests would be adequately represented during the negotiations and in the management of the WTO in general. This mandate presented the GC with the need to strike a delicate balance between overall WTO member representation and recognition of traditional experience and background attributes in considering candidates for chair positions.

MINISTERIAL CHAIRS AND THE DIRECTOR-GENERAL

While this study focuses on the chair appointments of the WTO GC and its many subsidiary committees, it is important to review briefly the pattern of MC Chair and the Director-General's appointments, since their impact on the entire decision-making process may be crucial. In addition, trends in these chair appointments may also affect the GC's appointments of other WTO committee chairs. Table 5.1 shows the eight WTO Ministerial Conference chairs, along with the WTO Director-General appointments from 1995 to 2016. Ministerial meeting arrangements and chair assignments reside in the WTO GC, which appears to maintain a pattern of geographical and developmental status balance in the selection of MC sites, and chairs when the meetings are held in Geneva. Political considerations also undoubtedly play a role. As noted above, the chair of a Ministerial is the chief trade official of the host country, while meetings in Geneva itself are generally chaired by an invited trade minister. So far, four chairs have come from developed countries (including

Table 5.1 WTO MINISTERIAL CONFERENCE CHAIRS AND DIRECTORS-GENERAL

A. WTO Ministerial Conference Chairs, 1996-2011

Site	Chair	Date
Singapore	Yeo Cheow Tong	Dec. 9–13, 1996
Geneva, Switzerland	Pascal Couchepin (Switzerland)	May 18–20, 1998
Seattle, USA	Charlene Barshevsky	Nov. 30–Dec. 3, 1999
Doha, Qatar	Youssef Hussain Kamal	Nov. 9–13, 2001
Cancun, Mexico	Luis Ernesto Derbez	Sept. 10–14, 2003
Hong Kong	John Tsang	Dec. 13–18, 2005
[Ministerial Conference Cancelled, 2007]		
Geneva, Switzerland	Andres Velesco (Chile)	Nov. 30–Dec. 1, 2009
Geneva, Switzerland	Olusegun Olutoyin Aganga (Nigeria)	Dec. 15–17, 2011

B. Directors-General of the WTO

Name	Country	Years of Service
Peter Sutherland	Ireland	1993–1995
Renato Ruggiero	Italy	1995–1999
Mike Moore	New Zealand	1999–2002
Supachai Panitchpakdi	Thailand	2002–2005
Pascal Lamy	France	2005–2013
Roberto Azevêdo	Brazil	2013

Singapore and Hong Kong, recently "graduated" to developed country status, according to the IMF listings), and four from the developing world. The
Ministerial chairs are also geographically diverse, representing East Asia,
Europe, North America, South America, and Africa. The GC thus established
its diversity approach to committee appointments in its decisions on location
and chair appointments for the MCs.

Recent practice suggests that the GC has come to approach the Ministerial
planning process with increasing care, especially since the MC chair can
affect the outcome of these important gatherings, as chapter 4's accounts of
the 1999 Seattle and 2003 Cancun MCs indicated. In contrast to these examples, WTO delegates and WTO scholars have pointed to the close and successful working relationships between the Ministerial chair, the GC chair,
and the Director-General in the preparation and management of the Doha
and Hong Kong Ministerials, which were successful by comparison (Odell
2009; Elsig 2011; Harbinson 2011; Kanitz 2011a). However, it is also noteworthy that the 2004 Framework Agreement was the result of a special GC
meeting chaired by Ambassador Shotaro Oshima of Japan and managed to
get the Doha Round back on track for a while after the Cancun debacle (see
Oshima 2011; Albin and Young 2012). This outcome suggested that major
WTO negotiating sessions may be more successful when held away from the
glare of a high-level Ministerial meeting. After the Hong Kong Ministerial,
plans for a 2007 Ministerial were actually scrapped, in view of the deadlock
in the Doha negotiations that had emerged in the meantime, and the 2009
and 2011 Geneva Ministerials were held in the wake of the final breakdown
of the comprehensive Doha negotiations in the summer of 2008, with scaled
back agendas and largely ceremonial roles for the invited chairs. It seems that
the ambitious WTO goal of holding high-level Ministerial summits every
two years, based on the notion that their frequency would push forward trade
liberalization more quickly and efficiently, have foundered on the "summit
syndrome," in which efforts to bring together each country's top officials prematurely, before the deal is closed (or nearly closed), are usually doomed to
failure. The WTO's regrettable experiences in this regard suggest that the GC
will carefully orchestrate future MCs, and not leave to chance an unscripted
chair's role when critical trade negotiation objectives are at stake.

The Director-General's role as head of the WTO Secretariat and chair
of the TNC has also evolved since the WTO's founding. The original WTO
Agreement described the Director-General appointment procedure simply as the decision of the Ministerial Conference (article VI.2), presumably
by consensus of the entire membership. Peter Sutherland of Ireland served
as the first Director-General, in a short transitional position at the end of
the GATT and beginning of the WTO period. However, over the next five

years, the Director-General selection process became increasingly politicized. The importance of the new organization and the potential influence of the Director-General's position, based on the GATT's history of strong Director-General's shepherding trade negotiations to conclusion, motivated large WTO members to take strong positions on particular candidates. The selection of Sutherland's successor followed the GATT tradition by going to a European, Renato Ruggiero, although Carlos Salinas of Mexico initially had US support and developing countries had become actively involved in the selection process. Another representational issue became a bargaining chip in the Director-General's selection as the United States agreed to Ruggiero on the conditions that the next Director-General not be a European, and that an additional (fourth) Deputy Director-General position would be created, with slots informally reserved for the United States, India, and two other developing countries (see Kahler 2001: 61). It is noteworthy that many WTO members were angry over such backroom dealing by large countries, and with regional issues and conditions dominating senior Secretariat positions. It was henceforth important to address geographical distribution in Director-General and Deputy Director-General appointments—and probably in GC decisions on chair appointments—without carving out geographical quotas for specific positions at the behest of specific countries.

As noted in chapter 4, the issue of developing country representation in the Director-General's chair reached a peak in the subsequent selection process, which led to a split term of three years each for Mike Moore of New Zealand and Supachai Panitchpakdi of Thailand, followed by Pascal Lamy of France, who served two consecutive four-year terms, from 2005 to 2013. Advocacy for developing, or developed, country agendas was not on the table in the selection of the Director-General during the Doha Round. In addition, to the extent that continued trade negotiations were possible at all, it was better not to switch the Director-General in mid-stream. After Lamy, however, there was from the beginning of the selection process a strong likelihood that the new Director-General would come from a developing country. Of the nine initial candidates, all but one candidate came from developing countries.[11] The final choice of Roberto Carvalho de Azevêdo of Brazil reflected both the personal standing of the candidate and Brazil's increasing role as a leading representative of developing countries in the WTO. In the post-Doha era, the choice may also be indicative of the WTO's membership view that progress in trade liberalization may require leadership from a representative of the emerging markets, as a possible bridge between the developing and developed world. However, the nationality of WTO negotiating committee chairs during the Doha Round has not necessarily indicated the chairperson's ability to bridge the gap between developing and developed country interests.[12]

AGGREGATE TRENDS AND DETERMINANTS OF
COMMITTEE CHAIRS

Each year from 1995 to 2011, the WTO GC announced the chairmanships of twenty-five to forty-six committees operating under it and its subsidiary councils, and also periodically appointed chairs of Working Parties for WTO accession for countries negotiating entry into the organization. The most chair appointments occurred during the Doha Round, when additional negotiating committees were formed under the TNC, which was chaired each year by the Director-General. Table 5.2 summarizes the national distribution of WTO chairmanships appointed through this GC process over this time period.[13] The tally counts each chair appointment for each year for each committee, since the GC process is to appoint new chairs to each committee annually.[14] The exception is the set of Accession Working Parties, which meet on an irregular basis according to the stage of the accession negotiations, and whose activities typically span several years. Each of these chairmanships thus counts in the tally as a single appointment, regardless of how long the chair served (turnover is common for long accession negotiations).

From 1995 to 2011, there were 732 committee chair appointments, an average of nearly five per WTO member country. The branch-and-stem breakdown of national representation of the chairs in Table 5.2 shows that a small number of countries accounted for most of the chairs. Out of 152 WTO members included in the study, the eleven countries with the most chair appointments, for example, accounted for fully one-third of the total, and the top twenty-three countries accounted for 57% of the total. At the same time, 52% of the chairs came from developing countries, and developing country representation did increase slightly, year by year, during this period, as described below. It is noteworthy that the top trading nations in the world are not among the top recipients of chair appointments, with the exceptions of Japan (26) and France (19). Germany, China, and the United States, the world's top three exporters, had relatively few chairs (although China did not accede to the WTO until 2001). The United States has in fact had fewer chairs than Bangladesh and many other developing countries! The General Council is evidently mindful of the political danger of appointing chairs from large countries, especially for negotiating or other high-profile committees. It is also likely that the large countries themselves prefer not to chair major committees, since the rules on chair neutrality would make it more difficult for them, with such high visibility, to pursue their national interests.

Overall participation among developing countries in terms of the number of countries with chairmanships has been limited, although it increased over the period. In 1995, there were just twelve different developing countries

Table 5.2 TOTAL WTO CHAIR APPOINTMENTS, BY COUNTRY, 1995–2011

Total	Country
38	New Zealand
26	Japan
27	Canada
23	Hong Kong
20	Uruguay
19	Australia, France
18	Chile, Norway, Pakistan, Singapore
17	Brazil
16	Philippines
15	Colombia, Switzerland, Thailand, United Kingdom
14	Costa Rica
13	Egypt, India, Mauritius, South Korea, Sweden
12	Argentina, Finland, Hungary, Mexico
11	Germany, Netherlands
10	Belgium, Nigeria
9	Barbados, Malaysia
8	Bangladesh, Czech Republic, Denmark, Turkey
7	Ireland, Jamaica, Kenya, Lesotho, Romania, United States of America, Zimbabwe
6	China, Iceland, Morocco, Poland
5	Guatemala, Israel, South Africa, Tanzania
4	Indonesia, Italy, Lithuania, Slovakia, Tunisia, Uganda, Zambia
3	Austria, Gabon, Ghana, Greece, Latvia, Peru, Senegal, Slovenia, Spain, Sri Lanka, Venezuela
2	Cote d'Ivoire, El Salvador, Estonia, Namibia, Paraguay, Taiwan, Trinidad
1	WTO Secretariat, Ecuador, Honduras, Madagascar, Mongolia, Nicaragua, Oman, Panama, Portugal

		Developing	Europe	Sub-Africa	NAfr-ME	EAsiaOceana	Americas
732	Total	378 (52%)	208 (28%)	76 (10%)	79 (11%)	191 (26%)	178 (24%)
4.8	Mean						
1	Median						
0	Mode						

SOURCE: WTO: http://www.wto.org/english/thewto_e/secre_e/current_chairs_e.htm, accessed July 27, 2012

represented among twenty-five total committee chair appointments. The number of developing countries represented in chairmanships increased steadily in subsequent years, peaking at twenty-four in 2009 (among forty-six chair appointments), and then declined, along with the cutback in WTO chair activity as the Doha Round was suspended. Even so, twenty different developing countries chaired twenty out of twenty-eight chairs in 2012, 71% of the total. It should also be noted, however, that 77% of the WTO membership consisted of developing countries at that time, and they are still underrepresented in this regard. Most of the developing country chair appointments have gone to Uruguay, Pakistan, and a relatively small number of emerging market countries, including Chile, Brazil, the Philippines, Columbia and Thailand. Sixty-nine WTO members, nearly all of them developing countries, did not have any chairmanships at all during this period. Some of the imbalance can also be seen in the geographical distribution of chairs. Sub-Mediterranean Africa (10% of total) and Northern African/Middle Eastern countries (11%) are underrepresented in comparison with Europe (28%), East Asia/Oceana (26%), and the Americas (24%).

A closer look at the trend in representation among developing countries and among the regional groupings shows that some improvement in the balance of chair distribution took place over this period. Figure 5.1 tracks the year-to-year representation ratio of developing countries and of the subsets of emerging markets and least-developed countries from 1995 to 2011. The representation ratio is defined as the proportion of committee chair assignments for that group in a given year divided by the share of that group's membership

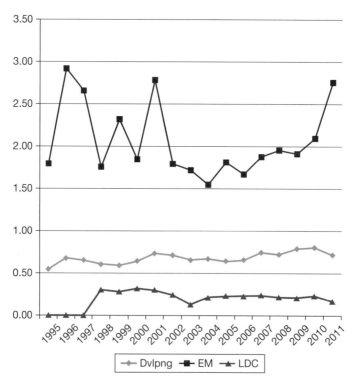

Figure 5.1 WTO Chairs Developing, Emerging Markets, and LDC Representation Ratios

in the WTO for that year. A representation ratio value of unity is therefore the benchmark for perfectly proportional representation for the group as a whole. Figure 5.1 shows that the overall developing country ratio has generally increased over the period, moving from.55 in 1995 to.72 in 2011. Many of the developing country chairmanships have been from a small group of fifteen emerging markets, whose representation ratios have ranged from 1.55 to 2.92 during this period. Very few chair appointments have gone to least-developed countries, which received their first chair appointment only in 1998; their representation ratio fluctuated between 0.13 and 0.32 for the rest of the period. Alternatively, it is also evident that in terms of trade shares in the world economy, developing countries are not underrepresented. Table 5.3 shows the trade representation ratio (share of chairs/share of global exports) of WTO developing country members over this time period. It shows greater than proportional representation by this measure, reaching a peak of 3.14 in 1997 and declining since then, based largely on their increasing share of global exports, especially after China's 2001 accession. Clearly, given the currently low, if growing, capacity to trade among developing countries, along with the sensitivity of "big country" representation on major committees, the GC is not going to rely on trade-weighted representation as a criterion in chair appointments.

The pattern of geographical representation has also revealed a trend toward increased balance, although countries' development status and economic interests are often not aligned along geographical lines. Dividing the WTO membership into five geographical regions—Europe, Sub-Mediterranean Africa, North Africa/Middle East, East Asia/Oceana and the Americas—figure 5.2 shows the representation ratio trends from 1995 to 2011 (see the Appendix for the groupings). Despite strong year-to year fluctuations, it is noteworthy that average representation ratios over this time period for Europe, North Africa/ Middle East, and the Americas have been close to unity, suggesting that GC chair appointments have sought a rough geographical balance for these areas over time. The mainly developed European countries' representation ratio has generally fallen during this period, from an initial high of 1.51 to values closer to unity by the end of the period. The North Africa/Middle East group generally had somewhat less than proportional chair representation on average, but with the highest variance of any region. The Americas region, with its mix of developed and developing countries, including several emerging market countries, had a chair representation ratio close to unity throughout the period. The two outliers are East Asia/Oceana and Sub-Mediterranean Africa. The strongly represented East Asia/Oceana region, with representation ratios well above 2.0 for most of the period, experienced slightly reduced proportional representation among WTO chairs toward the end of the period. This group contains many emerging markets and smaller open and otherwise trade-oriented

Table 5.3 TRADE REPRESENTATION RATIO IN WTO OF DEVELOPING COUNTRIES

	1995	1996	1997	1998	1999	2000	2001	2002	2003
Developing Share of WTO Chairs (A)	0.40	0.50	0.48	0.45	0.44	0.48	0.56	0.55	0.50
Developing Share of WTO trade (B)	0.24	0.25	0.15	0.15	0.16	0.17	0.21	0.22	0.23
Trade Representation Ratio (A/B)	1.63	1.97	3.14	3.00	2.82	2.91	2.63	2.47	2.17

	2004	2005	2006	2007	2008	2009	2010	2011
Developing Share of WTO Chairs (A)	0.51	0.49	0.50	0.57	0.56	0.61	0.62	0.55
Developing Share of WTO trade (B)	0.26	0.28	0.29	0.30	0.32	0.31	0.33	0.34
Trade Representation Ratio (A/B)	1.99	1.75	1.70	1.87	1.72	1.94	1.88	1.61

SOURCE: WTO: http://www.wto.org/english/thewto_e/secre_e/current_chairs_e.htm, accessed July 27, 2012, and yearly membership information compiled by the author.

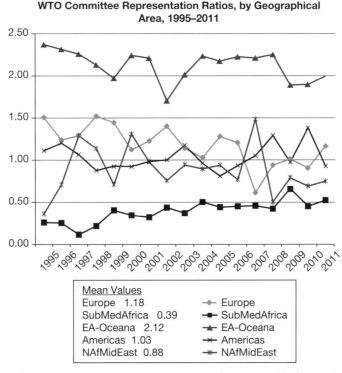

Figure 5.2 WTO Committee Representation Ratios, by Geographical Areas, 1995–2011

economies such as Japan, China, Hong Kong, Singapore, Thailand, Taiwan, the Philippines, South Korea, Australia, and New Zealand, all of which (except for China and Taiwan) are among the top WTO countries in terms of chair appointments. The mainly less developed group of Sub-Mediterranean Africa experienced increased ratios over the period, from an initial value of 0.24 to the most recent value of 0.61. This, the poorest of regions, clearly had the least chair representation.

A HUMAN CAPITAL HYPOTHESIS OF COMMITTEE CHAIR SELECTION

The importance of committee chairs in WTO negotiations and governance suggests that the GC will seek out the most qualified candidates, subject to a broad balance in overall WTO representation. Kahler (2001: 12–13), for example, observes the importance of merit in appointments to WTO leadership positions, subject to national diversity of representation. Official WTO documents themselves contain only vague indications of the qualifications for committee chairpersons, implied by the inherent powers of the chair to control the meetings and to discharge his or her role independently of home country interests. Those close to the process of selecting committee chairs emphasize the importance of diplomatic and organizational skills and experience, and familiarity with the substantive matters of the committee, with the WTO Secretariat, and with WTO procedures and rules (Lafer 2011: vii–xiii). These elements suggest the importance of the candidate's personal human capital in the selection of committee chairs. From the perspective of national representation in committee chair appointments, the selection process also implies the importance of the country's WTO mission capacity to support the activities of committee chairs among its delegates, which divert resources away from their normal duties. Larger missions thereby imply increased ability to support candidates for chair positions. Thus "human capital" may act as a determinant of WTO committee chair appointments both in terms of the qualitative attributes of individual candidates and the quantitative capacity of WTO member country delegations to support such appointments.

The committee chair selection process has been explored in the corporate governance literature (see Dunn 2012 and more generally Gatewood et al. 2008) and in studies of legislative committee appointments (Padro i Miquel and Snyder 2006). This chapter seeks to identify the distinctive elements of WTO committee chair selection through WTO member country characteristics. In the absence of individual educational and other personal background information on all potential candidates, testing this hypothesis requires the use of country-by-country statistical information that offers proxies for important selection criteria. The most important differentiator in this regard is likely to be the size of a country's Geneva mission to the WTO. Mission size itself may be linked with other explanatory variables, such as those described below, and this relationship will be tested with a separate regression. With regard to chair appointments, a larger mission provides greater capacity for chair appointments, as described above. Small delegations, for example, find it difficult just to keep up with the WTO's day-to-day meetings and deliberations, and it was very rare for any of them to receive a chair appointment.[15] In addition, during the sample period, twenty countries had no effective representation in Geneva at all, so chair appointments for them were impossible. Mission size may also signal the country's commitment to WTO representation, and therefore to developing trade diplomacy "assets" in the form of better educated and experienced trade diplomats.[16] In general, the shortfall in diplomatic "assets" in Geneva may explain in part the fact that sixty-nine WTO member countries did not have a single committee chair during the sample period. Further evidence of a higher value of a potential chair's human capital might be reflected in the country's length of experience in the GATT/WTO system, which presumably carries over into country staff members' familiarity with trade law and diplomacy. Economic indicators of a country's ability and willingness to invest resources in WTO representation could include GDP, GDP per capita, and perhaps more importantly, the country's share in world exports and the importance of trade in its economy (trade/GDP ratios). From the GC's point of view, prior experience in chairing a WTO committee will also enhance the individual's (or perhaps the delegation's) human capital, and thus the attractiveness, of a candidate (or perhaps candidates from countries that have previously had chair appointments). In general, the study focuses on chair selection based on the nationality of the chairperson, and how WTO-specific human capital indicators can be linked with the national delegation and with the country's economic profile.

Unobserved factors in chair appointments. In considering candidates, the GC can also be expected to consider special personal attributes of potential chairpersons, such as leadership, personality, and the ability of the candidate to command respect among fellow trade diplomats that may not be linked to mission size or other national delegation attributes. With the exception of documented previous committee chair appointments, which enters the Probit model estimations in the time series data, such individual attributes remain unobserved in the regressions. Political considerations in chair appointments, which may override human capital considerations, also remain unobserved.[17] In view of the presumed importance of diversity in national representation among committee chairs, particularly talented candidates from poorer, or otherwise underrepresented countries, for example, would be especially attractive to the GC. Such appointments may therefore be due to observed human capital factors associated with mission size or other national attributes, to previous chair appointments (in the probit regressions), or to unobserved human capital, personal, or political characteristics. Dummy variables for emerging market countries, for least developed countries, and for developing countries in general are included to test the hypothesis that these groups of countries receive greater or fewer chair appointments, independent of their mission size, GATT/WTO experience and economic determinants.

PATTERNS OF CHAIR REPRESENTATION USING AGGREGATE DATA

Taking the total number of chairs for each WTO country over this period as the dependent variable, and the simple averages of all explanatory variables during this time, table 5.4 reports the results of various regressions on its determinants. Based on the discussion so far, the hypothesis is that the size of the country's Geneva mission, a measure of the country's capacity to take on chairmanships,

Table 5.4 Determinants of Total Number of Chairs by Country Dependent Variable: Total Chairs, 1995–2011 (N = 152)

OLS

Variables	Variant 1	Variant 2	Variant 3
Constant	-4.378***	-3.210	-4.837***
P value	[0.000]	[0.148]	[0.000]
GenevaMis	0.719***	0.689***	0.659***
P value	[0.000]	[0.000]	[0.000]
Expsh2	0.574	0.572	...
P value	[0.327]	[0.332]	[...]
MnfExGDP	0.056**	0.052*	0.056**
P value	[0.030]	[0.062]	[0.023]
RealGDP	-0.958	-0.962	...
P value	[0.187]	[0.187]	[...]
GDPcap	0.087**	0.060	0.245***
P value	[0.020]	[0.229]	[0.004]

Poisson / Negative Binomial

Variables	Poisson Variant 1	Variant 2	Variant 3	Neg. Binomial Variant 1	Variant 2	Variant 3
Constant	-1.002***	-0.499**	-1.008***	-1.954***	-1.632**	-1.877***
P value	[0.000]	[0.022]	[0.000]	[0.000]	[.013]	[0.000]
GenevaMis	0.125***	0.112***	0.097***	0.220***	0.208***	0.186***
Marginal effect	0.366	0.313	0.283	0.537	0.501	0.460
P value	[0.000]	[0.000]	[0.000]	[0.000]	[0.000]	[0.000]
Expsh2	0.022	0.010	...	-0.085	-0.087	...
Marginal effect	0.064	0.028	...	-0.207	-0.210	...
P value	[0.566]	[0.793]	[...]	[0.504]	[0.484]	[...]
MnfExGDP	0.012***	0.010***	0.011***	0.022***	0.021***	0.019***
Marginal effect	0.034	0.029	0.031	0.053	0.050	0.048
P value	[0.000]	[0.000]	[0.000]	[0.002]	[0.005]	[0.005]
RealGDP	-0.115**	-0.103**	...	-0.084	-0.080	...
Marginal	-0.337	-0.287	...	-0.206	-0.194	...
P value	[0.017]	[0.034]	[...]	[0.626]	[0.632]	[...]
GDPcap	0.015***	0.006	0.045***	0.015	0.008	0.031
Marginal effect	0.044	0.017	0.130	0.037	0.020	0.076
P value	[0.000]	[0.137]	[0.000]	[0.110]	[0.557]	[0.184]

	(1)	(2)	(3)
AgExGDP	0.146	0.124	0.169*
P value	[0.106]	[0.182]	[0.059]
GDPcap_sq	...	...	-0.003**
P value	[...]	[...]	[0.042]
GattWto	0.087***	0.092***	0.088***
P value	[0.000]	[0.000]	[0.000]
EM	1.828	1.628	2.218
P value	[0.199]	[0.276]	[0.114]
Dvlpng	...	-0.681	...
P value	[...]	[0.690]	[...]
LDC	...	-1.175	...
P value	[...]	[0.317]	[...]
R^2	0.506	0.510	0.514

	(1)	(2)	(3)	(4)	(5)	(6)
AgExGDP	0.036***	0.029***	0.045***	0.053**	0.041	0.059**
Marginal effect	0.105	0.081	0.131	0.130	0.100	0.146
P value	[0.000]	[0.002]	[0.000]	[0.039]	[0.116]	[0.020]
GDPcap_sq	...	...	-0.001***	...	...	-0.0004
Marginal effect	...	...	-0.002	...	...	-0.001
P value	[...]	[...]	[0.000]	[...]	[...]	[0.343]
GattWto	0.026***	0.027***	0.025***	0.030***	0.032***	0.030***
Marginal effect	0.078	0.075	0.072	0.074	0.076	0.074
P value	[0.000]	[0.000]	[0.000]	[0.000]	[0.000]	[0.000]
EM	0.430***	0.382***	0.631***	0.674**	0.548*	0.735**
Marginal effect	1.492	1.233	2.376	2.164	1.640	2.451
P value	[0.000]	[0.001]	[0.000]	[0.033]	[0.090]	[0.020]
Dvlpng	...	-0.264*	...	...	-0.074	...
Marginal effect	...	-0.791	...	...	-0.182	...
P value	[...]	[0.098]	[...]	[...]	[0.874]	[...]
LDC	...	-0.809***	...	...	-0.581*	...
Marginal effect	...	-1.821	...	...	-1.195	...
P value	[...]	[0.000]	[...]	[...]	[0.079]	[...]
Pseudo R^2	0.428	0.443	0.433	0.123	0.128	0.122

* $P < 0.1$ significant at 10%;
** $P < 0.05$ significant at 5%;
*** $P < 0.01$ significant at 1%.

plays a prominent role in the number of chair appointments.[18] Other economic indicators, such as total GDP and GDP per capita, may also be related to the resource capacity of a country to develop trade specialists and diplomats as potential chairs. The number of years a country has been in the GATT/WTO system provides a measure of the country's experience and familiarity with the functioning and governance of the WTO, and thus readiness to assume positions as committee chairs. Finally, a set of trade indicators, including manufactures exports-to-GDP and agriculture exports-to-GDP, may show a country's inherent interest in negotiating market access, and therefore motivate it to seek and/or accept chair appointments. In addition, a set of dummy variables linked with a country's development status (developing country, LDC, emerging market country) are included to test the hypothesis that such status systematically affects the appointment process.

Table 5.4 reports the results of regressions on three sets of independent variables, using three estimation methods. In addition to the familiar Ordinary Least Squares (OLS) model, the presence of count data in the dependent variable suggests the appropriateness of testing Poisson (P) and Negative Binomial (NB) regressions as well.[19] In the P and BN regressions, the reported marginal effect for a variable shows the impact on the number of chairs of a one-unit increase in that variable above its mean, against the base of the fitted value using the mean of all tested independent variables. All estimation methods show the size of a country's Geneva mission (GenMis), and the number of years the country has been a GATT/WTO member, to be highly significant determinants of the number of total chair appointments from 1995 to 2011. An increase by one in GenMis results in an increase of about 0.7. (OLS), of 0.3 to 0.4 (P) and 0.5 (NB) in the number of chairs. When years of GATT/WTO membership increase by 10, chairs increase by 0.9 (OLS) and 0.7 to 0.8 (PandNB). An increase by ten in the percentage of manufactures exports to GDP (ManExGdp) leads to a highly significant increase in chairs by 0.3 and 0.5 in the P and NB models, respectively, less significantly by 0.5 to 0.6 in the OLS model. The P and NB models also attribute significant positive effects of the Emerging Markets dummy, increasing the number of chairs for that group by 1.2 to 2.4. The LDC Dummy decreases the number of chairs for that group by 0.6 to 0.8 in the NB and P models, respectively. The results for the Agricultural Exports-to-GDP are mixed: they are positive and highly significant in the P model, with about one additional chair for each additional ten percentage point increase in AgExGdp, but only occasionally significant in the NB, and not at all in the OLS, regressions. One interesting and apparently perverse result is the consistently negative coefficients for real GDP, suggesting that, the bigger the country's GDP, ceteris paribus, the fewer the chairs. However, as noted in the earlier discussion, larger countries may be deliberately passed over in certain chair assignments, especially in the GC and trade negotiating committees, due to the perception that the influence of already powerful countries in the WTO would otherwise be unduly enhanced. Another regression variant, using the square of per capita GDP as an additional variable, shows furthermore in OLS and P regressions that increasing per capita GDP may increase the number of chairs, but at a decreasing rate. Thus, developing countries will continue to receive more chairs as their income rises, but this number will peak at a certain level and then decline.[20]

If the P and NB regressions more accurately capture the statistical relationships, it appears that the OLS model tends to overestimate the impact of GenMis, GATT/WTO, and ManExGdp, while failing to identify the significance of the EM and LDC dummy effects. In general, however, the results support the hypothesis that a country's WTO "capacity," experience, and motivation for foreign market access for its manufactures positively influence the number of chair appointments it receives. These factors presumably make chair candidates from those countries both more attractive, and more eager to use their skills to promote trade liberalization. With regard to the dummy variables, or alternatively using the per capita GDP variables, it is not clear from the results whether EM candidates are "favored" by the selection process because of their EM status, or if perhaps they systematically invest more effort and resources into developing attractive chair candidates because of inherent EM interests in trade. The same question could be asked in the opposite way regarding the negative coefficient for LDCs. A meritocratic argument for chair appointments gives more credence to the latter view, that EM economic and trade interests amplify efforts to develop chair candidates, while LDCs, more poorly positioned to gain from trade in general, devote systematically fewer resources to this end.[21]

PROBIT RESULTS

Additional detail regarding the determinants of chair appointments is possible if data can be arrayed to show how each country's attributes affect the probability that it will receive a chair appointment in a given year. Table 5.5 shows representative results from Probit regressions using panel data, combining cross-section and time series data of WTO chair assignments. The dependent variable is a $(0,1)$ outcome for country i in time period j, with the value "1" representing at least one chair assignment for that country in that year, "0" representing no chair assignment.[22] Results are reported in terms of the estimated coefficients, plus a secondary calculation of the "marginal effect" of a change in the relevant variable by one unit (i.e., the increased

Table 5.5 PANEL REGRESSION (PROBIT): PROBABILITY OF WTO CHAIR APPOINTMENT. DEP. VAR.: CHAIR APPOINTMENT BY COUNTRY BY YEAR (0/1)

Variables	Variant 1	Variant 2	Variant 3	Variant 4	Variant 5	Variant 6	Variant 7	Variant 8
Constant	-2.550***	-2.592***	-2.585***	-2.513***	-2.579***	-2.434***	-2.950***	-2.450***
P value	[0.000]	[0.000]	[0.000]	[0.000]	[0.000]	[0.000]	[0.000]	[0.000]
GenevaMiss	0.113***	0.104***	0.110***	0.111***	0.114***	0.099***	0.111***	0.104***
Marginal effect	0.020	0.019	0.020	0.020	0.021	0.019	0.020	0.020
P value	[0.000]	[0.000]	[0.000]	[0.000]	[0.000]	[0.000]	[0.000]	[0.000]
MnfExGDP	0.008*	0.009**	0.008**	0.007*	0.008*	0.007*	0.008*	0.009***
Marginal effect	0.001	0.002	0.001	0.001	0.001	0.001	0.001	0.002
P value	[0.055]	[0.014]	[0.044]	[0.067]	[0.052]	[0.028]	[0.034]	[0.007]
AgExGDP	0.018	0.013	0.010	0.017	0.018	0.010	0.022	0.008
Marginal effect	0.003	0.002	0.002	0.003	0.003	0.002	0.004	0.002
P value	[0.252]	[0.410]	[0.502]	[0.256]	[0.249]	[0.471]	[0.159]	[0.546]
YrsGattWTO	0.018***	0.021***	0.022***	0.017***	0.019***	0.016***	0.018***	0.017***
Marginal effect	0.003	0.004	0.004	0.003	0.003	0.003	0.003	0.003
P value	[0.000]	[0.000]	[0.000]	[0.001]	[0.001]	[0.000]	[0.000]	[0.000]
EMdummy	0.691**	0.484*	0.437	0.711**	0.678**	0.322	0.756***	...
Marginal effect	0.125	0.088	0.080	0.129	0.123	0.061	0.137	...
P value	[0.014]	[0.066]	[0.120]	[0.012]	[0.016]	[0.153]	[0.007]	[...]

LDCdummy	...	-0.844***	-0.862***	...	...	-0.640**	...	-0.687***
Marginal effect	...	-0.153	-0.159	...	...	-0.121	...	-0.130
P value	[...]	[0.004]	[0.006]	[...]	[...]	[0.011]	[...]	[0.006]
Devdummy	-0.232	...	...	-0.292	-0.206	...	...	...
Marginal effect	-0.042	...	...	-0.053	-0.037	...	...	...
P value	[0.450]	[...]	[...]	[0.375]	[0.518]	[...]	[...]	[...]
Devdummy2000	...	...	...	0.063	...	...	...	...
Marginal effect	...	...	...	0.011	...	...	...	...
P value	[...]	[...]	[...]	[0.609]	[...]	[...]	[...]	[...]
Devdummy04	...	...	...	...	-0.031	...	...	...
Marginal effect	...	...	...	...	-0.006	...	...	...
P value	[...]	[...]	[...]	[...]	[0.767]	[...]	[...]	[...]
RealGDP	-0.144	-0.147	-0.147	-0.142	-0.145	-0.115	...	...
Marginal effect	-0.026	-0.027	-0.027	-0.026	-0.026	-0.022	...	...
P value	[0.145]	[0.134]	[0.134]	[0.151]	[0.141]	[0.167]	[...]	[...]
GDPcap	0.004	0.000	0.000	0.004	0.004	0.001	0.044**	0.009
Marginal effect	0.001	0.000	0.000	0.001	0.001	0.000	0.008	0.002
P value	[0.694]	[0.992]	[0.992]	[0.673]	[0.699]	[0.884]	[0.011]	[0.534]

(continued)

Table 5.5 CONTINUED

Variables	Variant 1	Variant 2	Variant 3	Variant 4	Variant 5	Variant 6	Variant 7	Variant 8
GDPcap–sq	...	...	...	...	...	...	-0.001**	-0.000
Marginal effect	...	...	...	...	...	...	-0.000	-0.000
P value	[..]	[..]	[..]	[..]	[..]	[..]	[0.032]	[0.394]
Lagchair	...	...	...	...	...	0.689***	...	0.695***
Marginal effect	...	...	...	...	...	0.130	...	0.132
P value	[..]	[..]	[..]	[..]	[..]	[0.000]	[..]	[0.000]
Expshare	0.115	0.058	0.121*	0.116	0.115	0.076	...	...
Marginal effect	0.021	0.011	0.022	0.021	0.021	0.014	...	...
P value	[0.105]	[0.280]	[0.081]	[0.103]	[0.105]	[0.222]	[..]	[..]
N of Obs	1986	2000	1986	1986	1986	1986	1994	1994
Pseudo R2	0.174	0.176	0.178	0.174	0.174	0.205	0.174	0.203

* P < 0.1 significant at 10%;
** P < 0.05 significant at 5%;
*** P < 0.01 significant at 1%.

probability of receiving a chair assignment associated with a unit increase in the independent variable). The results thus reflect not only cross-country differences (as the aggregate data did) but also the inter-temporal changes for a given country over the time period. This modeling also allows testing of time shift dummies, to show the possible impact of events such as the Seattle (1999) and Cancun (2003) MCs on chair assignments, and the impact of a lagged dependent variable.

As suggested by the regression results in table 5.4, the panel regressions using Probit in table 5.5 also indicate that GenMis, GattWto, and ManExGdp positively affect the probability that the country will have at least one chair appointment in that year. For example, an increase by one staff member in a country's Geneva mission increases the probability of its receiving a chair appointment by approximately 2%, an additional year as a member of the WTO increases this probability by 0.3 to 0.4%, and a one percentage point increase in its manufactures exports-to-GDP ratio increases the probability by 0.1 to 0.2%. Emerging market countries have an increased probability of 6 to 14% of receiving one or more chair appointments in a given year, while for LDCs the probability decreases by 12 to 16%. Coefficients for most other variables were usually insignificant. Notably, the dummies for post-Seattle (year 2000 +) and post-Cancun (year 2004 +), presenting the hypothesis that developing countries would experience a boost in chair appointments in the wake of these two crisis Ministerial meetings, were not significant in any regression that included GenMis.[23] Per capita GDP was rarely significant, except when tested in conjunction with its square (variant 7). Finally, the LagChair variable, which introduces the previous year's chair outcome (0 or 1) as an independent variable for the following year, shows a strong positive and significant effect: a country that received a chair appointment in the previous year has a 13% increased probability of receiving another chair appointment in the current year. Lagchair diminishes, however, the significance of the EM dummy, perhaps as it is picking up some of the repeat EM country appointments.

In summary, the same variables that influenced the number of total chairs over the entire period also increased the probability of a country receiving a chair appointment in a given year during the period. Thus, the panel data lend added support to the hypothesis that capacity, experience in the WTO system, and motivation to seek improved foreign market access play significant roles in a country's "WTO human capital endowment," thereby increasing its tendency to receive chair assignments. In addition, the panel data indicate that the GC did not systematically change the distribution of chair appointments between developed and developing (or within developing) countries in the post-Seattle and post-Cancun periods. The most interesting new information from the panel data was in fact that the GC tends to base its current appointment decisions in part on prior chair experience, either within the country, or by individuals under consideration.

DETERMINANTS OF MISSION SIZE

While the role of the individual is important, especially in the more prominent standing and negotiating committees, the regression results still show
that a country's mission size is of great importance in predicting a country
representation through chairmanships. This observation begs the prior question of what determines the size of a country's mission. Table 5.6 shows the
results of regressions on average mission size, using average values of the variables from 1995 to 2011, and rounding the average mission size to the closest
unit value for the Poisson (P) and Negative Binomial (NB) regressions. Using
this cross-sectional comparison among WTO member countries, export share
plays a consistently positive role. The OLS regressions imply that a one percentage point increase in a country's share in world exports (Expsh) increases
its Geneva mission size by one person, a result consistent with VanGrasstek's
estimate (2008). Under the P and BN assumptions of count data distribution,
the export share effect is somewhat smaller, evaluated at the mean value of the
independent variables. Years of GATT/WTO membership have a small but significant effect on mission size, adding 0.3 to 0.4 persons for every additional ten
years of membership. Emerging market country mission sizes are significantly
larger, by 3 to 4 persons, while LDC missions are 1.1 to 1.3 persons smaller.
Other variables tend not to be significant, although ManExGdp comes close in
some P and BN regressions.

Panel data regression results, using OLS and Poisson methods, combine
cross-section and time series data for all countries in the study and are shown
in table 5.7. The Emerging Markets and LDC dummies have similar results
to those of the average value regressions, as expected. Year-to-year impacts
for other variables differ, however. A one percentage point increase in global
export share increases mission size by.3 to.4 persons when considering combined cross-section and time series data, for example. Each additional year of
WTO membership adds about 0.1 to 0.2 members to the mission size, a much
larger effect than in the cross-sectional results. In addition, real GDP is positively associated with mission size in the OLS, but not the P regressions, while
per capita GDP is negatively associated with mission size in most panel regressions. Increases in mission size among the fastest growing emerging markets
may have been captured in the EM dummy, and in addition, rich country mission sizes are not proportionately larger than those of countries with low per
capita income. Given the impact of other factors, per capita income's marginal

Table 5.6 Determinants of Size of Geneva Mission, Aggregate Data, 1996–2011 Dependent Variable: Average Size of Geneva Mission, n = 152

Variables	OLS Variant 1	Variant 2	Variant 3	Variables	Poisson Variant 1	Variant 2	Variant 3	Negative Binomial Variant 1	Variant 2	Variant 3
Constant	2.298***	2.644***	3.940***	Constant	0.922***	1.023***	1.347***	0.859***	0.964***	1.246***
P value	[0.000]	[0.000]	[0.001]	P value	[0.000]	[0.000]	[0.000]	[0.000]	[0.000]	[0.000]
Expsh	1.014***	1.008***	0.961***	Expsh	0.141***	0.138***	0.129***	0.161***	0.158***	0.145**
P value	[0.001]	[0.001]	[0.002]	Marginal effect	0.582	0.566	0.524	0.660	0.642	0.591
				P value	[0.000]	[0.000]	[0.000]	[0.007]	[0.006]	[0.010]
MnfExGDP	0.015	0.013	0.007	MnfExGDP	0.004*	0.004*	0.002	0.005	0.004	0.003
P value	[0.295]	[0.341]	[0.651]	Marginal effect	0.016	0.015	0.009	0.020	0.018	0.013
				P value	[0.054]	[0.067]	[0.316]	[0.102]	[0.118]	[0.297]
RealGDP	0.331	0.316	0.319	RealGDP	0.001	0.000	0.004	-0.002	-0.005	-0.000
P value	[0.403]	[0.422]	[0.416]	Marginal effect	0.003	0.002	0.015	-0.010	-0.018	-0.001
				P value	[0.985]	[0.991]	[0.921]	[0.974]	[0.949]	[0.996]
GDPcap	-0.004	-0.018	-0.039	GDPcap	0.001	-0.003	-0.009*	0.000	-0.003	-0.008
P value	[0.851]	[0.395]	[0.148]	Marginal effect	0.005	-0.010	-0.035	0.000	-0.014	-0.034
				P value	[0.739]	[0.506]	[0.079]	[0.991]	[0.467]	[0.163]
AgExGDP	-0.022	-0.043	-0.040	AgExGDP	-0.010	-0.015	-0.013	-0.007	-0.013	-0.012
P value	[0.661]	[0.388]	[0.431]	Marginal effect	-0.041	-0.063	-0.053	-0.027	-0.053	-0.047
				P value	[0.301]	[0.121]	[0.193]	[0.578]	[0.288]	[0.341]

(continued)

Table 5.6 Continued

Variables	OLS			Variables	Poisson			Negative Binomial		
	Variant 1	Variant 2	Variant 3		Variant 1	Variant 2	Variant 3	Variant 1	Variant 2	Variant 3
YrsGattWTO	0.028**	0.034**	0.031**	YrsGattWTO	0.008***	0.009***	0.009***	0.009***	0.010***	0.010***
P value	[0.029]	[0.010]	[0.020]	Marginal effect	0.034	0.038	0.036	0.037	0.041	0.039
				P value	[0.000]	[0.000]	[0.000]	[0.002]	[0.000]	[0.001]
EM	3.675***	3.282***	3.458***	EM	0.665***	0.563***	0.612***	0.642***	0.545***	0.584***
P value	[0.000]	[0.000]	[0.000]	Marginal effect	3.582	2.882	3.186	3.405	2.753	2.993
				P value	[0.000]	[0.000]	[0.000]	[0.000]	[0.000]	[0.000]
Dvlpng	…	…	-1.196	Dvlpng	…	…	-0.320**	…	…	-0.268
P value	[..]	[..]	[0.194]	Marginal effect	…	…	-1.429	…	…	-1.173
				P value	[..]	[..]	[0.036]	[..]	[..]	[0.176]
LDC	…	-1.142*	-1.111*	LDC	…	-0.341**	-0.326**	…	-0.324**	-0.315**
P value	[..]	[0.071]	[0.078]	Marginal effect	…	-1.266	-1.210	…	-1.205	-1.170
				P value	[..]	[0.010]	[0.014]	[..]	[0.039]	[0.043]
R²	0.491	0.502	0.508	Pseudo R²	0.200	0.208	0.213	0.098	0.104	0.106

* P < 0.1 significant at 10%;
** P < 0.05 significant at 5%;
*** P < 0.01 significant at 1%.

Table 5.7 PANEL DATA: DETERMINANTS OF SIZE OF GENEVA MISSION IN A COUNTRY

OLS

Variables	Variant 1	Variant 2	Variant 3
Constant	0.139	0.423	0.766**
P value	[0.754]	[0.361]	[0.028]
MnfExGDP	-0.002	-0.000	-0.003
P value	[0.707]	[0.956]	[0.498]
AgExGDP	-0.033***	-0.035***	-0.032***
P value	[0.007]	[0.004]	[0.007]
YrsGattWTO	0.113***	0.118***	0.112***
P value	[0.000]	[0.000]	[0.000]
EMdummy	3.316***	3.093***	3.134***
P value	[0.000]	[0.000]	[0.000]
LDCdummy	...	...	-1.314**
P value	[...]	[...]	[0.032]

Poisson

Variables	Variant 1	Variant 2	Variant 3
Constant	0.559***	0.658***	0.699***
P value	[0.000]	[0.000]	[0.000]
MnfExGDP	-0.000	0.000	-0.000
Marginal effect	-0.001	0.002	-0.003
P value	[0.885]	[0.850]	[0.767]
AgExGDP	-0.019***	-0.021***	-0.019***
Marginal effect	-0.108	-0.122	-0.110
P value	[0.004]	[0.002]	[0.003]
YrsGattWTO	0.027***	0.030***	0.027***
Marginal effect	0.153	0.171	0.152
P value	[0.000]	[0.000]	[0.000]
EMdummy	0.619**	0.545**	0.565**
Marginal effect	3.492	3.136	3.204
P value	[0.016]	[0.039]	[0.029]
LDCdummy	...	...	-0.346
Marginal effect	...	...	-1.958
P value	[...]	[...]	[0.121]

(continued)

Table 5.7 CONTINUED

	OLS				Poisson		
Variables	**Variant 1**	**Variant 2**	**Variant 3**	**Variables**	**Variant 1**	**Variant 2**	**Variant 3**
Devdummy	0.361	0.165	...	Devdummy	0.074	0.014	...
				Marginal effect	0.419	0.080	...
P value	[0.262]	[0.624]	[...]	P value	[0.501]	[0.903]	[...]
RealGDP	1.096***	1.162***	1.051***	RealGDP	0.036	0.054	0.030
				Marginal effect	0.205	0.313	0.173
P value	[0.000]	[0.000]	[0.000]	P value	[0.420]	[0.237]	[0.498]
GDPcap	...	-0.029**	...	GDPcap	...	-0.011**	...
				Marginal effect	...	-0.061	...
P value	[...]	[0.042]	[...]	P value	[...]	[0.040]	[...]
Expshare	0.364***	0.373***	0.333***	Expshare	0.065***	0.065***	0.061***
				Marginal effect	0.366	0.377	0.345
P value	[0.000]	[0.000]	[0.000]	P value	[0.004]	[0.003]	[0.006]
N of Obs	1986	1986	1986	N of Obs	1986	1986	1986
R^2	0.374	0.366	0.392	Pseudo R^2	0.147	0.148	0.147

* $P < 0.1$ significant at 10%;
** $P < 0.05$ significant at 5%;
*** $P < 0.01$ significant at 1%.

effect, in itself, is apparently slightly negative. AgExGdp also becomes a significant but perhaps perversely negative determinant of mission size. While the effect is small, it may indicate a sort of trade liberalization pessimism over this period for agricultural exporters, who had seen their hopes dashed of the Uruguay Round promise of bringing agricultural trade under WTO discipline, as the early years of the WTO and the Doha Round dragged on with little progress on this issue.

The panel regressions in particular indicate that global export share, years of GATT/WTO membership, and the development status of emerging markets all have significant positive effects on the size of a country's Geneva mission using the pooled cross-section and time series data, while LDC status, per capita GDP, and the share of agricultural exports in GDP have negative effects. Mission size is therefore influenced by some, but not all, of the same determinants as the country's propensity to receive chair appointments. Export share is a strong determinant of mission size, and in most regressions on chair appointments, these two statistics are substitutes for each other, with mission size having the stronger impact and significance.[24] Years of GATT/WTO membership, on the other hand, appear to influence both mission size and chair appointments independently, as do emerging market status (positive) and LDC status (negative). All of these variables appear to provide the statistical measures that ultimately indicate a country's commitment to devote resources toward developing experienced and knowledgeable diplomats for chair positions.

MULTIPLE APPOINTMENTS

The regression results suggest that the GC tends to appoint WTO chairs from member countries that exhibit sufficient capacity, experience with the GATT/WTO system, and motivation to take an active role in trade negotiations and the WTO administration. There is also evidence that the GC considers previous chair experience. At the same time, the pattern of chair appointments seems to balance representation between developed and developing countries, and that some attention is also paid to the geographical distribution of chair nationalities, even though many countries never received a chair appointment. In general, the pattern of chair appointments suggests that nationality itself is not a primary determinant, but that the country's membership in a larger development or geographical group is. The chair positions are important to the functioning of the WTO, and it is important to appoint the right person for the job, based at least in part on individual qualifications, including, for the most important chair positions, experience.

The pattern of appointments to chair the GC itself, along with chairs for its coequal committees, the Dispute Settlement Body (DSB) and the Trade Policy Review Body (TPRB), show how such decisions, made annually, tend to reveal a deliberate process of sequencing and "grooming." Table 5.8 tabulates the chair appointments for these three committees from 1995 to 2012. Beginning in 1996, the preparation for appointment of GC chair began with the candidate's preliminary service as chair of the DSB, or in two cases, the TPRB. There have been just a few exceptions to this rule, and it has now become embedded as a predictable preparation for service as GC chair. Many of these same chairs had also previously served on the Goods, Services, or TRIPS Councils, so that senior level chairs are groomed through experience chairing subsidiary committees. Yet these high-profile chair positions also have symbolic importance in reflecting the overall membership of the WTO. The nationalities of these chair appointments have been balanced exactly between developed and developing countries over the period 1995–2012, with twenty-seven appointments for each group in the three main committees. For the Goods, Services, and TRIPS Councils, the balance was nearly even, with twenty-seven developed and thirty-three developing country chairs. Geographically, representation was not proportional to membership, but an effort in achieving some balance is evident. For the three main committees, fifteen appointments went to the Americas, fourteen each to East Asia/Oceana and Europe, eight to sub-Mediterranean Africa, and five to North African/Middle East. For the Goods, Services, and TRIPS Councils, fifteen went to the Americas, nineteen to East Asia/Oceana, sixteen to Europe, seven to Sub-Mediterranean Africa, and just one to the North African/Middle East region. Further unwritten rules for chair appointments to these six major committees appear to include provisions that there will be no consecutive reappointments of individuals to the same chair, no consecutive appointments to delegates from the same country, and no appointments for the US or chief EU ambassadors.[25]

Chairs of other WTO committees, however, often serve consecutive terms. Table 5.9 shows the number of consecutive years served by committee chairs by committee category. As noted above, consecutive terms do not occur on the six main committees, but on subsidiary committees to the GC, there were several multi-year consecutive term appointments. For the GC subsidiary committees (excluding the three Councils), 28 out of 123 annual chair appointments (23%) took the form of reappointments from 1995 to 2012. Consecutive chair reappointments to the subsidiary committees of the Goods and Services Councils were 15% and 10%, respectively, of the total, and reappointments to the two plurilateral committees accounted for 65% of total appointments. For these chairs, specialized knowledge of the committee's focus, accumulated experience, and continuity may have more weight (fewer member signatories for the

Table 5.8 Promotion Toward Chair of the WTO General Council, 1995–2012

Committee	1995	1996	1997	1998	1999	2000
General Council	Kesavapany Singapore	Rossier Switzerland	Lafer Brazil	Weekes Canada	Mchumo Tanzania	Bryne Norway
Dispute Settlement	Kenyon Australia	Lafer Brazil	New Zealand	Morjane Tunisia	Akao/Bryne Japan/Norway	Harbison HK,China
Trade Policy Review	Londono Columbia	Anderson Ireland	Akram Pakistan	Mchumo Tanzania	Noirfalisse Belgium	Chowdhury Bangladesh

Committee	2001	2002	2003	2004	2005	2006
General Council	Harbison HK, China	Marchi Canada	Perez del Castillo Uruguay	Oshima Japan	Mohamed Kenya	Glenne Norway
Dispute Settlement	Farrell/Bryn NZ/Norway	Perez del Castillo Uruguay	Oshima Japan	Mohamed Kenya	Glenne Norway	Noor Malaysia
Trade Policy Review	Hutanieme Finland	Mohamed Kenya	Whelan Ireland	Asavapisit Thailand	Stephenson Canada	Uribe Colombia

Committee	2007	2008	2009	2010	2011	2012
General Council	Noor Malaysia	Gosper Australia	Matus Chile	Gero Canada	Agah Nigeria	Johansen Norway
Dispute Settlement	Gosper Australia	Noor Malaysia	Gero Canada	Agah Nigeria	Johansen Norway	Bashir Pakistan
Trade Policy Review	Himanen Finland	Agah Nigeria	Major Hungary	Aran Turkey	Matus Chile	MunozGomez Colombia

Table 5.9 WTO Committees: Consecutive Reappointments, by Committee Type, 1995–2012

Length of appointment	Total number of years of repeat appointments					
	Main (GC, DSB, TPRB, Goods, Services, TRIPS Councils)	Other GC Subsidiary	Goods subsidiary	Services subsidiary	Plurilateral	Doha
Two-year	0	16	18	4	6	16
Three-year	0	2	8	0	4	6
Four-year	0	0	3	3	3	9
Five-year	0	4	0	0	0	16
Six-year	0	0	5	0	0	5
Seven-year	0	6	0	0	0	0
Eight-year	0	0	0	0	7	0
Total	**0**	**28**	**34**	**7**	**20**	**52**
Appointment opportunities	**108**	**123**	**232**	**69**	**31**	**88**
Percentage of appointment opportunities	**0**	**23**	**15**	**10**	**65**	**59**

source: WTO Committee Chair tables.

plurilateral agreements also play a role in the pattern of chair appointments those committees), while development status and geographical distribution still play important roles in the GC's appointment decisions.

Appointments to the Doha Round negotiating committees reflect the high value of continuity in the chair's position. The chair must bring all of his or her diplomatic skills, strategic thinking, and powers of persuasion to bear in the negotiations in order to move the committee toward consensus on the often contentious issues it faces, and the protracted nature of WTO negotiations typically requires longer periods of time for this task. Most chairs on Doha Round committees served two-year terms, but there were also numerous three-, four-, and five-year terms, and one six-year term. Overall, 59% of all chair appointments for these committees were consecutive reappointments. While the number of chair appointments given to developing countries was greater (thirty-six for developed, fifty-five for developing countries), the emphasis on continuity significantly reduced the geographical balance of the chairs. Counting each chair year separately, nine chairs came from Europe, five from sub-Mediterranean Africa, five from North Africa/Middle East, thirty-eight from East Asia/Oceana, and thirty-four from the Americas. The two-year terms often tended to coincide with the Ministerial meeting cycle, when the membership (and the GC) could take stock of the progress on various negotiating issues and decide if new leadership was called for. The frustration of the Doha Round, which lurched from one crisis-induced stalemate to the next, probably increased the amount of turnover in chair assignments.

The selection of Doha Negotiating committee chairs, with its presumed emphasis on the particular personal attributes needed to move the discussions toward consensus, focused on individuals, within the constraint of development status representation. In general, there appears to be a strong reliance on multiple and consecutive appointments for other committees as well. Of the 443 individuals identified as WTO committee chairs during the period 1995–2011, 284 served just once, 82 served twice, 44 served three times, and 11 served four times. Table 5.10 lists twenty-two trade officials who have each served five or more times as WTO chairs, counting each year on a committee chair as a separate appointment, except for Accession WP chairs, which count as one for the total time served. This group, representing about 5% of individuals who have served as WTO chairs during this period, has filled about 20% of the chair assignments. Nine are from developed, fourteen from developing, countries. Many of these individuals have served as chairs of the Doha committees and of the most prominent standing committees, such as the GC, DSB, and Goods and Services Councils, as well as the Working Parties on Accession. The GC, in its chair appointments, thus attains its goals of development status balance, and in most cases, geographical balance, in part through multiple

Table 5.10 WTO Chairmanships: Those Serving Five Times or More, 1995–2011

Name	Total	Country	GC Committees, Subcommittees	Doha Committees	Reappointments (years)	Accession WP
Saborio Soto	13	Costa Rica	CG, Region, TranspGP	D-DSB	Region (2), TranspGP (5), D-DSB (5)	
Falconer	10	New Zealand		Ag, Cotton	D-Ag (5), Cotton (5)	
Chambovey	8	Switzerland	CivAir		CivAir (8)	
Valles Galmés	8	Uruguay	Rules	Rules	Rules (7)	Algeria
Agah	7	Nigeria	TPRB, DSB, CG, CS, CTrips, GC	TRIPS		
Ahmad	7	Pakistan	BoP, ROO	TRIPS	TRIPS (5)	
Groser	7	New Zealand		D-Ag, Cotton, Rules	D-Ag (2), D-Cotton (2), Rules (2)	Lao P.D.R.
Harbinson	7	HK (3), Sec (3)	DSB, GC, CS, CTrips	D-Ag	D-Ag (2)	Tonga
Jenny	7	France	WGComp		WGComp (7)	
Major	6	Hungary	TPRB, CG, CS, CTrips, Enviro			Bosnia/Herz
Niggli	6	Switzerland	Specif		GovPro (5)	
Teehankee	6	Philippines	Enviro, TransfTech	D-Enviro	TransfTech (2), D-Enviro (3)	
Thorstensen	6	Brazil	ROO		ROO (6)	

			Devel	D-Enviro	D-Enviro (4)	
Ali	5	Bangladesh				FYROM
Bryn	5	Norway	DSB (twice), GC		Doha-Trips (2)	
Clarke	5	Barbados	CS, C-Trips, Devel, Trips			
De Mateo	5	Mexico		Services	Services (5)	
Hovorka	5	Czech Republic	CG (twice), BoP, AD, SCV			
Jara	5	Chile	Enviro	Services	Services (4)	
Jóhannesson	5	Iceland	TransfTech	NAMA	TransfTech (2), NAMA (2)	Russian Fed.
Perez del Castillo	5	Uruguay	DSB, GC, CG, CTrips			Algeria
Servansing	5	Mauritius	Devel, Enviro		Devel (3), Enviro (2)	
Total	143					

NOTE: Eleven individuals served as WTO chair four times, 44 served three times, 82 served twice, and 284 served once.

LEGEND: AD: Committee on Anti-Dumping; BoP: Committee on Balance-of-Payments Restrictions; CG: Council for Trade in Goods; CivAir: Committee on Trade in Civil Aircraft; Cotton: Sub-Committee on Cotton; CS: Council for Trade in Services; CTrips: Council for Trade-Related Intellectual Property; D-Ag: Special Session of the Committee on Agriculture; D-DSB: Special Session of the Dispute Settlement Body; D-Enviro: Special Session of the Committee on Trade and Environment; Devel: Committee on Trade and Development; DSB: Dispute Settlement Body; Enviro: Committee on Trade and Environment; GC: General Council; GovPro: Committee on Government Procurement; NAMA: Negotiating Group on Market Access; Region: Committee on Regional Trade Agreements; ROO: Committee on Rules of Origin; Rules: Negotiating Group on Rules; SCV: Committee on Subsidies and Countervailing Measures; Services: Special Session of the Council for Trade in Services; Specif: Committee on Specific Commitments; TranspGP: Working Group on Transparency in Government Procurement; TPRM: Trade Policy Review Body; TransfTech: Working Group on Trade and Transfer of Technology; TRIPS: Special Session of the Council for TRIPS; WGComp: Working Group on Trade and Competition Policy.

SOURCE: WTO Committee Chair Tables.

appointments of individuals from a relatively small number of countries, a process that also serves to increase the experience and quality of chairs for more important positions later.[26]

SUMMARY AND CONCLUSION

The GC decided on hundreds of WTO chair appointments from 1995 to 2011, and in the absence of any documentation of the deliberations, the statistical record provides indirect but substantial evidence that there are two basic elements to the decision: first, the quality and ability of a country's candidates to carry out a particular committee's chair functions, and second, achieving balance in representation, primarily between developed and developing countries, but also, over time, in membership geography. The first element, in turn, depends on the total and individual "human capital" embodied in a country's candidates. A country's mission size appears to capture at least some of this information, as larger missions can simultaneously support chair activities by a staff member, in addition to other WTO business. Larger missions may also indicate higher quality among the country's chair candidates. Rapidly growing, emerging market countries, in particular, appear to have invested heavily in supporting larger missions. In addition, the primary determinant of mission size appears to be global export share, which will motivate rapidly growing, globalizing economies to invest in trade negotiating "assets" and be ready and willing to accept leadership positions on WTO committees. Finally, one can expect individuals' personal attributes, presumably based on unobserved individual background, training, and leadership skills, and on observed prior WTO chair experience (or experience of others from the same mission), to enhance the candidate's attractiveness for a chair appointment. The role of these human capital elements is captured by the regressions results. Development status and geographical distribution factors appear in the observed patterns that point to the GC's balancing practices in chair appointments. Political and other unobserved factors regarding individual candidates are presumably behind the details of many choices, in filling chair positions.[27] In GC deliberations over chair assignments, strong objections by individual country delegations reportedly arise over disputes regarding previous policy and appointment decisions and even personal factors.[28] Accession committee chair appointments also appear to be driven by somewhat different criteria than those for other committees, due to the importance of bilateral negotiations and funding issues associated with the accession process.[29] Further research is required to identify the detailed choice criteria, based on the individual qualifications of candidates under consideration, and the political and other criteria that enter the GC's decision-making process.

While there is strong evidence that the GC carefully assembles a balanced roster of chair appointments each year, there is no evidence that it systematically favored (or disfavored) developing countries in its decisions after the Seattle and Cancun Ministerial meetings. Rather, it is evident that representation of developing countries in WTO chair appointments has increased over the years in large part on the basis of their increasing mission size and time as WTO members, leading to more experience and knowledge among their trade diplomats, and increasing resources to support their work and their countries' interests in the WTO. These results suggest the importance of increasing commitments by countries to their Geneva WTO missions, especially the poorer, under-represented developing countries, and to the development of expertise and experience in trade, trade diplomacy, and WTO affairs, as a way to increase their participation in WTO governance. In turn, the greater competency of WTO delegations, and their greater understanding of, and involvement in, WTO affairs, imply more informed negotiations and perhaps even a greater chance of achieving new multilateral trade liberalization. However, additional detailed research on the Doha negotiations themselves, including testimony from the negotiators, is required to determine how, if at all, the choice of critical committee chairs has affected progress in the Doha Round, and how this might inform future chair appointments. Yet the challenges of an enlarged membership, a more complicated agenda, and a shifting balance of power in the WTO may have put consensus beyond the reach of even the most talented chairs, and may point to the need for reforms in the structure of WTO negotiations.

The evidence of a meritocratic approach to committee chair appointments carries two further implications for the future of WTO multilateral negotiations. The technical expertise that has been developed especially in several subsidiary bodies of the Councils for Trade in Goods and Trade in Services could serve as a resource, not only of ideas and information for future negotiations but also as venues for deliberations on new issues as well. As noted earlier in this chapter, this would be a new approach to the negotiating process, but it may provide a direct way to explore paths for reform and compromise that are closer to those with the most knowledge on the subjects. One senior WTO trade official from a developing country has in fact suggested that the system of traditional trade negotiations and summitry by senior trade officials is no longer capable of identifying the best pathways for consensus on the increasingly technical issues of contemporary trade relations.[30] An "inversion" of committee leadership in the negotiations, with standing committees leading the negotiating groups, would allow for a more informed ongoing discussion of critical issues. Any cross-issue trade-offs would certainly require higher level political scrutiny, and in any case each country's delegation would have to be in close communication with its capital. However, an additional suggestion would be to follow several discrete paths to consensus on individual issues, allowing "rolling" negotiations in specific committees to lead to separate agreements. Institutionally, such an arrangement may in fact make it easier for experts to identify common ground on policy space in new and controversial areas of negotiation.

The meritocratic nature of committee selection also signals a warning to WTO members regarding the future of the organization in general. The results suggest that member countries will invest in the quality of their delegations in large part according to the benefits they hope to gain from WTO rules and trade liberalization. If the WTO were to become an ineffectual backwater for trade liberalization, its value could diminish and lead to members to deploy their trade diplomacy talent elsewhere. The implementation and dispute settlement functions of the WTO, to be sure, have remained strong and enjoy widespread support, but, as noted in earlier chapters, a failure of the trade negotiating function could eventually undermine these functions through the obsolescence of existing rules and global market access arrangements. Returning to the bicycle metaphor from chapter 1, trade organizations, like the negotiations they sponsor, need to keep moving forward, lest they fall over. Continued investments in trade diplomacy at the WTO are therefore required in order to maintain the organization's ability to negotiate future trade agreements.

APPENDIX: Rosters of Country Groupings

Groupings by Development Status

Developed Country WTO Members (35): Australia, Austria, Belgium, Canada, Cyprus, Czech Republic, Denmark, Estonia, Finland, France, Germany, Greece, Hong Kong, Iceland, Ireland, Israel, Italy, Japan, Lichtenstein, Luxembourg, Malta, Netherlands, New Zealand, Norway, Portugal, Singapore, Slovakia, Slovenia, South Korea, Spain, Sweden, Switzerland, Taiwan, United Kingdom, United States.

Developing Country WTO Members (117): Albania, Angola, Antigua and Barbuda, Argentina, Armenia, Azerbaijan, Bahrain, Bangladesh, Barbados, Belize, Benin, Bolivia, Botswana, Brazil, Brunei, Bulgaria, Burkina Faso, Burma (Myanmar), Burundi, Cambodia, Cameroon, Cape Verde, Central African Republic, Chad, China, Colombia, Democratic Republic of Congo, Republic of the Congo, Costa Rica, Cote d'Ivoire, Croatia, Cuba, Djibouti, Dominica, Dominican Republic, Ecuador, Egypt, El Salvador, Fiji, Gabon, Gambia, Georgia, Ghana, Grenada, Guatemala, Guinea, Guinea-Bissau, Guyana,

Haiti, Honduras, Hungary, India, Indonesia, Jamaica, Jordan, Kenya, Kuwait, Kyrgyzstan, Latvia, Lesotho, Lithuania, Macao, Macedonia, Madagascar, Malawi, Malaysia, Maldives, Mali, Mauritania, Mauritius, Mexico, Moldova, Mongolia, Morocco, Mozambique, Namibia, Nepal, Nicaragua, Niger, Nigeria, Oman, Pakistan, Panama, Papua New Guinea, Paraguay, Peru, Philippines, Poland, Qatar, Romania, Rwanda, Saint Kitts and Nevis, Saint Lucia, Saint Vincent and the Grenadines. Saudi Arabia, Senegal, Sierra Leone, Solomon Islands, South Africa, Sri Lanka, Suriname, Swaziland, Tanzania, Thailand, Togo, Tonga, Trinidad and Tobago, Tunisia, Turkey, Uganda, Ukraine, United Arab Emirates, Uruguay, Venezuela, Vietnam, Zambia, Zimbabwe.

Emerging Market WTO Members (18): Brazil, Chile, China, Colombia, Egypt, Hungary, India, Indonesia, Malaysia, Mexico, Morocco, Peru, Philippines, Poland, South Africa, Thailand, Turkey.

Least Developed Country (LDC) WTO Members (31): Angola, Bangladesh, Benin, Burkina Faso, Burundi, Cambodia, Central African Republic, Chad, Democratic Republic of Congo, Djibouti, Gambia, Guinea, Guinea Bissau, Haiti, Lesotho, Madagascar, Malawi, Mali, Mauritania, Mozambique, Myanmar, Nepal, Niger, Rwanda, Senegal, Sierra Leone, Solomon Islands, Tanzania, Togo, Uganda, Zambia.

WTO Geographical Country Groups

Europe (37): Albania, Austria, Belgium, Bulgaria, Croatia, Cyprus, Czech Republic, Denmark, Estonia, Finland, France, Germany, Greece, Hungary, Iceland, Ireland, Italy, Latvia, Liechtenstein, Lithuania, Luxembourg, Macedonia, Malta, Moldova, Netherlands, Norway, Poland, Portugal, Romania, Slovakia, Slovenia, Spain, Sweden, Switzerland, Turkey, Ukraine, United Kingdom.

Africa (Sub-Mediterranean) (40): Angola, Benin, Botswana, Burkina Faso, Burundi, Cameroon, Cape Verde, Central African Republic, Chad, Congo, Cote d'Ivoire, Democratic Republic of the Congo, Djibouti, Gabon, Gambia, Ghana, Guinea, Guinea-Bissau, Kenya, Lesotho, Madagascar, Malawi, Mali, Mauritania, Mauritius, Mozambique, Namibia, Niger, Nigeria, Rwanda, Saudi Arabia, Senegal, Sierra Leone, South Africa, Swaziland, Tanzania, Togo, Uganda, Zambia, Zimbabwe.

Middle East/Northern Africa (19): Armenia, Bahrain, Bangladesh, Egypt, Georgia, India, Israel, Jordan, Kuwait, Kyrgyzstan, Maldives, Morocco, Nepal, Oman, Pakistan, Qatar, Sri Lanka, Tunisia, United Arab Emirates.

East Asia/Oceana (22): Australia, Brunei, Cambodia, China, Fiji, Hong Kong, Indonesia, Japan, Macao, Malaysia, Mongolia, Myanmar, New Zealand, Papua New Guinea, Philippines, Singapore, Solomon Islands, South Korea, Taiwan, Thailand, Tonga, Vietnam.

Americas (34): Antigua & Barbuda, Argentina, Barbados, Belize, Bolivia, Brazil, Canada, Chile, Colombia, Costa Rica, Cuba, Dominica, Dominican Republic, Ecuador, El Salvador, Grenada, Guatemala, Guyana, Haiti, Honduras, Jamaica, Mexico, Nicaragua, Panama, Paraguay, Peru, St. Kitts and Nevis, St. Lucia, St. Vincent and the Grenadines, Suriname, Trinidad and Tobago, United States of America, Uruguay, Venezuela.

Sources: *Developed* (Advanced) and *Developing* countries: IMF listings, in IMF, *World Economic Outlook 2012*, available at http://www.imf.org/external/pubs/ft/weo/2012/01/pdf/text.pdf.

Emerging Markets: Based on joint listing by six or more of the following nine analysts: Next-11/BRIC, CIVETS, FTSE, MSCI, The Economist, S&P, Dow-Jones, BBVA, and Columbia University EMGP. These lists are compiled in the Wikipedia entry at en.wikipedia.org/wiki/Emerging_markets. Of countries meeting this criterion, Taiwan was excluded, as it is now listed by the IMF as a developed country.

Least-Developed Country WTO Members: http://www.wto.org/english/thewto_e/whatis_e/tif_e/org7_e.htm.

WTO Geographical Groups: Author's designation

Acknowledgments

The author acknowledges the assistance of Prof. Yunwei Gai in the econometric component of this chapter.

Regional vs. Multilateral Trade Liberalization

INTRODUCTION

This chapter addresses the role of regional trade agreements (RTAs) in the process of multilateral trade liberalization.[1] For most WTO members, RTAs represent the "best alternative to a multilateral trade agreement" (BAMTA). The problem is that such agreements are economically inferior to general multilateral trade liberalization because they are incomplete and possibly trade diverting. Yet RTAs do appear to allow progress on trade liberalizations while multilateral initiatives remain dormant. The question is whether, from a strategic and institutional point of view, RTAs might play a useful role in moving global trade talks forward, and even toward multilateral agreement. Politically, RTAs provide an extremely attractive alternative to WTO deals: they involve fewer countries that self-select the partnership, and they can often avoid politically sensitive issues and demands that are unavoidable in WTO negotiations. RTAs can therefore be more quickly negotiated and are often more politically acceptable than WTO agreements. While RTAs and WTO agreements may be seen as alternative ways to increase trade, the GATT/WTO system does not force the choice between the two. RTAs are also *complements* to multilateral trade agreements, in the sense that members are free to conclude or join such preferential agreements—subject to WTO rules—while enjoying the multilateral benefits and market access of WTO membership. The GATT/WTO system has in fact not only coexisted with RTAs for most of the postwar period through the Uruguay Round, but—based on some prominent examples from GATT's history—has arguably benefited from them as devices that create incentives for spreading trade liberalization to the multilateral level. In the post-Doha Round period, there is renewed interest in RTAs, but in a new trade environment of supply chains and the benefits of "deep integration" among trading partners, in which the nature of such agreements has changed. Can RTAs, under these new circumstances, promote global trade liberalization?

The following analysis sets out to address this question by focusing on the link between the two parallel institutional forms of trade liberalization, while addressing the perennial question of whether RTAs are "building blocs" or "stumbling blocs" in supporting institutions of trade cooperation that can achieve global, nondiscriminatory trade agreements. The role of the Doha Round in the current trend in RTA negotiations will also be examined, with a summary of the most important recent and proposed agreements, and their possible impact on future multilateral trade negotiations. The analysis will show that RTAs combine countries' desire for the gains from trade with the domestic political and foreign policy advantages of "playing favorites." The WTO will need to harness or channel these deeply embedded tendencies among its members in order to reconstruct its ability to deliver multilateral trade liberalization.

The discussion of RTAs begins with some definitions and an account of their institutional status under the GATT, followed by a brief review of the trend in RTAs, including the recent proliferation of RTAs since the beginning of the Doha Round. This section goes on to present a brief account of the role RTAs have played in the history of GATT negotiations, and why they have grown in popularity over the period. The discussion then turns to the economic and systemic effects of RTAs, based on the traditional attempts to measure trade creation and trade diversion, and more recent theories to determine their effects on GATT negotiations. The impact of recent changes in the role of supply chains on international production is then presented as an important development in the motivation for recent RTAs, and for trade negotiations in general. A summary section considers the institutional implications of RTAs, especially in terms of a possible revival of global WTO talks. The chapter's final section examines the proposed Trans-Pacific Partnership, Transatlantic Trade and Investment Partnership, and other RTAs and their potential impact on future WTO negotiations, concluding with an outlook for the role of RTAs in the WTO system.

THE ROLE OF RTAS IN THE GATT/WTO SYSTEM

Types of RTAs and Their Recent Proliferation

RTAs are generally categorized along a progressive scale of economic integration. Among WTO members, most RTAs are either Free Trade Agreements

(FTAs), focused largely on market access for the partners in goods, or more extensive Economic Partnership Agreements ("enhanced" FTAs) with deeper integration provisions in such areas as foreign direct investment, services trade, technical barriers to trade, health and safety standards, and/or bilateral dispute settlement. Bilateral investment treaties (BITs) represent a more limited scope of integration, defining the terms of foreign direct investment between an investor country and a host country, but often include deeper "behind-the-border" provisions associated with the foreign investment arrangement. They are not regulated in the GATT/WTO system, but are indirectly playing an increasing role in regional trade integration, as the following discussion will show. More advanced RTAs include Customs Unions (CUs), in which the partners agree to common external tariffs and other joint trade policy tools; Common Markets, in which there is also free internal movement of services and factors of production; and Economic Integration Areas (EIAs), in which the partner countries jointly administer common economic policies and regulations, including monetary union. The European Union is the main example of such an EIA, having created a single internal market among its members, conducting a joint trade policy from Brussels, and voting as a bloc of twenty-eight countries at the WTO. Despite the designation of RTAs as "regional," they include any bilateral or multiparty trade agreements regardless of the geographic proximity of the partners—the United States has FTAs with Israel, Morocco, Chile, Singapore, and other distant countries, and the European Union has FTAs with Cote d'Ivoire, Egypt, and Papua New Guinea/Fiji, for example.

The WTO rules for such arrangements are contained in GATT article XX1V (pertaining to goods trade) and General Agreement on Trade in Services (GATS) article V (pertaining to services trade), so there is a legal framework for the existence of RTAs, even though the GATT/WTO system maintains its emphasis on multilateral trade liberalization based on the most-favored nation principle. Technically, RTAs concluded by WTO members, except for those between developing country members, are required to pass muster according to the GATT article XXIV/GATS article V rules, but in fact few of them have been officially deemed compliant with the rules. RTAs involving only developing countries are exempt from these formal rules and must instead be reported under provisions of "special and differential" treatment of the Enabling Clause (see GATT 1979), which are much less rigorous than GATT article XXIV. The fact of the matter is that WTO members have allowed such agreements to proliferate without significant constraints, mainly because nearly every WTO member has concluded at least one, and usually several, RTAs. The number of RTAs reported to the WTO has in fact grown dramatically since 1991, just as the Uruguay Round of trade negotiations was ending. Subramanian and Kessler (2013: 9) report that the world's top thirty exporters send half of their exports to RTA partner countries. For some observers of the WTO this trend is seen as a great concern, since the entire GATT/WTO system is founded on the concept of nondiscrimination and global trade liberalization, in contrast to the discriminatory, limited trade agreements represented by RTAs.

As of July 2013, a total of 575 RTA announcements had been received over the entire history of the GATT and WTO, of which 379 were still in force at that time.[2] All but twenty-three of these agreements had been concluded since 1991. The oldest RTA on the books is the 1957 Treaty of Paris, founding what is today the European Union. Pomfret (2007) injects a note of caution in using the number of RTA announcements as the measure of the importance of RTAs in the trading system, or as a move away from multilateralism, since any RTA covering both goods and services must now be reported twice, under GATT article XXIV and GATS article V, as noted above, and any enlargement of existing agreements counts as a separate RTA report. Many RTAs, further-more, have little economic impact and often replace other existing regional trade pacts of various types. For example, from 1991 to 2000, about half of the seventy new RTAs still in force today involved the Russian Federation and other transition economies as they adjusted to new trade relationships among themselves in the decade after the dissolution of the Soviet Union. But the former Soviet Republics had previously traded internally as one country, and the Soviet-led COMECON trading arrangement had previously dominated trade in Eastern Europe. The new regionalist RTAs among former Soviet and other transition economies among themselves was certainly a change in trade regime, but not a move away from multilateralism, which many of them have since adopted independently by joining the WTO. In addition, many bilateral RTAs have little trade impact, either because of their overly modest liberalizing measures, or because the partner countries already had low tariffs and little to gain economically from the agreement.[3] Pomfret (2007: 933) cites the amusing example of the Japan-Thailand RTA, which had little other impact than allow-ing more Thai cooks to work in restaurants in Japan, hence its sobriquet, the "Japanese-Thai cooks agreement."

Yet during the surge in new RTAs in the 1990s there were important new agreements such as NAFTA, Mercosur, and Association of Southeast Asian Nations (ASEAN), as well as the major 1995 enlargement of the European Union and a number of smaller agreements. After 2000, there was yet another upsurge in new RTAs. For example, since 2000 the United States has con-cluded thirteen new RTAs, following a distinct US policy shift announced by US trade representative Robert Zoellick (2002).[4] During this same period, Japan, having previously refrained from any such agreements, began a regional integration strategy with thirteen RTAs of its own. The European Union has concluded twenty-eight new RTAs since 2001, both through expansion of its existing membership and through FTAs and other agreements, mainly with developing countries around the world. The European Free Trade Association (EFTA), a group of small European countries with trade ties similar to those of the European Union, concluded nineteen RTAs, and other OECD countries added thirty-four. While many of the agreements concluded by the United States, European Union, Japan, EFTA, and OECD were with developing countries, another fifty-seven RTAs were concluded between or among developing countries alone.

Nearly everyone, it seemed, was negotiating special preferential trade deals in the first decade of the twenty-first century. In the context of the ongoing multilateral trade negotiations, one might say that RTAs sprouted like mushrooms during and after the recurring storms of the Doha Round, even though other foreign and regional policy motivations, as well as the economic strategy of globalizing supply chains, probably also played a role. Yet the timing of the surge hardly seems coincidental. The beginning of the WTO era had signaled an increasing judicialization of trade relations, in which market access would be increasingly subject to binding WTO rules, with disputes subject to legal review under terms of the new Dispute Settlement System. As noted above, large new RTAs such as NAFTA, ASEAN, and Mercosur had been founded during the Uruguay Round, and the European Union had continued to expand. These agreements carved out spheres of trade policy influence for participating countries that would give them greater control over the terms and coverage of preferential market access. This form of trade diplomacy also implied increasing bargaining leverage by many RTA countries in WTO negotiations, although only the European Union has consolidated negotiating power systematically as an RTA, acting as a unified bloc in trade negotiations. RTAs also serve to secure market access agreements as a hedge against any failed multilateral negotiations in the future. Numerous regional groupings of (mostly smaller) developing countries in Africa, the Middle East, and Asia-Pacific regions also joined the RTA bandwagon during these pre-Doha years.[5]

When the Doha Round began to stall in the years following its launch in 2001, the stage was therefore already set to build on, and add partners to, the existing regional pacts. The larger players in world trade appeared to turn their trade policy attention increasingly away from the WTO and toward special trade deals with selected partners, as shown by the tally above, while certain regions exhibited growing matrices of bilateral trade arrangements. The twenty-seven countries in the Asia-Pacific region, for example, had concluded 180 overlapping RTAs by 2013 (Williams 2013). In Washington, DC, the focus among trade officials and lobbyists has shifted away from the WTO since the Doha Round was suspended in December 2011 and has turned toward the Trans-Pacific Partnership (TPP) negotiations, and more recently, the US-EU Transatlantic Trade and Investment Partnership (TTIP) negotiations. Meanwhile, the European Union has concluded RTAs with the Republic of Korea and Singapore, while beginning or continuing FTA negotiations with the United States, Japan, India, Canada, Mercosur, ASEAN, the Gulf Cooperation Council, and twenty-three other countries, in addition to Economic Partnership Agreements (EPAs), based on development cooperation, with African, Caribbean, and Pacific (ACP) countries. Japan had already concluded numerous RTAs among its neighboring countries and decided in early 2013 to join the TPP negotiations. In short, preferential trade liberalization now seems to be "where the action is" in global trade negotiations.

Early GATT History

Institutionally, RTAs have a fraught history with the GATT/WTO system. The original drafters of the GATT did not anticipate the subsequent popularity of such agreements, even though many such agreements had been concluded earlier and were still in effect (Finger 1993: 130).[6] More relevant to the GATT drafters in 1947 were the stirrings for regional economic integration in postwar Europe. In order to protect the principle of nondiscrimination in the GATT rules, a compromise was reached in which free trade areas would be allowed as part of the GATT system if they followed strict conditions. The requirements, however, turned out not to be particularly clear. Among the ambiguous requirements was a rule that a valid RTA must eliminate barriers to "substantially all the trade" between the partner territories (paragraph 8b).[7] Conceptually, the rules were meant to ensure that RTAs would represent bona fide steps toward nondiscriminatory and universal trade liberalization, but it was difficult for the GATT to fashion rules that could prevent RTAs from setting up more narrowly defined trade coverage (through exceptions), protectionist blocs (especially through non-tariff measures), and otherwise discriminatory regimes. The 1957 Treaty of Paris, establishing the European Common Market, represented a sort of showdown over the rules, since many provisions of the Treaty appeared to violate, or threaten to violate, GATT article XXIV. Yet Cold War politics trumped the GATT rules, as the United States saw the strategic value of the new Common Market as part of a western bulwark against communism in Europe. According to Finger (1993: 137), "the GATT blinked," and the official review of the Treaty was set aside. This was a watershed moment that set the stage for the subsequent spread of RTAs, although the flood did not start until much later.[8]

It is not difficult to understand why GATT/WTO rules designed to contain the use of RTAs have been unsuccessful. In the sociology of government trade policy, RTAs reveal the propensity of governments to play favorites and play politics in trade policy. Certainly this has resulted in part from the difficulty of concluding a comprehensive multilateral trade agreement under the WTO, as the Doha Round experience has shown. Countries find it quicker and easier to conclude trade agreements with a single country or group of countries. There are often negotiating advantages in bargaining with neighboring, friendly, economically similar, and/or strategically important partner countries, especially when the impact of increased trade does not threaten politically risky domestic adjustment costs. Large countries find it easier to pursue strategic trade policy interests in bilateral and regional settings, as they can exert their superior bargaining power with smaller RTA partners. Thus, the US agenda in recent RTAs has typically included environmental, labor, state-trading, and "WTO-plus" intellectual property measures that it could not pursue in WTO negotiations. If the large country can use its position as an RTA "hub," or as the leader of an expanding set of bilateral or regional RTA "spokes," it can set up the most advantageous rules to benefit its export industries, which its RTA partners would have to follow. The asymmetry in bargaining power in most RTAs points to their disadvantage for smaller, less developed and weaker countries, and highlights a major advantage of a WTO trade negotiating forum in providing a more balanced and "level" negotiating table for all countries. Still, for small and weaker countries, getting improved, guaranteed access to a large market is also a strong motivator to conclude RTAs, even if their "junior partner" status in the arrangement involves reduced bargaining power. In addition, the proliferation of regional developing country RTAs also suggests a strategy of creating forums for coalitions and joint representation on WTO and other international issues. There are, finally, domestic political motivations for governments to pursue RTAs, at least in democratic countries. Mansfield and Milner (2012) provide evidence that RTAs signal to domestic voters the independence of political leaders from protectionist forces. Depending on the partner country, RTAs may, to be sure, arouse strong protectionist opposition that may threaten the ruling party's political fortunes, but the ability of governments to judiciously choose their RTA partners, and to shape agreements to minimize domestic adjustment costs, makes them an important tool of domestic economic policy. In short, RTAs are more easily negotiated than WTO agreements and provide many advantages in trade, foreign, and domestic policy. They are not going away, whatever the WTO rules are, but the WTO rules do influence the pattern, timing, and content of RTAs, while RTAs, in turn, can also affect global trade negotiations.

ECONOMIC AND SYSTEMIC EFFECTS

Traditional RTAs, in the form of FTAs and other tariff-cutting agreements, increase reciprocal market access among the agreement's partners, capturing some of the potential gains from trade, but on a preferential (i.e., discriminatory) basis, which detracts from these gains. The traditional economic analysis of RTAs therefore distinguishes between their trade-creation effects (the gains from reducing tariff barriers with regard to the RTA partners) and their trade-diversion effects (the losses the RTA may impose by reducing more efficient import supply from non-partner countries).[9] For example, when Spain joined the European Union (known as the European Economic Community at the time) in 1986, it eliminated most trade barriers with its EU partner countries, resulting in economic welfare gains from trade creation with them. However, in joining the European Union, it also had to switch its source of corn and sorghum imports from the United States to less efficient EU sources, since EU-sourced corn and sorghum no longer faced Spanish tariffs, and US producers of these products now had to face higher EU tariffs in order to sell to Spain. Spain therefore lost economic welfare through trade diversion, that is, from foregoing the most efficient source of import supply, and the United States filed a GATT dispute case because of the losses to US exporters of these products. In a 1987 negotiated settlement the European Union provided compensating market concessions to the United States (see Haniotis 1990).

Another example illustrates perhaps the greatest trade diversion mischief arising from RTAs: the "spaghetti bowl" (in Asia often dubbed the "noodle bowl") effect on trade in intermediate goods (see Bhagwati 2008). Governments taking part in RTAs are wary of other non-RTA countries seeking to gain access to the new trade area by shipping their products to an RTA partner country with the purpose of then transshipping them duty-free to other RTA countries, thereby gaining "back door" market access to the RTA as a non-member. To prevent this sort of activity, governments participating in RTAs often establish rules of origin (ROOs) for imports from other RTA members that must document the origin of the components of the imported good, and usually require some minimum level of value-added transformation in the RTA region to be eligible for duty-free treatment. Such provisions often impose a protectionist cure that is worse than the alleged circumvention disease. The NAFTA, for example, has a "yarn-forward" rule that requires qualifying imports of clothing from other NAFTA countries to be made from materials from the yarn-production stage forward that are actually made in NAFTA countries. Yarn spun outside the NAFTA but imported by Canada and used to make a shirt for sale in the United States would not allow the shirt to qualify for NAFTA duty-free treatment, for example. Such ROOs are thus typically designed to protect domestic producers of both component inputs and the final goods, and their protectionist impact causes trade diversion in input markets. Labor union lobbies often cling tenaciously to these RTA provisions. The problem becomes even more complicated if countries take part in more than one RTA, with different ROOs for the different RTAs, hence the possible "spaghetti bowl" problem, particularly in a hub-and-spoke RTA network. The red tape and documentation of ROOs can be so onerous for firms located within the RTA that they often choose not to claim the duty-free benefits.

Theories about the overall impact of RTAs on trade and trade policy are legion, offering contrasting hypotheses, linking them variously to welfare-improving and welfare-decreasing outcomes, and to incentives for trade liberalization and for protectionism.[10] The "partial" nature of RTA liberalization, benchmarked against nondiscriminatory universal trade liberalization, leaves the welfare and incentive conclusions of economic theory on the razor's edge. The policy issue of whether RTAs are "building blocs" or "stumbling blocs" will therefore never be decided on theoretical terms. The empirical assessment of RTAs typically begins with a quantitative measurement of trade creation and trade diversion. The positive difference between trade creation and diversion will be larger, for example, as the number of partner countries and volume of intra-regional trade increases, the initial tariffs are lower, and efficient input suppliers are included in the agreement. One empirical measure of a negative effect would be large amounts of trade diversion, for example, which would indicate a reduction in global trade efficiency. Yet a study by Archarya et al. (2010) finds little trade diversion—and strong evidence of substantial trade creation—in recent RTAs. Freund and Ornelas (2010), reviewing the recent empirical literature on the topic, also find a preponderance of evidence that trade creation far outweighs trade diversion. Another possible measure of a negative impact of RTAs on global trade liberalization would be if countries' MFN (global) tariffs were systematically higher than their corresponding RTA tariffs, that is, that low RTA tariffs would be substitutes for high MFN tariffs. Baldwin and Seghezza (2010), however, find that tariffs tend to be complements rather than substitutes, although they acknowledge that both MFN and RTA tariffs may be high in politically sensitive, protectionist sectors. Most empirical studies of tariff effects of RTAs tend, in any case, to suggest that there are no strong negative or distorting impacts on domestic economic welfare of participant countries, or of strongly discriminatory RTA regimes.[11]

Economic analysis makes clear, however, that multilateral, nondiscriminatory trade liberalization is always superior to any partial liberalization through RTAs. For this reason, and also because of the ROOs problems described above, many economists have condemned RTAs as being inimical to a multilateral, nondiscriminatory system (see Bhagwati 2008; Krueger 1999). An RTA would be considered an institutional stumbling bloc if it merely partially substituted for, hindered or detracted from, multilateral trade liberalization. The inherent pessimism of this view is based on the observed tendency of RTAs to indulge domestic protectionist interests, through ROOs and special exclusions of politically sensitive products from free trade coverage, and the propensity of large countries, especially, to select RTA partners that will minimize domestic adjustment costs (and thus, in many cases, the gains from trade) and that will allow the large country to assert its superior bargaining power. Thus, RTAs led by the United States tend to exclude or minimize trade liberalization in such sensitive sectors as intercoastal maritime transport, clothing, and sugar, while insisting on environmental and labor clauses pushed by domestic import-competing industries and labor unions. The partner countries in most recent RTAs have tended to be small, with correspondingly minor impacts on trade, although this appears to be changing as the United States, European Union, and Japan have recently begun RTA negotiations with larger trading partners. One additional concern with RTAs, however, is that they may entail an opportunity cost in terms of government resources: political resource investments in RTAs, along with the personnel and expertise needed to negotiate them, take resources away from WTO negotiations. This may be true even for large countries with large trade bureaucracies: the best trade diplomats cannot adequately attend to both major RTA and WTO matters at the same time, especially if the RTAs become larger and more complicated.[12] An increasing focus on RTAs among WTO member countries in general may divert their best talent away from WTO affairs.

IMPACT ON MULTILATERAL TRADE NEGOTIATIONS

A historical review of the role of RTAs in the GATT/WTO system offers a generally optimistic assessment, however, in terms of the political process of trade liberalization. Large RTAs, despite their shortcomings, appear to have played a positive role in GATT negotiations. The conclusion of a large and significant RTA tends to focus the world's attention on multilateral trade talks, as such agreements engender "market access envy" among the outsiders. Thus, the formation of the European Union by the Treaty of Rome in 1957 helped motivate GATT members to agree to new trade talks in the 1960s, at the Dillon and Kennedy Rounds. In their willingness to bargain for greater market access to the European Union, the other GATT members also had to offer increased market access of their own, thus promoting multilateral liberalization (see Hufbauer 1990; Lawrence 1991). On the negative side of the ledger, the European Union also harmed world trade: recall the probable violations of GATT article XXIV, along with the fact that the more open European economies, Germany and the Netherlands, actually had to increase their tariffs in joining the European Union (see Winter 1993). In addition, the European Union's highly protectionist Common Agricultural Policy (CAP) has distorted both European and world food markets to this day. But in evaluating the overall impact of the European Union on trade liberalization, one must consider the counterfactual. Cold War politics, as mentioned earlier, prevented the GATT from stopping the formation of the European Union and the negative effects its internal rules created. One cannot, therefore, presume a global trading system without the European Union and its discriminatory rules. Given its existence, has its presence helped or hindered multilateral trade liberalization? Its influence on the GATT/WTO system has indeed been important, especially since its status of a customs union with an expanding membership has enhanced its bargaining power in trade negotiations. Such power can work either in favor of or against trade liberalization, and the temptation for an expanding economic area is to turn inward in response to the challenges of a rapidly changing world economy. The key to its role in the trading system—and this is important for any such RTA—has depended on its general outlook of the member countries' political leaders on trade and globalization. The presence of the United States as a large country backing trade liberalization has also been an important factor. In the end, trade policy decisions at critical moments push the outcome either toward or away from global trade liberalization. Fortunately, the internal consensus process of forging common EU trade policies has usually reflected the needs of its industries to remain open to technological advancement, growing world markets, and global competition. An additional beneficial factor lies in the European Union's ability, through its more advanced economic integration and governance, to settle internal differences that allow it to bargain externally for trade liberalization.[13] Since its founding, the European Union has on balance contributed significantly to trade liberalization in general, despite the CAP and concerns over the years that it would become a "fortress Europe." This fact is borne out in the general advancement of trade liberalization that occurred through most of the GATT/WTO era, which would not have been possible without EU support. For many years it has also been the most significant counterweight to US bargaining power, and as a result probably increased US trade liberalization measures as well.

Aside from the leadership effects of the European Union as a major influence in the WTO, RTAs may contribute to global trade liberalization through a number of economic incentives and political economy effects. Baldwin (2006b) identifies "domino" effects induced by RTAs, which tend to spur on further trade liberalization through the fear of trade diversion by those left out.

The resulting dynamic creates a "contagion" of proliferating RTAs (see also Baldwin and Jaimovich 2012). Baldwin (2006b) notes furthermore that the supply-chain phenomenon motivates RTA hub countries (through the interests of their manufacturers) to cumulate rules of origin among the many supplying countries so as to avoid the "spaghetti bowl" effect, yet another factor that tends to move RTAs toward further trade liberalization.[14] Reducing tariffs on a preferential basis then sparks a "juggernaut" effect (Baldwin 2006b) that motivates further trade liberalization on a multilateral basis. This occurs through a negotiating process of reciprocity and a political process by which the balance of lobbying power progressively moves in favor of exporters that favor lower domestic tariffs as the means for achieving lower tariffs and greater market access abroad. Baldwin (2006b) notes that the history of multilateral tariff cuts under the GATT went hand-in-hand with regional tariff cuts. The role of the European Union in the Dillon and Kennedy Rounds, described above, fits this pattern. In addition, EU internal tariff cutting also inspired the "domino" effect of non-EU members in Europe forming their own RTA, the European Free Trade Association (EFTA) in 1960.[15] Most of these countries have gone on to join the European Union in the meantime. The tandem of domino and juggernaut effects continued to drive regional and global trade liberalization through the Uruguay Round.[16] Many trade diplomats also recall the role of the NAFTA and APEC negotiations themselves in maintaining pressure on the negotiators in the Uruguay Round to move toward agreement (see Bergsten 1996).

Ironically, it is likely that WTO rules and trade liberalization have actually encouraged RTAs among its members—although this was not the intention—with positive feedback to multilateral trade negotiations. Countries enjoying the security of MFN treatment with the rest of the world economy have little to lose from concluding special trade deals with favored trading partners, especially since the lower tariffs negotiated under the GATT/WTO system have reduced the likelihood of trade diversion that might otherwise occur as a result of such agreements. In addition, the potential demonstration effect of RTA trade liberalization in new areas may encourage countries to use RTAs as a testing ground for later multilateral negotiations. NAFTA, for example, included new issues such as services, intellectual property, and investment that would also become part of the Uruguay Round, but also showed influences of the Uruguay Round negotiations on the NAFTA.[17] More recently, "deep integration" provisions of some RTAs have pioneered negotiations and created gains from trade that are not yet ripe or feasible for WTO negotiation. EU agreements on internal services trade, harmonized standards, internal migration, and competition rules represent current and possible future WTO agenda items on which there has been little multilateral progress so far.

The demonstration effect of successful internal trade liberalization in such behind-the-border measures can change the dynamic of multilateral negotiations through concrete results: RTAs show that agreements on new issues can be done and that the participants gain from them. The gains from trade, extended to new areas of negotiation, continue to provide a compelling incentive for countries to bargain for market access, at first on a regional, and then on a multilateral basis.

SUPPLY CHAINS, BITS, AND THE ADVENT OF THE "NEW" RTAS

The use of RTAs as laboratories for new trade topics reflects technological and policy trends that appear to be changing the nature of trade relations, and in particular the structure of RTAs. Recent scholarship on RTAs has identified a link between negotiations for "deep" integration and the increasing importance of international supply-chain specialization in manufacturing. Such agreements are typically between a large country and countries in its region (although partner countries may be more distant, so that the scope of the supply chain can be "global") that are all part of the supply chain, and include "WTO+" provisions that go beyond existing WTO commitments, as well as "WTO-X" obligations outside current WTO rules. Aside from the European Union itself, in which economic integration is most advanced among RTAs, "deep integration" agreements include US-Mexico provisions in the NAFTA, Japan's Economic Partnership Agreements with large ASEAN economies, and the European Union's Euro-Med Association Agreements (Baldwin 2011). The trend extends to many other recent RTAs, however, according to the WTO's *World Trade Report* (WTO 2011c), which concludes that dozens of agreements concluded since the beginning of the Doha Round in 2001contain WTO+ and WTO-X obligations in competition policy, intellectual property rights, investments, and movements in capital.

If the international supply chain is a major source of motivation for an RTA, not only final goods trade but also intermediate goods trade will be the subject of negotiations. It is important to keep mind that firms in the supply chain continue to be interested in multilateral trade liberalization, since both intermediate and final goods involved in the supply chain often face market access barriers that may not be easy to eliminate through RTAs alone. However, in view of the slow progress in WTO negotiations, attention has turned increasingly to securing market access and favorable investment conditions within international supply chains, through "behind-the-border" management and regulation of bilateral trade-related activities. As a result, the vertical links in supply chains also make foreign direct investment, intellectual property protection, and competition policy, as well as trade logistics (such as the management of port facilities) and trade in services, important components of the overall trade relationship. Domestic regulations of transportation, insurance, financial services, and health and safety standards often affect the transactions cost of import, export, and storage activities within the supply chain. Thus, the "new" RTAs are only partly about "concessions" of reciprocal market access. For this reason, the traditional consideration of trade creation and diversion becomes less important, since the focus is on a partnership within the supply chain, involving foreign direct investment and both imports and exports. This factor also changes the terms of the negotiations. For example, a supply-chain inspired RTA may typically require eliminating import tariffs on intermediate goods, which the importing country often gladly concedes in exchange for an arrangement by firms in the partner country to build manufacturing facilities to process the item for further export. In fact, the importing country has the economic incentive to eliminate such tariffs unilaterally if it attracts foreign direct investment that bestows economic benefits to the host. The more difficult concessions in RTA negotiations might include harmonizing its intellectual property standards to those of the partner country, or relaxing its services regulations or changing its competition policy to facilitate ancillary business activities of partner country firms linked with the supply chain.

BITs play an important role in the new supply-chain economics of trade, since there are no comprehensive global agreements on direct foreign investment. Such agreements usually follow templates established by each investor country, but each BIT can be tailored to address circumstances and concerns regarding individual host countries. Typically, they include provisions for nondiscrimination (national and MFN treatment for the investor country), expropriation, transferability of investment-related funds, performance requirements, nationality of managers, and dispute arbitration and settlement, usually through a special international tribunal established for this purpose.[18] Because of the specialized nature of each bilateral case, and the proliferation of foreign direct investment in recent years, the number of BITs has grown from a few hundred in 1985 to more than 3,000 in 2013.[19] Baldwin (2011) links the rapid proliferation of BITs during this period to the advent of international supply-chain integration, what he regards as a historic spatial "unbundling" of production locations, due to technological advancements in information technology and communications.[20] The spread of BITs reflects an interesting institutional development in response to the lack of multilateral disciplines regarding the treatment of foreign direct investment in host countries. There were efforts to establish such disciplines in the WTO Uruguay Round in the agreement on Trade Related Investment Measures (TRIMs), but these provisions were not comprehensive, and furthermore, many developing countries have failed to implement several provisions of the agreement (see Hoekman and Kostecki 2009: 264). A subsequent effort by OECD countries to establish a global Multilateral Agreement on Investment (MAI), beginning in 1995, encountered a strong political back-lash, spearheaded by anti-globalization NGOs (see Bonanno and Constance 2010: chapter 9). MAI negotiations had begun in the immediate post-Uruguay Round period, and developing countries, fresh from their frustrations with those negotiations (see chapter 4), harbored suspicions that the MAI repre-sented yet another attempt by wealthy OECD countries to set global rules favorable to themselves, at the expense of developing countries that would host FDI. At the same time, OECD countries themselves were not in agree-ment on many details of the proposed agreement, notably France, which had concerns regarding the protection of its national culture and sovereignty. In the end, France withdrew from the agreement in 1998, causing its collapse. In the absence of global rules, however, smaller bilateral and regional agree-ments on foreign direct investment have been concluded in the form of BITs, and some RTAs, such as the European Union (where investment integration is virtually complete), NAFTA Chapter 11, and the Republic of Korea-Chile and US-Australia FTAs.

The benefits of FDI and the accompanying gains from trade for the host coun-try appear to have motivated them to conclude BITs and similar agreements in large numbers, even if they remain suspicious of global disciplines. This trend suggests that there may be a growing basis for institutional convergence among both investor and host countries on the desirability of international disciplines on foreign investment, since MFN treatment and the consistent application of common rules would tend to improve global efficiency and improve the bar-gaining power of host countries collectively. In any case, the existence of some 3,000 BITs implies the possibility of finding some common ground for global rules. Yet recent WTO experience provides a reality check to this optimism. An extension of the TRIMs rules was a controversial item in the Doha Round, one of the "Singapore" issues, which led to the Cancun Ministerial collapse in 2003 and the elimination of investment from the agenda. In view of continued strong opposition among many developing countries, a global WTO agree-ment on investment is unlikely in the near future. However, the strong regional interest in supply-chain-based deep integration in TPP and TTIP negotiations, as well as other RTAs under negotiation, provide the opportunity to establish rules among participating countries that could serve as future templates for multilateral rules.

CLOSING THE INSTITUTIONAL LOOP: FROM RTAS TO THE WTO

The logical consequence of the growth in regional supply chains has been for countries to integrate these cross-border economic relationships—and/or deepen them—through intensified "deep integration" RTAs. Deeper international economic integration that goes beyond trade in goods to include services, domestic regulations, trade facilitation, intellectual property rights, and investment implies potentially large economic benefits for all parties to the supply chain, as suggested by the review of remaining unexploited gains from trade in chapter 1. Based on the economic gains alone, one would expect countries to pursue such agreements, regardless of their implications for the WTO system. The regional pattern of supply chains in Europe, North America, and Asia has led to numerous deep-integration RTAs in those areas, with particularly strong efforts still underway to consolidate gains from integration in Asia. This trend is likely to influence future WTO negotiating agendas. Institutional analysis suggests that only successful RTA negotiations contribute to trade liberalization progress on the multilateral front. This is because an RTA must establish its own "collective intentionality" among a group of countries that are presumably also WTO members, with an agenda and shared understandings of desirable goals and limits of domestic policy space that will make final consensus on an agreement possible. These factors will shape the RTA negotiating agenda and create a potential focal point for subsequent WTO negotiations. If consensus were not possible among a self-selected subset of "like-minded" partner countries, or those with strong supply-chain complementarities, and typically with a large country leading the negotiation, then one would not expect such a failed RTA negotiation to provide any prospect for success in a larger WTO negotiation on a similar agenda. We can also assume in this regard that prospective RTA participants would not want to waste the considerable investment in resources and effort in identifying a "zone of mutual agreement" in a failed RTA negotiation, one that would surely be more difficult to achieve at the WTO. Furthermore, the pattern of RTA negotiations since the beginning of the Doha Round suggests that countries are interested in getting gains from trade regionally that they were not getting through global negotiations, implying a general correspondence of bargaining preferences in regional and WTO negotiations. The benefit of successful RTAs therefore lies in their potential to pave the way to wider WTO agreements. Concessions that result in the successful conclusion of RTA negotiations set benchmarks for possible future bargaining patterns at the WTO.

Yet there are further institutional requirements in order for RTAs to be "building blocs" for global trade liberalization. As suggested in the institutional review of the Doha Round in chapter 3, an RTA (or a series of RTAs) would have to move WTO members closer to consensus on a trade agenda, specifically by closing the institutional gaps that emerged in the Doha Round: lack of collectively recognized limits on domestic policy sovereignty, an overloaded "single undertaking" agenda, a lack of a common understanding regarding the role of developing countries (particularly reciprocity), and the shift in WTO negotiating power. RTAs can address these issues by reducing the barriers to consensus, by narrowing participation to a set of self-selected RTA partners to the negotiation, and by adjusting the agenda to include only those items on which the parties agree to bargain. Traditional bargaining trade-offs raise the concern, however, that a particular RTA may be designed so that it forecloses a future WTO agreement on specific issues because the RTA agenda itself crosses "red lines" of countries not party to the RTA. To the extent that the RTA is in fact designed in this manner to form an exclusive trading bloc with a closed membership, it will tend not to contribute to multilateral trade liberalization. Baldwin (2011) and others raise the concern that current WTO bargaining conflicts may lead to large US- and EU-led regional blocs outside of WTO disciplines that would, for example, exclude or isolate China, India, and perhaps other developing countries, with the potential of increasing both global trade and political conflict. This sort of outcome is possible, but unlikely, insofar as economic growth among the large emerging and developing economies will make them attractive trading partners in the coming decades, not least to the United States, European Union, and Japan. There will be too much money left on the table by excluding these countries from future trade agreements.

The development divide does raise an important RTA issue, however. If RTAs are to address the institutional problems of the Doha Round, then the most direct way to make progress on the reciprocity issue is to conclude RTAs between major developing and major developed countries. Such a "crossover" RTA would seek an agenda that could establish reciprocal concessions of genuine value to both the developed and the developing parties, without the presumption of one-sided free market access provisions. This approach is based on the evidence over the entire history of the GATT/WTO system that market access is only worth receiving if it is paid for with reciprocal concessions. Large emerging markets such as China, India, and Brazil would therefore bargain as equal partners with the United States, European Union, and/or Japan.[21] The institutional goal would be to find bilateral means to make progress on the Doha Round problems of negotiating larger reciprocal access to emerging markets' policy space and tariff reductions. Large RTAs that cross the development divide would represent a major breakthrough for future WTO negotiations by offering a new foundation for reciprocal bargaining among major developed and developing trading powers.[22] While RTAs tend to be negotiated mainly on a regional basis, with like-minded or otherwise compliant partners dominated by a large country, the prospect of possibly even larger mutual gains from trade through RTAs between and among unlike-minded large countries at different levels of development should not be overlooked. Such agreements could in fact play a large role in motivating other developed and developing countries to return to the WTO negotiating table.

In this regard, even if the RTA includes provisions that go beyond the current limits of other WTO members to join the agreement, it may nonetheless establish a precedent and demonstration effect for future global (or plurilateral) agreements in modified form. One major test of this RTA attribute is its "openness" to new members (e.g., through a process of accession), or the ability of its provisions to be "multilateralized" in a future WTO agreement. Such a breakthrough would be particularly significant with regard to RTAs that establish new understandings among trading partners that draw back the limits of domestic policy space. Such progress in expanding trade liberalization into new areas will, however, also require progress at the domestic level of major trading countries, through increased economic flexibility in adjusting to trade, supporting trade adjustment policies, the active engagement of pro-trade interests, and political leadership that can forge coalitions for a platform that pushes the current policy boundaries of market access and trade rules. Weaker domestic political commitments to trade liberalization, in contrast, will lead to weaker RTAs that deliver lesser economic gains (or else to failed RTA negotiations), which in turn will diminish the prospects for progress in multilateral trade negotiations.

Thus, the greatest danger in principle from RTAs for the WTO system lies in the domestic connection between trade interests and trade policy. Given the regional nature of recent trends in economic integration, many of the most profitable business opportunities also have a strong regional dimension, based on the possibilities of more efficient supply chains and closer networks of customers and partnerships. Already, many business lobbying groups have focused their efforts on negotiating BITs and complementary business facilitation agreements in several countries of special interest to specific industries.[23] Such bilateral agreements, perhaps extended and enhanced by RTAs, may provide the greatest and quickest returns on their lobbying investment, when compared with the protracted and perhaps diluted benefits of WTO negotiations. While business interest in global market access and investment opportunity is still strong, the WTO as an institution runs the risk of losing the engagement of these, the most compelling supporters of multilateral trade liberalization, through the benign neglect of the member country governments. By focusing on RTAs in the face of frustration with WTO negotiations, governments are following paths of least (or in any case, less) resistance, which could lead to either politically safe, economically weak RTAs, or to expansive, innovative RTAs that point to larger, multilateral gains from trade. But it is still up to governments, in a world of negotiated market access and rules among sovereign countries, to persevere in WTO negotiations, and to find ways to build the requisite domestic political support for a global agreement.

THE MAJOR POST-DOHA RTA NEGOTIATIONS

While many countries began concluding RTAs well before the Doha Round began, they seem to have expanded their interests in such agreements since the Doha Round bogged down. More recently, a trend has emerged in which large countries are now negotiating RTAs with other large countries, and with larger numbers of countries, especially in Asia. RTA negotiations of this expanded scope in principle involve larger potential gains from trade, but also more difficult obstacles to an agreement, since they involve countries in which there is more equally balanced bargaining power. If the partners already trade extensively with each other, the RTA agenda will typically try to expand the scope of products and rules under negotiation, perhaps (with political will and effort) breaking new ground in trade cooperation, and possibly establishing precedents for future multilateral agreement in the WTO. In fact, the big RTAs in the post-Doha period appear to aspire to the sort of high-impact trade liberalization, on a regional scale, that the WTO could not deliver in the Doha Round itself. This section will focus on the two largest and most ambitious of these negotiations, the Trans-Pacific Partnership (TPP) and the Transatlantic Trade and Investment Partnership (TTIP).

The Trans-Pacific Partnership

The TPP was the most ambitious regional trade agreement under negotiation in 2013/14, when the talks included twelve countries: the United States, Canada, Mexico, Peru, Chile, Australia, New Zealand, Brunei, Malaysia, Singapore, Vietnam, and finally Japan, which joined most recently. It seems possible that the Republic of Korea will also eventually join the negotiations (Schott, Kotschwar, and Muir 2013), or perhaps accede to the agreement if it is concluded. TPP negotiations grew out of an earlier agreement that included Brunei, Chile, New Zealand, and Singapore, concluded in 2006. Australia,

Peru, the United States, and Vietnam joined this group in opening up negotiations for a larger agreement in 2008, subsequently joined by the other TPP
countries listed above. Because of the expanding roster of negotiating countries over time—and disagreements over several issues—the anticipated conclusion of the negotiations have been pushed back from its original target of
October 2013. After Japan joined the talks, further delays became likely, and
prospects for a TPP agreement as soon as 2014 (Schott 2014) faded during that
year. Nonetheless, the importance of the TPP lies in its ambitions to cover a
wide range of products and issues, which, if successful, could provide a blueprint and a precedent for global trade liberalization in the future. If successful,
it would represent the most comprehensive economic integration agreement
globally, next to the European Union. In addition, the TPP itself could expand
further to cover the entire Asia-Pacific region and perhaps even beyond that,
especially if it establishes an accession-based model of joining, similar to the
process for joining the WTO. Ultimately, it could also bring countries back to
multilateral trade negotiations in Geneva.[24]

Negotiations for a TPP agreement are part of a larger spectrum of trade
negotiations in the Asia-Pacific region, which seem to be moving toward progressive economic integration. The economic importance of the region has
increased dramatically in recent years, due especially to the supply-chain networks of production, intermediate goods trade, and assembly in East Asia.
Partly as a result of the cross-border economic interests in the supply chains,
there were 180 partially overlapping FTAs and over a thousand BITs in the
region (Williams 2013). Asia-Pacific Economic Cooperation (APEC), a loosely
structured forum of twenty-one countries[25] on the Pacific Rim, was founded
in 1989 with the general goal of promoting Asia-Pacific trade and economic
integration. While APEC itself is so broad an agreement that it has not served
as a forum for such negotiations, the participating countries did discuss plans
for a Free Trade Area of the Asia-Pacific (FTAAP) in 2006, sparked in part by
the glacial pace of the Doha Round. Since then, a smaller group of ten ASEAN
countries, which have their own FTA,[26] have pursued trade agreements with
other APEC members, with the goal of establishing a wider pan-Asian trade
agreement of their own, the Regional Comprehensive Economic Partnership
(RCEP), which currently includes the ASEAN countries plus their FTA partners: Australia, China, India, Japan, Republic of Korea, and New Zealand. This
agreement would also be open for additional countries to join. While talks
regarding such a sweeping agreement have remained in the early stages, plans
for a broader ASEAN agreement would include Japan, the Republic of Korea,
and China (ASEAN +3) or even this group plus Australia, New Zealand, and
India (ASEAN +6). Some ASEAN countries are also in the TPP talks (Brunei,
Malaysia, Singapore, and Vietnam), and ASEAN has also concluded FTAs with

other TPP countries (Australia and New Zealand), and with India. The overlapping nature of ASEAN and TPP integration efforts has raised the prospect that these efforts may eventually converge too form a pan-regional FTAAP (see Schott, Kotschwar, and Muir 2013; Petri, Plummer, and Zhai 2012).

The TPP is, however, particularly significant for the future course of global trade policy because of its ambitions for deeper integration among a large number of countries. While ASEAN countries and the associated FTAs have focused primarily on traditional market access measures, the TPP agenda is extremely broad in its coverage, more ambitious in several aspects than the Doha Round agenda. There are twenty-nine proposed chapters, covering trade in industrial goods, services, and agriculture, as well as labor, safety and environmental standards, rules of origin, and rules on intellectual property, competition policy (including state-owned enterprises), investment, government procurement and safeguards, and TPP dispute settlement procedures. If such an ambitious TPP is concluded (or close to being concluded), it will provide a test of one of the propositions discussed earlier in this chapter, that RTAs can, at their best, generate precedents for subsequent multilateral trade liberalization. First, however, participants in the TPP negotiations must reach agreement on a large package of measures, many of them controversial.[27] We must in this regard return to the questions raised by the Doha Round: are the TPP countries ready to negotiate market access in politically sensitive products and "behind-the-border" rules on sensitive domestic regulatory issues? The participating countries include several high-income and industrialized economies, but also middle- and lower-income developing countries such as Mexico, Chile, Malaysia, Peru, and Vietnam. Developed vs. developing country fault lines are likely on labor, environment and services issues, while terms of TPP agriculture and intellectual property agreements will reveal major disagreements among both developed and developing countries.

As with all RTAs, the value of a TPP agreement to the global trading system, and to the economic welfare of its participants, will depend on the details. Since most TPP countries have relatively low tariff barriers (with some exceptions, such as agriculture) and already trade extensively with each other (with many bilateral and sub-regional FTAs already in place among many participants), the additional welfare gains from trade from traditional market access liberalization will be relatively small, especially in the early years of a TPP agreement. It is only with the phase-in of comprehensive measures to harmonize regulations and deepen economic integration that the large payoff of an ambitious and successful negotiation would be realized. For all APEC countries, assuming the most optimistic case of a progressive realization of an FTAAP based on a consolidation of the TPP and Asian track models by 2025, the resulting increase in collective annual GDP for the region is estimated to be over $1.9 trillion (Petri, Plummer, and Zhai 2012).[28] The best outcome would be a comprehensive agreement that breaks new ground in services trade, market access in agriculture, and disciplines on domestic regulations that tend to restrict trade and disrupt trade relations. In particular, such an agreement would establish nondiscrimination among all participants, with rules of origin allowing input goods cumulation within the entire TPP. It would thereby avoid the "hub-and-spoke" syndrome of FTAs negotiated by large countries with smaller trading partners, which typically cause "noodle bowl" trade diversion due to differing terms of market access and differing terms of rule application. In addition, while some exemptions and waivers will probably be necessary, an ideal TPP agreement would cover "substantially all trade," in the spirit of the GATT article XXIV rule. Aside from these considerations, however, the deeper integration of the TPP proposal would address supply-chain efficiencies and the connections between investment, intellectual property protection, regulations, and trade in both goods and services.

The TPP negotiation contains a number of strategic dimensions for US trade and foreign policy. It contains the sort of trade agenda that the United States, unable to achieve in the WTO, is now attempting to spearhead on a regional basis in order to regain the initiative in global trade policy. It would establish standards for intellectual property, investment protection, labor rights, and environmental protection that could serve as models for other RTAs, and potentially for WTO agreements in the future, assuming that the WTO expands its mandate accordingly. It therefore focuses on sectors in which US comparative advantage in many services and IP-related products, and on its ability to benefit from foreign direct investment, while addressing critical areas in which US influence on WTO negotiations has been limited, but which are now important in order to get domestic political support for trade legislation, such as international labor and environmental standards. In addition, the TPP currently represents a counterweight to China's growing economic and political role in the region by providing an alternative to what are likely to be the China-dominated RCEP negotiations. Many WTO+ and WTO-X proposals in the TPP regarding state-owned enterprises, intellectual property protection, and regulation of other government involvement in the economy would prevent China from joining in the near future. If successful, the TPP negotiations would thus also allow the United States to "steal a march" on China in terms of influencing the future global trade agenda, perhaps forcing China into concessions on these issues once they become more widely acceptable among other WTO countries. This strategic impulse comes primarily from US concerns, but other countries in the Asia-Pacific region appear to be welcoming a regional agreement that is not dominated by China.

Yet there are serious obstacles to what has been described as the "gold standard" of regional deep integration proposed by the TPP. As noted earlier, the TPP negotiations break new ground on sensitive sectors and behind-the-border trade rules, even beyond the scope of the Doha Agenda. While it is true that the TPP countries are generally more open to trade than many other WTO members, and that the United States, in contrast to its diminished dominance in the WTO, is in a leadership role capable of guiding the TPP negotiations, it is not so clear that the same institutional barriers can be overcome. Schott, Kotschwar, and Muir (2013: chapter 4) list nine categories of "sticking points" involving serious differences among parties to the negotiations, including traditional protectionist sectors (textiles, apparel, and shoes),[29] new sectors (agriculture and services), WTO+ issues (intellectual property), WTO-X "trade and … " social issues (labor and environmental standards), and other rules not covered in the WTO (capital controls, state-owned enterprises, and investor-state dispute procedures). The institutional stretch required to reach consensus on many of these issues will also demand a new institutional understanding at the regional level of the legitimate reach of cross-border trade rules. US advocacy of creating or extending international disciplines on TPP members' trade and regulatory policies, for example, will almost certainly require flexibility by the United States in opening its own sensitive markets, in the face of potent protectionist lobbies. In addition, even US trade officials have noted privately that the United States has been accustomed to negotiating bilateral or regional trade agreements with small, or groups of small, countries, and typically dictating the agenda and most of the terms, but the large number of countries in the TPP talks, now including Japan, diminishes US bargaining power. Yet the TPP negotiations became significantly more valuable when the number and size of participants rose, so US leadership in global trade will have to begin at home, in constructing new momentum for trade liberalization. This would be the first step in shifting the institutional lines in the WTO system as well, if the TPP is to serve as a template for future multilateral negotiations.

Many of the political obstacles that stand in the way of an ambitious, ground-breaking TPP agreement reflect one of the main institutional barriers that plagued the Doha Round: the lack of a shared understanding among participants of the limits of domestic policy sovereignty in identifying bargaining chips. Some are new or recent issues, such as services, intellectual property, investment and state enterprises; others are the usual traditional suspects, including agriculture, textiles, clothing, and shoes. A TPP agreement that comes close to achieving new agreements on rules and market access on many of these "sticking points" would require enormous political will, not to mention domestic political risk taking by many of the participants, including the United States. Details of the negotiations, the twentieth round of which was completed in Ottawa in July 2014, have been generally kept secret, so it is difficult to gauge progress, but some hints of convergence on important issues began to appear at the Singapore Ministerial meeting of the TPP in December 2013 (Schott 2014). In the shadow of the stalled Doha Round, even a modest agreement, with marginal progress on market access and the beginnings of agreement on the new issues, would represent progress in trade liberalization. The Asia-Pacific area has become a laboratory for trade policy in the twenty-first century, due to its economic dynamism and the regional importance of trade-based supply chains and commerce. The tangle of overlapping FTAs and other preferential arrangements in the region provides a compelling case for consolidating these measures into a regional agreement that would truly liberalize trade in a non-discriminatory manner, with common terms of market access and the broadest rules of origin among all participants, and new deep integration rules. The TPP may not get the job done, but it can be a start.

The US-EU Transatlantic Trade and Investment Partnership

The agreement by the United States and European Union to launch negotiations on the Transatlantic Trade and Investment Partnership (TTIP) in July 2013 is another child of the suspended Doha Round. As recovery from the global financial crisis remained slow in the United States, and contributed (along with the Eurozone crisis) to stagnation in the European Union, both of these trading partners viewed a new trade agreement as a way to revitalize their economies. Like the TPP, its potential for expanding the gains from trade is enormous. The United States and European Union carry on the largest bilateral commercial relationship in the world economy, with approximately $1 trillion in bilateral trade annually and $3.7 trillion in joint cross-border foreign direct investment. While tariffs between the two trading partners are already very low on average, the long-standing and advanced state of their economic relationship suggests many areas in which further liberalization and harmonization of rules and standards would yield significant new gains from trade. An inter-governmental task force set up jointly by the US Trade Representative's Office and the European Commission outlined several areas of a comprehensive negotiation to increase trade and investment between the two areas (see HLWG 2013), including the elimination of most tariffs, liberalization of services trade, investment reforms, expanded access to government procurement, introduction of WTO+ rules on safety standards and technical barriers to trade, as well as the establishment of new rules on customs and trade facilitation, competition policy, state-owned enterprises, localization barriers to trade, raw materials, energy, small- and medium-sized enterprises, and transparency. An important part of the proposed agenda is regulatory reform and harmonization, bilateral negotiation of outstanding bilateral intellectual property rights issues, and joint discussion on environmental and labor standards. A study commission by the European Union (Francois et al. 2013) estimates the annual economic welfare gains from a comprehensive TTIP of approximately $153 billion for the European Union and $123 billion for the United States, with 80% of the gains coming from the reduction in red tape and other regulatory reforms. These estimates do not take into account possible productivity and dynamic market effects over time, which could increase the welfare gains. The report also estimates a strong positive spillover effect for the rest of the world of approximately $129 billion annually,[30] much of which comes from "MFN" effects of negotiated TTIP regulatory reforms, the benefits of which would apply to all trading partners of the European Union and United States.

The TTIP is of special interest to the future course of WTO negotiations for several reasons. As the two largest and wealthiest services-oriented economies of the world, with extensive cross-investment and embedded commercial interests in each other's markets, the negotiations provide the best hope of achieving progress in liberalizing services trade and reducing technical and regulatory barriers, which represent the largest impediments to trade between them. Trade liberalization in these areas could establish benchmarks for global liberalization later. Both have highly protected agricultural sectors that have posed major problems in WTO negotiations with developing countries; a mutual agreement to scale back such protection, especially through subsidy reductions, could remove a major impediment to further multilateral trade liberalization. The negotiations also provide an opportunity for the two sides to resolve long-standing disputes that have resisted satisfactory solutions at the WTO, such as the decades-long Boeing-Airbus subsidies battle; the fights over beef hormones and genetically modified organisms; lack of uniformity in access to government procurement contracts; and the conflict regarding geographical indications in intellectual property rights enforcement, especially in dairy products and wine. In general, a successful TTIP would establish precedents for new rules, create "market access envy" among other countries, contribute to a potential international services agreement, and possibly simplify future WTO negotiations in agriculture.

The bilateral TTIP negotiations are likely to be less complicated than multi-country TPP talks, even if the bargaining is equally contentious. Politically, the TTIP appears to face less resistance than the TPP in terms of domestic industrial and labor lobbies, thus increasing the chances that a breakthrough agreement with meaningful reforms. The exception to this generalization may be the farm lobby on both sides of the Atlantic, which is involved in disagreements over the general protection of agriculture, as well as the beef hormone, GMO, and geographical indications disputes. The United States and European Union have similar economic structures, and much of the trade competition between them is in the form of intra-industry trade, implying a less disruptive adjustment to trade liberalization. They also have a strong common interest in the enforcement of environmental and labor standards, issues that tend to hamper their relations with other countries.[31] In addition, Schott and Cimino (2013) note that both the United States and the European Union have concluded separate FTA agreements with Korea, providing a possible joint template for the TTIP, with some modifications. Finally, the United States and European Union countries are close allies on most political and military issues, and share many cultural and historical ties. These elements, taken together, do not guarantee an easy negotiation, but increase the chances for a substantial, final agreement, perhaps as soon as 2015.

And yet there are many impediments to a successful TTIP agreement. One might question, for example, why such obvious and large gains from trade between two broadly like-minded trading partners had not been negotiated already. In fact there have been previous attempts to conclude such agreements (see Transatlantic Task Force 2012: 18), but these efforts foundered on a negotiating strategy that relied on partitioned, issue-by-issue bargaining, on which differences on details could not be bridged, in the absence of larger trade-offs. The lesson from this experience is that a comprehensive agreement that spans all the issues is the only way to get a viable final agreement. The largest impediments to a TTIP in this regard are likely to lie in a remarkable tendency for both the United States and European Union to refuse to compromise on long-standing disputes, combined with squabbling at the regulatory and governmental levels. A close existing trade relationship such as this one evidently tends to generate a certain degree of contempt for the trade barriers that do prevail between them.[32] Institutionally, this problem illustrates yet again the problem of trying to expand the scope of domestic policy space available for bargaining in a trade negotiation. What, if anything, might persuade the European Union to modify its "precautionary principle" with regard to GMOs? What could persuade the US Congress to modify the latest Farm Bill in order to make a trade deal possible? Regarding the disputes mentioned above, both sides have usually counted on WTO "courtroom justice" to vindicate their positions, but in many of the long-standing cases it has long since become evident that an "out-of-court" compromise, now available in TTIP negotiations, promises a more lasting chance of resolving them. Leadership in the TTIP negotiations must prevent these and other politically touchy issues from derailing an agreement, either through stonewalling or—what is more likely—a pre-emptive removal from the agenda, which will lead to tit-for-tat withdrawals of other sensitive issues and a reduced scope for a meaningful agreement. The other major challenge is the unprecedented nature of negotiating behind-the-border regulatory reforms in the context of trade policy. The political logic of domestic regulatory regimes does not fit comfortably with the trade negotiating logic of reciprocal "concessions" to facilitate market access. New gains from trade may provide the bargaining chips needed for a deal, but corresponding exporter and other trade-opening interests must also be fully engaged in the negotiations in order to expand the scope of behind-the-border policy bargaining. Governments seeking gains from trade in these new areas must at some point build bridges between domestic regulatory reform (or harmonization) and trade liberalization, again placing a high premium on the creative strategy, vision, and leadership of US and EU trade authorities.

Other RTA Negotiations

The WTO's RTA database listed dozens of proposed new agreements as of early 2014, most of them bilateral negotiations that will have little impact on future WTO trade talks, at the same time exhibiting the continued efforts of both large and small countries to secure new market access in the wake of the Doha Round suspension.[33] Some of these proposed RTAs may influence the larger agreements discussed in this chapter, however. The preliminary EU-Canada trade agreement concluded in October 2013 and forthcoming EU-Japan negotiations may indicate, for example, some of the possibilities and difficulties that could arise in the TTIP talks and may provide "bridges" between the TTIP and TPP in the future. In addition, several countries in the Asia-Pacific region are conducting separate RTA negotiations, most of which go beyond simple market-access agreements to include investment, technical barriers to trade (TBT), SPS, and dispute settlement chapters. Some of these negotiations may influence the TPP, such as Australia-China, Australia-Japan, Japan-Korea, Canada-Singapore, Canada-Korea, and Mexico-Korea. Aside from providing information on the various countries' negotiating positions, such sub-regional RTAs may also provide alternatives, and therefore some leverage, for smaller countries in the TPP talks. In this regard EU-Malaysia, EU-Singapore, and EU-Vietnam may also play a role in the TPP. Perhaps the most encouraging RTA development in the region has been the 2013 conclusion of the Pacific Alliance (Dube 2013; O'Grady 2013), an economic integration agreement that includes Mexico, Chile, Colombia, and Peru. It is an FTA with commitments to reduce all tariffs on trade within the region to zero, with provisions for free movement of services, investments, capital, and people in the region, and consolidated cumulation on rules of origin among the members. Other Latin American countries are interested in joining, and the United States, Canada, Japan, Australia, and New Zealand are observer countries. The auspiciously named Pacific Alliance, though a small sub-regional agreement, would serve well as a model for the more ambitious goals of the TPP.

It is also important to take stock of RTAs involving the large emerging markets, especially Brazil, China, and India, since these countries' high rates of economic growth imply valuable future import markets, with corresponding importance for future WTO negotiations. These countries have also been pursuing RTA strategies, although not with the ambitious new coverage proposed by the TPP and TTIP. Brazil, as part of Mercosur, has concluded FTAs mainly in South America, but has also had on-again, off-again FTA negotiations with the European Union, which were revived in 2010. However, internal policy differences among Mercosur members and industrial market access issues may diminish the impact of any final agreement (Malamud 2013). China has focused its RTA strategy on the Asia-Pacific area and has started talks on a trilateral FTA with its two largest trading partners in the region, Japan and the Republic of Korea, but political and territorial differences make progress on an agreement uncertain. An EU-China "Partnership and Cooperation Agreement" was still underway in 2013, but little progress had been made to that point, while plans for a China-India FTA, which would also be of significance, remained an early stage of discussion. India itself also has an extensive list of RTA partners and ongoing negotiations, mainly in the East Asia-Pacific region. Its most significant post-Doha RTA negotiation, however, has been with the European Union. Given the importance of India in a broader WTO agreement, increased market and investment access for the European Union could open the door to trade reforms multilaterally. However, the negotiations have run into obstacles broadly associated with finding reciprocal terms for market access between a large developed area and a large developing country. Contentious issues have included automobiles, agriculture, foreign direct investment, information technology, and generic drugs (Khorana et al. 2010; Raihan 2009).

SUMMARY: THE INSTRUMENTAL ROLE OF RTAS IN THE GATT/WTO SYSTEM

The GATT/WTO system has provided participating countries with a foundation of rules and multilateral market access that has allowed hundreds of RTAs to be concluded over the years, most with little economic benefit, but imposing little damage to the system itself. The impulse for countries to conclude RTAs is strong and has grown stronger as trade liberalization has progressed.

Some RTAs, such as the European Common Market (later European Union) and NAFTA in fact played positive roles in maintaining momentum in concurrent multilateral trade negotiations. The recent proliferation of RTAs appears to be motivated largely by a desire among WTO members to achieve trade liberalization on a bilateral and regional basis while the Doha Round has in the meantime failed to deliver an agreement. While the gains from trade would be maximized through a comprehensive WTO agreement, it is important to allow countries to channel their desire for more trade through RTAs, as this same impulse can, under the proper conditions, be harnessed to revive WTO talks at some point in the future. The process of moving from regional to global negotiations requires major trading countries to pursue ambitious and expansive RTA market access and rules reform, with correspondingly large gains from trade, creating market access envy among countries left out of the RTA, and diminishing domestic protectionist resistance at home as the liberalization spreads. Unfortunately, this process is not entirely automatic. It requires leadership and initiative among major countries. They must creatively forge new trade coalitions to overcome domestic opposition, and must keep their ultimate focus on a global WTO agreement.

The two largest post-Doha RTA negotiations, the TPP and TTIP, have the potential to play such a role in reviving WTO-based multilateralism, covering substantial trade flows and proposing new rules and market-opening measures. A successful agreement on major new trade provisions would be likely to attract interest by other countries either in joining the agreement, negotiating similar agreements, or calling for WTO negotiations to multilateralize the provisions. Before such a felicitous outcome occurs, however, there is plenty of work to be done by countries negotiating the TPP and TTIP. The biggest danger is that the contentious issues will merely replicate Doha Round problems, leaving new deals to wither on the vine. This hazard is particularly acute for the TPP, its twelve nations comprising both developed and developing economies, large and small countries. Traditional market opening provisions have inflamed familiar protectionist passions in old-line manufacturing industries and agriculture, small countries have questioned the motives of the United States in spearheading the talks, and many countries carry long-standing resentments over prior trade agreements into the negotiations. For both the TPP and TTIP, the hard nub of new, behind-the-border measures will need to shrink the limits of sovereign policy space, a major institutional issue that must be resolved to capture new gains from trade. The new "collective intentionality" of a twenty-first-century trading system will require domestic political strategies to garner support for such changes in order to build a new foundation for regional, and perhaps then, multilateral consensus.

The job of achieving multilateral consensus is therefore not over until successful regional trade agreements can lead to wider agreement with countries outside the large RTAs. TPP and TTIP may indeed break new ground in trade liberalization, but, as business representatives in the United States have observed, "they won't get us into China or India." An RTA achieved on the strength of strong common interests among the partners, or regional hegemonic leadership and bargaining power, must contain elements for nurturing wider acceptance in order to move all WTO members closer to consensus. In the debate over the role of RTAs in multilateral trade liberalization, it is the capacity of governments standing behind the RTA to welcome new membership and further trade liberalization that makes the biggest difference, and this is a matter of the governments' political and economic attitude, confidence, outlook, and commitment. While the content of RTAs provides the potential for globalizing market access and rules, it is the decision by large trading countries to pursue a proper follow-up to their new RTAs to push for a WTO agreement that is perhaps the best indication that the RTA is in fact a "building bloc" for multilateral liberalization.

Trade, Embedded Liberalism, and Development

INTRODUCTION

Since the beginning of the GATT/WTO era, multilateral trade liberalization has depended on a political balance in key participating countries between forces favoring stability and particular national economic goals, on the one hand, and those favoring expanded trade opportunities, on the other. This balance, an essential feature of a successful global trade institution, has been maintained in part by macroeconomic and targeted sectoral and social safety net policies of participating countries, in combination with contingent protection measures, which together formed the "embedded liberalism" of the trading order, as described in chapter 2. In the meantime, this delicate political balance has been shaken by two major shifts in the trade environment. First, developed countries have had to face the challenges of globalized markets, combined with their own slower growth, expanding public debt, and the rapid growth of emerging market economies, creating anxiety and casting doubt on the ability of embedded liberalism to assure economic stability and well-being under trade liberalization. In addition, the developing countries—at various stages of economic development—have as the result of globalization and growth faced the challenge of taking part in trade negotiations as new partners but under old and at times contradictory rules. During the Doha Round, and especially since the talks collapsed in 2008, critical attention has focused on the divisions between developed and developing countries in their views on trade liberalization in general and also on the boundaries of legitimate "policy space" in trade negotiations.

This chapter examines these two issues, the connections between them, and possible ways to improve the situation, based on the need to renew traditional domestic embedded liberalism and to extend this concept internationally. The idea that supporting social safety net policies was a critical element of the success of the original GATT applied mainly to the industrialized countries, which were the only ones facing significant adjustment pressures from GATT-sponsored trade liberalization during those years. Now that developing countries have become an important part of the trading system, they face trade capacity, as well as adjustment, challenges, but in many cases without the domestic resources, institutions, or experience to capture fully the gains from trade. For the Doha Round, the holy grail of consensus necessary to forge a final agreement has remained frustratingly out of reach, in part over the question of developing countries' willingness to open their markets while pursuing policies in support of development. It is unlikely that future progress on global trade liberalization will be possible in the absence of a common framework for addressing this issue, particularly in light of the different levels of economic development represented by the developing country members of the WTO. Such a framework will require three elements. First of all, there must be a shared understanding about the link between trade and development—and the limits of this relationship. A second element will be an arrangement, perhaps differentiated according to national per-capita income, regarding expectations of reciprocity in trade negotiations. And in order for many countries to be willing to negotiate on reciprocal terms, there will also almost certainly need to be a workable system of transfers, through aid-for-trade or other types of assistance.

The chapter begins with a discussion of the concept of "embedded liberalism" and its role in trade liberalization, followed by an account of what the concept now means to the developed countries themselves. The discussion will then turn to the subject of trade and development, and the issue of whether the potential gains from trade liberalization, generally negotiated on a reciprocal basis, conflict with the perceived need for "policy space" to pursue development goals. The chapter then turns to the concept and possibilities of a new, extended and international embedded liberalism, based on transfers from richer to poorer countries that support trade capacity and adjustment. The prospects for harvesting a trade facilitation agreement from the Doha Round, and the advent of systematic aid-for-trade initiatives, will then provide the context for discussing a possible institutional approach to bridging the development gap in multilateral trade negotiations. A summary section, with prospects for future trade negotiations, concludes the chapter.

EMBEDDED LIBERALISM: THE CONCEPTUAL
FRAMEWORK

Trade liberalization operates within the confines of what Ruggie (1982) identified as the embedded liberalism of domestic policy goals. Ruggie shares
Searle's (2005) constructionist approach to international institutions, emphasizing shared social purposes as a component of the converging expectations
embodied in the institution (see Lang 2006). In the WTO, the principle of
post-Keynesian "policy space" continues to provide its members with the flexibility to pursue policies to prevent economic disruption while committing
to the principle of nondiscrimination and other rules of conduct in negotiating trade liberalization. At the domestic level, additional safety net policies
include social security or national pension plans, unemployment insurance,
subsidized public education and other services, and various forms of welfare
entitlements, as well as direct compensation, retraining and/or relocation
assistance for trade-related job and income losses through trade adjustment
programs. WTO policies also allow contingent and temporary trade restrictions against imports, through antidumping, countervailing duty, and safeguards measures. For the purposes of trade liberalization, the safety nets
provide insurance against losses that some workers may suffer as a result of
trade liberalization agreements.

Searle's constructivist approach draws links from the underlying collective
intentionality to the constitutive rules that will carry out that mandate, and
from there to the "output" or intended accomplishments of the institution.
Figure 7.1, based on elements of figure 3.1, illustrates these critical linkages.
The twin goals of realizing gains from trade and member countries' domestic
economic policy sovereignty imply the need for a set of constitutive rules that
support trade liberalization while providing for the requisite domestic "policy
space" to pursue social welfare programs and other foreign policy goals domestically. Policy space, in turn, has an embedded liberalism component (applicable primarily, but not exclusively, to developed countries), a development
priorities component (for developing countries, as set forth in GATT/WTO
rules), and an implicit "off-limits" policy component. What is off-limits is not
fully defined in the WTO, although the 1955 US waiver on agriculture and
the lack of inclusion of services in the GATT are examples of how such limits can be formalized. However, the political nature of what is "off-limits" cannot necessarily be overridden by fiat, as the shortcomings in extending global
trade liberalization to agriculture and services in the WTO—despite formal
frameworks—have shown. Together the policy space complex operates in tension with gains-from-trade forces to determine the degree of political support

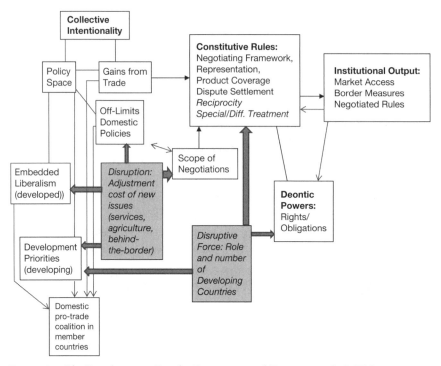

Figure 7.1 The Development Divide, Disruption and Tensions in the WTO Framework

for trade liberalization: the output of new market access and trade rules from WTO negotiations.

However, changes in the role of developing countries and the introduction of new and controversial issues into the negotiations can introduce disruptive elements in the alignment of institutional linkages shown in figure 7.1. These institutional disruptions were featured in the general discussion of the WTO's problems in chapters 2, 3 and 4; in this chapter the focus will be on the role of policy space and the potential role of embedded liberalism to address the problem. The increasing role and participation of developing countries in WTO negotiations has been institutionally disruptive insofar as this change has created a conflict between expectations of reciprocity, the traditional means of bargaining, and the special and differential (S&D) treatment of developing countries established under the GATT and carried over into the WTO. The constitutive rules of reciprocity and S&D treatment thereby come into conflict with each other, which disrupts the deontic nature of WTO membership. As a result, in negotiations, participants must ask what the rights and obligations of developing country members really are. The conflict also carries an impact in policy space: development priorities, which previously had not been a major constraint in trade negotiations, were in the Doha Round presented by developing countries as restricted policy space, reducing their willingness to offer reciprocal market access concessions. The introduction of new issues also disrupted policy space equilibrium in the negotiations, with some overlap on the development issue. For many countries, agriculture has continued to be essentially off-limits to meaningful trade liberalization. In addition, services trade liberalization failed to gain widespread support, as many countries insisted on keeping most of their services sectors, often tightly aligned with domestic regulatory regimes, exempt from import market incursions of foreign suppliers. Even beyond the Doha Round issues that proved to be politically off-limits, it is important to recognize the ongoing challenges that WTO members will face in coming years as many other new and potentially off-limits issues, especially sensitive behind-the-border regulatory measures, become the subject of trade liberalization proposals.

What sort of policies or measures—domestic or international—can serve to restrike a political balance in favor of new trade liberalization? Embedded liberalism is a concept that challenges the traditional economic analysis of trade policy, in that it relies on the use of a potentially broad array of government interventions—including contingent trade restrictions—to secure a political consensus on trade liberalization and the gains from trade. The problem lies in the conflict between the goal for all participating countries of achieving gains from trade and the political necessity of domestic government intervention in many countries to secure those gains. The intervention thus entails a cost-benefit analysis in political economy: it may distort market outcomes and impose social costs on the economy as a price for securing political support for the gains from trade. Opposition to increased trade arises among groups within countries suffering income losses and adjustment costs, and the policy challenge is to find efficient ways to compensate them to the extent that overall political support for trade can be secured. In economic terms, achieving this balance in principle theoretically comes down to finding the point where the marginal benefits of additional trade liberalization are equal to the marginal cost of increased government programs used to secure approval for it, a solution that would represent an economically optimal intervention. Corden (1974) first formulated this problem in terms of "market divergences," in which there is a gap between what a private laissez-faire market provides and what a socially optimal "corrected" market would provide. This gap can theoretically be closed or corrected with the appropriate policy intervention.[1] Unlike the policy treatment of discrete market failures, however, in which a tax or subsidy can close the gap between private and social values embodied in single market's demand or supply curves, the problem in this context is the lack of sufficient political support for trade liberalization in the broader domestic economy. Closing the gap in this case means providing guarantees of existing income distribution, as represented by what Corden termed a *conservative social welfare function*, implying that trade policies, in order to remain politically viable, should avoid reducing welfare for significant groups in the economy. Governments can pursue this goal through the use of various policy instruments, including trade intervention to benefit workers and other stakeholders in import-competing industries, trade adjustment assistance, subsidies, and other transfers, and broader social "safety nets" such as unemployment insurance, welfare payments, social security, and mandated health benefits.

Embedded liberalism, in this formulation, finds economic justification in the familiar observation that the gains from trade are typically large enough for the country as a whole to allow compensation, paid out of increased earnings of those who benefit from it, to those who lose from it. So far, so good: but economic danger lurks in the details. For example, how much trade restriction within embedded liberalism is needed to secure trade liberalization? Consider a common economic complaint along these lines, antidumping laws, which are designed to provide relief to import-competing firms in the form of special tariffs, and which may indeed provide a sort of "safety valve" for protectionist sentiment that is necessary to secure political support for general trade liberalization. Yet antidumping tariffs create market distortions and social costs, and an uncontrolled proliferation of cases and accommodating administrative rules could escalate these costs. Embedded liberalism thus runs the risk of creating economically illiberal outcomes. This problem is compounded by the apparent political need to establish a large and varied set of policies that address various components of trade-related income distribution in the economy. In pursuing the broad political goal of achieving a consensus favoring trade, it will be difficult to achieve economic precision when so many blunt policy instruments are involved.

Whatever the problems associated with antidumping and other contingent protection, embedded liberalism appeared to serve the original GATT system very well. It is also important to observe that "safety nets" were not entirely dependent on contingent trade protection, as broader welfare policies were also probably helpful in removing trade adjustment anxieties. In this regard, Corden's theory of divergences and optimal intervention provides a helpful framework in analyzing embedded liberalism. The best policy is one that addresses the market distortion or gap at its source, without creating new distortions in its wake. As new or different political requirements for a policy complex of embedded liberalism arise, it should in principle be possible to impose a set of policies that keeps economic distortion and cost to an acceptable minimum. It is clear, however, that such domestic policies are limited by the resources of the country. The ability of developing countries to provide such safety nets is of particular concern, to the extent that their absence may constrain governments' willingness to agree to market-opening measures. For this reason, the WTO carried forward S&D treatment provisions for developing countries in the amended GATT 1994, which modify WTO obligations for developing countries and grant them additional flexibility in imposing trade restrictions. Thus, S&D treatment has acted as a sort of partial substitute for embedded liberalism for developing countries. Even so, the development gap has revealed the traditional concept of embedded liberalism as a stabilizing feature primarily among high-income countries with sufficient resources to support social welfare programs. Many developing countries, in contrast, have more serious problems in securing the gains from trade, including basic infrastructure deficiencies, weak legal and governmental institutions, and inefficient finance facilities. They often have insufficient domestic resources to correct these problems, not only for the purpose of mitigating possible disruptions of trade liberalization, but to gain from trade in general.

EMBEDDED LIBERALISM FOR DEVELOPED COUNTRIES IN THE TWENTY-FIRST CENTURY

It is worth briefly reviewing the relevance of embedded liberalism for the high-income countries that presumably have the necessary resources to provide the safety nets that will vouchsafe the conclusion of new trade agreements. This optimistic view has turned out to be far from political reality in the WTO era. The rapid pace of technological change, anxiety over job security, and reduced economic growth have combined to make even rich countries vulnerable to adjustment pressures, whether from trade competition or other sources. The earlier discussion of figure 7.1 implies that the expansion of the trade agenda into new areas appears in at least some cases to have overstepped the boundaries for trade liberalization that are politically feasible in member states. This problem is not limited to developing countries. The original GATT balance between trade liberalization and embedded liberalism may no longer be capable of opening new and politically sensitive sectors to trade even in the richer countries, especially in cases when domestic regulatory regimes and their "behind-the-border" measures must be placed on the negotiating table. Furthermore, the increasingly prominent role of developing countries, which now have attractive import markets but are still constrained by limited domestic resources for adjustment and "safety nets," reframes the role of embedded liberalism. What if new transfers to those harmed by trade are required to complete a new global balance between further trade liberalization and embedded liberalism?

The most direct approach is to fill in the gaps with supporting domestic policies to support factor mobility, workforce training, and adjustment assistance.

Hays (2009) argues that, in an era of globalization and rapid economic change, the United States in particular has failed to uphold the role of embedded liberalism in its trade policy by neglecting to develop supportive domestic policies, thereby undermining the political support for trade liberalization. Since the United States remains an essential (if not the only) key to achieving a multilateral trade agreement, it will be necessary for it to provide its citizens with programs to prevent the adverse impact of trade on specific groups' economic welfare. Kletzer and Litan (2001) propose adjustment assistance, including transitional income compensation, as a safety net for workers at risk from increased import competition. In an increasingly globalized economy, achieving public support for trade liberalization in industrialized countries will also require governments to pay more attention to education, retraining, worker mobility, and labor market flexibility, so that the economy can continually respond to new trade and technology developments with correspondingly new patterns of specialization so that the gains from trade can continue.[2] Such structural measures are all the more important in view of fact that the increased share of capital in national income in many countries will make it more difficult for governments to finance adjustment assistance through taxation.[3]

Measures taken to shore up embedded liberalism in rich countries can at best address only half the problem, however. In much of the developing world, it is difficult to benefit from trade because of severe gaps in infrastructure, production methods, and domestic economic institutions, and many governments cannot afford generous fiscal policies to deal with disruptions that may accompany new import competition. So far the developed WTO members have attempted to offer developing countries S&D treatment as a substitute for traditional forms of embedded liberalism found in the developed world. Domestic political support for trade in resource-strapped countries would theoretically be nurtured by preferential market access, greater freedom to restrict trade, and lighter reciprocity requirements. However, experience has shown that these very measures have often sent the wrong signals, as they implied, for example, that valuable market access could be freely obtained without bargaining, or that the gains from trade come only from exports, or that trade preferences represent permanently preferential market access. In addition, S&D treatment has failed to address the underlying problems of deficient resources and institutions (trade capacity) in these countries.

THE DEVELOPMENT DIVIDE OVER TRADE

The use of the name, "Doha Development Agenda" (DDA) was an understandable, if ill-fated, attempt to portray multilateral trade negotiations as an exercise in development economics. It was part of a quiet acknowledgment among developed countries that the Uruguay Round, completed in 1994, had been disappointing to developing countries, particularly with regard to the unexpectedly limited benefits of textiles and apparel trade liberalization for most of them, along with a painful lack of progress in agricultural market opening by wealthy countries and costs and problems of implementing the TRIPS agreement. Developing countries needed to be brought on board with encouraging prospects for a new deal in the Doha Round that would deliver the goods for them. Initially dubbed the "Millennium Round" before the term "DDA" was adopted, the Doha plan was to show that the new trade talks would get the "development" aspect of trade right this time, hence the decision to pursue a public relations strategy of building it into the title of the trade negotiations.

However, developed and developing countries' views on the meaning of this concept diverged significantly. Developed countries tended to see the "development agenda" in part as a renewed effort to apply S&D treatment to developing countries, a sort of "affirmative action" program that would reduce the magnitude of the concessions the poorer developing countries would be expected to offer, while still opening markets in emerging-market and middle-income countries. In addition, the new round would finally liberalize agricultural trade, especially through reduced subsidies in the OECD countries, with more modest but significant reductions in tariffs in developing countries. Finally, the large new trade liberalization package would be, in itself, pro-development because it would be pro-trade, with the gains from trade contributing, ipso facto, to development. Many developing countries, on the other hand, still upset over the Uruguay Round results, saw the new "development round" as a way to correct what they saw as a bad and lopsided deal from the previous negotiations. In particular, their view of a "development agenda" was that it would require minimal market access concessions of their own, since many felt they had made too many concessions in the Uruguay Round, and besides, many regarded import competition itself as detrimental to their development policies. It is important to add that GATT/WTO negotiations had always been structured on such mercantilist principles, so everyone—developed and developing countries alike—viewed new export market access as the true "gain from trade," while the reciprocal offer of import market access to the other members was a "concession." The natural political inclination of every country's delegation was to maximize the gains and minimize the concessions. The problem was that a viable Doha Round agreement among all the members, with meaningful new export market access for all, would also require commensurate import market access *concessions* by all. This was, in fact, the only way that all the members could return home, trumpeting their hard-won new export market access to their national capitals, each declaring victory. To get a Doha deal done, developing countries, especially the large ones, would have to offer new access to their increasingly attractive import markets, which would be needed in the developed countries to win ratification by their domestic legislatures. Developing countries, for their part, insisted that their development priorities be honored, as the DDA implied, meaning, among other things, the right to continue protecting their strategically important domestic industries with high tariffs and to protect their domestic "policy space" from trade liberalizing measures.

This misalignment of expectations created a major institutional problem for the WTO, since reciprocity was one of the long-standing foundational principles of GATT/WTO negotiations, along with the consensus rule. It also reflected the implicit lack of agreement on the link between trade and development among WTO members, a major fault line in the organization. WTO members—both developed and developing—must ultimately address this issue in order for progress to be made in future trade liberalization between the two groups. The main point of misunderstanding in this regard is that trade is a *transaction*, while development is a *process*.[4] International trade, a commercial exchange between parties in which ownership of goods or services crosses borders, is the focus of WTO agreements, which seek to reduce the transaction costs of trade through market access and rules agreements. Development, on the other hand, is a complex process of transformation, as defined by Johnson (1967):

> The development problem of the less developed countries is one of converting a "traditional" society predominantly based on subsistence or near-subsistence agriculture and/or the bulk export of a few primary commodities, in which per capita income grows slowly or may even be declining as a result of population pressure, into a "modern" society in which growth of per capita income is internalized in the social and economic system through automatic mechanisms promoting accumulation of capital, improvement of technology, and growth of skill of the labor force. (Johnson 1967: 44)

What role does trade play in the process of development? The connection is through the gains from trade and its impact on the transformation, but the gains from trade are also achieved through a process executed domestically in the trading country. The process includes specialization, a series of market-driven actions that reallocates resources in production through changes in rewards to labor, capital, and other factors, and competition, another set of market-driven actions that realigns prices and consumption choices. WTO agreements facilitate trade as a transaction, but capturing the gains from trade relies on the domestic processes of its members. Clearly, the state of development affects the ability of a country to gain from trade, even as the gains from trade can also promote the development process. Specialization and competition are activities that rely on a system of property rights and contracts, as well as functioning financial and labor markets that efficiently channel factors of production toward activities of greatest reward. In addition, political stability and the quality of governmental institutions are critical elements of a country's business environment that facilitate its capacity for commercial activity. Trade liberalization, in terms of removing trade restrictions, is a necessary requirement for securing the gains from trade, but it is not always sufficient.

Thus, trade liberalization in principle improves a country's ability to promote the development process, but cannot guarantee that the complementary domestic processes will function properly. For this reason, empirical studies have not been able to establish a clear cause-and-effect link between trade and development, usually measured in terms of economic growth.[5] It is difficult to compare measures of discrete transactions-oriented policies (tariffs, etc.) with the effects of processes (development). A country's economic growth, for example, may be primarily the result of the expansion of a large internal market, despite high tariffs, or of the government's ability to mobilize a country's idle resources. Evidence of sustainable growth and development, which would be the result of what Johnson (1967) identified as the critical element of "automatic mechanisms," may not be evident until these initial boosts have run their course. The key to development, and the subsequent ability to gain from trade, may in fact lie mainly in domestic transformations, such as China's rural reforms (Huang 2012) and policy-driven sectoral shifts (Deckle and Vandenbroucke 2012). Agricultural productivity often plays a critical role in the structural transformation of developing economies (Dethier and Effenberger 2012). Trade liberalization should therefore not be oversold as the singular "key" to economic development.

This is not to suggest, however, that trade liberalization is irrelevant to development; trade provides price signals, economic incentives, access to technology, increased income, and consumption gains that can benefit even the poorest economies. Most reviews of the empirical literature find that there is no evidence that high tariffs and protectionist trade regimes, in themselves, promote sustainable economic development (see OECD 2009 and citations therein). Thus, while the gap in a country's capacity to achieve the gains from trade may give justification to modify the WTO's reciprocity rule for developing countries, it is difficult for all parties to the negotiation to agree on what, exactly, the terms of limited developing country reciprocity should be. Trade provides many additional benefits to countries as their development progresses, such as higher quality goods, more variety, exposure to new technologies, access

to more foreign direct investment, and better capital equipment and intermediate inputs. Developing countries, based on their membership in the WTO,
appear to acknowledge these gains from trade implicitly, and desire to take
part in the trade liberalization process, even if global import competition is an
unsettling proposition for many of them. The export side of the argument is
relatively uncontroversial: few in the developing world would oppose expanding export market access opportunities for developing economies as a way to
generate income and promote the growth of their agricultural, resource, and
industrial sectors. To argue, however, that trade liberalization for developing
countries should, or must, be limited to export market access alone, without a
reciprocal opening of domestic markets to imports, creates both an economic
and an institutional problem in WTO negotiations.[6] The economic problem
is that this approach denies the gains that come from imports listed above.
The institutional problem is that WTO negotiations are ultimately driven by
reciprocity.

Dani Rodrik (2007) in his book, *One Economics, Many Recipes*, exemplifies
the school of skepticism about trade liberalization for developing countries
that emphasizes the importance of domestic policy autonomy. While he does
not deny the gains from trade, or their importance for growth at later stages
of development, he rejects the need for trade liberalization before a country is
ready for it, hence the title of his book. He also takes an institutional approach
to economic development, so his analysis parallels the approach taken in the
analysis here, but he does not view the global trading system in the same institutional terms. His main point is that there are many institutional pathways
possible for a developing country to achieve economic efficiency and sustainable growth, citing examples such as Japan, China, Vietnam, India, and other
countries with interventionist government policies and periods of high trade
protection. Other poor countries, such as Haiti, which did liberalize their
trade policies, failed to grow, as indicated in much of the literature cited earlier.
Maximizing the gains from trade, he adds, assumes that several conditions are
in place, such as full employment, no market imperfections, and socially acceptable income distribution effects of trade (Rodrik 2007: 29–30). The conditions
should sound familiar to the reader, since they provide the main motivation
for embedded liberalism in developed countries. In fact, if trade liberalization depended on satisfying all of these conditions first, few countries, rich or
poor, would want to negotiate trade liberalization on a reciprocal basis, or for
that matter submit to WTO rules and other disciplines. Nonetheless, Rodrik's
observation inadvertently raises the point that developing country access to
some form of embedded liberalism would increase their willingness to agree
to trade liberalization. Instead, his position is that countries should be allowed
to liberalize trade at their own pace, without the constraint of WTO-based

reciprocity or rules that could compromise each country's domestic institutional path to development and growth.

This view of the WTO on development issues is unnecessarily narrow. While WTO trade agreements typically demand reciprocity in concessions, this requirement is waived for the poorest, least-developed countries (LDCs). In addition, other developing countries are not expected to reciprocate in a symmetrical fashion to their developed country counterparts, although the ambiguousness of this formulation, and its inability to differentiate along the continuum from higher-income emerging market to lower-income developing markets was a major problem in the Doha Round. In any case, S&D treatment rules provide developing countries with significant flexibility in their domestic policies. And while Rodrik repeats the oft-heard mantra, "trade is a means to an end, not an end in itself" (2007: 227), this statement can be applied equally to "autonomous protectionist policies" as well, which can easily become mired in rent-seeking trade regimes. Trade opening may in fact contribute to the development process as much through the means of providing incentives for better policies as in providing efficiency and welfare benefits on its own. Consider, for example, a domestic development-oriented policy to protect high-priced local production of soap from import competition for the sake of building domestic industries. If the soap factory is manifestly inefficient by global standards, does it really serve a country's development agenda to insist that protectionist measures be maintained, to the economic detriment of the entire population? Will the county's development benefit from systematically maintaining domestic relative prices that diverge radically with world prices, and thereby prevent businesses there from being competitive in the future? These questions, of course, must be decided by the developing countries' own governments, and WTO rules do in fact allow countries to follow different development paths. Yet when faced with the prospect of lowering its tariff on imported soap, the costs and benefits of that decision should balance whatever local or infant-industry production benefits would be lost against the consumer and efficiency gains, along with the bargaining chip advantages that may create new export market opportunities as well.

In addition, while the evidence shows that there are many recipes for countries to achieve (eventually) efficient economic growth, there are fewer recipes for securing the gains from trade. One way is through unilateral tariff cuts and other forms of trade liberalization, which some developing countries have in fact implemented.[7] Another is through RTAs, but as noted in chapter 6, developing countries tend to be at a disadvantage in those negotiations when the partner is a large developed country. Rodrik himself laments this aspect of RTAs (2007: 225), but in the end such agreements are the main alternatives to a WTO agreement, a factor that raises the value to developing countries of

multilaterally negotiated rules and market access. It is important to acknowledge that the global trading system is built on the self-interest of countries that
can influence the agenda and the negotiations. The rich countries used to run
the show, especially in the early GATT period, when the developing countries
had little to sell to them under the rules of the time, and were allowed to "free
ride" on tariff cuts negotiated among the developed countries. Now, however,
developing countries, especially the emerging market countries, have increased
their leverage to the point where both they and the developed countries have
value to put on the table, and are closer to being equal negotiating partners.
Yet meaningful and valuable access to developed countries' markets will not
be given away; it will require the active engagement of developing countries in
reciprocal bargaining.

AID-FOR-TRADE AS EMBEDDED LIBERALISM?

The value of embedded liberalism to the postwar trading system was that it provided a political framework for industrialized countries to agree to sweeping
multilateral trade liberalization over nearly five decades. Yet that framework
was essentially "home grown," internalized in each respective country's political processes, financed by growing postwar affluence and administered by
well-developed governmental infrastructure. It was a necessary complement to
the international cooperation that served as the institutional foundation of the
original GATT. The challenge in the twenty-first-century global trade environment is to create the conditions for a similar, outward-looking openness among
WTO members that can lead to consensus on further global trade liberalization. As noted earlier in this chapter, the developed countries have their part
to play in rebuilding domestic pro-trade coalitions through a renewal of traditional embedded liberalism. More creative efforts, however, will be needed in
order to apply this concept to developing countries, which to varying degrees
face resource and domestic institutional constraints in their trade policies.
Can transfers of financial and technical aid to resource-strapped developing
countries extend a new, international, embedded liberalism in support of trade
liberalization?

  There are many dimensions to this problem. Policy-oriented factors include
developing countries' debt burdens that constrain imports; preference erosion, in which global trade liberalization diminishes the relative advantage of
preferential tariff treatment; government revenue loss from negotiating lower
tariff rates; and domestic adjustment burdens from opening up domestic markets to trade (OECD 2009: 18). McCulloch, Winters, and Cireca (2001) view
the problem in terms of supply-side constraints, including the need to reduce

trade costs through infrastructure development, to build productive capacity, to improve access to credit, and generally, to improve the domestic business environment. Additional gaps include education and other investments in human capital (OECD/WTO 2013: chapter 3). There may also be shortfalls among developing countries in trade policy-making capacity (UN 2012) and in the ability to diversify their export portfolios and to recognize export opportunities (Page 2011). This broad array of development problems suggests that a country's capacity to gain fully from trade may involve nothing less than a comprehensive development program that rapidly accelerates progress. In fact, a serious question arises as to whether any external aid of technical assistance is capable of building embedded liberalism in countries that lack economic structures that can reallocate resources and income levels that can finance social safety nets. There are already several sources of private, governmental, and multilateral foreign aid that address many trade-related development issues separately, but the development process of social, political, and economic transformation may take many years. Ideally, economic growth among developing countries themselves would improve their domestic trade capacity, and perhaps even generate new sources of aid-for-trade support from large emerging markets such as China, India, and Brazil. For those developing countries that cannot create their own domestic embedded liberalism, however, support for further multilateral trade liberalization may have to begin with aid-for-trade transfers from a variety of sources.

The Coherence Problem in Delivering Aid-for-Trade

In attempting to bridge the development gap, however, the key is to find ways to make an impact. In this regard the concept of linking aid to trade serves as a useful focal point for promoting the process of gaining from trade in developing countries, as well as organizing and managing the resources, measuring the results, and evaluating the program's effectiveness. This conceptual approach has given rise to the aid-for-trade initiative, in which the WTO, World Bank, and other institutions have designed foreign aid programs specifically to support trade capacity (see OECD 2006; Prowse 2006). The WTO's Hong Kong Ministerial Declaration specifically called for such programs in support of the Doha Round (WTO 2005), although without specific commitments. One major problem in achieving the needed linkage is that it will require systematic institutional coordination, or coherence, between the WTO and the sources of funding. The WTO itself had established a specialized agency in 1997, now called the Enhanced Integrated Framework (EIF), to provide aid-for-trade exclusively for the world's forty-nine LDCs. Its programs are managed jointly with other aid organizations with a modest trust fund (totaling $241 million in 2013) provided by twenty-three country donors.[8] The focus of the EIF is to assist LDCs in participating in the global trading system, through "main-streaming" trade into their development programs, establishing governmental structures to implement trade-related policies, and identifying external aid partnerships. The EIF's programs do not affect WTO negotiations directly, since LDCs are not expected to reciprocate in multilateral trade negotiations. They also face the greatest challenges in terms of trade capacity and even administrative capacity, so progress in building functioning trade sectors for these countries at the early stages of development has been slow. Perhaps the biggest contribution of the EIF to the WTO has been its assistance in pre-paring four LDCs for the WTO's arduous accession process (beneficiaries include Nepal, Cambodia, Vanuatu, and Cape Verde), as well as its efforts to mainstream trade into the development policies of other LDCs in the WTO.[9] For purposes of future trade liberalization, EIF policies will be successful to the extent that participating LDCs internalize trade as an important compo-nent of their development process, and that they can "graduate" more quickly to higher income categories of development with this mindset.

Since the 2005 WTO announcement of an aid-for-trade initiative, the amount of global program disbursements has grown, despite the constraints of the global financial crisis, from an average of $24.8b from 2006 to 2008 to $33.6b in 2011 (OECD/WTO 2013: 351).[10] The OECD and WTO jointly issue an annual report with commentary, summary statistics, indications of program effectiveness, links to case studies, and topical essays. Aid-for-trade donors include individual governments and "multilateral" organizations, including the World Bank (by far the largest donor), regional development banks, UN agen-cies, and the EU institutions. The 2013 report lists eighty recipient countries. Of the top twenty recipients of aid in 2011, ten were LDCs and eight were in the lower middle income category (just above LDC). LDCs received 45% of the aid, with most of the rest going to lower middle-income countries, so the bulk of aid-for-trade is, as described earlier, unlikely to impact WTO negotia-tions directly. The largest category of aid in 2011 was economic infrastructure (transport and storage, communications, and energy generation and supply), followed by "building productive capacity" in sectors such as business services, financial services, agriculture, forestry, fishing, industry, mining, and tourism. A much smaller amount went to support trade policy and regulations, although this category includes trade facilitation (to be discussed below), which has a high priority among both donor and recipient countries as a policy issue.

The recent interest in aid-for-trade as a focus of development assistance has also given rise to increased attention to evaluation and assessment of these programs, which is probably the result of skepticism over the effectiveness of foreign aid in general (see, e.g., Easterly 2008; Moyo 2009). In principle, the problem of foreign aid devoted to improved trade capacity is that it may be diverting resources away from more productive uses, such as basic education, health services, and improvements in agricultural productivity. If development is in fact a process of fundamental social and economic transformation, shouldn't efforts be devoted to that goal, which may benefit more from basic legal and political reforms and policies to promote a better entrepreneurial and business environment? Furthermore, externally sourced and targeted aid may reflect the interests of the donors rather than the recipients and tends to bypass the process of internalized decision-making and resource allocation necessary for sustainable reforms in the developing country. These factors place aid programs in a different category from the traditional notion of embedded liberalism, which represents a domestic set of policies within a country to support market opening, based on an internalized political process of resource allocation.

A healthy dose of such economic skepticism will serve aid-for-trade programs well, including trade facilitation. Such efforts to support and improve trade capacity will be worthwhile as long as they serve the development process, through improved trade efficiency and performance, as well as engagement in the trading system. Despite criticisms that more detailed studies are needed of the many categories of aid-for-trade, and its interactions with other development policies, there have been numerous academic and case studies of the effectiveness of aid-for-trade. Most of these studies support the hypothesized link between aid-for-trade and actual trade flows, especially exports from the recipient countries (see OECD/WTO 2013 chapter 5 for a summary of recent results). The benefit of the aid appears to come from the fact that much of it tends to reduce the transaction costs of trade, facilitating greater trade, and therefore gains from trade for both importer and exporter. The mutual gains from increased trade strengthen the case for aid-for-trade. When trade is viewed as a transaction, as described in the discussion of development earlier, this result follows logically. Helble, Mann and Wilson (2012) and Busse, Hoekstra, and Königer (2012) conclude, in particular, that aid-for-trade focused on trade policy reforms, including improved customs processing, reduced "red tape," and improvements in trade administration, significantly reduces trading costs. Considering its relatively modest outlays, aid-for-trade appears to provide the largest payoff rate in terms of increased developing country exports.[11] World Bank and OECD case studies of aid-for-trade indicate that trade is increasingly being "mainstreamed" into recipients' development policies (see WTO 2011b). Recent aid-for-trade strategies have also begun to focus on the role of developing countries in regional supply chains, in which they can potentially take advantage of providing discrete production services, thus achieving gains from trade through international specialization, but with lower investment and resource requirements (see OECD/WTO 2013: chapter 3). Further contributions of aid-for-trade to the development process could include the link between trade efficiency and incentives for better resource allocation and economic policies, leading to new business opportunities, the reduction of corruption, and the promotion of development-oriented reforms promoting property rights and participatory democracy. All of these favorable possibilities and assessments must be tempered, however, by an acknowledgment that the level of development itself plays a crucial role in translating aid-for-trade into both an effective driver of trade, and through the development process, of generating sustainable growth:

> [I]t is clear that aid for trade is not effective in all country situations in attaining its intermediate outcome objectives of increasing trade, much less its impacts in promoting rapid growth and reducing poverty. Aid for trade is most effective at increasing trade and promoting trade-led growth when recipient countries have a supportive business environment, particularly stable macroeconomic policies and an investment climate that encourages private investment. (OECD/WTO 2013: 163)

The Bali Agreement: A Breakthrough for Aid-for-Trade Liberalization?

The contribution of aid-for-trade to trade performance and to trade's role in development policy plants the seeds for future engagement by developing countries in trade negotiations. Yet for the most part, the aid so far has not been coordinated, except in some cases of regional country groupings to take advantage of RTAs or regional supply-chain arrangements. While the OECD, through the Paris Declaration and other documents (OECD 2005, 2011), has developed a set of donor guidelines for the structure and accountability of trade development assistance, the many donors have allowed a thousand aid-for-trade flowers to bloom, with certain preferences shown by donors in particular forms of aid. Despite the demonstrable trade benefits, the sum total of global aid-for-trade cannot create the sort of embedded liberalism that could provide safety nets for developing countries and allow them to approach global trade negotiations with more confidence to engage in traditional GATT/WTO concessions bargaining. An alternative approach to this problem might be to introduce aid-for-trade into the trade negotiations themselves. Institutionally, it would indeed be tempting to structure trade deals that incorporate aid-for-trade in exchange for market-opening measures.[12] A successful deployment of aid-for-trade in the negotiations would thereby generate a more "coherent" global economic institutional structure. Aid-for-trade in fact played such a role in the Doha Round Trade Facilitation negotiations, which culminated in the Bali Agreement in December 2013. Technically, these negotiations focused on one component of aid-for-trade: improving the operation of member countries' trade administration, logistics, and freedom of transit, thereby reducing the transactions costs of trade.[13] The experience of trade facilitation negotiations in the Doha Round was particularly encouraging in this regard, as both developed and developing countries recognized the benefits of coordinating domestic rules on customs procedures with aid-supported infrastructure building (Wilson, Mann, and Otsuki 2005), as indicated in the previous section. The fact that the trade facilitation negotiations represented one of the few areas of progress after the Cancun Ministerial collapse in 2003 appears to have influenced the 2005 WTO announcement to pursue aid-for-trade as a more general initiative outside the trade negotiations.

Finger and Wilson (2007) have argued, however, that commitments of external aid are not possible as part of a comprehensive WTO trade agreement. As a practical matter, the trade diplomats in WTO negotiations do not come to the table with aid budgets in hand as bargaining chips, and the WTO's constitutive rules provide for formal reciprocal concessions only in terms of market access and related trade policy measures, not the exchange of funds, and in particular, not for specific capacity and infrastructure projects to support trade. In addition, WTO general rules, on their own, cannot support or protect aid-for-trade outcomes. Trade liberalization agreements are sweeping in nature, typically imposing cuts across thousands of tariff lines and reforms of rules on trade-related practices. Project aid such as aid-for-trade, in contrast, is highly targeted, detailed, and procedural, requiring specialized administration outside the WTO. Despite the general optimism over trade facilitation as a "win-win" proposition for both developed and developing countries, the negotiations ran into some difficulties over the institutional understanding of obligations and benefits. Since developed country aid is understood as a separate quid pro quo for ancillary trade capacity in the trade facilitation agreement, some developing countries argued during the negotiations that their obligations to improve trade efficiencies through policy reforms would represent uncompensated concessions, thereby requiring more developed country concessions in cross negotiations.[14] Using aid agreements as an internalized quid pro quo for trade liberalization appears to be difficult within the current institutional framework of the WTO, although the Bali Agreement will put this proposition to the test. The "division of labor" between aid organizations and trade organizations in the world economy had previously shown that foreign aid could at best supply indirect support for multilateral trade liberalization. Infrastructure and institution building in developing countries can certainly act as the handmaidens of trade liberalization, but in the absence of an ambitious merger of trade and aid organizations, direct issue linkage between aid and increased market access had always been problematical. In particular, the interests of aid donors and aid recipients are not always aligned, since donors are likely, for example, to focus their aid on larger and more advanced developing countries, with an eye toward larger payoffs for their exporters.[15] Therefore, establishing a level of coherence between aid and trade that can actually improve the operation of the WTO system requires aid measures in targeted sensitive areas, managed by aid institutions such as the World Bank, and well-coordinated with domestic reforms in these countries, and in anticipation of trade negotiations on related issues. This is a tall order, and one that must overcome the bureaucratic constraints of administrative cooperation across institutions.[16]

These constraints led to some awkward language in the Bali Agreement. The final trade facilitation text indicates, for example, that "[d]onor Members agree to facilitate the provision of assistance and support for capacity building to developing country and least developed country Members, on mutually agreed terms and either bilaterally or through the appropriate international organizations" (WTO 2013: section 9.1). Section 9 goes on to describe principles and suggested frameworks for planning, coordinating, and allocating financial assistance for capacity building, without specifying aid amounts, donors, and responsibilities (section 9.3). Thus, while amounts of total (and future) financial aid could not be included in the agreement, the aid that had already been delivered through established programs during the negotiations had advanced to the point where developing countries were willing to accept the reform obligations and conclude the agreement. As a result, trade-facilitation-earmarked aid would continue to flow. If such aid flows were to cease for some reason, or if disputes arose regarding the adequacy of financial or technical assistance, one might imagine that the recipient countries could withhold or reverse the reforms they had agreed to, but the Trade Facilitation Agreement goes on to establish review procedures that would presumably identify and address implementation problems (section 9.4). While such arrangements do not appear to provide airtight procedures for resolving disputes, the common interest among all parties in making trade facilitation work, and the potential of extending the aid and reforms in the future, may provide incentives for continued cooperation.

The Bali Trade Facilitation Agreement thus represents a watershed in WTO negotiations, by establishing a new bargaining paradigm that matches trade liberalizing reforms with targeted aid. In this regard it is also a test case, an experiment in trade-and-development coherence in multilateral negotiations. Based on past experience of foreign aid programs and the diversity of aid recipients, one can expect that the impact of trade facilitation reforms will vary from country to country. Will collaboration and cooperation on this issue be sustainable over time, in view of the mixed results? What happens to the agreement if there is significant protectionist backsliding by aid recipients in the future, or if for some reason aid flows diminish? Ideally, the up-front provision of aid-for-trade capacity building should allow future pay-offs as the aid stream fulfills its purpose and can be terminated. Will recipient countries hold future trade reforms, including those not related to trade facilitation, hostage in exchange for more aid? Will donor countries begin attaching new conditions clandestinely on trade or non-trade matters, in exchange for continued funding? A broader question is whether the bargaining principle of aid-for-trade can go beyond the narrow quid pro quo of specific procedural reforms to include a broader package of market-opening measures.

How should future WTO negotiations be structured to deal with activities such as aid-for-trade, which are complementary to its goals but outside its mandate? One possibility is that the World Bank or OECD could provide the needed channel for funding and project logistics through direct negotiation with the rich countries sponsoring the proposal and the developing countries receiving the aid. The World Bank had already begun this role outside the formal structure of the trade facilitation negotiations and will now have a chance to play a more formal role as the Trade Facilitation Agreement is implemented. Even this sort of arrangement may not be sufficient to complete a larger multilateral negotiation, however, unless there is confidence among all parties that funding support is reliably linked to negotiated WTO obligations. An agreement making this linkage, along with an agreement on financial burden sharing and implementation, would presumably require a new type of binding instrument in the WTO. Finger and Wilson (2007) suggest that it may be possible to conclude a plurilateral agreement among funding countries to support specific negotiations, while recipient country liberalization would be part of a multilateral WTO agreement. The Bali Trade Facilitation Agreement does not enumerate specific funding commitments, for the time being handling this issue informally, but a side agreement to guarantee funding may prove to be necessary in the future, either for its continuation or for other aid-supported agreements. Such an arrangement would include only self-selected donor countries willing to take part, but would presumably be structured to allow other countries to join later. Finger and Wilson (2007) also maintain that it would not be possible to specify particular aid commitments, which would have to be negotiated in separate non-WTO agreements with funding organizations such as the World Bank, unless perhaps such organizations could acquire the legal status to enter into WTO agreements. WTO plurilateral agreements appear in any case to provide a promising institutional avenue for new types of trade linkages. Similar agreements might be possible in arranging contingency

funds to compensate developing countries for reduced tariff revenues resulting from tariff liberalization, lost revenues due to preference erosion under
general WTO liberalization, or compliance costs of new WTO obligations.
As noted in chapter 4, the WTO has not added any new plurilateral agreements since its founding, so these are uncharted waters, but they are worth
exploring. The systemic demands of this coherence issue are likely, in one
way or another, to require more formal and perhaps binding obligations
from potential donor countries in the future, in order to overcome not only
the trade capacity "bottleneck" in WTO negotiations, but concerns over the
commitments and terms of actual aid transfers.

In addition to the major multilateral and bilateral government donors of
foreign aid, there are many other internationally active agencies involved in
transfers of funds, services, and technical assistance to developing countries
(see Jones 2010: chapter 6). While they may be peripheral in terms of major
project funding, they may nevertheless play a role in the development process, and in particular, in developing countries' capacity to engage in trade
liberalization. Various NGOs provide specialized development assistance,
expertise, and advice. Think tanks, research foundations, and universities
provide economic and trade information and analysis. Private consultancies
play a role in training and advising companies, governments, and organizations. This diverse population of international actors includes advocacy
groups of various stripes, including those that favor and those that oppose
trade liberalization. The developing world would benefit from the addition
of groups that can provide focused information and analysis for developing
countries regarding the impact of trade.

A GRAPHICAL ILLUSTRATION OF THE INSTITUTIONAL PROBLEM

Figure 7.2 illustrates the principal issues and difficulties involved in making coherence an integral part of trade liberalization. There is a presumed
resistance by many developing countries to trade liberalization, based on
the gap in trade capacity, ancillary costs of compliance, possible foregone
revenues, and uncertainties about the outcome of negotiations. All of these
factors raise the resistance threshold to reaching consensus in a multilateral
trade negotiation (MTN) in the WTO. Aid-for-trade activities would act
to alleviate the resource constraints and improve trade capacity, lowering
the resistance threshold. The graphical presentation in Figure 7.2 distinguishes between (1) independent bilateral and multilateral donor aid and
(2) "internalized," WTO-mandated aid and technical assistance beyond

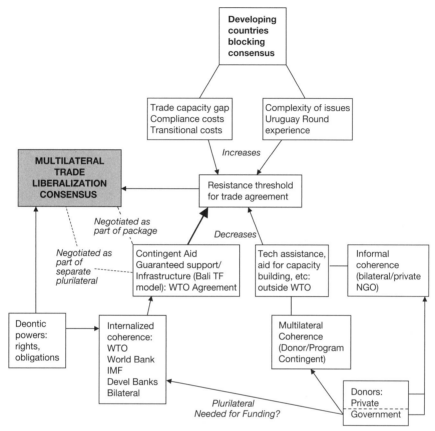

Figure 7.2 The Institutional Challenge of Harnessing Aid-for-Trade Liberalization
SOURCE: Concept based on Searle (2005).

the EIF, that is, aid that would be an integral part of a WTO trade agreement. The institutional innovation would be to have funding for adjustment, capacity-building, infrastructure, or transitional costs as part of the bargain, established through expanded rights and obligations (deontic powers) to offset compliance costs and revenue losses, and improve members' capacity to gain from trade. Currently, the Bali agreement establishes funding commitments informally as part of the Trade Facilitation Agreement. Alternatively, there could be separate, plurilateral agreements to establish more formal commitments. The benefit of internalized coherence would lie in its ability to systematically overcome the resistance threshold, assuming of course that the negotiations are successful. It is important to note that such an expansion of deontic powers would represent a major change in the foundational "collective intentionality" of the WTO, since it would thereby become a different sort of institution, with development and aid transfer mandates.

Additional challenges would lie in establishing institutional structures that coordinate, legitimize, and fund aid-for-trade activities, which would require an unprecedented level of cooperation and delegation of responsibility among the WTO and its partner institutions in the plan. Other challenges, not shown in Figure 7.2, include implementing the aid activity and making it effective. It should also be noted that aid-for-trade activities that fall outside the narrower confines of a WTO agreement, as well as other development aid activities, would continue on their own track, and would indeed continue to contribute to countries' trade capacity and performance.

SUMMARY AND CONCLUSION

Embedded liberalism, a key component of the political framework for global trade liberalization, appears to grow exclusively out of a country's domestic development and economic growth. It emerges from an internal political process that establishes a balance in the country between trade openness and an acceptable framework of income distribution and social welfare. A successful balance will facilitate the political support for trade openness that captures the gains from trade and globalization. Policies to support embedded liberalism often tend to be expensive, making it the province of richer countries, but even they struggle with meeting the adjustment challenges of globalization in periods of rapid change, lower growth, and larger public debt. For most resource-strapped developing countries, strengthening internal political and government support for trade liberalization will require a different sort of embedded liberalism, a system of infrastructure support based on international transfers. Foreign aid programs to build and support trade activities in developing countries (aid-for-trade) can, in this regard, contribute only marginally to the long-term process that culminates in high income and institutional development that will support the stabilization, adjustment, and safety net policies that can generate internal political support for trade liberalization. Sustainable support for trade openness that is associated with more advanced economies can come only from progress in the development process itself. Aid-for-trade programs can, however, remove financial constraints on building trade capacity and improve the recipient countries' ability to gain from trade, and may therefore prove to be instrumental in securing developing country support for trade liberalization in the future.

The December 2013 Agreement on Trade Facilitation was a groundbreaking achievement because it linked reforms by developing countries in trade processing and administration with their receiving financial and technical support to improve trade infrastructure. Trade facilitation measures address a small part of the trade capacity problem in developing countries, but this agreement could open the way for similar agreements in the future to link development assistance with other trade liberalizing measures. A note of caution is in order regarding the structure of the Trade Facilitation Agreement, since it does not specify funding responsibility or allocation, which may lead to disputes in the future. Further WTO institutional development may be required to correct this potential problem, including the establishment of legal status of multilateral aid organizations in WTO agreements and the use of plurilateral agreements to establish funding accountability. For this reason it remains uncertain whether aid-for-trade itself can serve as a direct incentive for trade liberalization beyond the limited scope of procedural reforms specified in the trade facilitation negotiations, since the WTO is institutionally ill-equipped to link aid with trade liberalization in a formal manner. This possibility will remain highly speculative until it becomes clear how new agreements of this type can be negotiated and can achieve consensus among the entire WTO membership in the General Council. Finally one must consider aid-for-trade as playing but one part in a larger process of development, in which the transformation of the country may depend on more fundamental changes in market processes and incentives. Aid-for-trade appears to have resulted independently in significant reductions in trade costs and increases in trade volumes across a wide number of developing countries, so this activity has, in itself, resulted in a form of trade liberalization, even without direct WTO involvement. In the annals of development economics, it has been difficult to find large-scale cross-border transfer activity that has led to such targeted and effective pro-growth outcomes, which furthermore enhance welfare in not only the recipient but the donor countries. Additional incentives for aid-for-trade are appearing in the form of new opportunities for regional supply-chain integration among developing countries. For that reason the aid-for-trade initiative should continue, with guidance from ongoing assessment and analysis in allocating the aid effectively. It should also expand to include more donor activity among emerging market countries, which are increasing their own commercial trade and investment activities in other developing countries. Instead of an ambitious but elusive "international embedded liberalism," the more modest but attainable goal of pursuing a sort of global "Marshall Plan" to build trade capacity and efficiency is more realistic. In addition, the engagement of various NGOs, universities, foundations, and other sources of funding and expertise can also play positive roles in building trade capacity in developing countries, through technical assistance, economic analysis, training, and advocacy.

The success of aid-for-trade notwithstanding, the development divide at the WTO persists. So far, WTO members have been unable to reconcile their evolving and divergent demands with a common understanding of reciprocity expectations, goals, and "policy space" guidelines that is consistent with the WTO's trade liberalizing mandate. Both the lower growth, often import-skeptical developed countries and the higher growth, import-skeptical developing countries fear the consequences of further trade adjustment in a seemingly volatile world economy. Efforts by developed WTO members to use an "affirmative action" approach toward developing countries as the way to secure their support for reciprocal market opening have not been successful, since this approach misaligns WTO rules and goals. This chapter has argued, in the end, that new incentives and foundations for pro-trade political support are needed in both developed and developing countries in order to bring them back to the multilateral negotiating table. So far, countries have focused their new trade efforts on RTAs, and with the exception of the Trade Facilitation Agreement, aid-for-trade will probably have to proceed in the foreseeable future on a parallel track to the WTO, rather than in the WTO itself. Establishing a truly global and coherent system of trade liberalization will be difficult in a world where shifts in growth to the developing countries clash with the legacy of political power of industrialized countries in the GATT/WTO system and with a still limited and largely uncoordinated system of foreign development aid.

Pathways Back to Geneva

GAMBLING AT THE TAHOE ROUND: A FABLE

A WTO multilateral trade negotiation is like a high-stakes poker game at the Big Table at Tahoe.[1] Poker is, of course, not really played at a big table, but this is a different sort of poker game. Unlike the typical zero-sum poker game, all the players at the Big Table can count on taking some winnings home: call them the gains from trade. In addition, the game isn't over until everyone determines, collectively, they have won as much as the game will allow. This also means, however, that most of the high rollers will have to come home with substantial gains; otherwise, they can't celebrate victory on their big triumph at Tahoe, and so might quit the game in disgust. The upshot of this is that the game can go on for a long time, as everyone is promised winnings at the end, if only they can find the right chips to put on the table. In the meantime, spouses and home governments get impatient. . .

The game as originally devised is played with chips of two sorts: export chips and import chips. They have the magical quality of changing from one into the other as they are played, enriching all the players. All of these chips are inherently valuable, but an odd political rule all the players seem to accept prevents them from counting the import chips as winnings. There is a troublesome group of gadflies, called economists, who, like card counters and others with an understanding of the mechanics of the game, are not generally allowed to play at Tahoe, but from the outside they look in through the windows and enjoy lamenting the nature of this rule.

In fact, the Tahoe casino makes the game more interesting by requiring a modified form of strip poker. In order to play the game, you have to make "concessions," which means putting import chips on the table—but this indignity also requires that you shed an article of clothing, curiously a humiliation only to that player's government and parts of its population called "import-competing lobbies." The good part is that, at the end of the game, you don't have to go home wearing a barrel; your winning gains-from-trade chips allow you and all the other players to get to wear more fashionable and valuable clothing than when you arrived! And the more you strip, the more beautiful clothes you gain when the game is finished! Often the new clothing is imported, but it's difficult to tell without peeking at the labels.

The Tahoe Big Table has run into trouble, however. Some players insist that their religion prevents them from disrobing in public, and so won't put any import chips on the table. Others say that the weather has turned cold and they'll get sick if they need to disrobe, even if it's temporary. There is also a side game going on called "services," with lots of chips available, but somebody came up with a rule that the game at the main table, called "Ag and NAMA," has to finish first. In the meantime, no one seems to want to play "services" anyway.

Someone suggests that the big game should break up and move upstairs, to the "plurilateral" rooms, where smaller games can be played. They are nice rooms with a beautiful view of the lake. Lots of players are interested, but the rules are that if you don't put any chips on the plurilateral table, you have to leave the room. That makes some players resentful and angry at being left out of the room if they don't like the game. But then they discovered that they can have the last laugh: you need everyone's key to open a plurilateral room, so any killjoy in the crowd can keep the door locked.

The real trouble, however, is that players, all members of the Tahoe Club, are leaving the building altogether, which is going to ruin the casino. Several of the players have already taken their chips and started their own private poker games at "Joe's FTA Bar," "TPP Palace," "Transatlantic TTIPsy Lounge," and places with similar names across from the casino. You don't have to play by all the silly Tahoe rules at these speakeasies and honky-tonks! The high rollers love these little "bilateral" games with their bootleg liquor, where they can sneak extra chips of their own onto the table. The smaller players shrug and say, "It's the only game in town now and at least I win something without waiting around forever." Tahoe Security tried years ago to shut them down by admonishing all the members that they were "bad places," but then decided that, like the irrepressible brothels at the other end of town, they could not be outlawed, and so they posted some rules of honky-tonk propriety they hoped would be followed.

In the meantime, the speakeasies have grown alarmingly popular, while, sadly, the Tahoe casino is emptying out. The members want to stay in the club: they especially enjoy common access to the rules wing and the well-appointed courtyards of the casino, where disputes can be settled peacefully, even if they don't always use them. But they don't seem interested in playing the big poker game there anymore. At the same time, some members have noticed that some of these parts of the Tahoe casino date from 1995, and, well, the paint is starting to peel and the grounds are due for some upgrading, while some also insist that the casino must expand into new areas to keep the membership happy. "We depend on proceeds from the Big Table to keep our maintenance up and finance expansion plans," says the management, "and traffic has been rather too thin lately for that."

Some of the economists, like revivalist preachers of yore, rain hellfire and brimstone sermons on the wayward gamblers who frequent the FTA bars, those pleasure pits of ill repute. Others, taking a different approach, say the best way to get the crowd back inside the Tahoe casino is by distributing something they call aid-for-trade chips and by changing the locks to make it easier to get into the plurilateral rooms. After all, they say, the Casino's food is better, the view is nicer, and for those who aren't high rollers, the fights and disagreements on the premises—a common occurrence—are dealt with more even-handedly in the casino courtyards than at the disreputable honky-tonks, where you're likely to get bullied about.

But finally, following the advice of their therapists, the whole group took the game to a South Seas island to play penny-ante poker with their new card dealer (called the "Director-General") to encourage them to keep on playing, so they could all get their mojo back. Lo and behold, they completed the low-stakes game and everyone went home with some winnings. They promised themselves that they would go back to Tahoe and pick up the Big Game again. And they guaranteed even bigger winnings for everybody . . . if only everybody would agree to come back and play the Big Game. Yet many of the players have returned with a gloomy face to the empty rooms and memories of the strip poker rules and the honky-tonk distractions. Small games are fine, but could the Big Game continue?

THE PROBLEM WITH MULTILATERAL TRADE NEGOTIATIONS

There is plenty of gains-from-trade fuel to drive global trade liberalization; the question is how to convert the fuel into bargaining energy in a multilateral negotiation. This problem describes the essential institutional challenge of the WTO. For many years, the GATT had provided the institutional formula for global trade liberalization. Partly because of the GATT's success, partly because the political and economic structure of that postwar era has passed, the formula stopped working. It could not be passed on to the WTO with all its increased ambitions. The ultimate source of the problem is that the WTO is a consensus-based system and achieving consensus has become elusive. The reasons for a lack of consensus, as described in the foregoing chapters, include an increasing diversity of trading interests, an overburdened single undertaking agenda, a lack of agreement on the terms of reciprocity for developing countries at different levels of development, leftover resentments from the Uruguay Round, sovereignty issues with sensitive domestic markets that are the main sources of new gains from trade, and the heightened legal exposure that countries now face in making binding WTO commitments.

The consensus problem is particularly frustrating because decision-making in the GATT had previously overcome numerous negotiating crises to conclude eight trade rounds, and then, in the new WTO system, this process seemed to grind to a standstill. It is as if the WTO's effectiveness had fallen victim to the sort of perpetual deadlock that the Security Council veto has imposed on the United Nations. But in the case of the WTO, the problem is doubly vexing because the gains from trade theoretically leave each participating country better off: why can't everyone, somehow, get to "yes?" Unfortunately, the GATT/WTO framework has always been based on mercantilistic bargaining for export market access vs. import market "concessions," which fostered zero-sum thinking. In earlier times, the GATT system had cleverly harnessed mercantilism to its advantage; by imposing a reciprocity rule on bargaining, everyone got to go home with a finished trade deal claiming victory in export market access. But in the Doha Round the difficulty (or unwillingness) of players to offer significant "concessions" has left the mercantilistic ethos to wreak havoc on the system.

The problems listed above suggest that the key to finding a solution lies in addressing the various institutional gaps or misalignments. Thus, if diversity is based on development gaps, then aid-for-trade might help to close these gaps. If the agenda is too big, then unpack it and negotiate deals on fewer, or on separate, issues. Another approach is to keep the agreements "in house" at the WTO with more creative use of "critical mass" or plurilateral negotiations; for broader agreements, some new understanding about reciprocity will be needed, perhaps through new (negotiated) rules linking reciprocal concessions based on a graduated development or income scale. The legal exposure issue could be alleviated by more flexible WTO safeguards measures, but of course this solution, in itself, would have to be negotiated in a new WTO deal. Similarly, changes in the rules that would provide more flexibility in adding plurilateral agreements, for example, would also require a consensus of the membership, a forbidding barrier. The discussion of possible solutions has shown that each of them has its own problems. In general, all the ideas for WTO reform seem to founder on the irreducible constraint of the consensus rule.

The institutional problems of the WTO and its failure to conclude the Doha Round are summarized in schematic fashion in figure. 8.1, based on the larger institutional sketch of the WTO in figure 2.1. The five principal elements of institutional misalignment are in the highlighted boxes: policy space, special and differential treatment on reciprocity obligations, the single undertaking, shifts in the balance of bargaining power, and judicialization of obligations under the Dispute Settlement Understanding. Together these factors raised high and seemingly insurmountable barriers to consensus in the Doha Trade Round, preventing a comprehensive, single undertaking multilateral trade agreement (shaded box), which then left WTO members to seek their "best alternatives to a multilateral trade agreement" (BAMTA) in order to pursue further gains from trade, or the possibility of institutional reforms. The three categories of institutional alternatives to a comprehensive Doha agreement include:

(1) RTA-type solutions outside the WTO (which could also include unilateral trade liberalization), which face low-to-medium thresholds of implementation;

(2) WTO incremental institutional adjustments, based on existing WTO rules and governance frameworks, such as the Bali model of a pared-down agenda, "critical mass" measures, plurilateral agreements, and aid-for-trade coherence initiatives, which face medium-to-high thresholds of implementation among WTO members; and

(3) WTO fundamental institutional reforms to modify the consensus rule or other constitutive rules that would require extensive deliberation and consensus among WTO members, thus implying a high threshold of implementation.

This book has examined elements of these three possible categories of adjustment, which may lead to new WTO frameworks for multilateral trade agreements. Additional factors may also need to be in place in order to improve the functioning of trade liberalization, such as improved domestic adjustment policies to achieve trade liberalization and improved representation through coalition building in the WTO decision-making process. All of these factors, on which progress depends largely upon the WTO members themselves, could indeed play an important role in bringing multilateral trade negotiations back on track. This section will focus, however, on institutional frameworks for liberalizing trade, given the stalemate on a comprehensive Doha agreement.

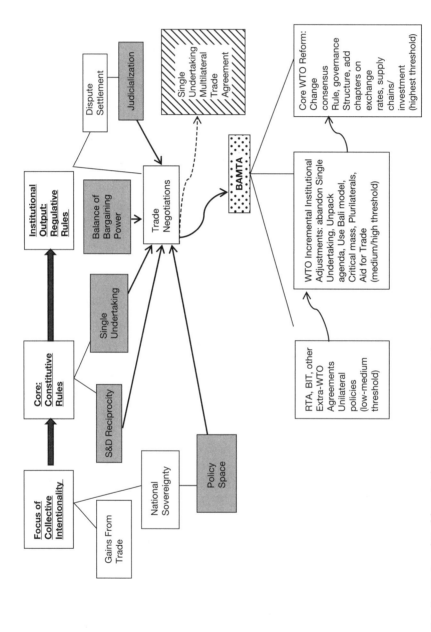

Figure 8.1 Institutional Problems in the WTO and BAMTA Alternatives

WTO members have resorted to a combination of the first two categories: BAMTA through RTAs; and incremental reforms, essentially through setting the single undertaking rule aside and attempting to create smaller agreements. For the December 2013 WTO Ministerial in Bali, they unpacked the trade agenda and whittled it down to a small number of items, including trade facilitation, some limited agricultural issues, and new features of special and differential treatment for developing countries, in order to achieve consensus more easily (see below). Negotiations for a new WTO (possibly plurilateral) International Services Agreement had also begun in 2013, as noted in chapter 4. Outside the WTO framework, ambitious RTA negotiations were continuing or beginning, as noted in chapter 6. These developments indicate that governments typically seek the institutional paths of least resistance in pursuing international trade agreements, even though the thresholds for agreement may still be daunting. Thus, the pared-down WTO "small game" agreement at Bali (with other such partial Doha "harvests" being considered), the services plurilateral, and the RTA talks, while more manageable than the unwieldy comprehensive Doha Round talks, still involve difficult policy space issues, with no guarantee of final agreement. Any far-reaching WTO reforms in the third category, on the other hand, would require significant institutional changes, any of which would require extensive negotiation and full affirmative consensus of the membership for approval.

RTAS: A PATH BACK TO THE WTO?

Trade liberalization has not stopped as a result of the suspension of comprehensive Doha negotiations, but most of the progress has taken place outside the WTO system. Global average applied tariff rates have fallen since the end of the Uruguay Round, but this is mainly the result of RTA and BIT agreements, which also involve new agreements and negotiations on deeper integration (see Baldwin 2012). As was noted in chapter 6, one can attribute at least some of this increase in international trade and investment to the stability established by the WTO system, whose member countries do not need to place the benefits of their current rules-driven global market access at risk by extending their trade relations on a bilateral or regional basis. But the fact is that, with the exception of the limited Bali Ministerial agreement in 2013, the WTO has not been actively contributing to multilateral trade liberalization since the Information Technology Agreement, Financial Services Agreement, and the Agreement on Basic Telecommunications Services of 1997. And so WTO members have turned increasingly to RTAs to pursue trade liberalization.

Multilateral trade agreements are generally superior to regional or bilateral trade agreements, implying the desirability of countries returning to the WTO to conduct trade liberalization on a systematic, global rules-based, nondiscriminatory basis. WTO multilateral negotiations do in fact have many advantages over RTAs:

(1) Based on the GATT trade rounds, a WTO deal is at least potentially a bigger deal than what RTAs can deliver, since it would establish global market access agreements and new rules that apply to all members. Once negotiated and agreed, ratification of a WTO deal would therefore tend to be attractive politically to member country legislatures and parliaments, since it would typically represent big gains for the country's exporters and progress toward a stable global trading order. This outcome would require, however, that the WTO deal deliver value in terms of liberalized trade that is commensurate with its global ambitions and sufficient to satisfy countries' political need to offset domestic opposition to increased imports.

(2) The WTO has a superior rules and judicial system, providing independent review and settlement of disputes. RTA dispute settlement is usually less comprehensive and subject to power imbalances among partner countries. The WTO system, unlike RTAs, also includes an appellate body, and allows third-party countries to take part in the proceedings. Furthermore, a judgment in a dispute case applies on a multilateral basis, as compared with the limited reach of any RTA dispute settlement. This systemic element is one of the most prominent benefits to WTO members. The rules and dispute settlement functions ultimately depend, however, on updated agreements that only a multilateral trade negotiation can deliver.

(3) The WTO has an extensive operational infrastructure, with a professionally staffed secretariat, to provide expert advice, research and administrative support to ongoing functions of the institution. Few RTAs have comparable secretariats, or standing committees of trade delegates, that have developed specialized knowledge of such a wide range of trade issues.

(4) The WTO is the *World* Trade Organization, providing a much more "level playing field" for its members than the typical RTA. Major RTAs are typically dominated by one large trading country or entity, which can then assert its bargaining power to minimize its own exposure to import competition and maximize the benefits to its exporters. In contrast, WTO members can significantly offset the bargaining power of a single country in a multilateral negotiation through coalition building and collective platforms on the issues.

These WTO advantages also imply that the decline of the WTO in favor of RTAs in negotiating new trade deals would impose significant costs on the world economy. While WTO rules and dispute settlement would continue, the lack of new agreements and updating would eventually trigger a slow process of entropy, in which the WTO framework would decline in relevance as trade disputes over new and emerging trade issues would have to be handled through alternative channels. Those alternative channels would be provided by a fragmented system of trade blocs or by unilateral policies of the larger countries. In the absence of a strong WTO negotiating forum, the major trading blocs, dominated by the United States and the European Union, perhaps also by China and Japan, may find it politically unattractive to bargain globally for more trade liberalization in key areas such as services, regulations, state trading, and environmental goods and technology.

In order to forestall such an outcome, what can be done to move countries back to the WTO multilateral negotiating table? One tempting strategy would be to use WTO rules to limit the negotiation of RTAs. After all, the WTO is a rules-based system, and stricter enforcement of GATT article XXIV could impose more discipline on behavior detrimental to the system. Unfortunately, the RTA genie is already out of the bottle, and there is neither the political will nor the inclination among WTO members to put it back in. Nearly all WTO members are complicit in the use—usually multiple use—of RTAs. As shown in chapter 6, RTAs have become a politically attractive and legitimized tool of most countries' trade policy. This will not change. It will be far better for all countries and observers to accept the fact that RTA negotiations, both large and small, will continue, and to focus on how they might serve to prepare a pathway that leads back to multilateral talks in Geneva.

Another approach is to change the rules and frameworks for bargaining, so that countries will find it easier or more attractive to participate in WTO negotiations. This has already begun, as the single undertaking has given way to an "unpacked" agenda, with agreement on a smaller set of Doha issues achieved at the Bali Ministerial, and continuing interest in wrapping up more "mini-Doha" agreements. Even if such agreements are not nearly large enough to compare with the results of previous trade rounds, WTO members may welcome the opportunity to harvest what can be agreed as soon as possible, and then to turn the page. Still, it is unclear that the political will exists in the WTO membership to bring closure to agreements beyond the modest accomplishment at Bali. In fact the danger now for the WTO system is for countries to invest significantly more time and resources in a vastly reduced set of Doha agreements that may take many more years to conclude. Such a spectacle would only cause many to view the WTO process as pathetic: seemingly endless negotiations over "small change" in terms of gains from trade. At some point in the near future, WTO members will have to find a way to declare the Doha Round to be over and start working on a new negotiation. Based on the WTO experience described in this book, the General Council would be well-advised not to call the new talks "Doha II" and not to nickname it the "development round."

One issue that has broken off into separate negotiations is services, with International Services Agreement (ISA) talks underway as a possible plurilateral or GATS article V agreement, as noted in chapter 4. Self-contained talks on services alone—a broad and varied sector in itself—offer the best chance for a multi-party, if less than universal, agreement on this rapidly growing area of trade. In order to avoid having to face the need for WTO consensus among all members for accepting a new plurilateral agreement, the ISA will have to pass the muster under GATS article V, thus as a broad agreement with no outright exclusion of any of the four modes of services delivery. This condition will make it more difficult to come to an agreement, but the participating countries will also know that the alternative is to have a lesser agreement presented as an annex 4 plurilateral, where it will almost certainly face a veto. Changing the consensus rule on plurilateral approval is, furthermore, extremely unlikely, which will therefore put the kibosh on many other plurilateral proposals. The point is that changing WTO rules moves the adjustment process shown in figure 8.1 into the "high threshold" area. Any proposal that calls for a significant change in decision-making in the WTO will inevitably run into the consensus rule stonewall. Any major institutional change of this sort would probably require a significant catastrophic or cataclysmic event, such as what was needed to launch the original GATT after World War II. [2]

So the institutional structure of the WTO, and the experience so far in the post-Doha period, suggest that major changes in decision-making rules or RTA disciplines will remain "non-starters." Minor changes in rules, and resort to alternatives within the rules, will probably have a limited impact on WTO negotiations. As noted, some progress is possible on mini-Doha and ISA negotiations, and there are some plurilateral proposals that may receive consensus support (see below). However, moving global trade policy and trade negotiations back into the WTO system will require more than incremental institutional reforms and negotiating *démarches*. It is very likely that it will take a systematic process of global institutional adjustment that creates new (or renewed) motivations for countries to return to comprehensive WTO negotiations. This sort of change in the world economy is difficult to manage because it depends on a series of circumstances, events, and policy choices that are largely beyond the control of one, or even of large groups, of players. Yet there are market forces and policy incentives in play that suggest that multilateralism can, under the proper circumstances and with the right policy choices, reassert itself as the driving force of global trade.

Bringing trade negotiations back to WTO multilateralism for large and significant MFN trade liberalization will not be easy, since the original institutional bargaining machinery of the GATT is no longer adequate. The wayward WTO members that have moved away from WTO "centricity" and resorted to RTAs will not be disciplined back to multilateral bargaining through tighter GATT article XXIV enforcement, nor will they be easily persuaded to change governance rules, especially the consensus rule, to allow the formation of new plurilateral agreements. They are also likely to remain unmoved by well-meaning lectures on the virtues of multilateralism, when WTO negotiations seem endless and RTAs can deliver politically attractive, second-best gains from trade more quickly. WTO members will return to the Geneva multilateral bargaining table when they are motivated to do so by the politics of trade liberalization, that is, when a global deal means being included in, rather than excluded from, the gains from trade. They will return when domestic political forces again make a compelling case for global rather than just regional openness. They will return when a global bandwagon, led by the large traders, again make multilateralism the prevailing force in global trade relations.

We can start with the fact that a certain process has already begun: the proliferation of RTAs, with further large and small RTAs under negotiation. From that starting point, a process that favors a return to the WTO "centricity" would include at least several of the following elements: (1) competitive liberalization among existing and new RTAs, (2) the engagement of China, India, probably Brazil, and perhaps other emerging markets in competitive liberalization, (3) the domestic re-engagement of exporter interests in multilateral trade liberalization, (4) effective domestic trade adjustment policies, (5) progress on building trade capacity and institutions in developing countries, (6) getting the right issues on the agenda, and (7) effective global leadership that bridges developed and developing countries.

The first element, competitive liberalization among RTAs, is based on the political economy described by Baldwin (2006b, 2012), as discussed in chapter 6. The quest for more efficient sources of supply, and broader markets for exports, tends to result in expanded liberalization beyond existing RTAs. The development of international supply chains on a regional basis has reinforced this part of the process, hence the long-term plans for a consolidated "mega-regional" Asian Economic Area, which could grow out of a merger of the proposed Trans-Pacific Partnership (which includes the NAFTA partners) and East Asian RCEP agreements. The European Union, for its part, has taken steps to extend economic integration to the Euro-Med countries. Many RTAs now incorporate "deep integration" provisions, which are expanding the reach of trade liberalization and can contribute to global liberalization in the future.

The more far-reaching and successful deep liberalization is in RTAs, the more momentum will build for wider agreements. Many of the deep integration provisions are motivated by international agreements to set up the supply chains generally include both RTAs and BITs. A distinctive feature of such agreements is that a high-income "technology" partner country agrees to build and support productive capacity in the "factory" country, which in return agrees to remove trade and investment restrictions in return. This quid pro quo differs from the traditional GATT/WTO bargain of reciprocal market access. This is one of the great challenges of the future of the trading system, since there is no institutional framework for global rules on such arrangements within value chains. Thus, Baldwin (2012) predicts the need for a "WTO.2" agreement to multilateralize such twenty-first-century supply-chain rules, in addition to the existing "WTO.1," which focuses on twentieth-century final goods market access.

In practice, however, it is unlikely that economic integration agreements will be parsed in this manner, even though they introduce the need for a global institutional balancing act. More and more RTAs include "deep integration" provisions that serve to facilitate and support foreign investments, but also open up the partner economies in general to arm's length commercial opportunities in both goods and services trade in final, as well as intermediate and supporting, products. The most desirable institutional arrangement, within the current WTO system, would be for participants in such regional supply chains to establish an annex 4 plurilateral agreement with rules to regulate the supply-chain motivated terms and obligations for both "factory" and "technology" countries in RTA and BIT agreements; this would be the "WTO.2" component.[3] The advantage of an annex 4 agreement is that it could regulate these agreements independently on the basis of its non-traditional reciprocity, with dispute settlement brought under the global WTO system.[4] "Technology" countries have an interest in establishing general agreements on the protection of their intellectual property in the host "factory" countries and would benefit from standardized rules on foreign direct investment and supporting services and regulations provisions across all participating host countries. "Factory" countries would benefit from collectively negotiated terms of sovereign control over their economies, so that they are not constantly played off against each other in negotiating their way into valuable supply chains. There should be no illusion that resolving these issues will be easy; the history of distrust over the ill-fated OECD-sponsored Multilateral Agreement on Investment (MAI) indicates that many countries would be wary of such a global agreement. Yet the intervening years have seen a huge expansion of BITs, suggesting that the time may finally be ripe, even from the host countries' point of view, for a global agreement, and a revitalized WTO could provide a more favorable forum for negotiating it.

An additional benefit of a WTO annex 4 supply-chain agreement would be that, by establishing global rules for international production networks, all countries involved in such arrangements would then be able to turn their attention to more traditional market access bargaining, thus returning to "WTO.1." Supply chains are likely to spur more development and higher incomes, with growing affluence and increased demand for final goods and services, and other welfare-enhancing forms of trade and regulations liberalization. Yet the consensus rule for approving a new annex 4 agreement still raises concerns: would there be sufficient interest among the many WTO members still not involved with international supply chains to support it? The trend in regional trade development suggests in fact that interest in such a plurilateral agreement could extend well beyond current supply-chain partners, as there are indications that other regional supply chains will develop in the future, especially in Africa, the Caribbean, and Latin America.[5] Aid-for-trade funding is building trade capacity in these countries, often with the explicit goal of developing regional production networks. Efficient supply chains may still take many years to develop in these areas, but when it comes to institutions and trade agreements, recent experience shows that a planning horizon of ten or twenty years must account for the possibility of change, even if it is not immediately on the horizon. The trend in international supply-chain economics suggests that many developing country WTO members may support such an annex 4 agreement, not necessarily out of immediate need, but with an eye on the future.

The process described above that would bring a supply-chain agreement into the WTO and facilitate a return to multilateral bargaining on other issues is certainly based on some blue-sky speculation about the course of future events and an extrapolation of current trends. Yet the international disaggregation of production appears to be here to stay, and along with the spread of trade liberalization through increasingly ambitious RTAs, suggests that liberalizing incentives will be strong. Even if a plurilateral supply-chain agreement is not concluded in the WTO, a less ambitious or less formal agreement could establish global standards for these arrangements that could still contribute to a return to multilateral trade liberalization.

RTA-Induced Fragmentation?

One of the most serious concerns of RTAs in general, and especially in light of the proposed "big RTA" supply-chain networks, is the possibility of fragmentation in the global trading system, the carving up of the world's regions into mutually exclusive trading blocs. In the post-Doha era, the dynamics of bargaining power raise the concern that major emerging markets, especially

China, India, and Brazil, will be systematically excluded from these big RTAs
by the way the United States, European Union, and Japan will negotiate the
rules, perhaps with the first-mover strategic goal of forcing the emerging markets to submit to the rules later. The proposed TPP, for example, has state trading and "WTO +" intellectual property provisions, and a conspicuous absence
of special and differential treatment provisions that would not survive a negotiation with major emerging market countries. These concerns are valid, but
are likely to be mitigated by the process of competitive liberalization. The fact
of the matter is that a country's leverage in market access negotiations comes
primarily through its economic growth prospects and the attractiveness of its
import market. In China and India especially, economic growth is projected to
outpace the OECD countries by a significant margin in the coming decades,
and their large populations include a new middle class that is growing by the
millions each year. Already these countries are producing technology-intensive
products that will make them attractive supply-chain partners with high
value-added components in the future.[6] Many economic surveys also rank
several other countries that are not already in, or negotiating to join, the TPP
and extended EU RTAs as "emerging markets": Colombia, Egypt, Indonesia,
Morocco, Philippines, Russia, South Africa, and Thailand. These countries
cannot match the growth rates of China or India, and many of them currently
suffer from domestic economic and political problems (as do China, India, and
Brazil), but they also represent potentially large and growing markets for consumer goods, and possibly venues for technology-intensive production, in the
future. The population of the emerging markets outside the TPP and EU networks is 3.4 billion and growing.

Exporters in the United States, European Union, and other advanced
OECD countries will want to have expanded access to these lucrative markets,
and entrepreneurs will want to pursue new investments and business opportunities there. In recent years, export-oriented organizations in the United
States and European Union had focused their lobbying efforts on regional
trade and investment opportunities, with waning interest in the WTO, which
appeared to be incapable of delivering on new agreements. The continued
absence of new WTO trade liberalization agreements, combined with the
exclusion of these growing markets from the big RTAs, will eventually lead
to market-access and foreign-investment envy among these exporters, which
in turn may finally move the business lobbies to push their governments
hard for multilateral deals. The large emerging markets, for their part, may
also become impatient with the fragmentation of global markets through big
RTAs, dominated by the large developed countries, and be willing to come
back to the WTO to get better deals on market and technology access than
they have gotten in their own RTAs. The emerging market countries could

quicken this process with creative, deep integration, big-RTA initiatives of their own, beyond the modest and limited agreements they have concluded so far, particularly if they initiate negotiations with a major trading power. India could have pursued such a strategy in the EU-India FTA, which is still under negotiation, but that agreement appears destined to produce a modest outcome at best, with limited liberalization based on India's insistence that it contain "special and differential" exclusions from major market-opening commitments. In contrast to this traditional strategy, the large emerging markets will need to embrace a stronger leadership role and "punch at their new weight," that is, recognizing that significant new gains from trade and investment for their large and rapidly growing markets will come only with greater opening of their own domestic markets. For both developed and developing countries, the interim during which comprehensive WTO multilateral negotiations have been moribund should provide a time for reflection about alternative systems of trade liberalization, and how much money is left on the table with the foregone opportunities of a large agreement, potentially bigger than the biggest mega-regional RTA.

LEADERSHIP AND DOMESTIC ADJUSTMENT

A New Model of Leadership and Collaboration. One element of an international institution such as the WTO appears to be the universal requirement for leadership within its ranks, which in the context of the WTO can be defined as providing, or contributing to, the public good of trade liberalization (see Narlikar 2011: 1608–1609). In an organization of sovereign countries, each dependent in turn on its own domestic institutions of governance, there seems to be little chance of creating the sort of spontaneous free trade order that Hayek advocated, although he knew it was a utopian proposition (see Hayek 1944: 219–240). Hayek in fact rejected the "constructivist" approach to institutions that this book has adopted (Hayek 1978: 3). In most countries' domestic political landscape of competing pro- and anti-trade forces, however, with a received tradition in most cases of mercantilism, there is typically a bias toward the status quo, which tends to discourage independent policies of trade liberalization. It took an economically self-confident, empire-building economy such as the United Kingdom to abolish the Corn Laws in 1846, sparking a period of trade liberalization in Europe, and an economically self-confident, victorious United States after World War II to lead the way in founding the Bretton Woods institutions, including the original GATT. It will also take leadership to bring global trade negotiations back to the WTO in the post-Doha Round era and move new negotiations toward consensus. Economic leadership in an age of

advanced globalization and convergence will, however, require a more collaborative effort among developed and developing countries.

The United States has lost a good deal of its expansive self-confidence as
leader of the world economy, in part, as noted in chapter 4, because its economic growth rate (along with those of most other OECD countries) and share
of global trade have declined in comparison with many developing, and especially with the emerging market, countries. Yet the increased trade and growth
rates in developing countries should rather be cause for celebration for the
United States and the rest of the developed world, since they represent in part
a victory of global liberalization championed by them in the GATT/WTO system. Increasing prosperity among developing countries will contribute both to
developed country growth and to global political and economic security. As for
the low US growth rate, that is a macroeconomic issue for which trade is part
of the solution, not the problem. In an environment of rapid global integration
and technological change, gains from specialization and efficiency will continue to contribute to higher standards of living in countries that embrace the
challenge and adjust to new trade opportunities. The danger lies in the United
States taking on a defensive posture in the world economy and viewing trade
and associated foreign investment as threats to its economy. The WTO will,
in any case, need the United States to maintain, or perhaps, regain, its leadership role in global trade negotiations. A retreat from this position will leave
the WTO as a trade liberalizing institution without momentum and without a
realistic chance of revival.

Yet the United States will need other countries to take on collaborative leadership roles as well. Collaboration in this sense does not mean that leadership
countries will form a bargaining alliance; its crucial aspect will be the ability
to find common ground on the terms and structure of the negotiation and the
agenda. The need goes beyond simply managing the framework of the negotiations, but also includes moving the negotiations toward consensus on an
agreement. There have been numerous suggestions for establishing a formal
representative WTO consultative body to act as a forum for negotiating issues,
including those that would otherwise be discussed in green room meetings
chaired by the Director-General.[7] Despite widespread support among WTO
observers and academics for such a standing consultative body, there is scant
support for it among WTO members themselves. They appear to be reluctant to
approve any formal decision-making body that would transfer voting proxies to
pre-determined representatives. In addition, even in green rooms, many countries are reluctant to depend on the Director-General to broker agreements,
a practice that was common in the GATT years. The best, and perhaps only,
way to establish deliberations and lines of communications outside the green
room, and also to complement the green room process, if necessary, is through

informal consultations, which will require a new sort of WTO leadership. The United States, in particular, and in conjunction with the European Union and other developed countries, will need to develop more effective working relationships with the key developing countries to manage WTO negotiations. A new arrangement along these lines is necessary in order to address not only the current leadership gap in the WTO but also the "trust" gap that has grown since the Uruguay Round. The ultimate goal is to create a leadership arrangement that can collectively contribute to the public good of multilateral trade liberalization.

A number of long-standing developed country partners in trade liberalization, including the European Union, Canada, Australia, Japan, and others, have played consultative roles in past negotiations. However, the diversity of the WTO membership will require a process of cultivating new leadership partners from the developing world that will have to begin (but not end) in the new Quad—United States, European Union, India, and Brazil, with the addition eventually of a fifth member, China. The relationship must go beyond the mere representation of divergent interests, and probably beyond the confines of the quad (or even "quint"), given the diversity of interests in the developing world. Developing countries will need to have meaningful representation in the agenda-setting stage of future negotiations, and the general terms of balancing concessions among participating countries must be negotiated at the outset, and well understood by all parties. Those countries—developing or developed—positioned to gain more should be prepared to give more as well and should take the lead in moving the negotiations toward consensus. It is certain that special and differential treatment will continue, with a full exemption for the LDCs and reduced reciprocity obligations for other developing countries. However, in the revived WTO negotiations, emphasis should be placed on achieving the capacity to reciprocate, with the large emerging markets setting the example. Increasing countries' trade capacity and engagement in the trade negotiations should therefore be a high priority (see below). As noted earlier, there also needs to be a new understanding about the obligations of reciprocity, with growing, higher income developing countries shouldering a greater burden.

The Leadership Gap: China. Which developing countries are best positioned to play WTO leadership roles, with 125 developing countries out of a total of 160 members? The single largest developing country trader is China, which has the most to gain from further trade liberalization and the most bargaining leverage in future global trade negotiations. China has shown that it is not inclined to take on this role at present, based on its focus on domestic and regional issues, historical wariness of global engagement, and lack of experience in multilateral trade diplomacy (see Shambaugh 2013). China has also maintained that it paid a high price of admission when joining in terms of trade liberalizing measures and kept a conspicuously low profile in Doha Round bargaining over new liberalizing measures. It is important to recognize, furthermore, that China is unlikely to be regarded as a developing country leader, since many other developing countries view China as a disruptive force in markets for their own exports, as well as for their import-competing industries. China unexpectedly captured the lion's share of gains from liberalized trade in textiles and clothing after the Uruguay Round, much to the chagrin of other developing country exporters. Its high-powered, export-driven economy and exchange rate policy have not endeared it to the developing world, which has filed more than half its antidumping cases against China since it joined the WTO in 2001.

Nevertheless future multilateral trade talks will benefit if China is persuaded to take on a stronger WTO leadership role, even if it will speak and act largely for itself. Exploring the conditions under which this would occur goes beyond the scope of this study, since they depend on multiple contingencies of future domestic and international policies and events. In general an expanded leadership role for China will depend in large part on how much progress it makes in its own internal economic reforms, especially regarding its inefficient state-owned enterprise sector, financial system, and management of its exchange rate. Inefficient domestic economic policies will prevent China from moving its economy forward into the new areas of comparative advantage necessary for continued economic growth and will leave its trading partners perpetually suspicious that the economy is being manipulated into generating large trade surpluses. Internal political reform is another unknown factor, as increasing per capita income appears to be making many Chinese impatient for democratic reforms, which, if enacted, could bolster support for increased imports of consumer goods. The course and handling of regional political and territorial rivalries and conflicts involving Japan, South Korea, North Korea, and Taiwan could spill over into trade relations. Finally, US policies toward China regarding trade, exchange rates, and military alliances will also set the parameters for possible Chinese cooperation on WTO issues. Subramanian (2013), for example, calls for the United States to forego policies he regards as intended to isolate China, such the TPP, in favor of purely multilateral engagement through the WTO, where China's growing bargaining power can be effectively counterbalanced by the other world trading powers. In this manner, China would be encouraged to play its proper leadership role in a rules-based multilateral system.[8] Yet, in view of the US current strategy to pursue TPP, it is perhaps more useful to focus on more immediate and compelling trade opportunities as the means for getting China, the United States, and its other trading partners to move toward multilateral negotiations, such as collaboration on high-tech investment and supply-chain trade, a large and growing Chinese middle class eager for consumption, growing world markets for future medium- and high-tech Chinese manufactures, and many services markets that can be opened to trade. Its increased engagement on the basis of its own interests, with the understanding that reciprocal market opening is the best path to its goals, will contribute significantly to WTO-sponsored trade liberalization.

India and Brazil. The two developing country members of the Doha Quad, India and Brazil, along with South Africa, will also be key players. These three countries formed an informal partnership, IBSA, in 2003, as emerging market representatives of the three main continents of the developing world. Their joint influence in the WTO emerged during the 2003 Cancun Ministerial, when they were instrumental in leading a coalition of developing countries that contributed to its collapse. Ironically, Vieira and Alden (2011) have noted that these three countries' economic dominance in their respective regions has not translated into an acceptance by other countries as regional leaders in representing their interests. This observation is consistent with other studies showing the diversity of trade interests within various regions, confounding efforts to establish a system of regional representation in the WTO (see Jones 2010: chapter 4). Furthermore, India, Brazil, and South Africa themselves have divergent trade interests based on their particular domestic economic circumstances and weaknesses. Unfortunately, their aspiration to represent third world interests collectively has led to the situation where they have determined that their legitimacy with the developing world is best maintained by blocking negotiations rather than moving them toward any sort of compromise and consensus.[9]

A continuation of the IBSA strategy of blocking consensus would be a serious obstacle to any future progress in WTO negotiations (see Efstathopoulos 2012). There may, however, be countervailing forces and incentives that could change the strategy's underlying dynamic.[10] Improved relations between developed and developing countries in planning future negotiations, as described above, could provide a new start, and an increased willingness of all developing countries to engage in WTO bargaining. The passage of time since the Doha Round, with few major export market opening opportunities for emerging markets and a limited bargaining power for small developing countries in RTA negotiations, could increase the attractiveness of WTO talks, in light of the alternatives. For emerging market countries, further progress in the development process could increase the value of reciprocal market opening on a multilateral basis. The impact of aid-for-trade to increase trade capacity and mainstream trade policy in developing countries could put trade liberalization in a new light, as a complement and contributing factor to development, rather than as a risk or burden imposed on them by developed countries. Increased participation in reciprocal bargaining by the emerging markets, combined with increased trade capacity and continued special and differential treatment (with lesser reciprocity) for other developing countries may then increase their willingness to take part in shared trade liberalization. This process of transformation among developing countries is by no means certain, and it will probably depend on a favorable combination of policy choices, a rebound in global economic growth, and increased self-confidence in key countries. On the other hand, one should not dismiss the possibility that, after the Doha debacle, all countries will come to recognize (or recognize anew) the value of multilateral trade liberalization.

Domestic Adjustment. The capacity of each WTO member to take advantage of and to adjust to new trade opportunities and trade competition is an essential component of its ability to muster the domestic political support for trade liberalization. This is an important element of trade liberalization that lies beyond the direct control of WTO rules and negotiations. For developed countries, as noted in chapter 7, the key is to ensure the flexibility of the economy when market forces change, including labor mobility, an updated system of education and training geared to emerging demands for particular skills, incentives for new investment and adoption of new technologies, and an environment conducive to new businesses and entrepreneurship. Policies to support economic flexibility are also likely to energize the country's export sector, whose political support is essential for trade liberalization. For many developing countries, creating the economic environment conducive to such flexibility is no less important. However, legal institutions are often not in place to support economic efficiency, and financial resources are often lacking to build the economic infrastructure to reduce transactions costs of trade. In such cases, policy reforms, aid-for-trade, and other development assistance will be needed to build trade capacity. Access to business financing will be critical in moving resources into profitable ventures, including those that use imported inputs and have output with export market potential. Improvements in basic elements of economic development, including health services, education, legal institutions, government effectiveness, and political stability will also contribute to building trade capacity. Linking trade opportunities to government support for trade is also an institutional issue. Typically, business organizations and lobbying groups will need to achieve a voice in the formulation of the country's economic and trade policy in order to provide incentives for its negotiators to bargain for export market opening.

MANAGING THE ISSUES: THE BALI MINISTERIAL

The attempt to cut the agenda down to size and achieve a partial harvest of Doha issues paid off at the December 2013 WTO Ministerial in Bali, Indonesia.

Consensus was finally achieved on a limited but significant portion of the Doha agenda, most importantly trade facilitation, which was probably the most valuable single issue in the Doha agenda, with potential economic welfare gains of $400–$1,000 billion. The agreement also included a "peace clause" to prevent dispute cases on food security measures until a broader agreement on agricultural issues could be reached by 2017, an issue of importance mainly to India. Otherwise there were a number of "best endeavor" agreements on developing country trade issues, including cotton, a waiver granting preferences to LDC services exports, and duty-free, quota-free market access for LDCs.[11] The agreement occurred only after last-minute threats and bargaining involving the United States, on the one hand, and India (over food security) and Cuba (over trade facilitation issues related to the ongoing US embargo against that country), on the other. In this regard, the Bali negotiations seemed like old times, when eleventh-hour drama typically preceded final GATT round agreements. However, the Bali agreement revealed all too clearly the new constraints on WTO bargaining. The small number of issues in the package focused the negotiations on a smaller set of controversies that seemed minor in comparison with the epic confrontations at the 2003 Cancun Ministerial, for example. The confrontation at Bali was also distinctive in that the largest impediment, India's objection to any WTO constraints on its food security policies, ran up against opposition from many other developing countries that stood to gain from trade facilitation. This juxtaposition of developing country interests allowed Director-General Azevêdo to avoid framing the issue as a poisonous North-South confrontation and convince India that concessions eventually offered by the United States on the food security issue would allow India to declare victory on food security while keeping trade facilitation gains for the developing world. Azevêdo, who rightly received credit for his efforts, thereby revived the traditional role of the Director-General in getting the parties to consensus. The positive outcome, which had eluded his predecessor, Pascal Lamy, can be attributed in part to the conjunction of a number of favorable factors: the timing of newly appointed Director-General Azevêdo's "honeymoon" period with the membership, the smaller agenda, his standing as a representative of the developing world, and the general weariness among the WTO membership over many years of Doha deadlock. The disagreements at Bali, such as they were, seemed in the end to be less important to the trade negotiators than the need to achieve, finally, an agreement, even if it would be limited, and show the world that the WTO is still a relevant force in global trade. It also helped that the smaller scale of the Bali controversies did not result in serious political ructions in the home capitals, thus allowing the trade negotiators the leeway to make needed compromises to close the deal.

The message from the Bali Ministerial appears to be that the WTO can still achieve trade liberalization, but for the foreseeable future, multilateral agreements will probably follow the Bali "small-game" model and remain limited in scope. The Bali declaration in fact included instructions for the TNC "to prepare within the next 12 months [in 2014] a clearly defined work program on the remaining Doha Development Agenda issues" (WTO 2013a: Part III). Finding manageable Doha sub-agendas for further negotiation will be difficult, however. The agriculture and NAMA talks would probably need to remain joined in order to provide trade-offs for meaningful bargaining, but WTO members appear to be no closer to consensus in 2014 on these issues than they were when the 2008 negotiations collapsed. Services have now been hived off as a separate issue and will probably follow separate negotiations among a subset of WTO members. Depending on the course of negotiations on these major issues, there is a substantial "built-in" agenda of other uncompleted Doha issues for a new trade round. At some point the remnants of the Doha Round will have to give way to new negotiations, with a more positive outlook, although earlier progress should be "bookmarked" to give the new talks a head start. Schott and Hufbauer (2012) propose a set of relatively "easy" issues from the Doha Round that could be concluded quickly, including issues from the Bali agreement, but also a phase-out of farm export subsidies, dispute settlement reforms; and food export controls. While agreement on these issues may not be so "easy" to conclude, would it not be advisable, in new negotiations, to seek out and secure closure on any less contentious issues first, in order to provide more positive incentives to tackle the harder issues? Or perhaps issues could be concluded and approved separately on a "rolling" basis, which would also be consistent with another proposal, to use standing WTO committees to hammer out agreements independently on technical issues.

There are also many new issues for WTO members to consider. One must distinguish between those that can "fit" into the WTO institutional framework, either through multilateral or plurilateral agreements, and those that will require separate agreements outside the WTO. One particularly difficult issue that will probably need to be addressed by the WTO, for example, is the emerging set of new environmental issues, including carbon border taxes, "green" subsidies, and certain energy export regulations (see Mattoo and Subramanian 2013). In terms of economic efficiency in the presence of externalities, environmental policy intervention is usually a domestic issue, but global commons considerations, along with the danger of protectionist capture of policies dealing with foreign countries' measures, will inevitably suck the WTO into the fray. Establishing a new "green box" category for subsidies benefiting products that contribute to environmental quality would defuse a number of antidumping and countervailing duty cases, for example.[12] WTO disciplines could also define the terms of any carbon tax assessments, based on the national treatment principle, as well as the terms of export restrictions on fossil fuels such as natural gas (ibid.). Other major topics for future WTO negotiations include the three "forbidden" Singapore issues: investment, competition policy, and government procurement. Developing country opposition caused these issues to be dropped from the Doha agenda in 2003, but many countries still have a strong interest in them. Government procurement negotiations have continued on a plurilateral track, and it is likely that negotiations on trade-related investment and competition policies will follow RTA tracks. In particular, supply-chain issues will continue to motivate interest in investment agreements. Similarly, the general issue of domestic regulations and their effect on trade in goods and services will continue to offer large potential gains from trade liberalization, currently being negotiated in some RTAs. Eventually, broader WTO agreements in all these areas may be possible if network and bandwagon effects generate momentum toward multilateralization.

One global issue that directly affects trade, but is unlikely to find a resolution in the WTO alone, is currency valuation. While GATT article XV formally prohibits "exchange action" that distorts trade, there is no precedent for dealing with this problem in the GATT/WTO rules (Mercurio and Leung 2009). Yet the history of the Bretton Woods system suggests that the system of fixed exchange rates under the US-led gold exchange standard may have provided a key element of stability for trade liberalization under the GATT (see Daunton 2012). The subsequent collapse of the Bretton Woods exchange rate system in 1973 did not appear to weaken continuing trade liberalization efforts. However, the subsequent combination of weakened US leadership and global macroeconomic imbalances in the world economy, China's managed exchange rate, and the financial recession beginning in 2008 appears to have brought currency issues back into the forefront of trade policy discussions. A plurilateral agreement on this issue, as proposed by Hufbauer and Schott (2012) is unlikely, due to the weak GATT/WTO legal foundation for it, the fact that China and perhaps other countries would veto it on an annex 4 vote outright, and the fact that all WTO members would want to retain their rights to be involved in negotiating the terms of the agreement. The IMF is the best venue for discussions on this issue, in conjunction with the WTO, although there is not a strong case for filing a complaint under IMF rules either (ibid.). While there is strong sentiment in favor of disciplining deliberate (as opposed, perhaps, to incidental) currency undervaluation, it is not clear how acceptable, consistent, and enforceable rules could be established to identify actionable violations. The best that can be hoped for in the current global system of exchange rates is probably a Code of Conduct with a framework for consultations. The WTO would probably need to play a role in such an arrangement, since governments typically threaten to use trade restrictions as a response to alleged currency manipulation.

AFTER BALI: POSSIBLE PATHWAYS BACK TO GENEVA

Figure 8.2 summarizes the foregoing discussion by sketching a set of incentive pathways that could ultimately lead back to WTO multilateralism. The process of motivating countries to return to global negotiations depends on both current trends and future initiatives and policy choices by governments. The outcome is therefore highly contingent on the course of the global economy and of political decision-making. Nonetheless, the advantages of the WTO system provide a strong undercurrent to the process. For example, discriminatory RTAs create both a "negative" motive, market-access and foreign investment

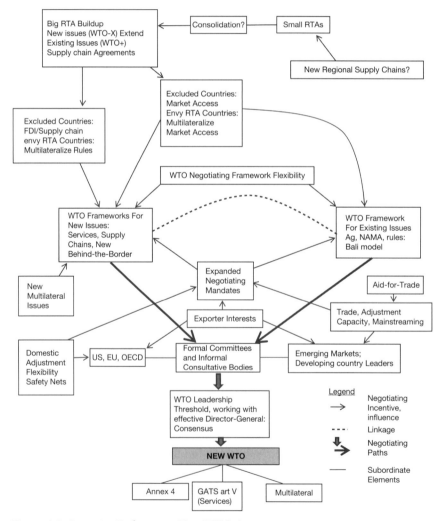

Figure 8.2 Incentive Pathways to New WTO Agreements

envy, and a "positive" motive, the preliminary negotiating frameworks for new issues, that can make global MFN negotiations more attractive and more manageable. An improved flexibility in the structure of future WTO negotiations should also make them a more attractive venue. This may be simply a matter of separating services into a separate negotiation, along with individual plurilateral agreements on supply-chain governance, trade facilitation funding, and other issues. WTO members may, on the other hand, mutually determine a more efficient grouping and sequencing of negotiating topics, or give more weight to ongoing technical negotiations in the standing committees, rather than in top-down, high-stakes bargaining and summitry. Figure 8.2 distinguishes between "new" WTO negotiations informed by groundbreaking work in deep integration RTAs and existing negotiations to extend previous agreements, but there is no reason that they could not contain crossover issues in any number of bargaining configurations. Aid-for-trade support that can increase trade capacity and cause trade policy to be "mainstreamed" in development policy will increase the incentive for trade bargaining in developing countries, just as effective domestic adjustment and economic flexibility will do the same in developed countries, which may also expand the scope of trade bargaining into non-traditional and behind-the-border areas. The increased or renewed political engagement of exporter interests in all countries will also probably be necessary in order to generate momentum for governments to make progress at the bargaining table. The new balance of bargaining power in the WTO is illustrated in the balance between US/EU/OECD members and emerging market/developing country leaders in both formal and informal consultations, which will define the effectiveness of the bargaining structure. With the still significant, but precarious, influence of the Director-General in brokering deals, more effort will be required from the leading WTO members in finding common ground and reconciling their differences. In the end, the effectiveness of "integrative" bargaining—securing for all participants new gains from trade—will determine whether the negotiating efforts pass the "WTO leadership threshold" necessary to move the membership toward consensus. Depending on the structure and partitioning of the negotiations, the resulting agreements will take the form of either annex 4 (plurilateral), GATS article V (services), or general multilateral WTO obligations and benefits.

Another way to describe the scenario presented in figure 8.2 is that a successful creation of the incentives to negotiate represents a strengthening of WTO institutions. Taking the traditional trade negotiating model and turning it around, a multilateral trade agreement on any given range of issues is, ceteris paribus, the best alternative to an RTA—as long as the WTO institutions are operating effectively. The gains from WTO liberalization and its associated trade rules are superior to those of an RTA, and its dispute settlement protection is more secure. These are two of the major goals that lie at the heart of the "collective intentionality" of WTO membership. Trade and invest- ment envy serve to reinforce the commitment to these goals. Increased trade capacity and more effective adjustment policies and flexibility reduce the sov- ereign policy constraint, thereby broadening the potential gains from trade. Increased exporter engagement strengthens the link between domestic politi- cal institutions and internal WTO decision-making in the process of moving toward consensus. Improved communication and trust in the processes of decision-making will likewise contribute to the process of achieving consen- sus, as will adjusting some unworkable internal rules and procedures, such as those that resulted in the requirement of single undertaking in combination with an overloaded agenda.

And what if this hopeful scenario does not materialize? Many things can go wrong. The changes are based on the assumption, for example, that govern- ments recognize the problem and have the political will to fix it, especially the leading countries, with the complication that a larger group of countries will need to share in this leadership. Many countries, both developed and devel- oping, reacted to setbacks in the Doha Round with anger and disdain at their counterparts across the table. The danger for the future of the WTO is that they will channel this discontent into defensive trade measures and RTA alliances, without risking any really new trade liberalization at all. The large RTAs will not serve the purpose shown in figure 8.2 if they are ultimately designed to exclude major emerging markets such as China and India, or to coerce them into rules asserted unilaterally by the United States and European Union, while establishing subordinate trade relations with the partner countries. They will also fail to serve any multilateral purpose if they eschew the more difficult trade liberalization issues regarding services, regulations, and traditional protection- ist strongholds in agriculture and basic manufacturing. It is possible, in other words, that trade liberalization progress through RTAs will be limited, thus making a return to Geneva less likely in the meantime. The course of global trade policy will depend, for better or for worse, on the political leadership in key developed and developing countries. In that case one can perhaps find some comfort in the observations of Jan Tumlir, Director of Economic Research at the GATT from 1967 to 1985, who viewed the course of global trade relations in terms of long historical arcs. Trade policy in the last two centuries, in his view, has followed a cycle of learning and unlearning, with remarkable initiatives by one or more countries to open their domestic markets to trade, followed by a period of liberalization among other countries; then a crisis, followed by col- lapse of the trade agreements and a period of retrenchment, before the next spark to liberalize trade anew. While the world trading system has certainly not collapsed into the protectionist abyss, it finds itself in a period of transition, in which its ability to gain from multilateral trade has weakened. Today's policy makers may have internalized the necessary lessons; otherwise there is more learning—and improvement—to look forward to in the future.

WHY THERE ISN'T MORE TRADE

This book began with the question: "why isn't there more trade?" In light of the overwhelming case for the mutual gains from trade and the human tendency to "truck and barter," what prevents human interaction from extending the process of specialization and exchange into areas of new international opportunity? The explanation presented in these pages has been that the problem lies with the institutions of international, and to a certain degree, domestic, trade policy making. In this regard the Doha Round has not failed because agreement is impossible, but because WTO members have not maximized the integrative potential of the issues (see Boyer 2012: 221). Building a stronger institutional foundation for the WTO is the best way to increase this potential. In recent years there has indeed been more RTA trade expansion because this is politically the best path available for pursuing the gains, even though the gains from trade are inferior to what a WTO agreement could theoretically accomplish. The Doha experience, in this context, shows that there isn't more multilateral trade expansion because changing the institutional environment of multilateral trade liberalization is hard work, and the efforts so far have not been up to the task. The internal gains from trade in local and domestic market exchanges usually rest on individual countries' well-established traditions and legal institutions. Yet the regulation of trade among sovereign countries has created the need for an additional set of international institutions in order to increase trade. Such institutions must establish common ground on the framework and scope for negotiations, and rules to achieve final agreement, and they require upgrading and updating when the negotiating environment changes. It is disappointing to reach the concluding pages of this study without identifying a clear set of institutional "fixes," a recipe of changes in WTO rules and procedures that will, on their own, get countries back to the negotiating table and somehow closer to consensus. The example of the WTO's failed negotiating function reveals that such fixes are not possible because the WTO as an institution has protected itself from internal change, through the consensus rule, when the underlying structure is no longer capable of functioning in a changed environment. The conclusions from this chapter, and from the institutional analysis of this book, can be distilled into the following recommendations.

Keep the WTO Fires Burning. It is essential that WTO members continue their active engagement in the WTO, lest the institution suffer from the entropy that follows neglect. A number of Doha issues could still be harvested, if on a smaller scale than originally planned—especially regarding agriculture and non-agricultural tariffs—and these efforts should continue as long as negotiations hold the realistic promise of an agreement. At some point, it may be worthwhile considering switching to critical mass or plurilateral negotiations to get an agreement. The smaller group of WTO members should also pursue ambitious ISA negotiations across all four services modes, which if successful seem destined for a GATS agreement, with an eye toward keeping the agreement open for both extensions in service sector coverage and accession-based WTO membership. Other important WTO-based negotiating opportunities include updates of the three existing "critical mass" agreements on technology products and financial services. It is in any case of critical importance to keep WTO negotiations, even at lower levels, in the forefront of its members' trade policy interests, so that there will be strong incentives to staff country delegations with capable trade diplomats and specialists, as suggested by the committee chair "human capital" analysis of chapter 5. There are already concerns that an inactive or irrelevant WTO can lead (or with regard to some countries, may already be leading) to a diversion of qualified personnel to other activities. Countries will commit their best people to WTO delegations if the payoff from WTO negotiations is worth it. The worst-case scenario is that delegations depleted of important issues to discuss, and qualified trade officials to discuss them, will cause the WTO General Council and its subsidiary bodies to deteriorate into a forum for ideological confrontation, unproductive argument, and procedural mischief.

  Stick to the (Old and New) Trade Knitting. The WTO is an institution based on the "collective intentionality" of its members to establish mutually advantageous trade rules and dispute settlement procedures and to increase their gains from trade. In this regard, there is no basis in the WTO agreements to pursue non-trade-related issues collectively, which is why it has been—and will most likely remain—impossible to negotiate new WTO chapters on the environment, human rights, and labor standards, for example. There are certainly areas in which trade and non-trade issues intersect, as defined by existing GATT exceptions, in which a balance must be struck between and among WTO rights and obligations, domestic policy sovereignty, and other international treaty commitments.[13] At the same time, the WTO negotiating and rules framework must maintain its ability to deal with new trade-related issues, such as aid-for-trade, foreign direct investment, carbon border taxes, government support for high-technology (including new environmental) industries, competition policy, and even global rules regarding exchange rates. However, the general conclusion of this book still applies: in order for there to be new trade-related agreements, there must be a sufficient institutional foundation to support them, including, if necessary, building bridges with other global institutions such as the World Bank and the IMF.

Prepare the Way for More Effective WTO Decision-Making. Within the WTO's decision-making structure, changes will come slowly, since the threshold for approving reform by consensus is so high. In the meantime, some practical procedures will need to change. For example, issue linkage will continue, but the Doha experience suggests that the comprehensive single undertaking straitjacket should be abandoned.[14] This means that agreements may no longer arrive in such large packages, and some individual agreements may be concluded sequentially. Divergences in the views of WTO members on a number of key issues (agriculture, the broad array of services sectors, behind-the-border measures, etc.) will have to narrow and the capacity to adjust to trade competition will have to improve, before broader agendas can again be linked in a single package. Negotiations on technical issues may in some cases eventually find a new home in standing WTO committees. In any case, by keeping WTO negotiations churning at various levels, member delegations should take the opportunity to build better working relationships and mutual understanding of the issues that divide them. Among the negotiating impediments during the Doha Round were divergences in the understanding and implications of terms such as "food security," "reciprocity," and "policy space."[15] Progress in economic development and in achieving better trade capacity and trade "mainstreaming" in development policy, which will continue to depend in part on external aid (see below), should contribute to bridging the gaps in understanding and negotiating positions between developed and developing countries. Improved prospects for achieving gains from trade may then allow developing country coalitions to take on positive, "integrative" negotiating platforms, rather than the blocking, "distributive" platforms that often stymied progress in the Doha negotiations. Greater flexibility in reciprocal bargaining among developing countries, in particular, will also facilitate more consistent coalition representation in green room meetings, and thus a stronger movement toward consensus. Better working and negotiating relationships among the United States, European Union, and emerging market economies, and especially between the United States and China, will be necessary in order to move new multilateral trade negotiations forward. Finally, the role of the Director-General in trade negotiations, which had declined during the Doha Round, should not be neglected. Despite the members' skepticism—and often distrust—of the Director-General's role in brokering agreements, it will be necessary for the major negotiating parties to develop a sound working relationship with him or her in order to facilitate future WTO deals, especially those that involve bargaining across diverse issues. Roberto Azevêdo's success in securing a compromise at the Bali Ministerial was perhaps a small accomplishment, but one that highlights the continued importance of personal trust and leadership in trade diplomacy.

Embrace the Opportunities of Regional Trade Agreements. RTAs are motivated by powerful political economy and foreign policy incentives and will remain a prominent feature of the global trading system for the foreseeable future. WTO members will need to take advantage of their potential multilateral dynamics to find pathways back to WTO negotiations. Negotiations on new issues for possible future WTO agreements, including services, behind-the-border regulations, and the currently taboo "Singapore" issues, will have to follow RTA or plurilateral pathways until the WTO membership is ready to consider them for global bargaining. The United States and European Union, in particular, must take on the responsibility of making their deep-integration, big-RTA negotiations ambitious, welfare-enhancing, and as open to new membership or multilateralization as possible. Otherwise, the "trade envy" effect on outsiders and eagerness of RTA participants to expand membership will not be effective, and the possibilities of new sectoral and behind-the-border coverage in WTO agreements will be reduced. Ambitious RTAs between the United States or European Union and one or more emerging markets would generate major "bandwagon" effects because of the attractive and growing import markets and investment opportunities in emerging markets. In addition, regional supply chains have become an important new feature of international trade and often play a major role in the negotiation of RTAs, although not completely in terms of reciprocal market access. They create added incentives to expand RTA membership, and to create multilateral services and goods market opening and investment liberalization rules, and can therefore play a future role in either multilateral or plurilateral WTO agreements.

Improve Domestic Adjustment Policies and Business Engagement. The Doha Round has revealed that the institutional foundation for global trade liberalization is highly contingent on the circumstances and domestic politics of its participants. Adjustments in the WTO rules themselves will have to come very slowly, and in the meantime, countries will be left to improve the situation through foreign aid initiatives, through government or multilateral lending channels, to improve developing countries' trade capacity, the improvement of domestic trade adjustment safety nets and market flexibility, and better (or renewed) business engagement in trade negotiations. Much of the effort to restore the WTO to its central position in world trade will therefore have to take place outside the WTO. Within the existing institutional structure, government policies and actions will need to change the underlying incentives so that the WTO again works as an institution, as shown by the hopeful presentation of aligned incentives in figure 8.2. Since the WTO as an institution was created by and for major governments in the world economy, progress toward the WTO's central role in it will depend on the committed efforts of the major governments responsible for the trading system to lead the way. This will require them to manage their own domestic trade institutions to support more trade, and to rediscover the gains from expanded trade in new areas and with new trading partners. The United States, European Union, and larger OECD countries must embrace this challenge, as must the emerging market countries, especially India, Brazil, and China. Other developing countries, which will continue to receive special and differential treatment, must nonetheless move toward a position of realizing the gains from reciprocal market access bargaining, where the real payoff from trade liberalization occurs.

Reconstructing the WTO for renewed multilateral trade liberalization will therefore require both interior work and foundational work. What the success of the GATT years concealed was the importance of common ground among participating countries in their understanding of negotiating boundaries and goals, in the process of translating business interests into reciprocal trade bargaining, and in foundation of trust in the formal and informal processes of reaching agreements. In the new WTO, the diverse membership must find common ground on new areas of negotiation, a process that must begin with domestic adjustment and development policies, and continue by harnessing all the available incentives, from RTAs to aid-for-trade, and by new forms of cooperation among developed, developing, and emerging market countries. The economic incentives for global trade liberalization remain strong, and the new global economy of more broadly shared economic power represents a major victory for its success in the GATT/WTO system. But history has shown that progress in global trade and trade relations does not necessarily follow a linear, upward path over time. The institutional challenge to achieve it in the future will require new domestic and international efforts with political vision, commitment, and leadership.

CHAPTER 1

1. See chapter 4. The Singapore issue included investment, competition, government procurement policies, and trade facilitation. Only trade facilitation survived to remain on the Doha agenda after the 2003 Cancun Ministerial and became the chief component of the 2013 Bali Agreement.

2. Simple unweighted averages of tariffs rates across broad categories may not capture individual tariff lines that apply to large volumes of trade, for example. In addition, when tariffs are weighted by trade volume, very large tariffs that reduce trade so much that they are nearly prohibitive would be given too little weight in the calculations. In both of these cases, the calculated mean tariff would underestimate the impact of tariffs.

3. A simple example is when the tariff is 0% on raw coffee beans, but 10% on ground coffee. If under free trade a $90 bag of coffee beans from a developing country is imported into a developed country to produce $100 worth of ground coffee, then the domestic value added for the coffee grinder is (100 – 90) = $10. The combination of a 0% tariff on raw coffee beans and a 10% tariff on ground coffee would raise the ground coffee price to $110, so that domestic value added is now $20. The 10% tariff on the final good has raised domestic value added by 100%, which is also called the effective rate of protection. The developing country with an interest in starting coffee grinding operations would have to significantly suppress its own domestic value added in order to export to the developed country. Grubel and Johnson (1971) offer a book-length discussion of effective tariff issues.

4. The WTO Agreement on Subsidies and Countervailing Measures spells out more detailed definitions, along with rules on prohibited subsidies, actionable subsidies, and non-actionable subsidies. See WTO (1999).

5. See Ferrantino (2006) for a review of the types of NTMs and the methodologies used.

6. The services trade restrictions index (STRI) ranges from 0 (completely free trade in the services item) to 100 (fully prohibitive trade restriction) and is based on data from twenty-four OECD and seventy-nine developing countries gathered by the World Bank.

7. The gains from trade discussed in this paragraph do not include the gains from permanent labor migration to the receiving country, with ambiguous results for the country of emigration. Permanent emigration/immigration is not part of the planned WTO services negotiations.

8. Based on an estimated global nominal GDP of $71.83 trillion (CIA World Factbook 2012).

9. See, for example, Evenett (2013), chapter 2. Evenett (2012) contains additional analysis and statistics on how protectionist measures grew over the crisis period.

10. While most developed country WTO members have bound their tariffs at applied levels, many developing countries often set applied rates below the bound rates, leaving them with the freedom to raise tariffs unilaterally without violating WTO rules.

11. Some of these types of government intervention may be subject to WTO rules, but only partially, or they may be actionable if certain conditions are met. There is a WTO plurilateral Government Procurement Agreement among some, but not all, WTO members, for example, which may allow some discriminatory procurement measures. Domestic subsidies may be subject to WTO rules, and export restrictions may be challenged in dispute settlement cases. See Evenett (2011: table 5).

CHAPTER 2

1. See McBrearty and Brooks (2000: 513–517), which dates evidence of distant trade to the middle Paleolithic era. See also Oppenheimer (2003: 127). Dillian and White (2010) contains several other studies of prehistoric trade.

2. History has shown, however, that allure of the gains from more distant trade in exotic and luxury goods, especially in the spice and silk trade that connected Europe with Asia, can outweigh fears of unfamiliar trading partners. See Findlay and O'Rourke (2007: chapters 3–5) and Bernstein (2008: chapters 3–7). Even in this case, however, countries often sought to gain control over both trading routes and the production sources of the exotic goods.

3. The Heckscher-Ohlin theory of trade assumes two countries, two goods, and two factors of production (labor and capital). The two countries produce identical goods, and based on their relative factor endowments, the opportunity to trade causes each to specialize production partially in its good of comparative advantage, which it exports to the partner country. Thus trade displaces production in the importable sector for each country, creating a motivation for protectionist policies. Furthermore, Stolper and Samuelson (1941) showed that one factor of production would benefit economically from trade, while the other would lose. These production and welfare effects have played major roles in the political economy of trade relations since the Industrial Revolution.

4. Baldwin (2011) traces the impact of what he describes as the historic spatial unbundling of production through information and communications technology on regional trade relations, and its implications for the WTO. See also the discussion on preferential trade agreements in chapter 6.

5. The major business institution that has resulted from global trade and investment opportunities, in conjunction with technological advancement, is the

multinational corporation. State institutions have also developed to intervene in the trading activity of firms, for example, through state ownership, support of "national champions," or enforcement of unfair trade laws. Given the resources of national treasuries and the regulatory power of governments, such policies are often the subject of negotiation and dispute among trading partners.

6. Searle (2005) provides the basic elements of his constructivist theory of economic institutions. Searle (1995) provides a book-length treatment. This section draws and expands on Jones (2010: chapter 1).

7. See Toye (2003). US negotiators had agreed to such conditional trade restrictions in the Havana Charter in order to attract more countries to it, especially from the growing developing world. The GATT, for its part, would also contain escape clauses and exemptions from trade liberalization commitments, as part of the agreement's "embedded liberalism" to be discussed below. However, the ITO included more explicit "policy space" exemptions; in addition, the ITO (unlike the GATT) contained foreign investment provisions that US business interests deemed insufficient to prevent expropriation by host governments, which influenced the US Senate's decision not to ratify it.

8. Aside from the United States and United Kingdom, Contracting Parties included Australia, Belgium, Canada, Chile, China, Cuba, Czechoslovakia, France, Lebanon, Luxembourg, the Netherlands, South Africa, Syria, India, Norway, Zimbabwe (then known as Rhodesia), Myanmar (then known as Burma), Sri Lanka (then known as Ceylon), Brazil, New Zealand, and Pakistan. China, Czechoslovakia, Syria, and Lebanon would later withdraw from the GATT, but Czechoslovakia's successor states, the Czech and Slovak Republics, joined again in 1993. China (along with Taiwan) joined the WTO in 2001, and Lebanon and Syria have applied for WTO membership.

9. While there are no specific references in the GATT to this provision, it is implied in the preamble, which acknowledges participating countries' goals of "raising standards of living, full employment, and a large and steadily growing volume of real income and effective demand." The GATT's role is one of "contributing to these objectives by entering into reciprocal and mutually advantageous arrangements."

10. A large country with price-making power on international markets can theoretically improve its own national welfare by restricting trade, thereby improving its terms of trade. The tariff level that maximizes welfare under these conditions is the "optimum" tariff. However, the improvement in welfare assumes that other countries do not retaliate with tariffs of their own. When other large countries also pursue optimum tariff strategies, the result would be a set of tariffs that leaves all countries worse off than they would be under free trade. The prisoner's dilemma comes from the fear of tariff "disarmament," in which the remaining tariff-imposing country gains at the expense of the free traders. A system of trade rules can overcome the prisoner's dilemma by establishing reciprocal trade liberalization, tariff binding, and dispute settlement, moving all participants closer to global welfare-maximizing free trade. Bagwell and Staiger (2002) formalize this analysis as an underlying motivation for establishing a GATT/WTO system.

11. Non-trade issues have arisen in GATT and WTO dispute cases, and the dispute panels have considered environmental issues in particular, which require

judgments that balance trade and environmental interests under international law. See Weinstein and Charnovitz (2001). GATT/WTO negotiations and rules focus squarely on trade, with some narrowly defined exceptions in GATT article 20.

12. Goldstein et al. (2007) emphasize the importance of participation in the GATT, and the deontic powers that this implied, rather than membership, per se. Under the original GATT, many countries that were not actual "Contracting Parties" enjoyed de facto GATT status, either through the sponsorship of colonies or former colonies by the metropole, provisional membership, or pending membership. The WTO subsequently introduced strict legal requirements for membership and the deontic powers that accompany it.

13. BAMTA is the author's variant of BATNA, "best alternative to a negotiated agreement," an acronym originally coined by Fisher and Ury (1981). The term crystalizes the issue of whether countries remain strictly within the multilateral GATT/WTO negotiating system, or are tempted to act unilaterally or pursue agreements on a preferential basis.

14. See Curzon (1965: 114–116); Dam (1970: 61–62).

15. The application of the safeguards provision in the original GATT allowed discrimination in practice, although it stipulated compensation to affected exporters in terms of a withdrawal of balancing trade concessions (see Dam 1970: 99–107). This was a perennially difficult balance to strike. The amended WTO safeguards clause required MFN treatment, with some exceptions (see Schott 1994).

16. GATT provisions, now incorporated with some modifications into the WTO, also allow countries to re-negotiate tariff concessions (GATT article 28), requiring a broader re-balancing of concessions with its trading partners. Finger (2002) notes that such re-negotiations were a common way to deal with pressures for new protection in the early years of the GATT, and Finger (2012) traces the evolution of other trade remedy provisions and their use in the GATT/WTO system, more recently favoring antidumping. Waivers from GATT/WTO obligations are subject to voting procedures in GATT article 25 and WTO article 9, respectively. For a general discussion of GATT/WTO "safety valves," see Hoekman and Kostecki (2009: chapter 9).

17. The United Nations Conference on Trade and Development proposed the GSP in 1968, and a GATT agreement approved an MFN waiver for it in 1971, made permanent in the "Enabling Clause" of the GATT Tokyo Round agreement in 1979. The GSP continues with unilateral rules imposed by the developed countries offering the preferences, often with attached conditions, to developing countries, subject to GATT/WTO disciplines and dispute settlement. See Hoekman and Kostecki (2009: chapter 12) and Michalopoulos (2001: chapter 3).

18. "Software" problems regarding informal rules and processes arose with the transition to the WTO, a subject for chapter 3.

19. Table 3.2 in chapter 3 will compare these GATT examples of institutional adjustment and their outcomes to comparable examples in the WTO.

20. There are some references to special treatment for agriculture in GATT articles 11 and 16, but they did not explicitly allow the widespread tariff and quota protection that prevailed during the GATT period. See Dam (1970: 260–262).

21. See Curzon (1965: chapter 7) and Dam (1970: chapter 15). As a result of such policies, high US agricultural prices were attracting foreign imports, which would have disrupted domestic agricultural production. The United States received in 1955 a broad waiver, allowed under GATT rules, for its import quota programs for agricultural imports, which squelched subsequent efforts to liberalize agricultural trade until the Uruguay Round.

22. The effective rate of protection accounts for trade in inputs along a product's supply chain and measures net protection of domestic value added. It is generally calculated as $(V'–V)/V$, in which V is the domestic value added under free trade for all inputs and output, and V' is the net domestic value added under a tariff regime on both inputs and the final output. A pattern of "cascading" tariffs, applied by many developed countries, sets tariffs on raw material inputs very low, but tends to escalate the tariff levels on intermediate goods, with highest tariffs on the final product in the supply chain, leading to high effective protection on the final good. This tariff regime often discourages downstream value-added processing by developing countries. See Curzon (1965: 228–231); Cordon (1971). For a comprehensive treatment, see Grubel and Johnson (1971).

23. See http://www.wto.org/english/thewto_e/whatis_e/tif_e/org7_e.htm. Currently, WTO member countries "self-declare" their developing country status, but this status can be challenged by other WTO members. Developed countries offering GSP benefits also have some discretion regarding the terms of "graduation." See Hoekman and Kostecki (2009: 542–544).

Chapter 3

1. Hudec, Kennedy, and Sgarbossa (1993) note that 88% of GATT dispute settlement cases were settled to the satisfaction of both parties, through consultations, concessions, or implemented panel decisions, emphasizing the importance of diplomatic deference to the dispute settlement process and the panels' decisions, even in the absence of a formal binding sanctions on countries found in violation of GATT rules.

2. See the discussion of this issue in chapter 4.

3. The term "Washington Consensus" was coined by economist John Williamson (1989) and described a set of policy prescriptions alleged promoted at the time by the IMF, World Bank, and US Treasury Department, including the desirability of open trade for developing countries.

4. There are two plurilateral agreements in the WTO, first concluded at the Tokyo Round, that do not include all WTO members: the agreement on Government Procurement and the agreement on Civil Aircraft. Other earlier GATT plurilateral agreements were folded into general WTO commitments. See Hoekman and Kostecki (2009: chapter 11).

5. Some cases may not result in a complete resolution of the dispute, especially those that involve large WTO players, such as the United States and European Union (agriculture, Airbus vs. Boeing, etc.). Equilibrium thus requires the disputants to partition the problem away from the general functioning of WTO trade relations, so that the dispute does not lead to unilateral retaliatory measures and a general breakdown of WTO rules.

6. See the discussion of Doha deadlock below and in chapter 4. Under the GATT, participating countries had also pursued RTAs during trade negotiations, but the difference in the Doha Round is the resort by large members to RTAs as a *result* of the failure of WTO negotiations. Statements by Zoellick (2003) and Lamy (see Price 2003) give credence to this interpretation.

7. The WTO's constitutive rule of a "single undertaking" implies that a comprehensive package deal is necessary to complete the Doha Round, but such partial agreements may be regarded as steppingstones to a broader agreement later. In addition, separate agreements among smaller groups of WTO members are possible as "plurilateral" agreements, which apply only to their signatories. Such agreements would represent new institutional "facts," but not as the sort of multilateral agreement outlined in the Doha Development Agenda.

8. The economic arguments for protecting IPRs lie in their contribution to incentives for innovation. Yet the merits of this case imply the need for the World Intellectual Property Organization (WIPO) to be responsible for global IPR protection. Unfortunately the WIPO has no effective enforcement powers, and it is unlikely that TRIPS will ever be carved out of the WTO.

9. An additional consideration is that all countries would benefit from the removal of US unilateral IP enforcement measures. Even so, on a present value basis, the bargain for developing countries was certainly questionable. See Maskus (2012) for an overview of the major TRIPS issues.

10. See the discussion of China in chapter 8, as well as in Vickers (2012). China was not completely absent from the negotiations and was influential in siding with India on the issue of Special Safeguard Measures for agricultural goods at the July 2008 negotiating session. Yet its large role in trade made its low profile for most of the Doha Round conspicuous. As a relatively new WTO member, China may have wanted to avoid a prominent role. Since it has such a strong interest in trade liberalization, however, it is curious that it was not more active in keeping the negotiations going.

11. The Special Safeguards clause made it easier to impose temporary trade restrictions against imports from China than under the "normal" WTO Safeguards provisions. It has been used in several cases involving textiles and clothing (United States, Peru, and Colombia), automobile tires (United States), and some additional cases filed by Turkey. There have been many antidumping cases under the special provisions. See Messerlin (2004) and Bown (2010).

12. Chapters 4 and 5 will examine this question in more detail.

13. The author has heard contesting points of view from trade officials close to the Doha negotiations on the issue of trust. A realist perspective would tend to hold that trust has nothing to do with a negotiation, which proceeds on the basis of national interests alone, and the objective means of securing them. While national interests may dominate the bargaining, however, in the advanced stages of deliberation a working relationship among negotiators needs to exist in order to close the deal, based on confidence in the reliability of offers and the perceived integrity of the heads of delegations and the Director-General. See Blustein (2009) for an account of the breakdown in the 2008 Doha negotiations, and the tensions among negotiators.

14. Anonymous interview with a US trade official, January 2013.
15. Chapter 4 provides a more detailed account of WTO members' attitudes toward the Director-General.
16. The most important part of the Bali Agreement, on Trade Facilitation, had been considered one of the least contentious issues earlier in the Doha Round, but had become mired in bickering over infrastructure funding. The breakthrough on this agreement will be discussed in chapters 7 and 8.

CHAPTER 4

1. Officially, WTO article IX requires unanimity on amendments to general principles such as the MFN clause, a three-quarters majority on interpretations of WTO provisions and waivers of disciplines, and a two-thirds majority on amendments to WTO provisions other than the general principles. All other issues require consensus.
2. Brown and Stern (2012) examine the issue of fairness in the WTO system, focusing on the principles of equality of opportunity and distributive justice.
3. They acquired the "green room" nickname from the green décor of the GATT Director-General's meeting room in Geneva in the old Centre William Rappard.
4. The green room meetings that led to the agreement to re-start the Doha negotiations in July 2004 were chaired by the Chairman of the General Council, Ambassador Tadamori Oshima, since the deliberations were part of an extended General Council meeting attended by several representatives at the ministerial level (source: correspondence with WTO official). Most green room meetings are held either in Geneva or at the locations of Ministerial meetings and are chaired by the Director-General.
5. Another type of informal meeting, outside the official negotiating framework, is the "mini-ministerial." See Wolfe (2005: 640–641) for a discussion of the distinction between mini-ministerial and green room meetings.
6. Martin Khor (2005) documents the following set of twenty-six green room participants at a pre-Hong Kong Ministerial session: the European Union, United States, India, Brazil, Japan, Canada, Switzerland, Hong Kong, Zambia, New Zealand, Australia, Korea, South Africa, Malaysia, Lesotho, Benin, Chad, Thailand, Argentina, Mexico, Costa Rica, Jamaica, Egypt, Kenya, Pakistan, and China.
7. For a review of the results of the Uruguay Round, see Schott and Buurman (1994). Jones (2010: chapter 2) discusses the institutional legacy of the Uruguay Round and its impact on the Doha Round.
8. The costs to developing countries came from the transfers of IP rents to developed countries, especially pharmaceutical firms, and from the cost of compliance in implementing IP legal and enforcement regimes, largely from scratch. See Finger and Schuler (2000).
9. Odell (2000: 27) discusses the importance of this concept in economic negotiations among countries and notes that the term originated with Fisher and Ury (1981).

10. Robert Zoellick, US Trade Representative during the early years of the Doha Round, made plain the alternative US strategy of concluding preferential trade agreements in attempting to motivate recalcitrant WTO trading partners to continue multilateral trade negotiations. See Zoellick (2003).

11. Cohn (2002: 5) presents a world trade governance pyramid with the United States and European Union at the top, followed by the G7/G8 (United States, Canada, United Kingdom, France, Germany, Italy, Japan, plus Russia), Quad, and OECD. The WTO system is subordinate to these countries in world trade governance, according to Cohn's paradigm. At the bottom is the G77 (developing countries group) and United Nations Conference on Trade and Development (UNCTAD). The emergence of China, India, and Brazil as major players in WTO negotiations indicates that Cohn's governance pyramid is outdated, although the United States, European Union, and other OECD countries may not have acknowledged it.

12. IMF estimates. See http://www.imf.org/external/pubs/ft/survey/so/2013/NEW100813A.htm.

13. See Bagwell and Staiger (2002: 18–41). It is important to remember that political considerations are central to the GATT/WTO mercantilist approach of reciprocity in trade negotiations, in which tariff reductions are regarded as trade "concessions." This aspect of the rules contradicts the traditional neoclassical analysis of the gains from trade. In a perfect world with no political constraints or price-making power, and with equal players and no market externalities, the optimum tariffs would theoretically always be zero.

14. As noted in chapters 2 and 3, trust in WTO negotiations appears to depend more on structural than on personal elements among the bargainers. In the case of a blocking strategy, the impact on "trust" may be a perceived signal that the blocking coalition is committed to a "distributive" strategy that will demand all, or the lion's share, of gains, with no concessions offered. As a result, other negotiators may discount any subsequent deliberations as insincere or futile, thus eroding "trust" in the negotiations. See Jönsson (2012).

15. Negotiating practice in the GATT/WTO system has come to focus on the need to achieve a balance of concessions won and yielded, implying an increased level of trade for each country balanced roughly between increased imports and increased exports. This approach typically satisfies political constraints while capturing at least some gains from trade. Trading concessions is thus not treated necessarily as a zero-sum swap, but as an exchange of foreign market access gains that must be "paid for" on a reciprocal basis.

16. Developed countries included Australia, Belgium, Canada, France, Luxembourg, the Netherlands, the United Kingdom, the United States, Norway, and New Zealand. The developing countries were Cuba, South Africa, India, Rhodesia (now Zimbabwe), Burma (Myanmar), Ceylon (Sri Lanka), Brazil, and Pakistan. The GATT's 1948 founding document had twenty-three signatories, adding Chile, as well as China, Lebanon, and Syria to the list. The last three later withdrew from the GATT.

17. Chapters 2 and 3 discuss the background of special and differential (S&D) treatment for developing countries in the GATT/WTO system. See Hoekman, Michalopoulos, and Winters (2004) for a critique of S&D in trade negotiations with regard to the interests of developing countries. Indirectly, S&D may have

contributed to the marginalization of developing countries in the green room process, since they were partially detached from the give-and-take of reciprocal trade concessions.

18. The first four negotiations used a line-by-line tariff approach, which became increasingly burdensome and was replaced by an across-the-board tariff-cutting approach in the Kennedy Round. For a discussion of early GATT negotiating history, see Curzon (1965) and Dam (1970).

19. See Hoekman and Kostecki (2009: chapter 4) for an overview of WTO negotiating procedures.

20. De Souza Farias (2013) comments on Wyndham White's effectiveness as Director-General, including the authority he enjoyed in managing the timing, length, agenda, and logistics of the various GATT committee meetings. See Curzon (1965: 50–51) and Dam (1970: 339–341), for more commentary on the role of Eric Wyndham White.

21. One US official, in conversation in 2012, declared that, if US strategy were accused of minimizing the power of the Director-General since the Uruguay Round, it stood "guilty as charged."

22. *Bridges Weekly Trade News Digest*, May 8, 2013, vol. 17(16), http://ictsd.org/i/news/bridgesweekly/163196/, reports that the first choice of both the United States and European Union was Herminio Blanco of Mexico, although they indicated that either candidate was acceptable.

23. Correspondence with a former trade official from a Quad country indicates that there were in fact several representatives from poor and other developing countries at the crisis-laden Seattle green room meeting. Thus, even a system of proportional representation would not necessarily satisfy countries left out of critical decision-making forums.

24. Despite the failure of the Doha MC to resolve important issues, it did represent a successful effort to prepare the MC summit for meaningful negotiation. See Odell (2009), who emphasizes the improved negotiating strategies among major countries of the Doha Ministerial, compared to Seattle, and Stoler (2011), chair of the General Council at the time, who emphasizes the pre-Ministerial preparation for the Doha Ministerial and the role of committee chairman in keeping negotiations on track.

25. Members included Argentina, Bolivia, Brazil, Chile, China, Colombia, Costa Rica, Cuba, Ecuador, Egypt, Guatemala, India, Indonesia, Mexico, Nigeria, Pakistan, Paraguay, Peru, Philippines, South Africa, Thailand, and Venezuela. See "The WTO under Fire," *Economist*, September 18, 2003, and Narlikar and Tussie (2004).

26. Other trade officials present at the green room meetings, in conversation with the author, dispute this assessment, noting in particular the role of the European Union in insisting on the Singapore issues agenda until it was too late.

27. Anonymous remarks, Geneva, October 2012.

28. The Special General Council session was chaired by Japanese Ambassador Shotaro Oshima. For his account, see Oshima (2011). See also Albin and Young (2012) for a comparison of agenda management between the 2003 Cancun Ministerial and the 2004 Geneva "July Package" Framework Agreement.

29. Some trade commentators suggest privately that the 2008 WTO negotiations came within a whisker of attaining an agricultural agreement, and but for that the Doha Round could have been concluded. This assertion is difficult to prove or disprove, but is certainly doubtful, given the number of other issues that were never resolved as part of a single undertaking to end the round.

30. Faizel Ismail (2009), Head of the South African delegation, blames the NAMA committee chair, Don Stephenson of Canada, for tilting the negotiations in favor of developed countries, while he credits Agricultural committee chair Crawford Falconer of New Zealand with a more inclusive and balanced approach regarding developed and developing country interests. Ismail represents a large number of developing countries in his criticism of WTO's alleged domination by developed country interests. Jawara and Kwa (2004) present an even harsher view of allegedly pervasive bias in the WTO system against the interests of developing countries. Chapter 5 of the present study examines representation patterns by nationality among WTO committee chairs.

31. Hufbauer and Schott (2012) propose modifying the operative constraint to that of securing a waiver (article IX.3) on the MFN rule, requiring an affirmative vote of 75% of the WTO membership. However, in 1995 the WTO General Council affirmed use of consensus in waiver decisions (WTO 1995a). Hoekman and Mavroidis (2013: 18) also favor reducing the threshold of WTO approval to some form of majority rule. However, like many other WTO reform proposals, such changes would almost certainly require a WTO consensus.

32. Much of the Civil Aircraft Agreement has been superseded by the WTO's Agreement on Subsidies and Countervailing Measures. Initially driven by the beginnings of the Boeing vs. Airbus disputes, the Civil Aircraft Agreement has not reduced tensions on these and similar cases (see Hoekman and Kostecki 2009: 526–529).

33. Jackson (1997: 224–228) notes that interest in the original Tokyo Government Procurement Code was limited to just thirteen countries. The Code was optional in both the Tokyo and Uruguay Round Agreements, and thus was not part of the general bargaining framework.

34. See *Inside U.S. Trade*, December 14, 2012, vol. 30(49) and March 29, 2013, vol. 31(13). The services negotiations began in early 2013 with twenty-two WTO members participating, including the European Union as one member, as well as Australia, Canada, Colombia, Costa Rica, Hong Kong, Israel, Japan, Mexico, New Zealand, Chile, Norway, Paraguay, Peru, South Korea, Switzerland, Taiwan, Turkey, the United States, Pakistan, Peru, and Iceland.

35. See Hoekman and Mavroidis (2013). Under GATS article V, an Economic Integration Agreement among a subset of WTO members can come into force without further approval of the entire WTO membership as long as it passes muster under the "substantial sectoral coverage" provision (GATS article V.1), with no a priori exclusion of any of the four modes of supply. If the agreement did not meet the coverage requirement, it would have to be submitted for annex 4 consensus approval. Yet the hundreds of RTAs among WTO members that include services provisions require a notification under GATS article V, so there is ample precedent for such an agreement among a "regional" subset of WTO members, even

if the purpose of the ISA is to establish a broader agreement among its signatories that goes beyond the membership scope of a typical RTA.

36. Finger (2007) suggested that the financing component of Trade Facilitation Agreement might be accommodated in a plurilateral. Hoekman and Mavroidis (2013) suggest that the entire Trade Facilitation Agreement could become a plurilateral, which would raise the questions of whether its provisions would apply on an unconditional MFN basis and how the financing of non-WTO oversight components would be incorporated. A Trade Facilitation Agreement was achieved at the 2013 Bali Ministerial, but the lingering issue of funding responsibility may persist into the future. See the related discussion of this issue in chapters 7 and 8.

CHAPTER 5

1. The WTO Secretariat provides support for these committees, through research, technical advice, and trade policy expertise, as well as translation, clerical, logistical, and administrative services. It also provides support for the Dispute Panels. A separate office, the Appellate Body, provides legal services and renders judgments in dispute cases. However, the WTO member countries control the organization's agenda, negotiations, and implementation of formal WTO rules and agreements. See Nordström (2005) and Elsig (2011) for more detailed discussions of the WTO Secretariat, including its underutilized potential to improve to the prospects and efficiency of trade liberalization.

2. Basic WTO organizational information is contained in WTO 1995b, article IV. References hereinafter will be to the "WTO Agreement."

3. See the WTO Agreement, Agreement on Implementation of Article VI, article 16.1 (Anti-Dumping Agreement), among many other examples.

4. Kanitz (2011b: annex V) also provides a comprehensive list of rules documentation for WTO committees.

5. Odell (2005) analyzes the role of WTO committee chairs, whose mediation tactics include passive, formulation, and at times manipulative elements.

6. The Trade Policy Review Body, one of the three co-equal principal committees of the WTO, along with the GC and DSB, is also largely a monitoring body with a formal mandate to review WTO members' trade policies. The Secretariat staff plays a prominent role in gathering information for these reports.

7. For the Goods Council their topics include market access, agriculture, sanitary/phytosanitary issues, technical trade barriers, investment measures, customs valuation, anti-dumping, rules of origin, import licensing, subsidies/countervailing measures, safeguards, and working parties on state trading and information technology. For the Services Council, subordinate committees include working groups on professional services, domestic regulations and GATS (services trade) rules, and committees on specific services commitments and financial services.

8. See Elsig (2011) for a discussion of principal-agent issues in the WTO.

9. See table 5.10. Based on this partial list, several chairs of Doha committees had previously served on administrative committees.

10. On intellectual property compliance costs, see Finger and Schuler (2000). On textiles and related issues, see Finger (2001). On green room issues, see Blackhurst

(2001). Jones (2010) has a more general discussion of the green room and Uruguay Round disappointments. Jawara and Kwa (2004) pursue this line of criticism into the Doha Round.

11. The nine candidates came from the Republic of Korea, Indonesia, Costa Rica, Mexico, Brazil, Ghana, Kenya, Jordan, and New Zealand, and included three women. The final choice was between Roberto Carvalho de Azevêdo of Brazil and Herminio Blanco of Mexico.

12. See, for example, Ismail (2009), who, as South Africa's representative on the Doha Market Access (NAMA) and Agricultural committees, praises the New Zealander Agriculture chair and heavily criticizes the Canadian NAMA chair for their differing approaches toward reaching consensus.

13. The tally of chairmanships in table 5.2 excludes appointments to plurilateral committees (Civil Aircraft, Government Procurement), since chairs are chosen from selected signatory countries to these agreements. In addition, the Appellate Body chair, appointed internally, is not included.

14. In cases where more than one chair is appointed to a committee within a given year, each appointment counts equally; thus the number of chair appointments shown in table 5.2 is greater than the number of annual committee chair positions.

15. Aside from EU countries (which enjoy joint representation as a bloc), the WTO member with average delegation size of four or less during the sample period that had the greatest chair representation was Costa Rica, with fourteen chair-year appointments, thirteen of them to Ambassador Saborio Soto, a fact some WTO diplomats are quick to cite as evidence of small delegations' ability to support chair positions. Other such countries with at least one chair appointment during the sample period include Honduras, Iceland, Madagascar, Namibia, Oman, Sri Lanka, and Tunisia.

16. Even wealthier countries are evidently carefully considering the costs and benefits at the margin of their mission sizes. According the Economist Intelligence Unit (http://www.iberglobal.com/files/cities_cost_living_eiu.pdf) Geneva was still ranked among the ten most expensive cities in the world in 2013. Based on interviews with WTO trade delegates, some smaller countries have chosen to reduce the size of their standing mission staff in Geneva and fly in trade specialists from the capital temporarily as needed for committee deliberations. For this reason the effective size of a country's WTO delegation may be underestimated in some cases in the WTO directory.

17. Elsig (2011: note 33), based on interviews with WTO delegates, reports that political factors also enter the deliberations over chair appointments.

18. The WTO E-Directory, a restricted document issued annually, identifies staff members for each country's delegation associated with the WTO. Some country delegations have separate, dedicated WTO missions in Geneva, and other, mostly developing countries, have no Geneva mission at all, managing their WTO affairs from other locations. Counting the number of Geneva WTO staff is straightforward in these cases. However, several Geneva missions will include staff for WTO, as well as staff for other Geneva-based international organizations (UNCTAD, ILO, etc.). Estimating the number of dedicated WTO staff is difficult in these cases. VanGrasstek (2008) suggests estimating that one-third of a consolidated

Geneva mission's staff are responsible for WTO affairs. The author gratefully acknowledges data provided by Elsig (2011), who compiled year-by-year estimates of Geneva WTO missions, incorporating a similar rule. The author has updated the information with the 2012 E-Directory.

19. OLS regressions assume a normal distribution of the dependent variable. Count data, in contrast, tend to exhibit Poisson distributions. Thus, OLS estimation techniques will tend to be biased in count data regressions. In Poisson regressions, the mean of the dependent variable is assumed equal to its variance. Binomial regressions relax this assumption to allow the variance to differ from the mean.

20. Based on the results in the OLS regression, ceteris paribus, a typical country achieves the highest number of chairs at a per capita income level of around $39,000, above which the number of chairs will decline.

21. There are surely exceptions to this general proposition. Those LDCs that do gain significantly from trade, such as Bangladesh, will devote additional resources to developing experienced and qualified trade diplomats. Many other resource-strapped LDCs with weak trade infrastructure at home may be expected to devote few resources to this effort.

22. Regressions were also attempted to measure the determinants of multiple (two or more) chair appointments for countries in a given year, but there were few such instances, given the large number of observations, and statistical results, hampered by modeling issues regarding the nature of the distributions, could not contribute further insight on chair appointments.

23. When GenMis is replaced with its highly correlated substitute variable, ExShare (the country's world export market share), some of the year-shift dummies appeared to be significant, but this was evidently because the dummies were then capturing the greater relative increases in developed country mission size over the years.

24. When regressed with mission size, export share is rarely (and then statistically weakly) significant in determining the number of chair appointments for a country, but then is highly significant, but not as strong a determinant as mission size, when regressed without mission size as an independent variable.

25. The European Union negotiates as a single unit at the WTO and has its own WTO mission in Geneva, but its staff do not serve as WTO committee chairs in that representational capacity. However, EU member countries also maintain missions of their own, and representatives of smaller EU countries (Belgium, Finland, Ireland, Hungary) have in fact served as chairs of the TPRB, but not of the GC or its "feeder" committee, the DSB.

26. At the May 2012 GC meeting, Ecuador and Cuba pointedly objected to the high incidence of chair reappointments (WTO 2012a), resulting in disproportionate representation by certain countries, and argued for a larger role for regional groups to determine chair appointments. See, however, notes 27 and 28, indicating that the GC is likely to continue the practice of focusing on candidates' leadership qualities and contributions to WTO processes, subject to geographical and development status balance.

27. OLS regression results generally exhibit R-squared values of .50 or less, with comparable pseudo R-squared "fit" diagnostics in the Poisson and Negative Binomial

regressions. Some of the unobserved determinants in the regressions are likely to reside in GC balancing by development status or geographical grouping. Unobserved political factors and personal attributes of candidates evidently also play a role, but the details of specific country and individual candidate choices remain discretionary aspects of the decision that are difficult to explain without direct knowledge of GC deliberations.

28. For example, some ASEAN countries reportedly blocked the appointment of the Singaporean ambassador to the DSB committee chair, contrary to the established succession practice described earlier, for overtly political reasons. Multiple anonymous interviews with WTO trade officials also indicate the importance of individual candidates' character and ideological position on trade matters as part of the GC deliberations.

29. I am grateful to Ambassador Reiter (Sweden) for this information. Many other WTO trade officials and ambassadors indicated that Accession committee chair appointments should be considered separately.

30. Anonymous interview, Geneva, October 2013.

CHAPTER 6

1. A note on terminology: The WTO distinguishes RTAs from Preferential Trade Agreements (PTAs), which are defined as non-reciprocal unilateral offers of preferential market access by one importing country or entity (such as the European Union) to other, usually developing, countries. Examples include the Generalized System of Preferences (GSP), duty-free access for Least Developed Countries (LDCs), and special regional programs such as the US preferential market access arrangements for Africa (AGOA), the Caribbean (CBER), and Andean (ATPA) areas. For a complete list of PTAs reported to the WTO, see http://ptadb.wto.org/?lang=1.

2. The WTO updates this information at http://www.wto.org/english/tratop_e/region_e/region_e.htm.

3. Trade impact alone is not the only benefit of an RTA, since the commitment and "lock-in" value of eliminating trade barriers (with possibly additional economic reforms) may be high, especially if it promotes deeper economic integration. Pomfret (2007) is skeptical, however, that many bilateral RTAs among smaller countries, for example, do much to advance trade liberalization or increase economic welfare.

4. See Schott (2004) for a review of US policy toward RTAs as it developed in the early WTO era.

5. From 1993 to 2000, six new RTAs came into force on the African continent (Economic Community of West African States, Common Market for East and South Africa, Economic and Monetary Community of Central Africa, West African Economic and Monetary Union, East African Community, and South African Development Community); the Pan-Arab FTA in the Middle East, the Economic Cooperation Organization in Central Asia, The South Asian Preferential Trade Arrangement, and the Melanesian Spearhead Group in the Pacific. See the WTO listing, with links to membership and other basic information for each RTA at http://rtais.wto.org/UI/PublicPreDefRepByEIF.aspx.

6. Hoekman and Kostecki (2009: 477–478) review the history of RTAs, as does Irwin (1993), who focuses on the interwar period and the discriminatory, protectionist RTAs during the Great Depression.

7. See Dam (1970: chapter 16), who is particularly critical of the ambiguity of the GATT rules. Curzon (1965: chapter 9), provides details on early cases of RTA review, and the difficulties of putting the discipline of the rules into operation.

8. According to Schott (1989), only four RTAs were ever formally deemed compatible with the rules, most in the early years of the GATT. While new RTAs still had to be formally reported to the GATT and later the WTO, no RTA has ever been formally disallowed as the result of an article XXIV review. In view of the increased number of RTAs under the WTO, the General Council established new guidelines on reporting new agreements, including more specific terms and import data. See WTO (2006a).

9. Viner (1923) developed the classic analysis of trade creation and diversion in RTAs. Baldwin (2010) reviews subsequent advances in the theory of preferential trade agreements.

10. Hoekman and Kostecki (2009: chapter 10) provide a balanced overview of the literature and review the main points of the debate. The WTO (2011a) provides an extensive analysis of RTAs and competing political economy theories.

11. A number of empirical studies have identified deleterious effects of RTAs on MFN tariff bargaining, but their results have raised methodological questions. Baldwin and Seghezza (2010) review the literature and present results that support a more benign view of RTAs. The state of the debate over RTAs is in any case unlikely to affect their popularity as a trade policy device.

12. Fred Bergsten (2012), in a November 2012 presentation on the Trans-Pacific Partnership, insists that the US government's trade policy establishment is capable of "waging" trade negotiations on two fronts, a reference to the US military's global capacity target of fighting on two major fronts if necessary. He cites the example of the simultaneous negotiation of the NAFTA and Uruguay Round agreements in the early 1990s. However, the United States faced three trade negotiations beginning in 2013: TPP, TTIA, and WTO (although the Doha Round has been scaled back). See also Yager (2003), who is more skeptical about the US trade bureaucracy to staff multiple trade negotiations.

13. For a discussion of EU internal bargaining over a unified trade policy position, see Meunier (2000). A coalition of governments within the European Union supporting trade liberalization could draw on compensating internal transfers, or "horse-trading" across policy issues, in order to secure sufficient political support for pro-trade EU policies. In addition, see De Melo, Panagariya, and Rodrik (1993) for a discussion of political economy effects in an RTA (especially a customs union) that tend to diminish protectionist influences on trade policy.

14. The motivation for these reforms is driven by the increased importance of the geographical dispersion of production through international supply chains (see below). Baldwin (2006a) traces the motivations for the Pan-European Cumulation System (PECS), consolidated rules of origin in the European Union network of

FTAs, and notes that the Asia-Pacific region may face similar pressures for such reform.

15. The original EFTA members included Austria, Denmark, Norway, Portugal, Sweden, Switzerland, and the United Kingdom, later joined by Finland, Spain, Iceland, Norway, and Liechtenstein. In the meantime, all EFTA members except Switzerland, Iceland, Norway, and Liechtenstein have joined the European Union, and the remaining EFTA members have extensive trade agreements with the European Union and many other countries.

16. Baldwin (2006b) notes the importance of reciprocity in maintaining the juggernaut's forward momentum, an observation that helps to explain the difficulties of the Doha Round, which lacked a clear understanding of the terms of reciprocal concessions between developed and developing countries. See the discussion at the end of this chapter.

17. See USITC (1997: 2–8 to 2–30), which discusses the correspondence between NAFTA and Uruguay Round provisions, and which identifies intellectual property rights, in particular, as a NAFTA provision adopted at a later stage into the final Uruguay Round agreement. Other new issues developed in parallel fashion between NAFTA and the Uruguay Round, and it is probably difficult to identify the direction of influence.

18. See Baldwin (2011: 14–15) and the website for the International Centre for Settlement of Investment Disputes (ICSID): https://icsid.worldbank.org/ICSID/Index.jsp. Information on the US template can be found at http://www.state.gov/documents/organization/117601.pdf.

19. The UNCTAD maintains a database of BITs and other investment agreements. See http://unctad.org/en/pages/DIAE/International%20Investment%20Agreements%20(IIA)/Research-and-Policy-Analysis.aspx.

20. See also Baldwin (2006a), who coined this term, and the historical discussion of trade institutions in chapter 2 of this book. Supply chains represent what Baldwin terms the "second unbundling" in the modern era of globalization, whose origins he traces to the "first unbundling" of the late nineteenth century, based on steam power and the sharp drop in transportation costs, allowing the geographic location of production and consumption to be "unbundled."

21. The European Union and India were still negotiating an RTA in 2014 (see discussion below). Other proposed EU-Mercosur, EU-China, and China-Japan RTAs showed few signs of progress as of 2014. Note that ambitious RTAs among large developing countries could also play a role in moving toward a WTO agreement, but such agreements do not appear to be in the offing. The 2012 China-Brazil partnership agreement has limited trade coverage, and possible China-India RTA remains at the discussion stage.

22. This approach appears to fly in the face of the principle of special and differential (S&D) treatment for developing countries, but large emerging markets could increase their gains from trade by waiving this provision. Numerous problems would remain in order to promote consensus among the entire WTO membership. Continued application of S&D could continue to apply to smaller low-income countries, especially LDCs, perhaps through a "critical mass" consensus rule. See also chapter 7.

23. See Vargo (2009), presenting the US National Association of Manufacturers testimony on BITs and *Corporate Europe Observatory*, July 2010, "The Battle to Protect Corporate Investment Rights," accessible at: http://corporateeurope.org/sites/default/files/sites/default/files/files/article/battle_to_protect_corporate_investment_rights.pdf.

24. Lim, Elms, and Low (2012) provide a collection of essays on the TPP, focusing on the negotiating and systemic issues.

25. Australia, Brunei, Canada, Chile, China, Hong Kong, Indonesia, Japan, Republic of Korea, Malaysia, Mexico, New Zealand, Papua New Guinea, Peru, Philippines, Russia, Singapore, Taiwan, Thailand, United States, and Viet Nam.

26. ASEAN countries include Brunei, Cambodia, Indonesia, Laos, Malaysia, Myanmar, Philippines, Singapore, Thailand, and Vietnam. It was founded in 1967 to promote regional economic cooperation, peace and security.

27. In December 2013 Wikileaks released confidential US negotiating documents pertaining to the TPP, highlighting areas of disagreement among the participating countries, especially over intellectual property. See https://wikileaks.org/IMG/pdf/tpp-salt-lake-extracts-.pdf and http://wikileaks.org/tpp/#start.

28. Petri, Plummer, and Zhai (2012) estimate annual gains in alternative scenarios by 2025 of $295 billion for a separate TPP agreement and $500 billion for a separate RCEP agreement.

29. The entry of Japan into the TPP negotiations has added automobiles to this list.

30. Other welfare gain estimates are much larger than those of Francois et al. (2013). The OECD (2013) estimates TTIP gains of approximately 3–3.5% of GDP for both the United States and European Union. Based on 2012 GDP figures, this would result in annual gains of $500–$580 billion for the European Union and $450–$530 billion for the United States. The Bertelsmann Institute (2013) estimates are even higher—5% for the European Union ($830 billion) and 13% for the United States ($1.95 trillion)—but also indicate a net loss to the rest of the world, implying significant trade diversion, contrary to the other studies.

31. There are regulatory differences between the United States and European Union on important issues, as exemplified by the EU airplane emissions taxation, opposed by the United States. However, beginning in late 2013 efforts were underway to resolve this issue through International Civil Aviation Organization emissions regulations. See Schott and Cimino (2013: 14).

32. Both the United States and European Union issue annual reports on foreign trade barriers, with special attention often paid to each other's trade restrictions. See USTR (2012) and European Commission (2012). In addition, the WTO website lists fifty-one dispute cases filed between 1995 and 2013 in which both the United States and the European Union were involved as either complainants or respondents. See http://www.wto.org/english/tratop_e/dispu_e/find_dispu_cases_e.htm?year=any&subject=*&agreement=*&member1=EEC&member2=USA&complainant1=true&complainant2=true&respondent1=true&respondent2=true&thirdparty1=false&thirdparty2=false#results.

33. See the RTA "Early Announcements" page: http://rtais.wto.org/UI/PublicEARTAList.aspx, which includes links to national trade ministry

webpages with additional information. The list appears to be incomplete, however. The European Union provides summaries of its many ongoing negotiations at: http://trade.ec.europa.eu/doclib/docs/2006/december/tradoc_118238. pdf. The EFTA provides similar information at: http://www.efta.int/free-trade/ ongoing-negotiations-talks.aspx.

Chapter 7

1. It is important to add that optimal intervention must be calibrated to close the gap exactly. Over-taxing or over-subsidizing a market activity could lead to outcomes inferior to those implied by the initial market distortion. Corden (1974) also notes that one can rank intervention policies according to how closely they correct the given market divergence.

2. Most economic studies indicate that technology plays a more important role than trade in job displacement, although their effects on labor markets are often linked. See Autor, Dorn, and Hansen (2013). Politically, however, heightened technological change, which is difficult to stop, may lead to more anxiety and opposition to trade liberalization, which is more directly subject to policy decisions, hence the need to fashion policy responses that take a holistic approach to the problem of adjustment and job displacement.

3. See Lawrence (2008: 47–49); Subramanian and Kessler (2013: 21–22). Weak economic growth and debt burdens in developed countries and the increasing international mobility of capital have reduced the ability of governments to tax capital. Subramanian and Kessler (2013: 38) suggest that greater international cooperation on taxation—another institutional challenge—will be necessary to protect national trade adjustment safety nets.

4. "Transaction" is defined (definition 2 of Webster's *Third New International Dictionary*) as "a communicative action or activity between two parties ... reciprocally affecting or or influencing each other." "Process" is (definition d) "a natural continuing operation or development marked by a series of gradual changes that succeed one another in a relatively fixed way and lead to a particular result or end."

5. OECD (2009) reviews much of the recent literature on trade, development, growth, and poverty reduction, with a discussion of the ambiguity of empirical research on these topics.

6. See chapter 2 for a discussion of the GATT's accommodation of infant industry protection for developing countries, along with the contradictions raised by the reciprocity rule and S&D treatment.

7. Unilateral trade liberalization may serve the purpose of establishing external market discipline to the economy, but also may be part of BITs or other supply-chain facilitation arrangements, as described in chapter 6.

8. The partner agencies include the World Bank, IMF, UNCTAD, ITC, and United Nations Development Program (UNDP). The EIF operates under a special trust fund, with a separate secretariat, and is not directly involved in trade negotiations. See its website at: http://www.enhancedif.org/.

9. The time from original application to final WTO membership ranged from eight-and-a-half years (Cape Verde) to nearly sixteen years (Vanuatu, which

actually deferred membership for several years before its final ratification notice). Much of the accession problem for LDCs is the need for institution building, which is required to implement WTO obligations. The thirty other LDCs that had earlier joined the GATT were automatically carried over into WTO membership in 1995, without having to undergo the more rigorous WTO accession process.

10. Amounts are in constant 2011 dollars. Aid disbursements peaked during this time period in 2010 at $34.9 billion.

11. Developing countries have complained about the fact that it also increases imports, according to discussions by the author with trade officials involved in the trade facilitation negotiations, providing an additional argument in its favor.

12. See Stiglitz and Charlton (2006), who oppose a quid pro quo approach to aid-for-trade programs and propose transfers from developed to developing countries independent of the trade bargaining agenda.

13. See http://www.wto.org/english/tratop_e/dda_e/draft_text_gc_dg_31july04_e.htm#annexd, annex D, for the modalities established for the trade facilitation negotiations, and WTO (2013b) for the final text of the Trade Facilitation Agreement.

14. See "WTO Members Far Apart on Bali Deal, Promise Cross-Cutting Effort in Fall," *Inside US Trade* 31, no. 30 (26 July 2013). India, for example, reportedly was using Trade Facilitation as a bargaining chip in parallel negotiations on food security subsidies, and other developing countries were seeking concessions in negotiations over their use of export subsidies.

15. See Hoekstra and Koopman (2012). Donor preferences may also target the wrong sorts of aid, focusing on expenditures in the recipient country that would typically enhance its own mercantilist interests. Theoretically, an efficient allocation of aid would require coordination through a process of multilateral governance to maximize the social returns of the aid activity.

16. Winters (2007) is skeptical that successful coordination and funding among various agencies can be successful when transaction costs are high and the ultimate benefit of the aid-and-trade-liberalization package is not the central focus. Winters (2007) and Laird (2007) conclude that coordinated aid-for-trade projects, including the WTO's Integrated Framework, have had very limited success in supporting and promoting global trade liberalization itself.

CHAPTER 8

1. The limited gambling opportunities in Calvinist Geneva do not include poker, and there is, of course, no gambling at all in Doha. And so by Joycean phonetic reversal Doha becomes Tahoe, a scenic gambling venue on the shores of its own lake in Nevada.

2. One can argue that the September 11, 2001, attacks on the United States played a significant role in motivating WTO members (by a whisker) to begin the Doha Round a few months later, but even this event was not sufficient to sustain a joint commitment among them to complete an agreement over the next several years.

3. See Nakatomi (2012), who proposes an agreement that might also exist outside the WTO.

4. BITs currently have their own international court system, which allows firms to file cases directly against governments, a provision that the firms would not easily give up. Dispute settlement arrangements would therefore be an important, and potentially difficult, issue to negotiate in any such agreement. According to St. John (2012), BITs are lawyer-driven, while the WTO is policy-driven.

5. See OECD/WTO (2013: chapter 4), which discusses aid-for-trade efforts to build trade capacity in Africa and in the Caribbean, in order to support supply-chain development in those respective regions. See Flores and Valliant (2011) for an account of Latin American supply-chain prospects. Some countries in Latin America are also involved in TPP negotiations, indicating their intentions of joining Asian supply-chain networks.

6. China's growing status in this area is reflected in the attention it is drawing in anti-dumping cases, particularly in solar panels. Trade and investment partnerships between China and US and EU technology companies would reduce this sort of conflict.

7. See Schott and Watal (2000), Blackhurst (2001), Sutherland et al. (2005), and Jones (2010: chapter 4).

8. Subramanian (2013) goes on to propose measures to reform the IMF and promote the Renminbi as a reserve currency, which would further anchor China in the global economic system. Like many WTO reform proposals discussed in this chapter, its success depends on institutional changes that are unlikely in the foreseeable future.

9. See Narlikar (2011) for an account of India's insistence on blocking the 2008 Geneva negotiations, convincing (or shaming) Brazil into solidarity with this strategy, despite Brazil's inclination to seek a compromise. Narlikar (2012) provides a more general discussion of coalition strategies, and the tendency of developing country coalitions in the WTO to lead to deadlock.

10. See Vickers (2012) for an account of the roles, contrasting interests, and capacity for leadership of Brazil, India, and China in WTO governance.

11. For WTO documentation of the Bali agreements, see https://mc9.wto.org/draft-bali-ministerial-declaration. See also "WTO Approves Bali Package," *Inside US Trade* 31, no. 49 (13 December 2013).

12. Mattoo and Subramanian (2013) mention the antidumping case against Chinese solar panels. This case is likely to be the tip of the iceberg of environmental technology-related disputes, which would seriously compromise global efforts to improve environmental quality.

13. GATT article XX provisions regarding natural resources and prison labor are examples. Dispute settlement panel rulings have sought to reconcile such legal conflicts. Yet the WTO is ill-equipped to enforce new obligations in non-trade areas.

14. The single undertaking requirement was part of the Ministerial Declaration at Doha in 2001 (WTO 2001: paragraph 47), which set out the organization and management of the work program, although this provision did not preclude the conclusion of smaller agreements. New WTO negotiations could therefore set up different provisions for reaching a final agreement.

15. A recent study by Eagleton-Pierce (2013) examines the power structure in the WTO based on dominant countries' control over "knowledge claims," including the use of language in negotiations. While the study sticks to a dialectical approach of rich vs. poor countries that will be familiar to students of ideologically based WTO criticism, it illustrates divergences in perception that will require improved efforts by all WTO members in reaching a common understanding of, and mutual agreement on, the consequences of trade liberalization.

BIBLIOGRAPHY

Acemoglu, Daron, and James Robinson (2012). *Why Nations Fail: The Origins of Power, Prosperity and Poverty*. New York: Crown Publishers.

Acemoglu, Daron, Simon Johnson, and James Robinson (2005). "The Rise of Europe: Atlantic Trade, Institutional Change and Economic Growth." *American Economic Review* 95(3): 546–579.

Acharya, Rohini, Jo-Ann Crawford, Maryla Maliszewska, and Christelle Renard (2010). "Landscape," in Jean-Pierre Chaffour and Jean-Christophe Maur (eds.), *Preferential Trade Agreement Policies for Development*. Washington, D.C.: World Bank.

Albin, Cecilia, and Ariel Young (2012). "Setting the Table for Successor Failure? Agenda Management in the WTO." *International Negotiation* 17(1): 37–64.

Anderson, Kym, and Ernesto Valenzuela (2008). "Estimates of Global Distortions to Agricultural Incentives, 1955 to 2007." World Bank, Washington, D.C., October. http://www.worldbank.org/agdistortions.

Aoki, Masahiko (2007). "Endogenizing Institutions and Institutional Changes." *Journal of Institutional Economics* 3(1): 1–31.

Autor, David, David Dorn, and Gordon H. Hanson (2013). "Untangling Trade and Technology: Evidence from Local Labor Markets." NBER Working Paper No. 18938.

Bagwell, Kyle, and Robert W. Staiger (2002). *The Economics of the World Trading System*. Cambridge, Mass. and London: MIT Press.

Baldwin, Richard E. (2006a). "Globalisation: The Great Unbundling(s)," Chapter 1, in *Globalisation Challenges for Europe*. Helsinki: Secretariat of the Economic Council, Finnish Prime Minister's Office.

Baldwin, Richard E. (2006b). "Multilateralising Regionalism: Spaghetti Bowls as Building Blocs on the Path to Global Free Trade." *The World Economy* 29(11): 1451–1518.

Baldwin, Richard E. (2010). "Understanding the GATT's Wins and the WTO's Woes." CEPR Policy Insight No. 49, June. http://www.cepr.org.

Baldwin, Richard E. (2011). "21st Century Regionalism: Filling the Gap between 21st Century Trade and 20th Century Trade Rules." Staff Working Paper ERSD-2011-08. Geneva: WTO.

Baldwin, Richard (2012). "Trade and Industrialisation after Globalisation's 2nd Unbundling: How Building and Joining a Supply Chain are Different and Why it Matters." CEPR Discussion Papers 8768.

Baldwin, Richard, and Simon Evenett, eds. (2009). *The Collapse of Global Trade, Murky Protectionism, and the Crisis: Recommendations for the G20.* London: Centre for Economic Policy Research. http://www.voxeu.org/epubs/cepr-reports/collapse-global-trade-murky-protectionism-and-crisis-recommendations-g20.

Baldwin, Richard E., and Dany Jaimovich (2012). "Are Free Trade Agreements Contagious?" *Journal of International Economics* 88(1): 1–16.

Baldwin, Richard E., and Elena Seghezza (2010). "Are Trade Blocs Building or Stumbling Blocs?" *Journal of Economic Integration* 25: 276–297.

Beghin, John, Anne-Celia Disdier, Stephan Marette, Frank Van Tongeren (2012). "Welfare Costs and Benefits of Non-Tariff Measures in Trade: A Conceptual Framework and Application." *World Trade Review,* suppl. Symposium Issue: Standards and Non-Tariff Barriers in Trade 11(3): 356–375.

Bergsten, C. Fred (1996). "Competitive Liberalization and Global Free Trade: A Vision for the Early 21st Century." Working Paper 96-15. Washington, D.C.: Institute for International Economics.

Bergsten, C. Fred (2012). "A Trans-Pacific Partnership and the Future of the Asia Pacific Region" (video remarks). Washington, D.C.: Peterson Institute. http://www.piie.com/events/event_detail.cfm?EventID=166.

Bernstein, William J. (2008). *A Splendid Exchange: How Trade Shaped the World.* New York: Atlantic Monthly Press.

Bertelsmann Institute (2013). Press Report, June 16. http://www.bertelsmann-stiftung.de/cps/rde/xchg/SID-30139407-D63FD557/bst/hs.xsl/nachrichten_116768.htm.

Bhagwati, Jagdish (2008). *Termites in the Trading System: How Preferential Agreements Undermine Free Trade.* Oxford and New York: Oxford University Press.

Blackhurst, Richard (2001). "Reforming WTO Decision Making: Lessons from Singapore and Seattle," in Klaus Gunter Deutsch and Bernhard Speyer (eds.), *The World Trade Organization Millennium Round: Freer Trade in the Twenty-First Century.* London: Routledge.

Blackhurst, Richard (2005). "The Future of the WTO: Some Comments on the Sutherland Report." *World Trade Review* 4(3): 379–390.

Blustein, Paul (2009). *Misadventures of the Most Favored Nations: Clashing Egos, Inflated Ambitions and the Great Shambles of the World Trade System.* New York: Perseus/Public Affairs.

Bonanno, Alessandro, and Douglas H. Constance (2010). *Stories of Globalization: Transnational Corporations, Resistance, and the State.* University Park: Penn State Press.

Borchert, Ingo, Batshur Gootiiz, and Aaditya Mattoo (2012). "Policy Barriers to International Trade in Services: Evidence from a New Database." Policy Research Working Paper 6109. Washington, D.C.: World Bank.

Bouët, Antoine, Yvan Decreux, Lionel Fontagné, Sébastien Jean, and David Laborde (2008). "Assessing Applied Protection across the World." *Review of International Economics* 16(5): 850–863.

Bown, Chad P. (2010). "China's WTO Entry: Antidumping, Safeguards, and Dispute Settlement," in Robert C. Feenstra and Shang-Jin Wei (eds.), *China's Growing Role in World Trade*. Chicago: University of Chicago Press for the NBER.

Bown, Chad (2011). "Introduction," in C. Bown (ed.), *The Great Recession and Import Recession: The Role of Temporary Trade Barriers*. Washington, D.C.: World Bank.

Brown, Andrew, and Robert M. Stern (2012). "Fairness in the WTO Trading System," in Amrita Narlikar, Martin Daunton, and Robert Stern (eds.), *The Oxford Handbook of the World Trade Organization*. Oxford and New York: Oxford University Press.

Busse, Mattias, Ruth Hoekstra, and Jens Königer (2012). "The Impact of Aid for Trade Facilitation on the Costs of Trading." *Kyklos* 65(2): 143–163.

Cadot, Olivier, Sebastian Saez, and Maryla Maliszewska (2010). "Non-Tariff Measures: Impact, Regulation, and Trade Facilitation," in Gerard McLinden (ed.), *Modernizing Border Management; Washington*. Washington, D.C.: World Bank, 2010. Available at: http://works.bepress.com/ocadot/24.

Capling, Ann, and John Ravenhill (2011). "Multilateralising Regionalism: What Role for the Trans-Pacific Partnership Agreement?" *The Pacific Review* 24(5): 553–575.

Charnovitz, Steve (2007). "Mapping the Law of WTO Accession." GWU Legal Studies Research Paper No. 237. Washington, D.C.: George Washington University.

Cohn, Theodore H. (2002). *Governing Global Trade: International Institutions in Conflict and Convergence*. Aldershot, Hampshire, and Burlington, VT: Ashgate.

Corden, Max [1974] (1997). *Trade Policy and Economic Welfare*, 2nd ed. London and New York: Oxford University Press.

Cot, Jean-Pierre (1972). *International Conciliation*. London: Europa.

Curzon, Gerard (1965). *Multilateral Commercial Diplomacy: The General Agreement on Tariffs and Trade and Its Input on National Commercial Policies and Techniques*. New York: Praeger.

Dam, Kenneth W. (1970). *The GATT: Law and International Economic Organization*. Chicago: University of Chicago Press.

Das, Dilip (2002). "The Global Trading System: From Seattle to Doha." *International Journal* 57(4): 605–623.

Daunton, Martin (2012). "The Inconsistent Quartet: Free Trade vs. Competing Goals," in Amrita Narlikar, Martin Daunton, and Robert Stern (eds.), *The Oxford Handbook of the World Trade Organization*. Oxford and New York: Oxford University Press.

Dekle, Robert, and Guillaume Vandenbroucke (2012). "A Quantitative Analysis of China's Structural Transformation." *Journal of Economic Dynamics & Control* 36(1): 119.

Del Castillo, Carlos Perez (2011). "The WTO Chairman during a Ministerial: Views from the Bench and Lessons Learned," in Roberto Kanitz (ed.), *Managing Multilateral Trade Negotiations: The Role of the WTO Chairman*. London: Cameron May.

De Melo, Jaime, and Arvind Panagariya (1993). *New Dimensions in Regional Integration*. Cambridge, UK: Center for Economic Policy Research and Cambridge University Press.

De Melo, Jaime, Arvind Panagariya, and Dani Rodrik (1993). "The New Regionalism: A Country Perspective." Policy Research Working Paper Series 1094, World Bank.

De Souza Farias, Rogério (2013). "Mr. GATT: Eric Wyndham White and the Quest for Trade Liberalization." *World Trade Review* 12(3): 463–485.

Dethier, Jean-Jacques, and Alexandra Effenberger (2012). "Agriculture and Development: A Brief Review of the Literature." *Economic Systems* 36(2): 175–205.

Diego-Fernandez, Mateo (2008). "Trade Negotiations Make Strange Bedfellows." *World Trade Review* 7(2): 423–453.

Dillian, Carolyn, and Carolyn White, eds. (2010). *Trade and Exchange: Archaeological Studies from Prehistory and History.* New York: Springer.

Dube, Ryan (2013). "The Pacific Alliance: Market-friendly Integration." Latin Trade, May 30. http://latintrade.com/2013/05/the-pacific-alliance-market-friendly-integration.

Dunn, Paul (2012). "The Role of Gender and Human Capital on the Appointment of New Corporate Directors to Boardroom Committees: Canadian Evidence." *International Business Research* 5(5): 16–25.

Eagleton-Pierce, Matthew (2013). *Symbolic Power in the World Trade Organization.* Oxford: Oxford University Press.

Efstathopoulos, Charalampos (2012). "Leadership in the WTO: Brazil, India and the Doha Development Agenda." *Cambridge Review of International Affairs* 25(2): 269–293.

Elsig, Manfred (2009). "WTO Decision Making: Can We Get a Little Help from the Secretariat and the Critical Mass?" in Debra P. Steger (ed.), *Redesigning the World Trade Organization for the Twenty-first Century.* Waterloo, Canada: Wilfrid Laurier University Press.

Elsig, Manfred (2011). "Principal-Agent Theory and the World Trade Organization: Complex Agency and 'Missing Delegation.'" *European Journal of International Relations* 17(3): 495–517.

Ericson, Jonathon, and Timothy Earle, eds. (1977). *Exchange Systems in Prehistory.* New York: Academic Press.

Evenett, Simon J. (2011). "Did WTO Rules Restrain Protectionism during the Recent Systemic Crisis?" Discussion Paper Series No. 8687, International Trade and Regional Economics. London: Centre for Economic Policy Research. http://www.cepr.org/pubs/dps/DP8687.asp.

Evenett, Simon J., ed. (2012). *Débâcle: The 11th GTA Report on Protectionism.* London: Centre for Economic Policy Research.

Evenett, Simon J. (2013). *What Restraint? Five Years of G20 Pledges on Trade: The 14th GTA Report.* London: Centre for Economic Policy Research.

Faure, Guy Olivier, ed. (2012). *Unfinished Business: Why International Negotiations Fail.* Athens: University of Georgia Press.

Ferrantino, M. (2006). "Quantifying the Trade and Economic Effects of Non-Tariff Measures." OECD Trade Policy Papers, No. 28, Paris: OECD Publishing. http://dx.doi.org/10.1787/837654407568.

Findlay, Ronald, and Kevin H. O'Rourke (2009). *Power and Plenty: Trade, War and the World Economy in the Second Millennium.* Princeton: Princeton University Press.

Finger, J. Michael (1993). "GATT's Influence on Regional Arrangements," in Jaime deMelo and Arvind Panagariya (eds.), *New Dimensions in Regional Integration.* Cambridge: Cambridge University Press and Centre for Economic Policy Research.

Finger, J. Michael (2001). "Implementing the Uruguay Round Agreements: Problems for Developing Countries." *The World Economy* 24(9): 1097–1108.

Finger, J. Michael (2002). "Safeguards: Making Sense of GATT/WTO Provisions Allowing for Import Restrictions," in Bernard Hoekman, Aaditya Mattoo, and Philip English (eds.), *Development, Trade and the WTO: A Handbook*. Washington, D.C.: World Bank.

Finger, J. Michael (2007). "Implementation and Imbalance: Dealing with Hangover from the Uruguay Round." *Oxford Review of Economic Policy* 23(3): 440–460.

Finger, J. Michael (2012). "Flexibilities, Rules and Trade Remedies in the GATT/WTO System," in Amrita Narlikar, Martin Daunton, and Robert Stern (eds.), *The Oxford Handbook of the World Trade Organization*. Oxford and New York: Oxford University Press.

Finger, J. Michael, and Philip Schuler (2000). "Implementation of Uruguay Round Commitments: The Development Challenge." *The World Economy* 23(5): 511–525.

Finger, J. Michael, and John S. Wilson (2007). "Implementing a Trade Facilitation Agreement in the WTO: What Makes Sense?" *Pacific Economic Review* 12(3): 335–355.

Fisher, Roger, and William Ury (1981). *Getting to Yes: Negotiating Agreement Without Giving In*. Boston: Houghton Mifflin.

Flores, M., and Marcel Valliant (2011). "Global Value Chains and Export Sophistication in Latin America." *Integration and Trade* 32(15): 35–48.

Francois, Joseph, and Bernard Hoekman (2010). "Services Trade and Policy." *Journal of Economic Literature* 48(3): 642–692.

Francois, Joseph, Miriam Manchin, Hanna Norberg, Olga Pindyuk, and Patrick Tomberger (2013). *Reducing Transatlantic Barriers to Trade and Investment: An Economic Assessment*. Final Project Report, for the European Commission, March. London: Centre for Economic Policy Research.

Freund, Caroline, and Emanuel Ornelas (2010). "Regional Trade Agreements." Working Paper No. 5314. Washington, D.C.: World Bank.

Gallagher, Peter, and Andrew Stoler (2009). "Critical Mass as an Alternative Framework for Multilateral Trade Negotiations." *Global Governance* 15: 375–392.

Gatewood, Robert, Hubert Field, and Murray Barrick (2011). *Human Resource Selection*, 7th ed. Mason, Ohio: South-Western.

GATT (1979). "Differential and More Favourable Treatment, Reciprocity and Fuller Participation of Developing Countries, Decision of 28 November." Document L/4903.

Goldstein, Judith, Douglas Rivers, and Michael Tomz (2007). "Institutions in International Relations: Understanding the Effects of the GATT and the WTO on World Trade." *International Organization* 61: 37–67.

Greif, Avner, and David D. Laitin (2004). "A Theory of Endogenous Institutional Change." *American Political Science Review* 98(4): 633–652.

Grubel, Herbert G., and Harry G. Johnson, eds. (1971). *Effective Tariff Protection*. Geneva: GATT and Graduate Institute of International Studies.

Haberler, Gottfried, James Meade, Jan Tinbergen, and Roberto da Oliveira Campos (1958). *Trends in International Trade* (the "Haberler Report"). Sales No. GATT/1958-3. Geneva: GATT.

Hamilton, Colleen and John Whalley (1989). "Coalitions in the Uruguay Round" *Weltwirtschaftliches Archiv* 125: 547–562.

Hamilton, Carl, and P. Kniest (1991). "Trade Liberalization, Structural Adjustment and Intra-Industry Trade." *Weltwirtschaftliches Archiv* 127: 356–367.

Haniotis, Tassos (1990). "European Community Enlargement: Impact on U.S. Corn and Soybean Exports." *American Journal of Agricultural Economics* 72(2): 289–297.

Harbinson, Stuart (2009). "The Doha Round: 'Death-Defying Agenda' or 'Don't Do it Again?'" European Centre for International Political Economy (ECIPE) Working Paper No. 10.

Harbinson, Stuart (2011). "The Role of the Chairman of WTO Negotiations. A Broad Perspective: Representative, Chairman, Secretariat," in R. Kanitz (ed.), *Managing Multilateral Trade Negotiations: The Role of the WTO Chairman*. London: Cameron May.

Hartwick, John M. (2010). "Encephalization and Division of Labor by Early Humans." *Journal of Bioeconomics* 12: 77–100.

Hayek, Friedrich A. (1944). *The Road to Serfdom*. Chicago: University of Chicago Press.

Hayek, Friedrich A. (1978). *New Studies in Philosophy, Politics, Economics and the History of Ideas*. Chicago: University of Chicago Press.

Hays, Jude. C. (2009). *Globalization and the New Politics of Embedded Liberalism*. Oxford and New York: Oxford University Press.

Helble, Mattias, Caterine L. Mann, and John S. Wilson (2012). "Aid-for-Trade Facilitation." *Review of World Economics* 148: 357–376.

HLWG (High Level Working Group on Jobs and Growth) (2013). Final Report, February 11. Washington and Brussels: USTR and European Commission.

Hoekman, Bernard (2012). "Proposals for WTO Reform: A Synthesis and Assessment," in Amrita Narlikar, Martin Daunton, and Robert Stern (eds.), *The Oxford Handbook of the World Trade Organization*. Oxford and New York: Oxford University Press.

Hoekman, Bernard, and Michel Kostecki (2009). *The Political Economy of the World Trading System*, 3rd ed. Oxford and New York: Oxford University Press.

Hoekman, Bernard, and Petros C. Mavroidis (2013). "WTO 'à la carte' or WTO 'menu du jour'? Assessing the Case for Plurilateral Agreements." EUI Working Paper RSCAS 2013/58. San Domenico di Fiesole, Italy: European University Institute.

Hoekman, Bernard, Will Martin, and Aaditya Mattoo (2010). "Conclude Doha: It Matters!" *World Trade Review* 9(3): 505–530.

Hoekman, Bernard, Constantine Michalopoulos, and L. Alan Winters (2004). "Special and Differential Treatment of Developing Countries in the WTO: Moving Forward after Cancun." *The World Economy* 27(4): 481–506.

Hoekman, Bernard, Francis Ng, and Marcelo Olarreaga (2001). "Tariff Peaks in the Quad and Least Developed Country Exports." World Bank Development Research Group Working Paper, February.

Hoekstra, Ruth, and Georg Koopmann (2012). "Aid for Trade and the Liberalization of Trade." *Journal of World Trade* 46(2): 327–366.

Hudec, Robert E., Daniel L. M. Kennedy, and Mark Sgarbossa (1993). "A Statistical Profile of GATT Dispute Settlement Cases, 1949–1989." *Minnesota Journal of Global Trade* 2(1): 1–113.

Hufbauer, Gary C. (1990). "Chapter 1: Overview," in Gary Hufbauer (ed.), *Europe 1992: An American Perspective*. Washington, D.C.: Brookings Institution.

Hufbauer, Gary C., and Jeffrey J. Schott (2012). "Will the World Trade Organization Enjoy a Bright Future?" Policy Briefs PB12–11, Peterson Institute for International Economics.

Hufbauer, Gary C., and Jeffrey Schott (2013). *Payoff from the Global Trade Agenda, 2013*. Washington, D.C.: Peterson Institute of International Economics.

Irwin, Douglas A. (1993). "Multilateral and Bilateral Trade Policies in the World Trading System: A Historical Perspective," in Jaime de Melo and Arvind Panagariya (eds.), *New Dimensions in Regional Integration*. Cambridge: Cambridge University Press and Centre for Economic Policy Research.

Irwin, Douglas (2010). *Free Trade under Fire*, 3rd ed. Princeton and Oxford: Princeton University Press.

Ismail, Faizel (2009). "The Role of the Chair in the WTO Negotiations from the Potsdam Collapse in June 2007 to July 2008." *Journal of World Trade* 43(6): 1145–1171.

Ismail, Faizel (2012). "Is the Doha Round Dead? What is the Way Forward?" BWPI Working Paper 167. Manchester: Brooks World Poverty Institute.

Jackson, John (1989). *The World Trading System: Law and Policy of International Economic Relations*. Cambridge, Mass.: MIT Press.

Jackson, John H. (1997). *The World Trading System: Law and Policy of International Economic Relations*, 2nd ed. Cambridge, Mass.: MIT Press.

Jawara, Fatoumata, and Aileen Kwa (2004). *Behind the Scenes at the WTO: The Real World of International Trade Negotiations/Lessons of Cancun*, updated edition. London and New York: Zed Books.

Jones, Kent (1994). *Export Restraint and the New Protectionism: The Political Economy of Discriminatory Trade Restrictions*. Ann Arbor: University of Michigan Press.

Jones, Kent (2004). *Who's Afraid of the WTO?* New York: Oxford University Press.

Jones, Kent (2009). "The Political Economy of WTO Accession: The Unfinished Business of Universal Membership." *World Trade Review* 8(2): 279–314.

Jones, Kent (2010). *The Doha Blues: Institutional Crisis and Reform in the WTO*. New York: Oxford University Press.

Jönsson, Christer (2012). "Psychological Causes of Incomplete Negotiations," in Guy Olivier Faure (ed.), *Unfinished Business: Why International Negotiations Fail*. Athens: University of Georgia Press.

Kahler, Miles (2001). *Leadership Selection in the Major Multinationals*. Washington, D.C.: Institute for International Economics.

Kanitz, Roberto (2011a). "Between Theory and Practice," in R. Kanitz (ed.), *Managing Multilateral Trade Negotiations: The Role of the WTO Chairman*. London: Cameron May.

Kanitz, Roberto, ed. (2011b). *Managing Multilateral Trade Negotiations: The Role of the WTO Chairman*. London: Cameron May.

Kenworthy, James (2000). "'Reform' of the WTO: Basic Issues and Concerns." *Trade Trends*, Washington International Trade Association (Summer/Fall): 2.

Khor, Martin (2005). "Mood at WTO Gloomy as Ministerial Green Room Convenes." Third World Network Information Service, November 9. http://www.europe-solidaire.org/spip.php?article829.

Khorana, Sangeeta, N. Perdikis, W. A. Kerr, and M. Yueng (2010). *The Era of Bilateral Agreements: The EU and India in Search of a Partnership*. Cheltenham and Northampton, Mass.: Elgar Publishing.

Kindleberger, Charles P. (1973). *The World in Depression*. Berkeley: University of California Press.

Kindleberger, Charles P. (1981). "Dominance and Leadership in the International Economy: Exploitation, Public Goods, and Free Rides." *International Studies Quarterly* 25: 242–254.

Kingston, Christopher, and Gonzalo Caballero (2009). "Comparing Theories of Institutional Change." *Journal of Institutional Economics* 5(2): 151–180.

Kletzer, Lori, and Robert E. Litan (2001). "A Prescription to Relieve Worker Anxiety." Brookings Policy Brief No. 74. Washington, D.C.: Brookings Institution.

Krueger, Anne O. (1999). "Free Trade Agreements as Protectionist Devices," in J. Moore (ed.), *Trade, Theory and Econometrics: Essays in Honor of John S. Chipman*. London: Routledge.

Krugman, Paul (1995). "Dutch Tulips and Emerging Markets." *Foreign Affairs*, July/August.

Laborde, David, Will Martin, and Dominique van der Mensbrugghe (2011). "Measuring the Benefits of Global Trade Reform with Optimal Aggregators of Distortions." World Bank. http://siteresources.worldbank.org/INTRANETTRADE/Resources/Internal-Training/287823-1256848879189/6526508 1283456658475/Will_Martin_ Sep28_ 2010.pdf.

LaCarte Muro, Julio (2011). "Interview," in Manfred Elsig and Thomas Cottier (eds.), *Governing the World Trade Organization: Past, Present and Beyond Doha*. Cambridge: Cambridge University Press.

Lafer, Celso (2011). "Preface," in R. Kanitz (ed.), *Managing Multilateral Trade Negotiations: The Role of the WTO Chairman*. London: Cameron May.

Laird, Sam (2007). "Aid for Trade: Cool Aid or Kool-Aid?" UNCTAD G-24 Discussion Paper No. 48. Geneva: UNCTAD.

Laker, Joan Apecu (2013). *African Participation at the World Trade Organization: Legal and Institutional Aspects, 1995–2012*. Leiden: Martinus Nijhoff.

Lamy, Pascal (2011). "Forward," in Sue Arrowsmith and Robert D. Anderson (eds.), *The WTO Regime on Government Procurement: Challenge and Reform*. Cambridge: Cambridge University Press.

Lang, Andrew T. F. (2006). "Reconstructing Embedded Liberalism: John Gerard Ruggie and Constructivist Approaches to the Study of the International Trade Regime." *Journal of International Economic Law* 9(1): 81–116.

Lang, Andrew, and Joanne Scott (2009). "The Hidden World of WTO Governance." *European Journal of International Law* 20(3): 575–614.

Lawrence, Robert Z. (1991). "Emerging Regional Arrangements: Building Blocks or Stumbling Blocks?" in Richard O'Brien (ed.), *Finance and the International Economy: 5*. New York: Oxford University Press.

Lawrence, Robert Z. (2008). *Blue-Collar Blues: Is Trade to Blame for Rising US Income Inequality?* Washington, D.C.: Peterson Institute.

Lim, C. L., Deborah K. Elms, and Patrick Low, eds. (2012). *The Trans-Pacific Partnership: A Quest for a Twenty-first Century Trade Agreement*. Cambridge and New York: Cambridge University Press and World Trade Organization.

Low, Patrick (2011). "WTO Decision Making for the Future." World Trade Organization: Staff Working Paper ERSD-2011-05.

Malamud, Carlos (2013). "The Future of the EU-Mercosur Negotiations: How Important are Politics? Mercosur European Union Dialogue. Brasilia: Apex Brasil/ Brazilian Trade and Investment Promotion Agency.

Mansfield, Edward D., and Helen V. Milner (2012). *Votes, Vetoes, and the Political Economy of International Trade Agreements.* Princeton and Oxford: Princeton University Press.

Martin, Will, and Aaditya Mattoo, eds. (2011). *Unfinished Business? The WTO's Doha Agenda.* Washington, D.C.: World Bank.

Maskus, Keith (2012). "Trade-Related Intellectual Property Rights," in Amrita Narlikar, Martin Daunton, and Robert Stern (eds.), *The Oxford Handbook of the World Trade Organization.* Oxford and New York: Oxford University Press.

Mattoo, Aaditya, and Arvind Subramanian (2013). "Four Changes to Trade Rules to Facilitate Climate Change Action." Policy Brief No. PB13-10. Washington, D.C.: Peterson Institute for International Economics.

Mattoo, Aaditya, Francis Ng, and Arvind Subramanian (2011). "The Elephant in the Green Room: China and the Doha Round." Policy Brief PB11-3. Washington, D.C.: Peterson Institute for International Economics.

Mavroidis, Petros C. (2011). "Doha, Dohalf or Dohaha? The WTO Licks its Wounds." *Trade Law and Development* 3(2): 367–381.

M'Bow, Amadou-Mahtar (1978). "The Practice of Consensus in International Organizations." *International Social Science Journal* 30(4): 893–903.

McBrearty, Sally, and Alison S. Brooks (2000). "The Revolution that Wasn't: A New Interpretation of the Origin of Modern Human Behavior." *Journal of Human Evolution* 39: 453–563.

McMillan, John (1988). "A Game Theoretic View of International Trade Negotiations: Implications for Developing Countries," in J. Whalley (ed.), *Rules, Power and Credibility.* London: Macmillan.

Meléndez-Ortiz, Bellmann, and Rodriguez Mendoza, eds. (2012). *The Future and the WTO: Confronting the Challenges.* Geneva: International Centre for Trade and Development.

Mercurio, Bryan C., and Celine Sze Ning Leung (2009). "Is China a 'Currency Manipulator'?: The Legitimacy of China's Exchange Regime under the Current International Legal Framework." *The International Lawyer* 43(3): 1257–1300.

Messerlin, Patrick (2004). "China in the World Trade Organization: Antidumping and Safeguards." *World Bank Economic Review* 18(1): 105–130.

Meunier, Sophie (2000). "What Single Voice? European Institutions and EU–U.S. Trade Negotiations." *International Organization* 54(1): 103–135.

Michalopoulos, Constantine (2001). *Developing Countries in the WTO.* Houndmills and New York: Palgrave.

Moyo, Dambisi (2009). *Dead Aid: How Aid Is Not Working and How There Is a Better Way for Africa.* New York: Farrar, Straus and Giroux.

Nakatomi, Michitaka (2012). "Concept Paper for an International Supply Chain Agreement (ISCA): Improving Global Supply Chains by an Issues-based Plurilateral Approach." Tokyo: Research Institute of Economy, Trade and Industry. http://www.rieti.go.jp/users/nakatomi-michitaka/policy-proposal_ 3_en.pdf.

Narlikar, Amrita (2003). *International Trade and Developing Countries: Bargaining Coalitions in the GATT and WTO.* London and New York: Routledge.

Narlikar, Amrita, ed. (2010). *Deadlocks in Multilateral Negotiations: Cases and Solutions.* Cambridge: Cambridge University Press.

Narlikar, Amrita (2011). "Is India a Responsible Great Power?" *Third World Quarterly* 32(9): 1607–1621.

Narlikar, Amrita (2012). "Collective Agency, Systemic Consequences: Bargaining Coalitions in the WTO," in Amrita Narlikar, Martin Daunton, and Robert Stern (eds.), *The Oxford Handbook of the World Trade Organization.* Oxford and New York: Oxford University Press.

Narlikar, Amrita, and Diana Tussie (2004). "The G20 at the Cancun Ministerial: Developing Countries and their Evolving Coalitions in the WTO." *The World Economy* 27(7): 947–966.

Narlikar, Amrita, and Peiter van Houten (2010). "Know the Enemy: Uncertainty and Deadlock in the WTO," in Amrita Narlikar (ed.), *Deadlocks in Multilateral Negotiations: Cases and Solutions.* Cambridge: Cambridge University Press.

Nordström, Hakan (2005). "The World Trade Organization Secretariat in a Changing World. *Journal of World Trade* 39(5): 819–853.

North, Douglass (1990). *Institutions, Institutional Change and Economic Performance.* Cambridge and New York: Cambridge University Press.

North, Douglass (2005). *Understanding the Process of Economic Change.* Princeton: Princeton University Press.

Odell, John S. (2000), *Negotiating the World Economy.* Ithaca, N.Y.: Cornell University Press.

Odell, John (2005). "Chairing a WTO Negotiation." *Journal of International Economic Law* 8(2): 425–448.

Odell, John S. (2009). "Breaking Deadlocks in International Institutional Negotiations: The WTO, Seattle, and Doha." *International Studies Quarterly* 53: 273–299.

Odell, John (2010). "Negotiating from Weakness in International Trade Relations." *Journal of World Trade* 44(3): 545–566.

OECD (2006). "Aid for Trade: Making it Effective." Paris: OECD.

OECD (2013). "The Transatlantic Trade and Investment Partnership: Why Does It Matter? http://www.oecd.org/trade/TTIP.pdf.

O'Grady, Mary Anastasia (2013). "The Next Big Free-Trade Breakthrough." *Wall Street Journal*, July 15.

Oppenheimer, Stephen (2003). *Out of Eden: The Peopling of the World.* London: Robinson.

Oshima, Shotaro (2011). "Wrapping the July 2004 Package," in R. Kanitz (ed.), *Managing Multilateral Trade Negotiations: The Role of the WTO Chairman.* London: Cameron May.

Otsuki, T., J. Wilson, and M. Sewadeh (2001). "Saving Two in a Billion: Quantifying the Trade Effect of European Food Safety Standards on African Exports." *Food Policy* 26: 495–514.

Padro I Miquel, Gerard, and James M. Snyder (2006). "Legislative Effectiveness and Legislative Careers." *Legislative Studies Quarterly* 31(3): 347–381.

Patterson, Gardner (1966). *Discrimination in International Trade: The Policy Issues 1945–1965*. Princeton: Princeton University Press.

Panagariya, Arvind (2013). "Challenges to the Multilateral Trading System and Possible Responses." *Economics* 7(10). http://dx.doi.org/10.5018/economics-ejournal. ja.2013.10.

Petersmann, Ernst-Ulrich, ed. (2005). *Reforming the World Trading System: Legitimacy, Efficiency, and Democratic Governance*. Oxford and New York: Oxford University Press.

Petri, Peter, Michael Plummer, and Fan Zhai (2012). "The Trans-Pacific Partnership and Asia-Pacific Integration: A Quantitative Assessment." Washington, D.C.: Peterson Institute Policy Analyses in International Economics, No. 98 (November).

Pfetsch, Frank R. (2009). "Chairing Negotiations in the World Trade Organization." *Négociations* 11(1): 121–141.

Pinker, Steven (2011). *The Better Angels of Our Nature*. New York: Viking.

Pomfret, Richard (2007). "Is Regionalism an Increasing Feature of the World Economy?" *The World Economy* 30: 923–947.

Price, Niko (2003). "World Trade Organization Trade Talks Collapse; Poor Countries Declare Victory Over West." Associated Press, September 14.

Prowse, Susan (2006). "Aid for Trade: A Proposal for Increasing Support for Trade Adjustment and Integration," in Simon J. Evenett and Bernard M. Hoekman (eds.), *Economic Development and Multilateral Trade Cooperation*. Washington, D.C.: World Bank.

Putnam, Robert D. (1988). "Diplomacy and Domestic Politics: The Logic of Two-Level Games." *International Organization* 42(3): 427–460.

Raihan, Selim (2009). "European Union-India Bilateral Free Trade Agreement: Potential Implications for the Excluded Low-income Economies in Asia and Africa," in *Challenges and Opportunities for Trade and Financial Integration in Asia and the Pacific*, vol. 67. New York: United Nations Economic and Social Commission for Asia and the Pacific (ESCAP).

Robinson, Sherman, Zhi Wang, and Will Martin (2002). "Capturing the Implications of Services Trade Liberalization." *Economic Systems Research* 14(1): 3–33.

Rolland, Sonia E. (2010). "Redesigning the Negotiation Process at the WTO." *Journal of International Economic Law* 13: 65–110.

Ruggie, John (1982). "International Regimes, Transactions and Change: Embedded Liberalism in the Postwar Economic Order." *International Organization* 36(2): 379–415.

Ruggie, John (1998). "What Makes the World Hang Together? Neo-Utilitarianism and the Social Constructivist Challenge." *International Organization* 52(4): 855–885.

St. John, Taylor (2012). "Summary of Proceedings," in *Multilateral Liberalization through Bilateral Treaties: A Workshop on Global Investment Governance*. Oxford: Blavatnik School of Government, Oxford University.

Schott, Jeffrey J. (1989). *Free Trade Areas and U.S. Trade Policy*. Washington, D.C.: Institute for International Economics.

Schott, Jeffrey J. (1994). *The Uruguay Round: An Assessment*. Washington, D.C.: Institute for International Economics.

Schott, Jeffrey J., ed. (2004). *Free Trade Agreements: US Strategies and Priorities.* Publication number 375. Washington, D.C.: Peterson Institute for International Economics.

Schott, Jeffrey J. (2014). "A Step Forward for the Trans-Pacific Partnership?" Interview, January 10. Washington, D.C: Peterson Institute. http://www.piie.com/publications/interviews/interview.cfm?ResearchID=2547.

Schott, Jeffrey J., and Johanna W. Buurman (1994). *The Uruguay Round: An Assessment.* Washington, D.C.: Institute for International Economics.

Schott, Jeffrey, and Cathleen Cimino (2013). "Crafting a Transatlantic Trade and Investment Partnership: What Can Be Done." Policy Brief PB13–8 (March). Washington, D.C.: Peterson Institute for International Economics.

Schott, Jeffrey J., and Gary C. Hufbauer (2012). "Will the World Trade Organization Enjoy a Bright Future?" Policy Brief 12–11. Washington, D.C.: Peterson Institute for International Economics.

Schott, Jeffrey J., and Jayashree Watal (2000). "Decision Making in the WTO," in Jeffrey J. Schott (ed.), *The WTO after Seattle.* Washington, D.C: Institute for International Economics.

Schott, Jeffrey, Barbara Kotschwar, and Julia Muir (2013). *Understanding the Trans-Pacific Partnership.* Policy Analysis in International Economics No. 99. Washington, D.C.: Peterson Institute for International Economics.

Schwab, Susan (2011). "After Doha: Why the Negotiations are Doomed and What We Should Do about It." *Foreign Affairs* 90(3): 104–117.

Searle, John (1995). *The Construction of Social Reality.* New York: Free Press.

Searle, John (2005). "What Is an Institution?" *Journal of Institutional Economics* 1(1): 1–22.

Shambaugh, David (2013). *China Goes Global: The Partial Power.* New York: Oxford University Press.

Steger, Debra P., ed. (2010). *Redesigning the World Trade Organization for the Twenty-First Century.* Waterloo, Canada: Wilfrid Laurier University Press.

Steinberg, Richard H. (2002). "In the Shadow of Law or Power? Consensus-Based Bargaining in the GATT/WTO." *International Organization* 56(2): 339–374.

Steinberg, Richard H. (2010). "The Hidden World of WTO Governance: A Reply to Andrew Lang and Joanne Scott." *European Journal of International Law* 20(4): 1063–1071.

Stewart, Richard B. (2011). The World Trade Organization: Multiple Dimensions of Global Administrative Law." *International Journal of Constitutional Law* 9: 556–586.

Stoler, Andrew (2011). "The GATT and WTO Chairmen," in Roberto Kanitz (ed.), *Managing Multilateral Trade Negotiations: The Role of the WTO Chairman.* London: Cameron May.

Stolper, Wolfgang, and Paul A. Samuelson (1941). "Protection and Real Wages." *Review of Economic Studies* 9(1): 58–73.

Subramanian, Arvind (2013). "Preserving the Open Global Economic System: A Strategic Blueprint for China and the United States." Policy Brief PB 13-16. Washington, D.C.: Peterson Institute.

Subramanian, Arvind, and Martin Kessler (2013). "The Hyperglobalization of Trade and its Future." Working Paper WP 13–6. Washington, D.C.: Peterson Institute.

Sutherland, Peter, et al. (2004). *The Future of the WTO: Addressing Institutional Challenges in the New Millennium.* Geneva: WTO.

Tallberg, Jonas (2010). "The Power of the Chair: Formal Leadership in International Cooperation." *International Studies Quarterly* 54: 241–265.

Toye, Richard (2003). "Developing Multilateralism: The Havana Charter and the Fight for the International trade Organization, 1947–1948." *The International History Review* 25(2): 282–305.

Transatlantic Task Force on Trade and Investment (2012). *A New Era for Transatlantic Trade Leadership.* Washington, D.C. and Brussels: German Marshall Fund and European Centre for International Political Economy.

United States International Trade Commission (USITC). (1997). *The Impact of the North American Free Trade Agreement on the US Economy and Industries: A Three-year Review* (Vol. 3045). US International Trade Commission.

VanGrasstek, Craig (2008). *The Challenges of Trade Policymaking: Analysis, Communication and Representation.* Policy Issues in International Trade and Commodities Studies No. 36. New York and Geneva: United Nations.

Vargo, Franklin (2009). Testimony submitted to the Interagency Model Bilateral Investment Treaty (BIT) Review Panel Co-Chaired by the Department of State and the Office of the U.S. Trade Representative, July 31. http://www.nam.org/~/media/FBB5CB94BA2847BD95DE654555B17F5E/Comments_on_Interagency_Bilateral_Investment_Treaty_Review_Panel.pdf.

Vickers, Brendan (2012). "The Role of the BRICS in the WTO: System-Supporters or Change Agents in Multilateral Trade?" in Amrita Narlikar, Martin Daunton, and Robert Stern (eds.), *The Oxford Handbook of the World Trade Organization.* Oxford and New York: Oxford University Press.

Vieira, Marco Antonio, and Chris Alden (2011). "India, Brazil, and South Africa (IBSA): South-South Cooperation and the Paradox of Regional Leadership." *Global Governance* 17(4): 507–528.

Viner, Jacob (1923). *Dumping: A Problem in International Trade.* Chicago: University of Chicago Press.

Warren, T., G. Hufbauer, and E. Wada (2002). *The Benefits of Price Convergence: Speculative Calculations.* Policy Analyses in International Economics 65. Washington, D.C.: Institute for International Economics.

Warwick Commission (2007). *The Multilateral Trade Regime: Which Way Forward?* Warwick: University of Warwick.

Weinstein, Michael, and Steve Charnovitz (2001). "The Greening of the WTO." *Foreign Affairs* 80(6): 147–156.

Wilkinson, Rorden (2006). *The WTO: Crisis and the Governance of Global Trade.* London and New York: Routledge.

Wilkinson, Rorden (2012). "Of Butchery and Bicycles: The WTO and the 'Death' of the Doha Development Agenda." *The Political Quarterly* 83(2): 395–401.

Williams, Brock R. (2013). "Trans-Pacific Partnership (TPP) Countries: Comparative Trade and Economic Analysis." Congressional Research Service, Report R42344, June 10.

Williamson, John (1989). "What Washington Means by Policy Reform," in John Williamson (ed.), *Latin American Readjustment: How Much has Happened.* Washington, D.C.: Institute for International Economics.

Wilson, John S., Catherine Mann, and Tsunehiro Otsuki (2005). "Assessing the Benefits of Trade Facilitation: A Global Perspective." *The World Economy* 28(6): 841–871.

Winters, Alan (1993). "The European Community: A Case of Successful Integration?" in Jaime deMelo and Arvind Panagariya (eds.), *New Dimensions in Regional Integration*. Cambridge: Cambridge University Press and Centre for Economic Policy Research.

Winters, Alan (2007). "Coherence and the WTO." *Oxford Review of Economic Policy* 23(3): 461–480.

Winters, Alan L., T. Walmsley, Z. Wang, and R. Gyrnberg (2002). "Negotiating the Liberation of the Temporary Movement of Natural Persons." Sussex: University of Sussex.

Wolfe, Robert (2005). "Decision-Making and Transparency in the 'Medieval' WTO: Does the Sutherland Report Have the Right Prescription?" *Journal of International Economic Law* 8(3): 631–645.

Wolfe, Robert (2010). "Sprinting During a Marathon: Why the WTO Ministerial Failed in July 2008." *Journal of World Trade* 44(1): 81–126.

WTO (1995a). "Decision-Making Procedures under Arts, IX and XII of the WTO Agreement." Decision of November 15, Document WT/L/93 (November 24, 1995).

WTO (1995b). *Final Act of the Uruguay Round of Trade Negotiations*. Geneva: WTO.

WTO (1996). *WTO Rules of Procedure for Sessions of the Ministerial Conference and Meetings of the General Council*. Document WT/L/161, July 25. Geneva: WTO.

WTO (1999). *The Legal Texts: The Results of the Uruguay Round of Multilateral Trade Negotiations*. Cambridge, UK, and New York: Cambridge University Press.

WTO (2001). Ministerial Declaration, November 20. WT/MIN(01)/DEC/1.

WTO (2003). "Procedures for the Appointment of Directors-General." WT/L/509.

WTO (2005). Doha Work Program, Ministerial Declaration in Hong Kong. WT/MIN(05)/W/3/Rev.2. December 18.

WTO (2006a). "Transparency Mechanism for Regional Trade Agreements." WT/L/671, December 18.

WTO (2006b). *World Trade Report 2006: Exploring the Links between Subsidies, Trade and the WTO*. Geneva: WTO.

WTO (2007). *World Trade Report 2007*. Geneva: WTO. http://www.wto.org/english/res_e/publications_e/wtr07_e.htm.

WTO (2011a). "Elements for Political Guidance." Ministerial Conference, Eighth Session, Geneva, December 15–17. Document WT/MIN(11)/W/2. Geneva: WTO.

WTO (2011b). "Aid-for-Trade Work Programme, 2012–2013: Deepening Coherence." November 15. Document WT/COMTD/AFT/W/30.

WTO (2011c). *World Trade Report*. Geneva: WTO.

WTO (2012a). General Council Minutes of Meeting, May 1, 2012. Document WT/GC/M/136.

WTO (2012b). "Current WTO Chairpersons." http://www.wto.org/English/thewto_e/secre_e/current?chairs_e.htm.

WTO (2013a). "Bali Ministerial Declaration." December 7. Document WT/MIN(13)/DEC.

WTO (2013b). "Agreement on Trade Facilitation." December 7. Documents WT/MIN (13)/36; WT/L/911.

Yager, Loren (2003). "Human Capital: Significant Challenges Confront U.S. Trade Agencies." Testimony before the Subcommittee on the Oversight of Government Management, the Federal Workforce and the District of Columbia. Washington, D.C.: General Accounting Office.

Yarbrough, Beth, and Robert M. Yarbrough (1992). *Cooperation and Governance in International Trade*. Princeton: Princeton University Press.

Young, Alisdair R. (2010). "Transatlantic Intransigence in the Doha Round: Domestic Politics and the Difficulty of Compromise," in Amrita Narlikar (ed.), *Deadlocks in Multilateral Negotiations: Cases and Solutions*. Cambridge: Cambridge University Press.

Zoellick, Robert (2002). "Unleashing the Trade Winds." *The Economist*, December 7, 27–29.

Zoellick, Robert B. (2003). "Final Press Conference: World Trade Organization Fifth Ministerial Meeting." *The Soy Daily*, September 14, 2003. http://www.thesoydaily.com.

DATA SOURCES

Global Trade Alert. http://www.globaltradealert.org/14th_GTA_report.

International Monetary Fund, World Economic Outlook, http://www.imf.org/external/pubs/ft/weo/2012/01/weodata/index.aspx.

World Trade Organization, Blue Book (later E-Directory), various years (restricted distribution).

World Trade Organization, Chairpersons listings, 1995–2012. http://www.wto.org/english/thewto_e/secre_e/current_chairs_e.htm.

World Trade Organization, Statistical Database, Time Series. http://stat.wto.org/StatisticalProgram/WSDBStatProgramHome.aspx?Language=E.

Figures and tables are indicated by an "f" and "t" following the page number.